Praise for *Peril*

"The book details how Mr. Trump's presidency essentially collapsed in his final months in office, particularly after his election loss and the start of his campaign to deny the results."

—Michael S. Schmidt, *The New York Times*

"We know that the period between the election and the inauguration was a time of great domestic turmoil. And what *Peril* does is it shows that this was also a grave national security crisis."

—Isaac Stanley-Becker, *The Washington Post*

"Explosive new details about former President Donald Trump's actions around last year's election and the January insurrection."

—PBS

"A Bob Woodward book is like a large Christmas tree with dozens and dozens and dozens of unique ornaments that you've never seen before, news media headlines immediately focused on the biggest and most important ornaments on that tree, and we all eagerly read those first news reports about a Bob Woodward book. But the reason to read the book, the reason to order this book tonight or get it at your bookstore tomorrow is to see how the whole story fits together and see all of those ornaments on the tree that the news media never gets to because there are just too many of them."

—Lawrence O'Donnell, MSNBC

"Woodward and Costa got an exclusive transcript of the call. Pelosi has the same concerns that Milley does. The phone call is dramatic. It's blunt. And Pelosi wants Milley to reassure her that the nuclear weapons are safe."

—Jamie Gangel, CNN

"Excerpts of the Woodward/Costa book in *The Washington Post* and CNN make the Trump administration's operations in January 2021 sound like a bewildering blend of *King Lear, The Decline and Fall of the Roman Empire, Dr. Strangelove* and *Veep*."

—Olivier Knox, *The Washington Post*

"The clear theme of *Peril* is not a rehash or account of what transpired over the past year or so. It is a waving red flag designed to warn the electorate and chattering class that this story is far from over."

—*Mediaite*

"The explosive new book . . . that rocked Washington and the world with its headlines . . . you've done it again."

—George Stephanopolous, ABC

"Extraordinary new book . . . chockful of scoops . . . iconic pieces of reporting. . . . A collaboration we have been waiting for. It lives up to all of our hopes and expectations. . . . It is stunning."

—Nicolle Wallace, MSNBC

"Woodward and Costa make a powerful case that America has had a narrow escape. It leaves all Americans, in particular the Republican Party, with some thinking to do."

—Justin Webb, *The Times*, UK

ALSO BY
BOB WOODWARD

Rage

Fear:
Trump in the White House

The Last of the President's Men

The Price of Politics

Obama's Wars

The War Within:
A Secret White House History, 2006–2008

State of Denial

The Secret Man
(*with a Reporter's Assessment by Carl Bernstein*)

Plan of Attack

Bush at War

Maestro:
Greenspan's Fed and the American Boom

Shadow:
Five Presidents and the Legacy of Watergate

The Choice

The Agenda:
Inside the Clinton White House

The Commanders

Veil:
The Secret Wars of the CIA, 1981–1987

Wired:
The Short Life and Fast Times of John Belushi

The Brethren
(*with Scott Armstrong*)

The Final Days
(*with Carl Bernstein*)

All the President's Men
(*with Carl Bernstein*)

PERIL

Bob Woodward
Robert Costa

Simon & Schuster Paperbacks
New York London Toronto Sydney New Delhi

Simon & Schuster Paperbacks
An Imprint of Simon & Schuster, Inc.
1230 Avenue of the Americas
New York, NY 10020

First Simon & Schuster trade paperback edition January 2023

For information about special discounts for bulk purchases, please contact Simon & Schuster Special Sales at 1-866-506-1949 or business@simonandschuster.com.

The Simon & Schuster Speakers Bureau can bring authors to your live event. For more information or to book an event, contact the Simon & Schuster Speakers Bureau at 1-866-248-3049 or visit our website at www.simonspeakers.com.

Manufactured in the United States of America

1 3 5 7 9 10 8 6 4 2

Library of Congress Cataloging-in-Publication Data is available.

ISBN 978-1-9821-8291-5
ISBN 978-1-9821-8292-2 (pbk)
ISBN 978-1-9821-8293-9 (ebook)

Always for the parents:

Alfred E. Woodward and Jane Barnes

Tom and Dillon Costa

Contents

"We have much to do in this winter of peril."

President Joseph R. Biden Jr. in his inaugural address, January 20, 2021, at the United States Capitol

Authors' Personal Note

Claire McMullen, 27, a lawyer and writer from Australia, worked as our assistant on this book. She was our full collaborator on the investigative reporting and the research, pushing us to dig deeper, ask further questions, and to be more precise. At every stage, she was focused, resourceful and steady, even during challenging moments, and determined to execute each step with meticulous care.

Claire's creative devotion to hard work cannot be required. She chose to give it every day, every hour. She readily came in early, stayed late at night, and worked countless weekends with us. She also brought to this project her brilliant insights on human rights, foreign policy, and human nature. Her career is limitless in its promise. She is the best.

We will always appreciate her friendship and dedication.

PROLOGUE

Two days after the January 6, 2021, violent assault on the United States Capitol by supporters of President Donald Trump, General Mark Milley, the nation's senior military officer and chairman of the Joint Chiefs of Staff, placed an urgent call on a top secret, back-channel line at 7:03 a.m. to his Chinese counterpart, General Li Zuocheng, chief of the Joint Staff of the People's Liberation Army.

Milley knew from extensive reports that Li and the Chinese leadership were stunned and disoriented by the televised images of the unprecedented attack on the American legislature.

Li fired off questions to Milley. Was the American superpower unstable? Collapsing? What was going on? Was the U.S. military going to do something?

"Things may look unsteady," Milley said, trying to calm Li, whom he had known for five years. "But that's the nature of democracy, General Li. We are 100 percent steady. Everything's fine. But democracy can be sloppy sometimes."

It took an hour and a half—45 minutes of substance due to the necessary use of interpreters—to try to assure him.

When Milley hung up, he was convinced the situation was grave. Li remained unusually rattled, putting the two nations on the knife-edge of disaster.

The Chinese already were on high alert about U.S. intentions. On October 30, four days before the presidential election, sensitive intelligence showed that the Chinese believed the U.S. was plotting to secretly attack them. The Chinese thought that Trump in desperation would create a crisis, present himself as the savior, and use the gambit to win reelection.

Milley knew the Chinese assertion that the U.S. was planning a secret strike was preposterous. He had then called General Li on the same back channel to persuade the Chinese to cool down. He invoked their long-standing relationship and insisted the U.S. was not planning an attack. At the time, he believed he had been successful in placating Li, who would pass the message to Chinese president Xi Jinping.

But now, two months later, on January 8, it was evident China's fears had only been intensified by the insurrection.

"We don't understand the Chinese," Milley told senior staff, "and the Chinese don't understand us." That was dangerous in itself. But there was more.

Milley had witnessed up close how Trump was routinely impulsive and unpredictable. Making matters even more dire, Milley was certain Trump had gone into a serious mental decline in the aftermath of the election, with Trump now all but manic, screaming at officials and constructing his own alternate reality about endless election conspiracies.

The scenes of a screaming Trump in the Oval Office resembled *Full Metal Jacket*, the 1987 movie featuring a Marine gunnery sergeant who viciously rages at recruits with dehumanizing obscenities.

"You never know what a president's trigger point is," Milley told senior staff. When might events and pressures come together to cause a president to order military action?

In making the president the commander in chief of the military, a tremendous concentration of power in one person, the Constitution gave the president the authority single-handedly to employ the armed forces as he chose.

Milley believed that Trump did not want a war, but he certainly was willing to launch military strikes as he had done in Iran, Somalia, Yemen and Syria.

"I continually reminded him," Milley said, "depending on where and what you strike, you could find yourself in a war."

While the public's attention was on the domestic political fallout from the Capitol riot, Milley privately recognized the U.S. had been thrust into a new period of extraordinary risk internationally. It was precisely the kind of hair-trigger environment where an accident or misinterpretation could escalate catastrophically.

It was all unfolding fast and out of public view, which in some ways resembled the tensions during the Cuban Missile Crisis of October 1962 when the U.S. and the Soviet Union almost went to war.

Milley, 62, a former Princeton hockey player, burly and ramrod straight at 5-foot-9, did not know what China would do next. But he did know, after 39 years in the Army and many bloody combat tours, that an adversary was the most dangerous when they were frightened and believed they might be attacked.

If an adversary like China ever desired, he said, "They could choose to do what's called a 'first-move advantage' or a 'Pearl Harbor,' and conduct a strike."

The Chinese were investing in a sweeping expansion of their military to almost superpower status.

Just 16 months earlier at a stunning military parade in Tiananmen Square in Beijing, President Xi, the most powerful Chinese leader since Mao Zedong, had said there is "no force that can stop the Chinese people and the Chinese nation forging ahead." The Chinese also revealed their latest "game changing" weapon, a hypersonic missile that could travel at five times the speed of sound.

Milley told senior staff, "There are capabilities in cyber or in space where you could do some really significant damage to a large, industrial complex society like the United States and you could do that very, very quickly through some very powerful tools that are out there. China is building all of these capabilities."

China was also aggressively staging war games and sending military planes daily toward the island of Taiwan, the independent offshore nation that China considered theirs and the U.S. had pledged to protect. The previous year, General Li had announced that China would "resolutely smash" Taiwan if necessary. Taiwan alone was a powder keg.

In the South China Sea, China was on the march like never before, placing military bases on man-made islands, aggressively and, at times with breathtaking risk, challenging U.S. naval ships in important global shipping lanes.

Upcoming U.S. Navy Freedom of Navigation exercises around Taiwan and the South China Sea, and a U.S. Air Force bomber exercise, deeply worried Milley.

Such simulated attacks duplicated war conditions as much as possible and were often macho, goading endeavors, with U.S. naval ships deliberately, at high speeds, challenging China's claims on internationally recognized territorial waters.

Infuriated, Chinese captains frequently tried to push the U.S. ships off course by closely following or darting in front of them. Due to the size of the ships, any quick turns were inherently dangerous—accidents waiting to happen that could precipitate a disastrous chain reaction.

The chairman of the Joint Chiefs is the highest-ranking military officer in the armed forces and principal military adviser to the president. By law, the chairman's role is one of oversight and adviser. The chairman is not in the chain of command. But in practice, the post is one of enormous power and influence held by some of the most iconic figures in military history, including Generals Omar Bradley, Maxwell Taylor and Colin Powell.

Shortly after speaking with General Li on January 8, Milley called Admiral Philip Davidson, the U.S. commander of the Indo-Pacific Command that oversees China, on a secure line.

Phil, Milley said, reminding him that as chairman he was not a commander. "I can't tell you what to do. But you might reconsider those exercises right now. Given what's going on in the United States, that could be considered provocative by the Chinese."

Davidson immediately postponed the exercises.

The planned operations potentially had echoes of a similar 1980s incident when leaders in the then-Soviet Union believed the U.S. and the United Kingdom were going to launch a preemptive nuclear strike. A NATO military exercise called ABLE ARCHER greatly magnified those Soviet suspicions. Robert Gates, later the CIA director and defense secretary, said, "the most terrifying thing about ABLE ARCHER was that we may have been at the brink of nuclear war."

It was that brink that worried Milley. He was living in it.

China was, by far, the most sensitive and dangerous relationship in American foreign policy. But U.S. intelligence showed the January 6 riot had not only stirred up China but caused Russia, Iran, as well as other nations to go on high alert to monitor the American military and political events in the United States.

"Half the world was friggin nervous," Milley said. Many countries were ramping up their military operating tempo and cueing spy satellites. The Chinese already had their Intelligence, Surveillance and Reconnaissance (ISR) satellites looking intently to see if the U.S. was doing anything erratic or unusual or preparing to conduct any kind of military operation.

Milley was now on full alert every waking moment, monitoring space, cyber operations, missile firings, ship, air and ground movements, and intelligence operations. He had secure phones in nearly every room of Quarters 6, the chairman's residence at Joint Base Myer-Henderson Hall, Virginia, that would connect him instantly to the Pentagon war room, the White House, or combatant commanders throughout the world.

Milley told his service chiefs of the Army, Navy, Air Force and Marines—the Joint Chiefs—to watch everything "all the time."

He called National Security Agency (NSA) director Paul Nakasone and described his call with Li. NSA monitors worldwide communications.

"Needles up," Milley said, "keep watching, scan." Focus on China, but make sure the Russians are not exploiting the situation to "make an opportunistic move."

"We're watching our lanes," Nakasone confirmed.

Milley called CIA director Gina Haspel and gave her a readout on the call with Li.

"Aggressively watch everything, 360," Milley said to Haspel. "Take nothing for granted right now. I just want to get through to the 20th at noon"—the inauguration of Joe Biden as president.

Whatever happened, Milley was overseeing the mobilization of America's national security state without the knowledge of the American people or the rest of the world.

Milley had misled General Li when he claimed that the United States was "100 percent steady" and the January 6 riot was just an example of a "sloppy" democracy.

To the contrary, Milley believed January 6 was a planned, coordinated, synchronized attack on the very heart of American democracy, designed to overthrow the government to prevent the constitutional certification of a legitimate election won by Joe Biden.

It was indeed a coup attempt and nothing less than "treason," he said, and Trump might still be looking for what Milley called a "Reichstag moment." In 1933, Adolf Hitler had cemented absolute power for himself and the Nazi Party amid street terror and the burning of the Reichstag parliamentary building.

Milley could not rule out that the January 6 assault, so unimagined and savage, could be a dress rehearsal for something larger as Trump publicly and privately clung to his belief that the election had been rigged for Biden and stolen from him.

Milley was focused on the constitutional countdown: 12 more days of the Trump presidency. He was determined to do everything to ensure a peaceful transfer of power.

Unexpectedly, Milley's executive officer came into the office and passed him a handwritten note: "Speaker Pelosi would like to speak to you ASAP. Topic: Succession. Twenty-fifth amendment."

Speaker Nancy Pelosi, a California Democrat, was second in line to succeed the president after the vice president and received detailed briefings on the command and control of U.S. nuclear weapons. The 34-year House veteran was steeped in all national security, military and intelligence matters.

Milley picked up the Pelosi call on his personal cell phone, an unclassified line, and put it on speakerphone so one of his advisers could also listen.

What follows is a transcript of the call obtained by the authors.

"What precautions are available," Pelosi asked, "to prevent an unstable president from initiating military hostilities or from accessing the launch codes and ordering a nuclear strike?

"This situation of this unhinged president could not be more dangerous. We must do everything that we can to protect the American people from his unbalanced assault on our country and our democracy."

Pelosi said she was calling Milley as the senior military officer because Christopher Miller, recently installed by Trump as acting secretary of defense, had not been confirmed by the Senate.

"I can tell you that we have a lot of checks in the system," Milley said. "And I can guarantee you, you can take it to the bank, that there'll be, that the nuclear triggers are secure and we're not going to do—we're not going to allow anything crazy, illegal, immoral or unethical to happen."

"And how are you going to do that? Going to take the football away from him or whatever it is?" she asked.

She well knew that the football is the briefcase carried by a senior military aide to the president containing the sealed authentication launch codes for using nuclear weapons and a so-called black book that lists attack and target options.

"Well," Milley said, "we have procedures. There are launch codes and procedures that are required to do that. And I can assure you, as Chairman of the Joint Chiefs of Staff, I can assure you *that* will not happen."

"So if you had some concern that it could, what would be the step you would take?"

"If I thought even for a nanosecond that—I have no direct authority," he said, "but I have a lot of ability to prevent bad things from happening in my own little . . ."

Pelosi interrupted, "The American people need some reassurance on this, General. What are you prepared to say publicly about this?"

"I don't, candidly, Madam Speaker. Publicly, I don't think I should say anything right now. I think that anything that I would say as an individual, I think would be misconstrued in ten different ways."

"Well, let's just talk about it objectively and not about any particular president," Pelosi said. "With all the power that is invested into the president to have that power—to use the word twice—what are the precautions here?"

"The precautions are procedures that we have in place," he said, "which require authentication, certification, and any instructions have to come from a competent authority and they have to be legal. And there has to be a logical rationale for any kind of use of nuclear weapon. Not just nuclear weapons, use of force.

"So I can assure you that we have rock solid systems in place. That there's not a snowball's chance in hell this president, or any president can launch nuclear weapons illegally, immorally, unethically without proper certification from . . ."

"And you said not only nuclear, but also use of force?" she asked.

"Absolutely," Milley said. "A lot of people are concerned about, and rightly so, concerned about a potential incident in say Iran. I'm watching that as close as a hawk. Every single hour watching things overseas. The same thing domestically, with things like martial law stuff, the Insurrection Act.

"This is one of those moments, Madam Speaker, where you're going to have to trust me on this. I guarantee it. I'm giving you my word. I can't say any of this publicly because I really don't have the authorities and it would be misconstrued in 50 different directions, but I can assure you that the United States military is steady as a rock and we're not going to do anything illegal, immoral or unethical with the use of force. We will not do it."

Pelosi interjected. "But he just did something illegal, immoral and unethical and nobody stopped him. Nobody. Nobody at the White House. This escalated in the way it did because of the intent of the president. The president incited it and nobody in the White House did anything about it. Nobody in the White House did anything to stop him."

"I'm not going to disagree with you," Milley replied.

"So you're saying you're going to make sure it doesn't happen?" the speaker asked. "It already did happen. An assault on our democracy happened and nobody said, you can't do that. Nobody."

"Well, Madam Speaker, the launching of nuclear weapons and the incitement of a riot . . ."

"I know they're different. Thank you very much. What I'm saying to you is that if they couldn't even stop him from an assault on the Capitol, who even knows what else he may do? And is there anybody in charge at the White House who was doing anything but kissing his fat butt all over this?"

She continued, "Is there any reason to think that somebody, some voice of reason, could have weighed in with him? So for this, we are very, very affected by this. This is not an accident. This is not something that you go, well, now that's done, let's go from there. Let's move on. It ain't that. This is deep what he did. He traumatized the staff. He assaulted the Capitol and the rest of that. And he's not going to get away with it. He's not going to be empowered to do more."

Pelosi brought up President Richard Nixon, who had been forced to resign in 1974 because of the Watergate scandal.

"Nixon did far less and the Republicans said to him, 'You have to go.' Not even in the same league of things. 'You have to go.' The Republicans are all enablers of this behavior and I just wonder does anybody have any sanity at the White House? Say don't go there.

"They put up this fraudulent—this uh—'he says he doesn't have anything to do with it' video yesterday because they know they're in trouble. This is bad, but who knows what he might do. He's crazy. You know he's crazy. He's been crazy for a long time. So don't say you don't know what his state of mind is. He's crazy and what he did yesterday is further evidence of his craziness. But anyway, I appreciate what you said."

"Madam Speaker," Milley said. "I agree with you on everything."

"What can I tell my colleagues who are demanding answers

about what is happening to deter him from engaging in launching any kind of initiation of hostilities in any way, in any way, and including taking his hand off that power?

"And the only way to do that is to get rid of him because there's nobody around with any courage to stop him from storming the Capitol and inflaming, inciting an insurrection. And there he is, the president of the United States in there. And you've answered my question. Thank you, General. Thank you."

Pelosi paused and asked, "Is that fool at the Department of Defense, the acting Secretary, does he have any power in this regard? Is it worth any second even to call him?"

"I agree 100 percent with everything you've said," Milley replied. "The one thing I can guarantee is that as the Chairman of the Joint Chiefs of Staff, I want you to know that—I want you to know this in your heart of hearts, I can guarantee you 110 percent that the military, use of military power, whether it's nuclear or a strike in a foreign country of any kind, we're not going to do anything illegal or crazy. We're not going to do . . ."

"Well," Pelosi asked, "what do you mean, illegal or crazy? Illegal by whose judgments of illegal? He already did and nobody did anything about it."

"So I'm talking about the use of the U.S. military," Milley said. "I'm talking about us striking out, lashing out militarily. U.S. military power domestically and/or internationally."

"I'm not going to say that I'm assured by that," she said, "but I'm going to say that I asked you about it—just so you know. Because . . ."

"I can give you my word," Milley said. "The best I can do is give you my word and I'm going to prevent anything like that in the United States military."

"Well," she said, "I hope you can prevail in the insane snake pit of the Oval Office and the crazy family as well. You'd think there'd been an intervention by now. The Republicans have blood on their hands and everybody who enables him to do what he does has blood on their hands and the traumatic effect for our country.

"And our young people who are idealistic and who work here, I will tell you the people on both sides of the aisle have been traumatized to the nth degree because this man is a nut and everybody knows it and nobody will act upon it. So we'll just keep pushing for the 25th Amendment and for some Republican leadership to replace the president.

"But it is a sad state of affairs for our country that we've been taken over by a dictator who used force against another branch of government. And he's still sitting there. He should have been arrested. He should have been arrested on the spot. He had a coup d'état against us so he can stay in office. There should be some way to remove him. But anyway, it's no use wasting your time on this. I appreciate that. Thank you, General. Thank you."

"Madam Speaker, you have to take my word for it. I know the system and we're okay. The president alone can order the use of nuclear weapons. But he doesn't make the decision alone. One person can order it, several people have to launch it.

"Thank you, Madam Speaker."

Pelosi had a case, Milley realized. Her profound worries were well founded. Since the dawn of the nuclear age, the procedures, techniques, even the means and equipment, of controlling the possible use of the nukes had been analyzed, debated, and, at times, changed.

Milley often said that the use of nuclear weapons had to be "legal" and the military did have rigorous procedures.

But no system was foolproof, no matter how finely tuned and practiced. Control of nuclear weapons involved human beings and he knew that human beings, including himself, made mistakes. As a practical matter, if a president was determined to use them, it is unlikely a team of lawyers or military officers would be able to stop him.

Former defense secretary William J. Perry had been saying for years that the president has sole control of the use of U.S. nuclear weapons.

In an article published in early 2021, Perry said, "Once in office, a president gains the absolute authority to start a nuclear war. Within minutes, Trump can unleash hundreds of atomic bombs, or just one. He does not need a second opinion."

Now, with Pelosi's challenge and the clear alarm from China, Milley wanted to find a way to inject, if not require, that second opinion.

He developed a phrase, what he called "the absolute darkest moment of theoretical possibility."

It was both nuanced and real. There was a dark and theoretical possibility that President Trump could go rogue and order military action or the use of nuclear weapons, without going through the required procedures.

Milley felt no absolute certainty that the military could control or trust Trump. Milley believed it was his job as the senior military officer to think the unthinkable, take any and all necessary precautions.

He considered himself a closet historian and had thousands of books in his personal library.

"Pulling a Schlesinger" was what he needed to do to contain Trump and maintain the tightest possible control of the lines of military communication and command authority.

The move was a reference to an edict by former secretary of defense James Schlesinger to military leaders in August 1974 not to follow orders that came directly from President Nixon, who was facing impeachment, or the White House without first checking with Schlesinger and his JCS chairman, General George Brown.

Two weeks after Nixon resigned because of the Watergate scandal, *The New York Times* broke the story headlined: "Pentagon Kept Tight Rein in Last Days of Nixon Rule."

Schlesinger and General Brown feared Nixon might go around the chain of command and independently contact officers or a military unit to order a strike, putting the country and the world in jeopardy. They had been unwilling to take the risk.

Milley saw alarming parallels between Nixon and Trump. In 1974, Nixon had grown increasingly irrational and isolated, drinking heavily, and, in despair, pounding the carpet in prayer with then Secretary of State Henry Kissinger.

Milley decided to act. He immediately summoned senior officers from the National Military Command Center (NMCC). This is the war room in the Pentagon, used for communicating emergency action orders from the National Command Authority—the president or his successor—for military action or use of nuclear weapons.

The NMCC is part of the chairman's Joint Staff and is manned 24/7 with rotating teams on five shifts headed by a one-star general or admiral.

Soon a one-star officer and several colonels who were designated senior NMCC operations officers filed into Milley's office. Most had never been in the chairman's office. They seemed nervous and bewildered to be there.

Without providing a reason, Milley said he wanted to go over the procedures and process for launching nuclear weapons. Only the president could give the order, he said.

But then he made clear that *he*, the chairman of the JCS, must be directly involved. Under current procedure, there was supposed to be a voice conference call on a secure network that would include the secretary of defense, the JCS chairman and lawyers.

"If you get calls," Milley said, "no matter who they're from, there's a process here, there's a procedure. No matter what you're told, you do the procedure. You do the process. And I'm part of that procedure. You've got to make sure that the right people are on the net."

If there was any doubt what he was emphasizing, he added, "You just make sure that I'm on this net.

"Don't forget. Just don't forget." He said that his statements applied to any order for military action, not just the use of nuclear weapons. He had to be in the loop.

By way of summary he said, "The strict procedures are explicitly designed to avoid inadvertent mistakes or accidents or nefarious, unintentional, illegal, immoral, unethical launching of the world's most dangerous weapons."

It was his "Schlesinger," but he did not call it that to the assembled NMCC officers.

Make sure everyone on duty and in each shift gets this review, he said.

"They're in place 24/7, every day, all day long." The watch teams practiced the procedure multiple times a day.

Any doubt, any irregularity, first, call me directly and immediately. Do not act until you do.

He pointed to himself.

Then he went around the room, asking each officer for confirmation they understood, looking each in the eye.

"Got it?" Milley asked.

"Yes, sir."

"Got it?" he asked another.

"Yes, sir."

"Got it?"

"Yes, sir."

"Got it?"

"Yes, sir."

Milley considered it an oath.

Suddenly, about 12:03 p.m., Milley noticed the news crawl on the television in his office tuned to CNN with the sound off:

PELOSI SAYS SHE SPOKE TO JOINT CHIEFS CHAIRMAN ON PREVENTING TRUMP FROM "INITIATING MILITARY HOSTILITIES" OR "ORDERING A NUCLEAR STRIKE."

"What the fuck?" an officer asked.

As Milley listened to the CNN story, he quickly saw Pelosi had not revealed what he had said to her—and only shared part of what she had said to him. She did not mention her reference to Nixon. But what she had said publicly was correct as far as it went.

In these final days, Milley wondered, could Trump prompt the undermining of American democracy and the world order, carefully built in the years since World War II?

Milley was not going to allow an unstable commander in chief, who he believed had engaged in a treasonous violation of his oath, to use the military improperly.

The Schlesinger revival, 47 years after Nixon, had been necessary, a wise check, carefully calibrated, Milley was sure.

Was he subverting the president? Some might contend Milley had overstepped his authority and taken extraordinary power for himself.

But his actions, he believed, were a good faith precaution to ensure there was no historic rupture in the international order, no accidental war with China or others, and no use of nuclear weapons.

ONE

Nearly four years earlier, Joe Biden was knocking around his beach house in Rehoboth, Delaware, the weekend of August 12, 2017, when he caught snatches of President Trump on television. The president was insisting the violent brawls between marching white supremacists and counter-protesters in Charlottesville, Virginia, were the fault of both sides.

Speaking before four American flags at his New Jersey golf club, Trump declared there was "hatred, bigotry and violence on many sides, on many sides."

Incensed, Biden grabbed the phone and called "Mike D.," Mike Donilon, his closest political confidant, who at 59 had the look and manner of a neighborhood priest. Gray hair, bushy eyebrows, glasses, hushed voice.

Like Biden, Donilon had grown up in an Irish-Catholic family. His mother was a local union organizer in South Providence, Rhode Island, and his father was president of the school board. Over four decades, he had become Biden's gut check and a blend of John F. Kennedy's two key advisers: his younger brother and strategist, Robert F. Kennedy, and Theodore Sorensen, his wordsmith.

Donilon moved to the deck at the back of his house because his cell phone had poor reception inside his Alexandria, Virginia, home.

Jolting videos of white nationalists streamed seemingly nonstop on cable news. Many carried flaming torches and chanted "Jews will not replace us" and the Nazi slogan, "blood and soil."

They marched defiantly onto the campus of the University of Virginia on the eve of the "Unite the Right" rally, protesting the removal of an outsized statue of Confederate general Robert E. Lee.

Heather Heyer, a 32-year-old counter-protester, was killed on August 12 as the clashes continued and a self-avowed anti-Semite rammed his Dodge Challenger into a downtown crowd holding signs that read "Love," "Solidarity" and "Black Lives Matter."

"I have to speak out on this," Biden told Donilon. "This is different. This is darker. It is more dangerous. This is really a fundamental threat to the country."

Donilon could hear the profound alarm in Biden's voice. Biden was often stirred emotionally and long-winded, but on Charlottesville, he was going on and on, even more than his usual length.

"What's different about this moment in history is that the American people are going to have to stand up and defend the country's values and the Constitution because they don't have a president who is going to do it."

Biden had never seen anything like Trump's response, maybe in his lifetime. The president of the United States had given moral equivalency to those who stand against hate and the haters—safe harbor for white supremacists and Nazis who were willing to come out in the open.

"Unprecedented," he said, using one of his favorite words. "Trump is breathing life into kind of the darkest, worst impulses in the country."

"They didn't even bother to cover their faces!" Biden exclaimed. "The reasons they felt they could do it there was because they believed they had the president of the United States in their corner."

He was not going to sit idle. Could Donilon help him draft something—an article, an op-ed, a speech?

Up until then, Biden, age 74, a full six feet, had been out of office for seven months, after serving eight years as vice president. His hair was snow white and his face weathered by the years.

Biden had been trying to abide by the traditional rule for a previous administration: avoiding public comment on a new president. Let them get their sea legs. But he told Donilon the rule no longer applied.

"I have to speak," he said. "I need to be a very clear voice."

Biden argued if people stayed silent, the nation's civic fabric would grow threadbare, with more terror in the streets. Trump was systemically attacking the courts, the press, and Congress—a vintage move by an autocrat to dismantle institutions constricting his power.

"Okay," Donilon said. "I've got to get writing." The old Biden was engaging again as if he still held office.

As Donilon went to work, Biden issued a tweet at 6:18 p.m. that Saturday: "There is only one side."

It was classic Biden—declarative and righteous. And it picked up some traction on social media. But it was hardly a sensation. A former vice president was a fading brand.

Trump would not let go. On August 15, during a press conference at Trump Tower in New York, he maintained "there is blame on both sides" and there were "very fine people on both sides."

Drafts flew back and forth between Biden and Donilon.

Donilon mulled over how to convey Biden's urgency. What was the language? They agreed Biden needed to sound an alarm without sounding hysterical. How could he best confront—to use a phrase Biden had famously whispered after the passage of the Affordable Care Act in 2010—this disturbing, "big fucking deal" American moment?

They were looking for a larger theme, even a framing that invoked Biden's Catholic faith and spirituality. Something visceral, with a values component. Something that captured Biden's optimism and the nation's spirit. But what?

Donilon landed on "soul," a word no one identified with Trump. Biden loved the word. Just right.

Within two weeks, an 816-word piece under Biden's name ran in *The Atlantic*, with the headline, "We Are Living Through a Battle for the Soul of This Nation."

"The crazed, angry faces illuminated by torches. The chants echoing the same anti-Semitic bile heard across Europe in the 1930s," Biden wrote. "The neo-Nazis, Klansmen, and white supremacists emerging from dark rooms and remote fields and the anonymity of the web into the bright light of day."

In the aftermath of the march, he wrote, "America's moral conscience began to stir."

After the essay ran, there was a new, rising intensity in Biden's private speeches.

"Who thinks democracy is a given?" Biden asked corporate leaders at a closed event on September 19, 2017. "If you do, think again."

Known as Mr. Silent, Donilon was an unusually good listener. Biden aides often forgot Donilon was on conference calls until Biden would wonder, "Mike D., are you there?"

Yes, just taking it all in, trying to think it through, Donilon would say.

But the silence served a purpose—crystallizing Biden's aspirations. And this time, Donilon felt they had hit on something powerful with "soul." In speechwriting, sometimes you did, sometimes you did not.

"The battle for the soul of the nation" did not resonate like JFK's famous inaugural command, "Ask not what your country can do for you. Ask what you can do for your country." But it asked deeper, more fundamental questions: What is your country? What has it become under Trump?

TWO

Republicans were at a crossroads that summer of 2017, pleased to be holding power across Washington but increasingly unnerved about Trump and his response to Charlottesville. One of them was Paul Ryan, who had been Mitt Romney's running mate in the 2012 presidential election.

Ryan, a tall, dark-haired Midwesterner, was the opposite of Trump in many ways. He was a devotee of the grueling "P90X" workout regimen, a straitlaced family man, and an insider on Capitol Hill since his early twenties. He had been elected House speaker in October 2015.

Trump's personality confounded Ryan, who told friends he had never met another human being like him.

Throughout the 2016 campaign, Ryan had been supportive of the Republican nominee, whom most GOP leaders doubted would be able to win. But his support of Trump started to crack that October, when Ryan publicly said he was "sickened" by Trump's lewd, caught-on-tape comments about women, which were revealed by *The Washington Post*.

Once Trump won, Ryan was caught off guard. He now had to deal with him. Ryan, as speaker, was second in the line of presidential succession, right behind Vice President Mike Pence. There was no avoiding it.

Ryan began, on his own, to research how to deal with someone who is amoral and transactional. The exercise initially was difficult. Ryan liked to call himself a "policy guy," but his wonkiness did not extend from the realm of Social Security and Medicare into psychiatry.

Then a wealthy New York doctor and Republican donor called Ryan and said, "You need to understand what narcissistic personality disorder is."

"What?" Ryan asked.

The doctor sent Ryan a memo and an email with his "thoughts on how to best deal with a person with anti-social personality disorder." He also sent along hyperlinks to dense articles in *The New England Journal of Medicine*.

The memo contained material from the *International Statistical Classification of Diseases and Related Health Problems*, 10th edition, called "ICD-10." Ryan studied them for weeks, convinced Trump had the personality disorder.

Ryan's main takeaway: Do not humiliate Trump in public. Humiliating a narcissist risked real danger, a frantic lashing out if he felt threatened or criticized.

Ryan tested out his research on December 9, 2016. He and his senior aides, including soon-to-be chief of staff Jonathan Burks, arrived at Trump Tower in Manhattan for a transition meeting with the president-elect.

Ryan, Burks and others stepped into the gleaming elevator and said nothing. Burks wondered if the elevator was bugged. Trump had a reputation for secretly recording.

Once upstairs, they were ushered into Trump's office on the 26th floor. Burks stood up to close the door so the speaker and president-elect could have a private meeting.

"Oh, no, we leave that open," Trump said.

"Okay," Burks said, sitting down.

Trump shouted at his longtime administrative assistant, Rhona Graff.

"Rhona! Rhona! Get the coffee. Get the good stuff. It's Paul Ryan," Trump bellowed. "We've got to get the good stuff for him!"

A parade of Trump people kept strolling in, then walking back out. Steve Bannon, the unkempt conservative strategist who had migrated into Trump's orbit from *Breitbart*, a hard-right and anti-Ryan website. Incoming national security adviser Michael Flynn. Ivanka Trump.

Well, this is New York, Burks thought.

Trump nodded as Ryan spoke earnestly about taxes and health care, then looked down at his cell phone, which was ringing. It was Sean Hannity of Fox News. He answered the call as Ryan and his advisers sat silent.

"Yeah, I'm here with Paul," Trump told Hannity. "Oh? You want to talk with him?"

Trump looked at Ryan then put the call on speakerphone. "Sean, talk to Paul," he told the host, and Hannity did for about seven minutes.

The pattern of disjointed behavior continued once Trump became president. Trump kept erupting with erratic decisions and anger about perceived slights.

On April 26, 2017, Ryan got word that Trump was ready to announce that the United States would leave the North American Free Trade Agreement, NAFTA, the pact linking the U.S., Canada and Mexico. Ryan told Trump he risked public humiliation.

"You're going to crash the stock market," Ryan warned. Trump pulled back.

A lasting rupture came on August 15, 2017. On a hiking trip with his family in Colorado, a member of Ryan's eight-person security team approached with the satellite phone.

On the line, an adviser had bad news: Trump was at it again, blaming "both sides" for Charlottesville. The media was asking for a comment. Ryan sighed. This time, he had to pop Trump publicly.

Standing alone on the side of a mountain, Ryan began to dictate a cutting statement that was then tweeted out.

Once back in normal cellular range, Ryan's phone buzzed. It was Trump.

"You're not in the foxhole with me!" Trump screamed.

Ryan yelled back. "Are you finished? May I have some time to speak now?

"You're the president of the United States. You have a moral leadership obligation to get this right and not declare there is a moral equivalency here."

"These people love me. These are my people," Trump shot back. "I can't backstab the people who support me."

There were white supremacists and Nazis in Charlottesville, Ryan said.

"Well, yeah, there's some bad people," Trump said. "I get that. I'm not for that. I'm against all that. But there's some of those people who are for me. Some of them are good people."

Ryan later spoke to John Kelly, Trump's chief of staff and a retired four-star Marine general. Kelly said Ryan did the right thing with his tweet.

"Yeah, you need to hit him for that," Kelly said. "Don't worry about it."

On March 21, 2018, Ryan went through another tiring episode when the president threatened to veto a $1.3 trillion spending bill, known in Washington as the "omnibus." Trump had heard pundits pan it on Fox News. A veto could shut down the government. Ryan headed to the White House.

When he arrived, Trump started yelling immediately. He said he despised the omnibus and was now crosswise with his core voters.

"This is a terrible deal! Who signed off on this piece of shit?" Trump asked. No one answered.

"This is a piece of shit, a bad fucking deal," Trump said, working himself into a rage.

"The wall! It's not in here!"

"You have to sign this, we just passed it," Ryan said. "I mean, we discussed this already. This is the military. This is the rebuild. This is veterans."

When Trump again complained about only getting $1.6 billion for the border wall in the omnibus, Burks said the number in the bill was the number the president had asked for in his own budget.

"Who the hell approved that?" Trump asked.

No one spoke.

An hour in, Ryan asked, "Are you going to sign this bill or not?"

"Yeah. Fine. I'll sign it," Trump said.

As Ryan and Burks left, they huddled with Marc Short, a Pence adviser for decades who had agreed to serve as Trump's legislative director.

"What the hell was that?" Ryan asked.

"It's like this every day around here," Short said.

"Oh my God. Jesus," Ryan said.

Two days later, an unhappy Trump dithered again when it was time to formally sign the bill.

On Fox News that morning, conservative commentator Pete Hegseth, a veteran, had called it the epitome of a "swamp budget." Steve Doocy, one of the co-anchors of *Fox & Friends*, lamented "there's no wall" in the legislation. Trump tweeted he was "considering a veto."

If Trump did not sign the bill by midnight, the government would shut down.

Ryan phoned Jim Mattis, then secretary of defense. "Mad Dog," the president called him.

"You've got to get your ass over there and sit on him and make sure he signs this thing," Ryan said. "If you're standing there, he'll do it." Mattis cleared his schedule and spent hours with Vice President Pence and Marc Short, urging Trump to sign. Trump eventually did.

By early 2018, Ryan had had enough. Tax reform had been passed and signed by Trump. Ryan's three kids back in Wisconsin were still young enough to spend time with him. Growing up, his dad had died when he was a teenager.

On April 11, 2018, Ryan announced he would not seek re-election. He was 48 years old. The political-media world was stunned. Ryan was considered a possible presidential candidate, or, at the least, a Bob Dole–type who could spend years atop the Republican leadership.

Ryan soon went to meet with Senate Majority Leader Mitch McConnell of Kentucky. The speaker and leader had worked together to manage Trump. McConnell, 76 and known for being guarded and calculating, also found Trump bizarre, resistant to logic and advice.

When Ryan entered the majority leader's office, he thought McConnell might cry.

"You're a very talented guy," McConnell said. "We had a first-class relationship." But he was distressed. He and Ryan were the two leaders of the Republican Party in Congress. The coaches on the field.

With Ryan exiting, would Trump now be unbound? Who else would try to hold him back?

"I hate to see you abandon the playing field," McConnell said.

THREE

Joe Biden's first two runs for the presidency, in 1988 and 2008, were disasters, plagued by plagiarism charges in the first and by mangled remarks on race in the second.

Following his second botched candidacy, Biden wrote a new prologue for the paperback version of his 365-page campaign autobiography, *Promises to Keep*. His own words tell the story of a man who kept moving through the reeling dramas of life and presidential politics, going back to the horrific death of his first wife, Neilia, and baby daughter, Naomi, in a 1972 car accident, when he was 30 and newly elected to the Senate.

Biden's father, Joe senior, never gave up and never complained during Biden's childhood in Scranton, Biden wrote. "He had no time for self-pity.

"*Get up!* That was his phrase, and it has echoed through my life. The world dropped you on your head? My dad would say, *Get up!* You're lying in bed feeling sorry for yourself? *Get up!* You got knocked on your ass on the football field? *Get up!* Bad grade? *Get up!* The girl's parents won't let her go out with a Catholic boy? *Get up!*

"It wasn't just the small things but the big ones—when the only voice I could hear was my own. After the surgery, Senator, you might lose the ability to speak? *Get up!* The newspapers are calling you a plagiarist, Biden? *Get up!* Your wife and daughter—I'm sorry, Joe there was nothing we could do to save them? *Get up!* Flunked a class at law school? *Get up!* Kids make fun of you because you stutter Bu-bu-bu-bu-bu-Biden? *Get up!*"

Biden's 2008 failure offered a consolation prize: then Senator Barack Obama of Illinois, soon to be the nation's first Black president, picked him to be his running mate. He gave Biden important roles in foreign policy and budget negotiations, seemingly setting up Biden for his clearest shot at making another run for the presidency.

But nearing the end of his second term, President Obama was hinting strongly it was Hillary Clinton's turn. She had almost beaten Obama for the nomination in 2008 and then ably served as his secretary of state. He also flatly told Biden it would be tough to beat her.

Biden kept the idea on the table. He liked Obama. They were close. But he told his aides he never felt like he had to follow his cues on another run.

Biden's youngest son, Hunter Biden, and his then wife, Kathleen, came to dinner Friday night, February 6, 2015, at Woodward's home in Washington. Woodward's wife, Elsa Walsh, and Kathleen had become friends through Sidwell Friends, a private Quaker school their children attended.

Hunter's alcoholism, drug addiction and financial problems would later generate headlines. But neither Woodward nor Walsh were much aware of them, other than a brief October 2014 story that Hunter, a Yale Law School graduate, and lobbyist, had been discharged from the U.S. Navy Reserve after testing positive for cocaine. Nor did they know of the brain cancer threatening Hunter's brother, Beau, a secret held closely by the family.

At dinner, Walsh asked them, is your father going to run for president?

Hunter—45 and thin, with jet-black hair—quickly answered yes. Sitting and speaking confidently at the dining room table, Kathleen recounted how several days earlier, her father-in-law had called and said he wanted to come for dinner. He had important news.

Kathleen, who worked with domestic violence victims, said she scooped the already plated spaghetti back into the pot to await the arrival of "Pop" at their nearby home.

Once there, the vice president explained he had decided to run. Hunter and Kathleen seemed thrilled. This might finally be Joe Biden's time.

In his 2021 memoir, *Beautiful Things*, Hunter Biden wrote "Beau and I always knew that Dad wouldn't retire until he became president. That was the collective dream of the three of us." Beau and Hunter, who had also been in the car that day, had been injured but survived the 1972 crash. Hunter also wrote he detested the doubters inside the West Wing who "undercut" his father.

Woodward and Walsh were not particularly surprised. Presidential hopeful was embedded in Biden's character. It seemed he was always running for president.

When told later about Hunter's assertion that February, Biden advisers insisted they were not aware of Biden's decision at the time. But Biden often kept his latest thinking tight, in the family.

A few months later, on May 30, 2015, Beau Biden died at age 46, ending a life that included a Bronze Star for military service in Iraq and two terms as Delaware's attorney general.

Joe Biden was devastated.

"This is going to be a very tough time personally," Biden told Steve Ricchetti, his chief of staff for nearly three years and another principal in Biden's political brotherhood.

"The only way I'm going to be able to get through this," he said, "and we'll be able to get through it as a family, is if we just, you know, you have to keep me working and busy."

Ricchetti—like Donilon, gray-haired and balding, and averse to appearing on television or on the record—loved Biden. The resilience, the generosity, the friendliness. If Biden said he needed to work, he knew how to keep the vice president busy. Schedule. Action.

Ricchetti later reflected to others that "sometimes, it sounds almost cruel."

But keeping busy meant taking another hard look at a presidential campaign.

Biden asked Donilon to make an honest assessment of whether there was still enough time to run and win.

In the final "go or no-go" meeting on October 20, 2015, Donilon ventured that Clinton was vulnerable in a general election and even vulnerable in a Democratic primary race against Biden.

Donilon recalled to others, "I never wavered from the view that I thought he could run, and I thought he could win."

But as Donilon looked at Biden, he could see how the heavy burden of Beau's death weighed on him—the loss of a second child and the third member of his family gone. Biden was taut with pain, the usual easy smile now a jaw clenched.

"I don't think you should do this," Donilon finally told him.

It was the first time in years that Donilon had advised him against running. Biden took it as the best advice from a friend, and Donilon left with instructions to put together a statement.

The following day, Biden stood in the White House Rose Garden, with President Obama at his side, and announced he would not run for president.

FOUR

Biden began to look toward something utterly unfamiliar: a life out of office. But others were skeptical. "A fish is going to swim, a bird is going to fly, and Biden is going to run," a friend of Biden's once said.

Biden told Ricchetti, "All I want to do is keep doing what I've always done. How can I still work on the things that I have spent my life working on, the things that I care the most about?"

Biden and Ricchetti sketched out pillars of his coming life: the Biden Foundation, the Biden Cancer Initiative, the Penn Biden Center for Diplomacy and Global Engagement at the University of Pennsylvania, and the Biden Institute at the University of Delaware.

"Hillary's going to be elected and we'll find a way to contribute," Biden said.

A year later, on November 8, 2016, Biden assembled his top advisers at the Naval Observatory, the vice presidential residence, to watch the returns.

The night started off well with projections pointing toward a Clinton win. Biden's wife, Jill, relaxed and headed upstairs with a book and a glass of wine.

Jill and Joe Biden had been married since 1977. He had spotted her, then a teacher and part-time model in the Philadelphia area, on an advertising billboard at the airport and sought out her phone number. He proposed five times before she agreed to marry him.

Jill helped him raise his two boys, and they had a daughter together named Ashley. She eventually earned a doctoral degree in education and taught English at Northern Virginia Community College. She was an avid runner, and considered herself an introvert, uncomfortable in the spotlight giving speeches, yet an ardent defender of her husband.

As the evening wore on, the needle swung toward Trump. Joe Biden was unsettled. Trump won Ohio at 10:36 p.m. and Florida at 10:50 p.m. At 2:29 a.m., the Associated Press declared Trump the winner, and a shocked Hillary Clinton soon conceded.

Biden immersed himself in phone calls. "My God, the world has just turned upside down," he said.

As Biden ambled around the first floor of his home, he told friends he had sensed trouble for Clinton for a long time. Trump had seemed to be stealing away the party's support among rank-and-file labor workers without much of a fight.

"You didn't hear a single solitary sentence in the last campaign about that guy working on the assembly line making 60,000 bucks a year and a wife making $32,000 as a hostess in a restaurant," Biden said later, at a 2017 appearance at Penn.

On January 20, Biden sat through Trump's stark "American carnage" inaugural address and then turned to writing a second memoir, *Promise Me, Dad*. It was a chance to think and talk about Beau, a "search for a way forward in his own life," as Ricchetti explained it to others. Biden wanted to show a person could get through even the most debilitating tragedy and find purpose in the memory.

Soon, the Biden family was back in the news. Hunter's wife, Kathleen, had quietly filed for divorce in December, citing drug use and infidelity, and filed a new motion asking the court to freeze his assets. On March 1, the *New York Post* first reported that Hunter was dating Beau's widow, Hallie.

Joe Biden issued a statement to the New York newspaper: "We

are all lucky that Hunter and Hallie found each other as they were putting their lives together again after such sadness. They have mine and Jill's full and complete support and we are happy for them."

It was a bleak time for Hunter. In his memoir, he wrote his daughters were rattled by his conduct and his business began to collapse. Clients deserted him. "Worse yet, I started backsliding" into drugs.

Promise Me, Dad, Joe Biden's second book, was published that November, three months after Charlottesville. It was raw, and Biden charted the inner emptiness overwhelming him. But this time, it was Beau, at the end of his life, saying, *Get up!*

"You've got to promise me, Dad, that no matter what happens, you're going to be all right. Give me your word, Dad," Beau Biden said, according to the book.

"I'm going to be okay, Beau," Biden replied.

"No, Dad," Beau Biden said. "Give me your word as a Biden. Give me your word, Dad. Promise me, Dad."

"I promised," Biden wrote.

Although Beau was speaking of his father's well-being, the book's title was interpreted by many as Beau asking Biden to promise to run for president.

Biden began his national book tour in the middle of the 2018 congressional campaign season.

Cedric Richmond, 44, the only Democratic member of Louisiana's congressional delegation and chairman of the powerful Congressional Black Caucus, asked Biden to go on the road for Black Democrats.

Richmond was a rising star in the party and a skillful strategist whose colleagues in the House thought he might one day become the first Black speaker. He loved the backroom talks on policy, the mapping of relationships across the House and the party.

Richmond also had the build and easy swagger of a star athlete. He had been a center fielder and pitcher at Morehouse College before going to law school. During the annual Congressional Baseball Game, he had a reputation for being the only truly good player.

Richmond noticed Biden was welcome everywhere. Other big names prompted caution in certain slices of the country. But with Biden, he told others, "there wasn't a district in the country that didn't want him." Liberal New York, the Midwest, conservative suburban enclaves, the South.

Mike D. also monitored Biden's reception. There was a practical political reality to a former vice president actively supporting 65 candidates in 24 states. The key question Donilon asked was: "Did Biden still have real standing in the party and in the country?" The answer, he concluded, was yes. The book hit No. 1 on the *New York Times* bestseller list for one week. Biden was drawing crowds.

Donilon and Ricchetti kept nudging Biden to consider another campaign. They told him the data showed a path in a fast-changing party. Trump had changed some Democratic voters' motivations and priorities. Most of all, they wanted Trump gone.

Biden's pollster, John Anzalone, a son of Teamsters in Michigan who had worked with Biden since his unsuccessful 1988 campaign in Iowa, produced slides, known as "Anzo's decks," for Biden to take on the road and flip through with candidates and donors.

On one slide, Anzalone wrote "Democratic primary voters tended to support more traditional, establishment candidates over progressive firebrands."

A final slide concluded, "Importantly, there is no urgent demand for a younger generation of leadership among voters."

Biden would not say whether he would run. He was coy, and let the slides make the argument.

"Cedric, is there anything I could do for you when I come down for the book tour?" Biden asked Richmond ahead of his June 2018 book stop in New Orleans.

"I don't need a fundraiser," Richmond said. His seat was safe. Instead, he proposed a round of golf at the Joseph M. Bartholomew Golf Course, a historic public golf course named after the Black architect who had designed many of Louisiana's best country club courses but could not play on them in the segregated South.

When Biden showed up, Richmond noted he was dropped off by a single publishing representative. No security, no aides.

After the first nine holes, rain started to fall, and the group moved inside the clubhouse where 30 older Black golfers were waiting for Biden. Richmond had trays of food and drinks brought in.

Richmond studied Biden as he went around the room asking questions. What do you do for a living? Are you retired? The curiosity seemed genuine. Some were Vietnam veterans and Biden told them his late son was an Army lawyer who had volunteered for duty in Iraq. He described Beau's brain cancer and the wound left by his loss. He gave no political speeches.

"You should run," one of the men said. Another agreed, then another. "Run!" voices said, building to a crescendo.

"I'm not making any commitment on running," Biden said. "I just want to get us to a place where we can beat Donald Trump. I don't have to be the person to beat him."

Biden spent two hours with the men. It was as honest a human encounter that Richmond had ever seen from a politician.

FIVE

That same summer, Mitch McConnell labored to keep Trump in line, particularly on judges. Steering the federal judiciary to the right could be the keystone of his legacy.

Trump usually aligned with McConnell and Trump's White House counsel, Don McGahn, who worked closely with the Senate leader to fill up the judicial pipeline with conservative nominees. But Trump's commitment to the enterprise was never grounded in ideology, only in winning, leaving him susceptible to changing his mind.

Trump nominated Brett Kavanaugh to fill the seat being vacated by Justice Anthony M. Kennedy. Just before Kavanaugh's Senate Judiciary Committee hearing, Christine Blasey Ford, a college professor, stepped forward on September 16, 2018. She accused Kavanaugh of sexually assaulting her when they were teenagers.

Blasey Ford was soon scheduled to testify before the committee on September 27.

Trump called McConnell that morning. Should he pull the Kavanaugh nomination?

"Why don't we talk after Dr. Ford testifies?" McConnell asked. "Think of that as halftime."

Trump agreed. He would wait.

Blasey Ford, careful and hesitant, was widely seen as credible during her testimony. Trump, uneasy, stayed in touch with McConnell. He would wait to hear from Kavanaugh. Kavanaugh's testimony, that same day, was charged and defensive, and praised on the right.

Trump placed another call after both Blasey Ford and Kavanaugh testified.

"How do you feel about Kavanaugh?" Trump asked.

"I feel stronger about Kavanaugh than mule piss," McConnell said.

"What?" Trump asked.

In Kentucky, nothing is stronger than mule piss, McConnell said. "We ought to stick with him."

Besides, he said, "We need to wrap this one up one way or the other because we don't know whether we'll still be in the majority after November."

McConnell needed a swift confirmation vote on Kavanaugh. He was convinced that would be the only way to have enough time to approve another nominee before the election. If Kavanaugh lacked support or dropped out of the running, there was no guarantee he could get it done.

The Senate voted to confirm Kavanaugh on October 6, 50 votes to 48 votes.

The exhilaration of being out campaigning drove Joe Biden to hit 13 cities in the last six days of the 2018 congressional elections. And November 6 brought blue gains. Democrats won 40 additional House seats and took control, handing Nancy Pelosi the speaker's gavel for a second time. Republicans held on to the Senate majority.

Richmond and Virgil Miller, his chief of staff, made an appointment to see Biden at his office in Washington at 101 Constitution Avenue, steps from the Capitol.

"You may be the only person who can beat Donald Trump," Richmond said. "I think you should do it." Run and beat him.

Richmond was friends with Senators Cory Booker of New Jersey and Kamala Harris of California, two Black Democrats who were expected to run. But he kept coming back to Biden. For Richmond, electability was paramount. You cannot govern if you don't win first, he would say.

"I'm not sure I'm the right person," Biden replied. Richmond sensed genuine reluctance on Biden's part. "I don't have to be the person. It's not about me. Somebody else can do it."

Richmond said topic one with the Congressional Black Caucus was beating Trump. Many would support you, he said. You have a great relationship with the Black community. He reminded Biden of his visit to the Bartholomew Golf Course.

Richmond pushed. "Look, African Americans appreciate, one, your authenticity. Two, they appreciate that you had Barack Obama's back. And three, they know how much our community has to lose if Democrats can't beat Trump."

Richmond added that Biden's support extended not just through the Black Caucus but to the Hispanic Caucus and to moderates. He had a base.

By Thanksgiving 2018, the pieces were being assembled, albeit tentatively. Greg Schultz, wiry and not yet 40, was the informal campaign manager for a possible Biden campaign. He was the opposite of Donilon—a young tactician, focused on the mechanics of ground organizing and data, not soul.

A Cleveland area native, Schultz had helped guide Obama to back-to-back victories in Ohio as his state director and later joined Biden's vice presidential office as a senior adviser.

Biden would bounce around ideas and grievances with his older crew, but they counted on Schultz to keep the Biden political machine humming. Schultz had his challenges. It was a creaky machine, and campaign talent was signing up with other candidates who thought Biden's time had passed.

It was not an assessment without merit: Biden was popular on the campaign trail, but he was never a successful fundraiser. His social media following was what you would expect for a well-liked former vice president, but his political presence was almost nonexistent.

Schultz and his deputy, Pete Kavanaugh, sent Biden a detailed 11-page memo in December 2018 on the steps to set up a national campaign. It included decisions on a headquarters, scheduling, travel, staff. Clinton's campaign in Brooklyn four years earlier had been a mammoth beast. Biden's was a small cadre of loyalists.

A campaign announcement and launch were proposed for the first week of March 2019.

Richmond kept making appearances at 101 Constitution.

"I'm 74 percent in," Biden said at one point. Soon after, he said, "I'm 82 percent in."

What the hell are these percentages? Richmond asked himself. This is crazy.

Next, it was 85 percent, then 88 percent.

Oh, shit, he's running for sure, Richmond realized. It was Biden's way to get to yes.

SIX

At the close of 2018, President Trump appointed General Milley, then the Army chief, as chairman of the Joint Chiefs, a year before the official end of the term of Marine General Joseph Dunford Jr.

Trump made it clear to his aides that he felt Milley, with his broad shoulders and outgoing persona, was his kind of general. David Urban, a West Point graduate and lobbyist whom Trump credited with helping him win Pennsylvania in 2016, and who was a constant booster for Trump on CNN, had given Milley a hearty recommendation. Jim Mattis, Trump's defense secretary, had been pushing for Air Force Chief of Staff David L. Goldfein. Trump sided with Urban.

During Milley's confirmation hearing before the Armed Services Committee, Senator Angus King, independent of Maine, said, "General Milley, given the risks that you have articulated and that the National Defense Strategy articulates, I consider your job the second most important in the United States government because we are living in a dangerous world. And your position as principal advisor to the president in a time of heightened international tension and risk is incredibly significant and important. You know what my question is going to be."

"Are you going to be intimidated?" Milley responded.

"That is the question," King said. "What is the answer?"

"Absolutely not, by no one ever. I will give my best military advice. It will be candid. It will be honest. It will be rigorous. It will be thorough. And that is what I will do every single time."

Milley was self-righteous and relished proclaiming his independence. But nothing prepared him for Trump. There was no training course, no preparatory work, no school for handling a president who was a total outsider to the system. Trump simultaneously embraced military imagery and language but could be harshly critical of military leaders. Trump had isolationist and unpredictable instincts when it came to policy. America First often meant America Only.

As he settled into his new job, Milley believed his central mission was to prevent a great powers war. One large bookcase in his hallway at Quarters 6 held hundreds of thick books just on China.

The job also meant being the top military adviser to Trump, a responsibility that prompted Milley to think about a doctrine called "movement to contact," where you navigate through smoke in a battlespace and try to feel out the unknown, step by step, learning as you go. Milley had practiced it before Trump, now it was a way of life.

Mattis once called Trump's tendency to wander off during briefings "Seattle freeway off-ramps to nowhere," where Fox News items were "more salient to him."

Trump would not let up on both the largest and smallest matters. He became obsessed with the USS *Gerald R. Ford* aircraft carrier—its cost and the placement of the "island," the flight command center, that sits upright on the deck.

The generals and admirals were horrible businessmen, Trump complained repeatedly, and particularly terrible at acquisition and deal making on big ships, ensuring the military was always being ripped off.

The *Ford*, named after the 38th president, was a prime example of these white elephant business practices, Trump said. He lashed out about almost everything about the *Ford*—the elevators that raised and lowered ammunition on the ship, the catapults used for launching aircraft from the deck.

"I was in the construction business," Trump told military

leaders in one meeting. "I know about elevators. If water gets on them," they could malfunction.

But it was the redesigned placement of the island, more to the rear of the deck, that set the president off.

"It doesn't look right. I have an eye for aesthetics," Trump said at a dinner with Milley.

Trump then rubbed his own hair.

"Can't you tell?" he said in a jovial way.

Top naval officers later explained to Trump that the island was set to the rear to expand the runway space for the aircraft that landed on the deck. If the island were in the center, they said, it would funnel the wind in a way that made it more difficult for pilots.

"It just doesn't look right," Trump said.

Trump returned to the topic of the *Ford* many times, and Milley would listen. What was there to say? The president did not like a ship's look. He had to endure it, just let him vent.

Trump had announced on December 7, 2018, that he would nominate William Barr to be his next attorney general to replace Jeff Sessions. Barr, 68, had been attorney general 26 years earlier for President George H. W. Bush from late 1991 to early 1993, then served as general counsel for Verizon for 14 years.

A conservative Republican, Barr was one of the strongest advocates for the executive power of the president, and he was a firm supporter of Trump's policies, tax cuts and deregulation. And he had publicly criticized Robert Mueller's special counsel investigation of alleged collusion between Trump and Russia for infringing Trump's power—a gesture even some Republicans saw as deliberately ingratiating.

"My first choice since day one," Trump had said. "There is no one more capable or qualified for this role."

In his interview with Trump, Barr had underscored that the

president and the White House had to keep their distance from criminal investigations conducted by the Justice Department and supervised by the attorney general.

Criminal prosecutions had one rigorous standard: proof beyond a reasonable doubt. That was the basis on which someone was charged or not charged. Barr said it was in the interest of the president, the White House, the attorney general, and the Justice Department to keep a wall between criminal justice decisions and politics. He said he had learned this the first time he was attorney general. There could be no exceptions and he would not tolerate any effort by anyone to break through that wall. It was the one absolute.

Just so it was clear, Barr said again that he would not tolerate the president trying to monkey around with the criminal justice process—who to prosecute, who not to prosecute. "I don't want to hear about it," Barr said. "If there's something that's appropriate for you to know, I'll tell you."

Trump acknowledged Barr's declaration, but Barr was not sure the president understood it.

"Under the regulations, Bob Mueller could only be terminated for good cause," Barr testified a month later at his confirmation hearing before the Senate Judiciary Committee. For decades, he had known Mueller, who had been FBI director for 12 years. Mueller's reputation was sterling, he was an independent workaholic. "Frankly, it is unimaginable to me that Bob would do anything that gave rise to good cause."

Barr added, "I believe right now the overarching public interest is to allow him to finish." More pointedly, "I do not believe Mr. Mueller would be involved in a witch hunt." Before Barr was nominated, Trump had called the Russia investigation a "witch hunt" 84 times.

Barr intentionally did not take shots at Mueller. During a

break about two hours into the hearing, he went back to a holding room. His team of advisers said he was really kicking ass out there, doing a great job.

Barr's chief of staff came up and said he just got a call from Emmet Flood, who had recently served as the president's acting White House counsel. "He said he has a client problem."

"Why?" Barr asked.

"The president's going crazy. He thinks he made a mistake picking you because of what you've been saying. You said nice things about Bob Mueller."

At the White House, First Lady Melania Trump offered a contrary opinion to the president.

"Are you crazy?" she asked her husband. "This guy's right out of central casting. Look," she pointed at Barr, "that's an attorney general."

The contrast with the mousy Sessions was clear.

Now Melania was speaking the language of the president, who put a premium on appearance. Barr, six feet and with an extraordinarily large belly, came across as the sober, knowledgeable lawyer, she said.

Trump later told Barr of his wife's remarks and how important they were to him. "You do come out of central casting." He seemed to excuse Barr's otherwise slothful appearance. Barr knew he came across as Big, with a powerful, confident voice.

Trump, who was on the chunky side himself, said to Barr about his weight, "You hold it well, Bill. You carry it well. Be careful because if you lose too much weight, your skin is going to start becoming saggy."

Mueller finally finished his report in March 2019, and under the law and rules delivered the 448-page document to Barr as the attorney general. Barr and his top aides read it.

"You're not going to believe this," Barr said in a call to Judiciary Committee chairman Lindsey Graham. "After two fucking years he says, 'Well, I don't know, you decide.'"

Barr said Mueller found no evidence that Trump or his aides worked illegally or colluded with Russia. But on the critical question of whether Trump had obstructed justice, Mueller wrote one of the most convoluted lines in the history of high-profile investigations: "While this report does not conclude that the president committed a crime, it also does not exonerate him."

The attorney general was a believer in what he called the "shit or get off the pot" rule for prosecutors. They either charged or did not charge. Prosecutors were not supposed to make judgments about exoneration. Barr released a letter stating that he and his deputy "have concluded that the evidence developed during the Special Counsel's investigation is not sufficient to establish that the President committed an obstruction-of-justice offense."

The four-page summary letter and that conclusion became more controversial than the Mueller report itself. Many were outraged, calling Barr a sycophant and loyalist dutifully protecting the president, and cleaning up Trump's mess.

"It was a complete and total exoneration," Trump said, contradicting Barr's letter, which quoted the Mueller report's statement that it "does not exonerate him."

Mueller himself complained that the Barr letter distorted his findings. Next, 700 former federal prosecutors weighed in, saying the Mueller report showed multiple acts of obstruction of justice by the president, and that the president was not charged because of the Justice Department policy of not indicting a sitting president.

In a Freedom of Information Act lawsuit, a federal judge said that Barr "distorted the findings in the Mueller Report," another critique accusing Barr of carrying water for Trump.

For practical purposes, the Mueller investigation was over

though it would be debated for years. Trump was not charged, nor was he ever impeached as a result of the findings in the Mueller probe.

Trump had weathered a real threat to his presidency. He told Woodward in a taped interview, "The beautiful thing is, it all evaporated. It ended in a whimper. It was pretty amazing. It ended in dust."

SEVEN

Biden continued deliberating whether to run. In early 2019, he invited Anita Dunn, a veteran of the Obama White House and managing director at SKDK, a political and communications firm in Washington, to meet him at the estate he rented in the Virginia suburbs.

Dunn—married to Bob Bauer, who had served as Obama's White House counsel—was a defender of the party's centrist wing. She considered herself a proud liberal, but she was not in lockstep with the progressives who were increasingly gaining power after Senator Bernie Sanders of Vermont built a movement with his 2016 primary campaign against Clinton.

Sanders and his supporters defined their politics as "progressive" and to the left of "liberal." The term "progressive" carries an anti-establishment and anti-corporate protest spirit—and a more forceful, left-wing approach to economic and cultural issues. Progressives often embraced ideas such as "Medicare for All" and wealth taxes, although the label lacked a specific credo.

At 61, Dunn was in the same age range as Donilon and Ricchetti and had gotten her start in presidential politics inside Jimmy Carter's White House. Dunn was known as formidable, opinionated, tough, and smart.

Dunn had one central message for Biden: The Democratic Party is significantly misreading the 2018 midterms if it thinks the party regained control because a progressive wave is sweeping the country.

While a 28-year-old democratic socialist, New York's Alexandria Ocasio-Cortez, had upset a House Democratic leader in a primary and other Sanders allies were making inroads, there is no such wave, Dunn said.

Pay attention to Biden-type Democrats who had won, she said. She pointed to Virginia's Abigail Spanberger, a former CIA operations officer, and others who had won back long-held Republican seats.

Biden expressed hesitation. Am I too late? Will the campaign talent really be there? He was careful and nervous, no doubt remembering how much of the Obama staff had flocked to Clinton in 2015.

I'll support you if you run, Dunn told him. Biden had one clear advantage: Most candidates struggle with the message. In his case, he was the message.

But Biden's lack of direction troubled Dunn. He was notoriously slow to make decisions, and he was not building the operation he would need to start the race in a position of strength. No one appeared to be empowered to offer people jobs, and he seemed uncomfortable asking people to sign up for a maybe campaign.

She concluded that if an alternative, standout candidate emerged who Biden thought could beat Trump, he might not run.

In early March, Biden summoned Ron Klain, who had served as chief of staff in the vice president's office during the first two years of the first term.

"Come up and talk to me about the campaign," Biden said.

Klain, 55, with wavy dark hair, had the persona of a university president who had spent years on the faculty. Comfortable with power, but even more comfortable in the policy weeds. Easygoing and social, but sharp-elbowed if anyone tried to scramble his agenda.

Klain had entered Biden's orbit more than two decades earlier, serving as chief counsel to the Senate Judiciary Committee when Biden was chairman. He was one of Biden's Ivy League high achievers—magna cum laude from Harvard Law School, editor of the *Law Review*, and Supreme Court law clerk to Justice Byron White.

He also was keenly attuned to the Washington pecking order and Biden. He once candidly noted, "Joe Biden ran for president in 2008. And you do not run for president if you don't think you could be president, right? Obviously, 99 percent of Democrats thought someone else should be president, but he thought he should be president. And you bring that with you when you become vice president."

Klain had backed Hillary Clinton's presidential bid in 2016 when Biden took too long to decide, and the break had been painful for both men.

"It's been a little hard for me to play such a role in the Biden demise," Klain wrote to Clinton campaign chairman John Podesta in October 2015, a week before Biden announced he would not run. "I am definitely dead to them—but I'm glad to be on Team HRC." The email was part of a trove of Podesta exchanges hacked by Russians.

Klain, who was working for an investment firm run by AOL founder Steve Case, hopped in his car at his home in Chevy Chase, Maryland, and drove the two hours to Wilmington.

A couple hours analyzing Biden's alternatives would be a high-road, intellectual-political exercise, catnip to Klain, who belonged to that semipermanent club of politicos in Washington who went into the private sector but leapt at the chance to return to presidential politics.

"I just feel like I have to do this," Biden said as they sat down. "Trump represents something fundamentally different and wrong about politics."

Biden's next words would stick forever with Klain: *"This guy just isn't really an American president."*

Biden's certainty surprised Klain. He had anticipated Biden's usual exhausting back-and-forth, picking at the pluses and minuses of important decisions.

Klain was also struck by how different this Biden sounded from the Biden of that first presidential run back in the late 1980s. Then, conversations centered on gaming what kind of candidate could win. The theory was that Biden, then at age 44, was the right generation. He had the look, and *National Journal* had put him on its cover as a Kennedyesque figure, a significant accolade at the time.

The calculus in 1988 was all politics—the marketing department's version of what it would take to win the White House. It was a disaster.

Now, Klain felt differently. This was not a political conversation. It was to fix what Trump broke, a mission. They did not talk about the states Biden could win, the blue Democratic wall or the Electoral College.

Others running were saying the country needed to turn the page from Trump. Biden said he was going to talk about Trump regularly, perhaps endlessly.

"This is going to be brutal on your family," Klain told him. "The one thing about Trump is there will be no rules. He will throw every lie, every harsh thing, every mean thing he can at you and your family."

Some of the dark side of Hunter had already made it into the press: alcohol and addiction, messy foreign finances, a relationship with Beau's widow, massive credit card and tax debts. His former wife, Kathleen, had accused him of squandering their finances on drugs and other women.

Klain pressed. "Is your family really ready for what's coming?" It was a delicate nod to those Hunter issues.

Yes, Biden insisted. They understood.

"Are you ready for what's coming?" Klain asked. "This isn't like any campaign you have ever run before."

When Biden was on the ticket in 2008, he and Senator John McCain, then the Republican nominee, would have off-the-record, back-channel exchanges to smooth the waters.

"There's going to be no phone calls here," Klain said. "This is going to be a battle to the death. Nothing off-limits. Trump will use every possible tool, legitimate and illegitimate, fair and unfair, true and false to try to destroy you and your family."

Biden was dug in. He had crossed the decision line. He was running.

Time was running out on a formal announcement. Top campaign hands had gone to work for Senator Harris and Senator Elizabeth Warren of Massachusetts, whose progressive credentials made her a force. Pete Buttigieg, the 37-year-old mayor of South Bend, Indiana—gay and a veteran and a Rhodes Scholar—was drawing rave reviews. Biden was being privately dismissed by some donors and rivals as the past.

After about 4 p.m., after talking for six hours, Biden and Klain were done.

"I will win," Biden told Klain.

EIGHT

"You know," Joe Biden once told Mike Donilon during that period, "the family will make the decision."

Joe and Jill called a family meeting in early February 2019 that included their five grandchildren, a signal to advisers that he was inching closer.

"What do you think?" Jill asked her grandchildren. "Pop's thinking about this."

The Biden grandkids were excited. "Pop has to run! He has to do this." But Joe and Jill Biden held back. They knew if Biden got in, the race risked becoming torturous, with malicious attacks on the family.

We understand, Pop, his grandchildren assured him. Biden recalled later that year each youngster "gave their own story that they had written out, a note as to how mean they knew it was going to be," but also why Biden and the family should be all-in on a run.

Biden's grandson Robert "Hunter" Biden II handed him a photo taken of the two of them at his father, Beau's, funeral. He was then nine years old, and Biden had bent down to comfort him with his hand cupping the boy's chin.

Corners of the right wing online had lit up with wild allegations about Biden's gesture, suggesting Biden was a pedophile. The younger Biden told his grandfather he knew a campaign could be nasty.

"We do everything by family meetings," Biden told an audience at the University of Delaware on February 26, 2019, saying there was a "consensus" he should run.

"They, the most important people in my life, want me to run."

What Biden did not disclose was that his family also was in severe crisis. Hunter Biden was in the throes of addiction to crack cocaine. Biden's closest friends confided to each other that Hunter seemed to be on Biden's mind every hour.

Hunter had dropped out of his treatment center and was holed up in a New Haven, Connecticut, motel. He was smoking as much crack as he could score, roaming the streets late at night or taking long drives in his Porsche. He wrote in his memoir he had a "death wish," seeing his ability to "find crack anytime, anywhere" as a "superpower."

"It was nonstop depravity."

Joe Biden frequently texted and called Hunter, asking about his well-being and whereabouts.

"I'd tell him everything was fine," Hunter wrote. "All was well. But after a while, he wasn't buying it."

In March 2019, the family staged an intervention.

"One day, out of the blue, three or four weeks into this madness, my mother called," Hunter wrote in his memoir.

"She said that she was having a family dinner at the house, that I should come, even stay in Delaware for a few days. It would be great; we hadn't had everyone together in ages. I was in lousy shape, but it sounded appealing.

"I believe I arrived on a Friday night. I walked into the house, bright and homey as always." He was surprised to see his three daughters—Naomi, Finnegan and Maisy. "I knew then that something was up. . . . I then saw my mom and dad, smiling awkwardly, looking pained."

Hunter spotted two counselors in the room. He recognized them from a rehabilitation center in Pennsylvania.

"Not a chance," Hunter said. He recalled Joe Biden looking at him, terrified.

"I don't know what else to do," his father pleaded. "I'm so scared. Tell me what to do."

"Not fucking this," Hunter said.

"It was awful. I was awful," Hunter recounted, and the evening "devolved from there into a charged, agonized debacle," with Joe Biden chasing Hunter down the driveway as he tried to leave, grabbing his son and hugging him tightly, crying. One daughter grabbed his car keys.

To end the scene, Hunter agreed to go to a nearby rehab center in Maryland. "Anything, please," Joe Biden pleaded.

But minutes after he was dropped off, Hunter called an Uber ride and returned to his hotel room where he smoked more crack cocaine. "For the next two days, while everybody who'd been at my parents' house thought I was safe and sound at the center, I sat in my room and smoked the crack I'd tucked away in my traveling bag."

Hunter then booked a flight to California, and "ran and ran and ran." He was, he wrote, "vanishing."

NINE

With a green light, Mike Donilon prepared a memo about the pitfalls Biden would face. It came down to ignoring the noise on Twitter and from reporters. The memo's bottom line: "You need to run as Joe Biden."

Donilon verbally summarized the memo to Biden. He was direct.

"Look, you've got to run on who you are. And guess what? You've been vice president of the United States, you start this campaign with a profile with the voters, which is extraordinarily strong, and you got that by being who you are. And you try to change it, you may as well go home. Don't bother."

They came back to the concept of "soul." By then, it had become ingrained not just in Biden's rhetoric but as an idea with a bestselling following, thanks to historian Jon Meacham's 2018 book, *The Soul of America*.

When Meacham moderated the conversation with Biden at the University of Delaware that winter, Meacham told him, "I wrote the book because of Charlottesville."

Meacham, who lived in Tennessee, had also grown friendly with Biden and Donilon behind the scenes, providing insights on language and historical tidbits in phone calls. As Meacham defined it, soul was a set of values, a force that pulled Americans toward grace.

Biden and Donilon relished the input. Meacham seemed to get Biden, unlike many of the pundits who were constants on cable news, and he slowly became the informal Arthur M. Schlesinger Jr., dubbed the historian of power, for the not yet announced Biden campaign.

"I'm going to announce," Biden said to the three-person Delaware congressional delegation in March 2019, all Democrats. Biden had asked the state's two senators, Chris Coons and Tom Carper, and Delaware's lone House member, Lisa Blunt Rochester, to lunch at 101 Constitution.

Coons, who held degrees from Yale Law School and Yale Divinity School, always felt he understood Biden. They were both spiritual men, Delaware men.

He had known Biden for 30 years and had been elected to the New Castle County Council, the same office that had given Biden his start. He and Beau Biden also had been friends, and Beau had asked Coons to run for his father's Senate seat in 2010 when Joe Biden resigned to become vice president.

Coons was not surprised to hear Biden was in. Biden spoke about Charlottesville, about the country's alarming divisions. His basic pitch was being honed.

Carper and Blunt Rochester left after lunch, but Coons hung back. He and Biden talked Delaware.

"Joe," Coons said, looking Biden in the eyes, "I've got a piece of advice for you. And you know, you may not want to hear this, but Lisa is a congresswoman in her own right." Blunt Rochester was the first woman and first Black person to hold the at-large Delaware seat. "She's an elected statewide official."

"Yeah," Biden said. "What's your point?"

"You talked about her dad who had been city council president. You talked about how close you are to John Lewis," the Georgia congressman and civil rights icon. "You talked about how you're going to get endorsed by this person and that person.

"You needed to give *her* the respect of looking *her* in the eyes and saying, 'Congresswoman, I would be honored to have your support.' "

Biden blinked and turned to look out the window.

"I thought I did that," he said.

"No, you did not do that," Coons said. "It's uncomfortable for you because you don't want her to say no. And it's uncomfortable for us because we don't want to be taken for granted. But I'm telling you, you need to invest time in actually respecting her and asking for her support."

Coons worried for a moment that Biden would be angry. Coons paused and pulled back. Biden looked at Coons.

"You know, that's what Beau would have said if he were here."

Biden grew quiet. "This is going to be harder than I thought because I don't have anyone to give me that kind of advice. I want you to promise me, when you see me do something like that, you will tell me, even if it pisses me off, even if I don't want to hear it."

Coons promised.

"I'm just wondering how you felt that lunch went," Coons later said in a phone call to Blunt Rochester.

There was silence. Coons asked if she thought Biden was respectful in how he asked for their support.

"Hell, no," she said. "It's like he was telling me that I should support him because my dad supported him. And I'm not my dad."

"Yes," Coons said, "that's what I heard." Although he had already spoken with Biden, he asked, "Would you be offended if I conveyed this to the vice president?"

"That would be helpful because I was a little upset," she said.

Blunt Rochester was soon invited to visit Biden at his home on Saturday. She had serious questions about Biden as a presidential candidate. "Is he really ready for this?" she thought. "Is he the one?" She knocked on his door. Nobody answered but she could hear dogs barking.

Suddenly, she saw Biden driving down the hill, carrying coffee and bagels. I didn't know if you ate, he told her. They then went into his study. She noticed a picture of Beau in his bomber jacket.

Biden told her he wanted hard questions.

She asked him how he would bridge the gap between progressives and moderates in the party. What kind of people are you going to have run this campaign? Who would you be looking at for your cabinet?

His answers were not particularly original, but she was struck by the intensity of his engagement. He wanted her to ask him more questions. He almost looked pained when he talked about his family, what cost they would pay and how they were encouraging him to run. On domestic policy, he said he wanted to expand Obamacare.

I would want a woman as my running mate, Biden told her. That was a surprise to Blunt Rochester and was not something he had yet said publicly.

Biden said people were pressuring him to say he would only serve one term, but he had resisted.

After two and one half hours, Biden walked her to her car. Before leaving, she asked that they say a brief prayer together. And so they prayed. She drove away feeling that Biden was born for this moment.

Blunt Rochester soon endorsed Biden and went to multiple states and churches to campaign for him, from Harlem to the heartland. She campaigned harder for Biden than Coons did. Biden asked her to be one of the co-chairs for his campaign and later to be on his vice presidential selection committee.

Once Biden was elected, she knew he had lots of incoming—advice, special pleadings, recommendations. But she stayed close to him, ever judicious about his time. "I've always felt that he would listen," she said.

Biden's past habits hovered. His penchant for hugging and kissing women he met, including candidates and elected officials, was being newly scrutinized as the Me Too movement exposed sexual harassment and assault.

Biden had long dismissed criticism of his conduct as a crude attempt by Republicans to sexualize his interactions with women. But on March 29, 2019, it was not a Republican but a former Democratic state assemblywoman in Nevada who accused Biden of "demeaning and disrespectful behavior" for kissing the back of her head at a 2014 event.

"An Awkward Kiss Changed How I Saw Joe Biden," read the headline of a story written by Lucy Flores, the Nevada Democrat, for *New York* magazine. Biden was floored.

On a call with staff, Biden sounded hurt and exasperated. "I never meant . . ." he began, his voice drifting off.

Then, in a speech a few days later, Biden joked about being given permission to hug the president of the association who had introduced him. He also told reporters he was "not sorry for anything I've ever done." The reaction was fierce. Biden stopped making the joke.

In her book, Jill said her husband comes from a family of huggers. But after the Flores episode, and public complaints from six other women who said Biden's touching and kissing made them feel uncomfortable, Jill was firm with Joe: You need to change, fast.

"He needs to give people their space," Jill Biden later told *CBS This Morning*. She called the women who came forward courageous. "Joe has heard that message."

TEN

By April 2019, Biden and Donilon were under pressure to launch. Already, 19 Democrats had jumped into the race, the largest field in decades.

Donilon initially thought Biden should give a speech in Charlottesville. But complications arose with using the University of Virginia as a backdrop. Biden instead played against type: a controlled, three-and-a-half-minute taped video shared on social media. Something younger, more contemporary.

In a suit jacket and open-collared shirt with dramatic background music, Biden said "Charlottesville, Virginia, is home to the author of one of the great documents in human history," Thomas Jefferson. It is "also home to a defining moment for this nation in the last few years.

"If we give Donald Trump eight years in the White House, he will forever and fundamentally alter the character of this nation. Who we are. And I cannot stand by and watch that happen."

Notable was what was not included. No biography. No discussion of policy. Just Charlottesville, the "soul of the nation," and Trump as a moral aberration.

News coverage of the announcement had a check-the-box quality. The forever candidate. Many political reporters found Biden unexciting, like a grandfather they liked but who told too many folksy stories. Progressives outwardly detested him as a relic of Democratic mistakes on Iraq and the 1994 tough-on-crime bill, which disproportionately affected people of color. Most remembered was his much criticized handling of Anita Hill's allegations of sexual harassment by Supreme Court nominee Clarence Thomas.

Inside Biden's circle, there was private grousing about the subtle dig behind the news coverage: Old white man, with a record of failing and dropping out early, enters the most diverse presidential primary contest. Couldn't they see he was taking the fight straight to Trump?

Biden jumped on the Amtrak train from Washington to Wilmington, the route he had traveled most evenings while in the Senate to be home with his family. He stopped at Gianni's Pizza, ordered a pepperoni pizza to go, and talked with locals. And he called Heather Heyer's mother, Susan Bro, around 4:30 p.m., and spoke of loss.

Biden then headed to a campaign fundraiser in Philadelphia. The next day, his campaign reported it raised $6.3 million in the 24 hours following his announcement, more than any other Democratic candidate raised on their first day.

Donilon saw hope amid the naysaying, particularly about the "soul" theme being too vague and old-fashioned. It was who Biden was. The last thing Donilon wanted was another Democrat running another typical presidential campaign on promises for the economy or health care. Something bigger was at work.

The Trump White House reacted with surprise. What a lost opportunity for Joe Biden, Kellyanne Conway, the controversial Trump counselor, told the president, dissecting Biden's video. Charlottesville?

Trump agreed. He found it ridiculous.

"His fast lane," Conway told Trump, "was to remind everybody that he and he alone was Barack Obama's number two." Had his back. Remind people that he had the perfect Washington résumé. Instead, Biden made no mention of Obama or his experience.

She saw a better approach and went into automatic campaign mode. Biden should have said, "Trump is what happens when you don't have enough Washington experience. Trump is what happens when you don't know your way around Capitol Hill like I do. For those of you who miss the Obama years, I'm your guy."

Conway called it a blown announcement. "Biden missed a second opportunity," she said. "He should have energetically and enthusiastically made six or seven stops the day he announced in some of the states Obama-Biden carried two times and that you carried in 2016."

They knew the states well—Michigan, Wisconsin and Pennsylvania—and Trump's margin of victory. "He should have had union guys behind him. Biden should have said to the voters, 'Listen, I want you back.'"

Trump nodded and hit Biden as a candidate of likely little or no consequence, wildly out of step with his party. But he also knew Biden had a brand. If anyone understood the power of a brand, it was Trump. Obama-Biden had won two national races. He'd keep watch.

"Welcome to the race Sleepy Joe," Trump said on Twitter. "I only hope you have the intelligence, long in doubt, to wage a successful primary campaign. It will be nasty—you will be dealing with people who truly have some very sick & demented ideas. But if you make it, I will see you at the Starting Gate!"

A few days later, Trump stopped to speak with reporters on the White House lawn before boarding Marine One. The helicopter's blades were whirring. The president was buoyant, his tone taunting.

"I just feel like a young man. I'm so young. I can't believe it," Trump told them. "I'm a young vibrant man.

"I look at Joe. I don't know about him."

When Biden, appearing on ABC's *The View* that day, was told of Trump's comment, he playfully dipped his head for a second, blinked twice in exasperation, and smiled.

"Look," Biden joked, "if he looks young and vibrant compared to me, I should probably go home."

Biden's eye was on Trump. In late April 2019, he traveled to Pittsburgh to serve up his middle-class arguments to a boisterous crowd at Teamsters Local 249.

"I am a union man," he told the rank and file. "If I'm going to be able to beat Donald Trump in 2020, it's going to happen here."

But by the summer, Anzalone came back with poll results from Iowa, the first contest. "Soul" was a flop. Iowa Democrats craved a bolder economic message.

Donilon would not budge, and Biden never asked for a change. "Soul of the nation" was it.

ELEVEN

Cedric Richmond's political mentor, House Majority Whip James Clyburn, heard the critics. Biden again? Why not new blood? Shouldn't Black Democrats rally behind one of their own?

But this was not a normal year to the South Carolina Democrat, two years older than Biden and the highest-ranking Black leader in Congress. Trump had to be defeated.

Clyburn, a sturdy orator going back to his childhood and his days as a public school teacher in Charleston, also prized his private time. Lately, he had been studying up on fascist histories, with a focus on Italy. He saw Trump as America's Benito Mussolini in waiting.

Clyburn wondered if Trump would leave the White House if he lost reelection.

On a humid Friday, June 21, 2019, Biden arrived in Columbia, South Carolina, for Clyburn's annual fish fry, a gathering that had become a must-stop for Democratic presidential hopefuls. The crowd was mostly Black, eating fried whiting filets with hot sauce.

Biden needed a bounce and a show of support from the South Carolina party king.

News coverage of Biden's campaign had taken its worst turn. That week, Biden had said there was "some civility" years ago in Washington. He cited his experience of working with segregationist senators.

"I was in a caucus with James O. Eastland," Biden said at a fundraiser, referring to the late Mississippi senator and segregationist. "He never called me boy, he always called me son."

Biden also recalled the late Georgia senator and segregationist Herman Talmadge, "one of the meanest guys I ever knew.

"You go down the list of all these guys. Well guess what? At least there was some civility. We got things done. We didn't agree on much of anything. We got things done. We got it finished. But today, you look at the other side and you're the enemy. Not the opposition, the enemy. We don't talk to each other anymore."

When later pressed on his remarks by a gaggle of reporters, Biden was defensive.

"I ran for the United States Senate because I disagreed with the views of the segregationists," he said.

They asked him whether he would apologize.

"Apologize for what?" Biden asked, raising his eyebrow. "There's not a racist bone in my body."

Clyburn made sure to defend Biden when reporters came up to him at the fish fry. Biden was a good man, period. But he did not endorse him, following his tradition of not announcing a favorite in the primary race.

When Clyburn returned home that night, he gave a rundown to his wife of 60 years, Emily, who was nearing the end of a decades long struggle with diabetes. He noted the crowd roared for Joe Biden.

Emily, a librarian, was an astute political observer, Clyburn's eyes and ears. When they attended church together, she brought a notebook and recorded how others reacted to her husband. She liked to give him a readout.

"If we really want to win," and beat Trump, "our best candidate would be Joe Biden," Emily Clyburn told him that night, her voice soft.

"You're probably right about that," Clyburn told her. "But that would be for the general. The problem is getting him out of the primary."

A week later in Miami, Mayor Buttigieg spotted Biden, his head down, touch the rosary beads on his wrist before stepping onstage at the first Democratic presidential primary debate.

Biden turned and told Buttigieg that they were Beau's.

Biden seemed to be in all the candidates' sights. It was a rough outing. The hardest hit came from Senator Harris, who tore into Biden's long-ago opposition to school busing.

"So on the issue of race," Harris said, "I couldn't agree more that this is an issue that is still not being talked about truthfully and honestly."

She paused and looked to her right. "I'm going to now direct this at Vice President Biden. I do not believe you are a racist. And I agree with you when you commit yourself to the importance of finding common ground.

"But it was hurtful," she said, "to hear you talk about the reputations of two United States senators who built their reputations and career on the segregation of race in this country. And it was not only that, but you also worked with them to oppose busing.

"And, you know," she said, her voice filling with emotion, "there was a little girl in California who was part of the second class to integrate her public schools, and she was bused to school every day. And that little girl was me."

Harris left a mark.

Members of Biden's family were surprised and indignant. Senator Harris, the former California attorney general, had been close with Beau when he was Delaware's AG.

How could she?

By the next week, a Quinnipiac University poll showed Harris jumping up, landing in a virtual tie with Biden for the lead in the race, with Biden at 22 percent and Harris at 20 percent among Democratic voters.

TWELVE

Progressives were on the march, eager to pull the party away from Wall Street and the foreign policy hawks—and from Biden. Senator Harris's bump to the top tier did not last, and by early fall, Senators Sanders and Warren were the two leading lights of the left wing in the race.

While Sanders still had a fervent following from his 2016 campaign, when he had seemed close to beating Clinton, his progressive rivals now saw him as vulnerable. His October 1 heart attack during a Las Vegas campaign stop, at age 78, only led to more questions about whether he would stay in the race.

Sanders, however, recovered quickly—and concentrated on Biden. Sanders, a former track star, was always running, going back to long-shot, unsuccessful statewide campaigns in the 1970s and then his out-of-nowhere victory in Burlington, Vermont's mayoral race in 1981.

If he muscled through the fall campaign, Sanders and his team envisioned a head-to-head match against Biden, perhaps deep into 2020.

"Over time, Senator, he's the perfect foil for you," Faiz Shakir, Sanders's trusted campaign manager, told him. They could position Sanders as a progressive on the correct side of history, and Biden as the past.

Sanders agreed. Buttigieg and others were straining to be the centrist alternative to Biden. So was billionaire Michael Bloomberg, the former New York mayor, who was moving toward a run. But Sanders never thought they would outlast his former Senate colleague.

"Joe Biden's the one we're going to have to defeat," Sanders said.

Shakir later told others that Sanders "always believed it, always felt it.

"Every debate. Every kind of conversation we had about the race, it was always Biden, Biden, Biden. It wasn't like Bloomberg or Warren or somebody else," Shakir said. "He was always, you know, 'How's Joe Biden doing? How is his operation doing?' was always what he wanted to know."

Donilon kept resisting persistent calls for a shakeup of the message. He organized a set of focus groups in South Carolina, the state believed to be Biden's firewall.

Donilon showed them videos: the announcement videos, and another video on the "soul of the nation."

The participants were mostly older Black women, the voters Clyburn said would be crucial. When the videos were screened, the women began to cry. They said that's the America we're living in. That's what we're scared of. That's what we're worried about. That's our life. That's why we want Biden to win.

Donilon was heartened as he discussed the results with colleagues, and later said, "I always remember that single piece of information about how powerful this message was and how clear and resonant it was with these voters, in particular African American voters and older, African American women in South Carolina."

Outside of the intense echo chamber on Twitter, Donilon said, "there's a fundamental fear" at the crux of this presidential race.

Donilon informed Biden, reporting, "They cried."

Biden, though, seemed open to advice. He knew he was straddling generations.

"Just be yourself," Speaker Pelosi told him at the funeral service for Maryland congressman Elijah Cummings in October. "Do so in a way that shows your authenticity. After all is said and done, that's what people want to see. The sincerity. The genuineness."

She had been watching his campaign, watching him flail early on. She would be neutral in the primary race but did not hide her affection for him, personally or politically.

"You know," Pelosi added, "these young people now, they have a smaller attention span. So, we all have to be briefer in how we speak."

By the end of the year, before any votes were cast, Senator Harris and former Texas congressman Beto O'Rourke had dropped out despite their enthusiastic beginnings.

Biden had survived but his campaign was still stuck in gear, with Sanders, Warren and Buttigieg now surging in the early voting states.

To complicate matters, Bloomberg, who jumped into the race in November, was sinking millions of dollars into advertising and on-the-ground operations. Due to his late entry, he was gambling on an unorthodox approach and bypassing competing in the early voting states.

Biden allies like Congressman Tim Ryan, an Ohio Democrat, were nervous. Biden seemed to have been washed out of the news.

"Trust the plan," Biden told Ryan when they crossed paths at a Pittsburgh airport.

During a December 5, 2019, Oval Office interview for Woodward's book, *Rage*, Trump asked Woodward to predict who would be his Democratic opponent. Woodward passed on answering.

"I'll be honest with you, I think it's a terrible group of candidates," Trump said. "It's an embarrassment. I'm embarrassed by the Democratic candidates. I may have to run against one, and who knows? It's an election. And I'm looking pretty good right now."

THIRTEEN

In January 2020, Biden was campaigning full-time in Iowa ahead of the caucuses.

In between stops, he met regularly with Tony Blinken, his longtime top foreign policy adviser, for briefings on the world.

Blinken had served as No. 2 in the State Department during the Obama years after first working for Biden in the vice president's office. He kept in touch with the foreign policy and intelligence establishments as well as anyone outside government.

While known for his smooth diplomacy in both professional and personal dealings, Blinken kept his hair long and played in a dad-rock band.

That January, news of a virulent virus emerged from China. On January 23, China locked down Wuhan, one of its most populated cities, and restricted its population of 11 million people to their homes to control the outbreak.

Blinken told Biden a global health emergency could explode, perhaps into a pandemic. He urged Biden to speak out on it.

Biden talked with Klain, who had overseen the Ebola crisis for the Obama administration in late 2014 and early 2015. Klain had led efforts to track individuals from Ebola-stricken countries and worked closely with the Centers for Disease Control and Prevention.

Get out in front of it, Klain suggested to Biden. Blow the whistle loudly.

These outbreaks are always harder and take more time than

anyone thinks, Klain said. It is not over until it is over, and you risk over-responding or under-responding.

They agreed it was precisely a governing, organizing matter that Trump could not handle. But Biden could.

Biden and his team drafted an op-ed and placed it in *USA Today*, the daily newspaper aimed at travelers who would be alarmed about a worldwide health crisis.

It ran on January 27. The headline: "Trump Is Worst Possible Leader to Deal with Coronavirus Outbreak." Biden blasted Trump for tweeting "it will all work out well" and for proposing "draconian cuts" to the CDC and the National Institutes of Health. He pledged, if elected, to "always uphold science, not fiction or fearmongering."

The next day, Trump's national security adviser, Robert O'Brien, warned him, in a top secret Presidential Daily Briefing, that the mysterious pneumonia-like virus outbreak would be seismic.

Sitting at the Resolute Desk, Trump looked intently at O'Brien.

"This will be the biggest national security threat you face in your presidency," O'Brien said.

"What do we do about it?" Trump asked, turning to Matthew Pottinger, the deputy national security adviser, who had been a *Wall Street Journal* reporter in China. Pottinger said his excellent sources in China believed the U.S. could suffer hundreds of thousands of deaths from the virus.

Cut off travel from China to the United States. A major health crisis was coming, Pottinger said, that could resemble the Spanish flu pandemic of 1918 that killed an estimated 675,000 Americans.

Three days later, Trump curtailed travel with China, but the president remained distracted. There was the upcoming Super Bowl, the Democratic presidential field, his State of the Union address—and his Senate impeachment trial.

At the heart of the trial was Trump's angst about Biden. Trump publicly dismissed Biden, but he and his senior advisers knew Biden, unlike Hillary Clinton, had a strong base among blue-collar voters. Since Trump had narrowly beaten Clinton, any erosion of Trump's support with those voters could be crippling to his reelection chances.

On July 25, 2019, Trump had called recently elected Ukrainian prime minister Volodymyr Zelensky, who was seeking a commitment of military aid from the United States in Ukraine's conflict with Russia.

In the call, a transcript of which Trump later ordered released, Trump asked Zelensky to talk with Attorney General William Barr and the president's personal attorney, Rudy Giuliani, about an investigation of the Bidens, particularly Hunter Biden's work for Burisma, a Ukrainian energy company that faced legal trouble.

In early February, Trump was acquitted by the Republican-controlled Senate of impeachment charges that he abused his power and obstructed Congress, falling 10 votes short of the 67-vote, two-thirds majority required by the Constitution to remove the president from office.

Jake Sullivan, previously a top national security aide to Biden and to Hillary Clinton, was another super high-achiever inside Biden's campaign.

Sullivan, 42, was Yale Law School, a Rhodes Scholar, and a law clerk to Supreme Court Justice Stephen Breyer. Rail thin, he was cautious and serious. In meetings, Biden often asked, "Jake, what do you think?"

Sullivan had studied the upcoming caucuses and primaries. They were obviously unfriendly terrain for Biden—mostly white and rural.

Early on, Sullivan came up with a strategy, one he wrote down and kept:

4-3-2-1

Fourth in Iowa, third in New Hampshire, second in Nevada, and first in must-win South Carolina.

By February 2020, the 4-3-2-1 plan was on the brink of collapsing entirely, and campaign manager Greg Schultz was under mounting pressure.

Biden, averse to the drama of a public shakeup, kept Schultz on board, but dispatched Anita Dunn to the campaign's Philadelphia headquarters to take charge of a demoralized campaign with a shoestring budget. She was now de facto campaign manager.

The Iowa caucuses on February 3 were a drubbing—the expected fourth-place finish. Biden won just 16 percent of the vote, slumping behind Buttigieg, Sanders and Warren. That trio took 70 percent of the vote in the state.

As the New Hampshire primary neared, Dunn warned others that Biden may not be able to compete if Bloomberg began to make gains nationwide. Super Tuesday, a battleground with 1,357 delegates in 14 states, lay ahead on March 3, following the first four contests.

Biden was not pointing fingers or blaming people. Dunn saw no self-pity. Instead, he asked, "What is our plan and how are we going to do this?"

With scant funds, Dunn shut down Biden's Super Tuesday efforts. Field staff east of the Mississippi were sent to South Carolina. Those to the west of the Mississippi were sent to Nevada, where Biden was looking to kindle labor support.

Buttigieg, surging in the polls after a narrow delegate win for him in Iowa, saw the New Hampshire primary on February 11 as a chance to take the lead.

To try to slow him, the Biden campaign pulled together a brutal attack video called "Pete's Record," comparing his record with Biden's. The ad's narrator said both Biden and Buttigieg had "taken on tough fights."

"Under the threat of nuclear Iran, Joe Biden helped negotiate the Iran deal," the narrator said. Then the background music lightened up, like a cartoon track. "And under the threat of disappearing pets, Pete Buttigieg negotiated lighter licensing regulations on pet chip scanners."

It went on, the music alternating, touting Biden's work on the economy and Obama stimulus package, "saving our economy from a depression" while "Pete Buttigieg revitalized the sidewalks of downtown South Bend by laying out decorative brick."

The campaign, though, had no money to run the ad on television. Donilon argued to Biden that it was politically necessary to release it to the media and on YouTube. The pickup could be greater than a paid ad.

"I hate it," Biden said, but agreed the video could be released.

About six hours later, Biden called Donilon: "Take it off. Take it back. I don't want it airing any longer. Take it down!"

It was too late. The media was running the ad, with some commentators saying it showed Biden's desperation. Buttigieg's aides labeled the attack as a classic example of snarky, dirty Washington politics.

Biden was polling fifth in New Hampshire. On top of that, campaign finances were dwindling.

On the eve of the New Hampshire vote, Jake Sullivan and Biden communications director Kate Bedingfield sat in a bar in Manchester, New Hampshire. Sullivan wrote a new sequence on a napkin:

4-5-2-1

New Hampshire was a catastrophe. Sanders and Buttigieg each received about 25 percent of the vote, and Senator Amy Klobuchar of Minnesota, another moderate, exceeded expectations and took 20 percent. Warren finished fourth.

Biden, with about 8 percent of the vote, in fifth place, left New Hampshire that night and dashed toward South Carolina.

FOURTEEN

On Sunday, February 23, the Congressional Black Caucus had a gathering on the USS *Yorktown*, a massive, decommissioned aircraft carrier docked in Charleston. It was six days until the South Carolina primary.

Biden needed Clyburn to get off the fence, now, and endorse him. He arrived at the ship late at night. In a tucked-away room, Clyburn was waiting.

Clyburn got right to the point. This meeting was about hard politics. If Clyburn were going to play savior, he wanted a political guarantee in exchange: Biden would make Black voters his priority, in the campaign and in the White House.

Clyburn also thought Biden was rusty and needed a kick in the ass.

"There are three things I'd like for you to do that, I think, would really make this endorsement work," Clyburn told Biden.

"I'm listening," Biden said.

"The first thing is, you should really shorten your speeches and get more to the point."

Biden stayed mum.

"My advice is the advice my dad gave me," Clyburn said, recalling his minister father. Keep it simple, keep it short.

"He would tell me, 'Just remember, when you speak, the Father, the Son and the Holy Ghost. Don't go beyond those three things," Clyburn said.

"My second point is about 10-20-30," Clyburn said. Biden

knew the reference. It was Clyburn's signature antipoverty plan for federal spending, allocating "at least 10 percent of funding from any given federal program to counties where 20 percent of the population has lived below the poverty line for 30 years or more."

"You need to adopt 10-20-30," Clyburn told him. "Now, it's in your platform, but you've got to run on it.

"Finally, the third thing, is I've three daughters.

"I'm very proud of my three daughters and it's a little bit disconcerting for us to be at this particular juncture in our history and there has never been an African American woman on the Supreme Court.

"Four women. No African Americans. There is something wrong with that."

"I played a role in having the first Latina on the Supreme Court and I look forward to doing that with an African American woman," Biden said.

Biden and Clyburn shook hands.

The remaining Democrats convened in Charleston on February 25 for the final debate before the primary.

Biden was in the spotlight. But so was Sanders, who won the Nevada caucuses on February 22, where Biden had come in second place. With two outright victories in New Hampshire and Nevada, and a near tie in Iowa, a Sanders nomination, a seeming fantasy five years earlier, was imaginable.

At the debate, Clyburn sat up front. His endorsement had been offered to Biden with conditions, and all but sealed. But nothing had so far leaked out. If Biden flopped or failed to follow through, Clyburn could hold back.

Clyburn cringed as he watched. Biden whiffed on numerous chances to bring up the Supreme Court pledge.

During an intermission, Clyburn told a friend he was heading to the restroom. He instead strolled backstage and pulled Biden aside.

"Man, there have been a couple instances up there tonight where you could have mentioned having a Black woman on the Supreme Court," Clyburn said. "You can't leave the stage without doing that. You just got to do that."

Of course, Biden said, you got it.

In his final answer, Biden hit the mark.

"Everyone should be represented. Everyone," he said. "The fact is what we should be doing—we talked about the Supreme Court. I'm looking forward to making sure there's a Black woman on the Supreme Court, to make sure we in fact get every representation."

The crowd roared. Clyburn nodded.

The next day, Clyburn spoke in North Charleston.

In a dark suit and bright gold tie, he looked out and saw two of his daughters, Jennifer and Angela. They were sitting a seat apart, with a vacant seat between them. Clyburn thought of his late wife, Emily, who had died in September.

"I know Joe," Clyburn said. "We know Joe.

"But most importantly," he said, his voice raspy and his right index finger punctuating the air, "Joe knows *us*.

"I know his heart. I know who he is. I know who he is!" Clyburn said. "I know where this country is."

Biden stood over to Clyburn's right, his hands clasped. Biden's eyes welled up with emotion as he listened to Clyburn offer a passionate endorsement. It was everything he needed at that moment. And it was a political explosion.

For months, there were constant complaints about Biden's campaign. Too old, too slow, not enough energy. Too centrist. The past. Party officials, the press corps—they all had that refrain. No more. Biden was now the candidate positioned to fend off Sanders. The one who could rally Black Democrats. The one who could beat Trump.

During an interview with CNN that Friday, on the eve of the primary, Clyburn made a jarring statement: Biden needed to win by at least 15 or 16 points. Cedric Richmond chided him over drinks that evening.

"Don't do us any favors," Richmond said. "We haven't won one yet. And now all of a sudden, you want us to beat the field by 15 or 16 points? You've just upped the ante."

Clyburn was sure Biden would finish well over that. "I know South Carolina," he said. He also knew Sanders, while making strides with Black voters since stumbling in 2016, had not yet found a way to galvanize them in the same way he excited white progressives.

A day later, February 29, Biden won 48.7 percent of the South Carolina vote, a colossal victory. Sanders plummeted from being the near front-runner, carrying just 19.8 percent of the vote, a lackluster second. Buttigieg and Klobuchar finished in the single digits.

At Biden's primary night rally, a beaming Jill Biden gave Clyburn a hug as she and Joe Biden took the stage. Curtis Mayfield's "Move on Up" blared loudly, and supporters lifted their blue Biden posters.

"My buddy, Jim Clyburn! You brought me back!" Biden told the crowd. "And we are very much alive."

Buttigieg and Klobuchar raced to meet Biden in Dallas and endorse. So did Beto O'Rourke, the young Texan who loved to jump on tables to give speeches.

It would be a unity rally on March 2, the day before the Super Tuesday showdown.

Sanders's fear was suddenly the reality. Many Democrats were rushing to back Biden and end the race—and stave off a Sanders comeback. Sanders, they believed, would lose to Trump in a general election.

Biden was moved as his rivals arrived.

"I don't think I've ever done this before, but he reminds me of my son, Beau," Biden said at an event before the rally, standing next to Buttigieg, clean-cut with his crisp white shirt and dark blue tie. Buttigieg had served in Afghanistan in the Navy Reserve.

"I know that may not mean much to most people. But to me, it's the highest compliment," Biden said.

Backstage, Klobuchar and her husband, John Bessler, met with Joe and Jill Biden. Their exchanges were gracious. Then Klobuchar noticed Cameron Smith, her campaign's young photographer, was crying.

"Cam, it's okay," Klobuchar said. "This is good."

Biden walked over to Smith and put his arm around her in a fatherly way. "Cam, we're all going to work together. You're going to be okay."

Jill Biden also cried backstage. It was catharsis. Everything had come together.

Klobuchar told Jill Biden that she often looked at Jill during debates because she was a "good face," warm and upbeat. And, she noted with a smile, Jill would nod agreeably from time to time at her answers.

After the rally, O'Rourke and his wife, Amy, joined Biden for a late bite at Whataburger, a fast food chain. Biden was ebullient, shaking hands with the workers behind the counters and signing autographs.

Sitting down for burgers and shakes, they talked kids. O'Rourke's were growing fast. Biden noted that college was coming and recalled visiting campuses decades ago.

Biden remembered his dad did not like the elite Amherst College in Massachusetts, one of the little Ivies, even though Biden was interested in attending.

"He said, 'You'd have to work in the dining hall serving rich kids,'" Biden told them.

Biden added that his father, who had a high school education from St. Thomas Academy in Scranton, was just not interested in visiting Amherst. His father would feel uncomfortable, out of place.

"That fucking got me," O'Rourke, who graduated from Columbia University, later remarked about the exchange. "Because that obviously got Biden." Feeling a father's shame, 50 years on.

O'Rourke noted in a journal entry that evening that "Biden's ability to understand that feeling his dad had is part of his genius."

FIFTEEN

Faiz Shakir, Sanders's campaign manager, soon got a phone call from his old boss, former Senate majority leader Harry Reid of Nevada. Reid was endorsing Biden.

"Listen, Faiz," Reid said. "I just hope you appreciate that I got a lot of pressure."

Shakir called Sanders. "If Harry Reid is moving to Joe Biden," Shakir said, "it means that there's a lot of other movements occurring. Harry Reid doesn't move alone." Party leaders, donors, officials—they wanted this over.

Super Tuesday brought 10 more states for Biden, picking up wins from the South to the Midwest to New England, and winning in Texas. Michigan's March 10 primary was critical, and Biden won there, too. It was not just the brass making a statement. It was voters.

That night, on a flight, Sanders motioned for Shakir to come over. It was time to call the Biden people.

"Just ask them if there's a role for progressives to play in their campaign," Sanders said, his voice low. "Just ask them that. Let's see where they want to go with this."

Unlike in 2016, when he and his allies warred with Clinton's campaign all the way to the convention and viewed her as elitist and moderate, Sanders wanted to play ball and endorsed Biden. Maybe he could nudge Joe toward going big, toward transformation, toward an agenda that incorporated progressive ideas.

Biden would be spared a Democratic civil war. It was one of the most dramatic turnarounds in presidential campaign history.

Biden faced a new world: He was now effectively the Democratic presidential nominee. But the pandemic upended his campaign's plans.

Biden suspended in-person campaigning in mid-March as the virus spread and governors across the map began to ban large gatherings. He focused on virtual events.

The shift was strange, from busy marathon days with flights and rallies to a life of seclusion, working from his home in Delaware surrounded by Secret Service. He spoke with aides and supporters throughout the day, by phone and video, in lieu of events. He did TV interviews. Trump made fun of Biden, calling him "Basement Biden."

Even with Sanders in the fold, holding Democrats together was a priority. Biden needed to keep his onetime rivals close, to make sure the left felt welcome. To beat Trump, no one could stay on the sidelines.

Senator Elizabeth Warren's older brother, Don Reed, died in late April 2020 from the coronavirus. He was an Air Force veteran who had seen action in Vietnam.

Warren, who had dropped out after Super Tuesday in March, fielded dozens of calls—paint-by-numbers condolences.

Then Joe Biden rang.

"This is just wrong. This is just goddamned wrong!" Biden told her.

Biden said he did not know Don Reed, but he said he was "quite sure he was fiercely proud" of her.

He told her brothers and sisters have special relationships. He talked about his sister, Valerie, and how they would ride bicycles together.

"These internal relationships that you form when you're so little, last forever," he said. He then laughed. "And here we all are in our seventies.

"But those things that tied us together as children, tie us together as human beings, even after death."

Biden turned the conversation toward the pandemic and the economy. He said the country was on the precipice of a calamity on both unless significant action was taken.

Warren, a progressive who had built a campaign on "plans" for wholesale economic reform and an influx of federal spending, perked up. Was Biden signaling he was moving toward her?

"This is bad and we're on the edge," Biden told her. "And this guy," Trump, "is trying to deny it."

Biden said he was desperate to do something. Something that would have an impact.

Biden expressed thanks to her and others in the party for backing him. It meant a lot to see the Democrats come together. Warren could sense he was touched.

"I couldn't be doing this without you, kid," Biden told her. The conversation had lasted 30 minutes.

On April 27, 2020, Tony Fabrizio, a premier Republican pollster working for the president, sent an unvarnished and pointed three-page memo to Brad Parscale, then the Trump campaign manager. It was a document worthy of the political campaign hall of fame.

"We have seen the enemy and the enemy is us," Fabrizio wrote. They were failing to define Biden and allowing him free rein over his own image.

The memo offered an ominous forecast to the Trump campaign: Trump was on the road to epic defeat.

At the outset, Fabrizio wrote, "you are probably tired of me sounding alarmist, but I think what I've laid out below makes a compelling case for us to immediately ramp up our efforts to define Biden.

"We are at a low point. . . . The collapse of optimism about the economy and the impact of the CV [coronavirus] overall and more specifically, how POTUS is perceived as handling it, have been a triple whammy on us. Conversely, Biden has been largely MIA and by going around to the national media and directly to local market media, he has steadily rehabilitated his image across the board."

He added, "Absent a miraculous 2-month recovery for the economy or Biden literally imploding, there is little chance that we will find ourselves back in the position we were in February without a full-throated engagement of Biden."

Fabrizio summarized the campaign's polling and research to date in 10 points. He warned that Trump's leadership on the pandemic was a handicap:

> *And while POTUS started off in a strong position on his handling of the [coronavirus], even though he continued to dominate the conversation and drew huge audiences with his daily briefings, the controversies and conflicts that came out of them were often the only take-aways for voters.*

Fabrizio underscored his conclusion:

> *As we have seen many times before, it isn't POTUS policies that cause the biggest problem, it is voters' reactions to his temperament and behavior.*

Fabrizio also dismissed the rumor that Democrats would replace Biden at their convention. That chatter had spread in right-wing media circles and drifted into the Oval Office. Trump brought it up constantly.

"I know POTUS tends to share this opinion," Fabrizio wrote. But he said the idea was absurd.

"Short of an utter and complete implosion on his part," Biden would be the nominee, Fabrizio wrote. In May, a "sustained attack of several weeks with meaningful weight to move numbers" was necessary.

Fabrizio did not expect Parscale to follow his advice. Parscale was close to Trump's son-in-law and adviser, Jared Kushner, who Fabrizio believed routinely hid uncomfortable political truths from the president.

Fabrizio, stout with a gray beard, decided to deliver the bad news directly to Trump in the Oval Office.

"Mr. President, every day this race is about you, we're losing," he said. "Every day the race is about Joe Biden, we're winning. And right now, Joe Biden's not doing anything, so the race is constantly about you."

SIXTEEN

After 15 months running the Justice Department for the president, Attorney General Bill Barr was also worried in April 2020 that Trump was sabotaging his reelection chances. He needed a come-to-Jesus meeting.

Barr consulted two people about what he should say to Trump, first his wife of 47 years, Christine, a librarian, who was close friends with Robert Mueller's wife, Ann.

"You can't save someone from themselves," Christine told her husband. "This guy is set in his ways and he is what he is, and you're not going to change that."

"I know," Barr said. "I'm going to try." He would continue to run Justice the way he thought was in the best interest of both Trump and the administration, and then, "hopefully, he'll have a shot at being reelected."

Barr confided, though, that he felt a little bitter. "I've been around long enough not to hold grudges, but I feel I and a lot of others went in there to help this guy, sort of acclimate him to the Washington system." Guide Trump about its boundaries. The problem, he said, was Trump's "own pigheadedness and his blindness."

Barr remembered how he mounted a similar effort 28 years ago with President George H. W. Bush, when Barr had been attorney general for the first time.

Jack Kemp, then the housing secretary, and Barr had gone to see Bush after a cabinet meeting in March 1992, when Bush was leading in the polls for his own reelection bid.

"Mr. President, on the current trajectory, we think you're going to lose," Barr said. Kemp echoed him. Bush had been shocked. Their message was that he had to pay a lot more attention to domestic affairs and the economy. It turned out to be good advice. Bush lost in part because he failed to have a coordinated message on the economy.

Barr checked with Jared Kushner, who said the way was clear to go talk to Trump alone. Kushner said Trump needed to hear it, and he was going to have other officials swing by. But Barr would be the leadoff batter of the soft intervention because he might get a hit.

Barr went into the little dining room off the Oval Office and took a seat. He steeled himself because Trump's usual approach when the president detected someone coming with an unwelcome recommendation, or something he didn't want to hear, was to filibuster.

"No filibustering, Mr. President, please," Barr said. "I really hope that you take to heart what I say, because it's important for me that you listen."

Trump nodded and signaled he would listen.

"Mr. President, I think you're on a trajectory to lose the election. I travel probably more than any other cabinet secretary around the country. And I'm talking to Joe Six Pack kind of guys. You know, cops and stuff like that. I have yet to meet one of your supporters who doesn't come up to me and, say, 'You know, we love the president, we love you. We want our selfie. You know, thank God. God bless you.' "

But Barr said "these people whisper, 'Would you please tell the president to dial it back? Would you please tell him not to tweet as much? He's his own worst enemy.'

"This election is about the suburbs," Barr said. "You know you're going to bring in your base and you don't gain anything by continuing to be more and more outrageous. And I think you have some repair work to do among Republican and independent voters who like your policies generally."

Barr paused and delivered his summary line: "They just think you're a fucking asshole."

Trump did not seem taken aback or insulted.

"In my opinion," Barr said, "this is not a base election. Your base is critical, and you'll get it out. And there are a lot of people out there, independents and Republicans in the suburbs of the critical states that think you're an asshole. They think you act like an asshole and you got to, you got to start taking that into account.

"You know, you pride yourself in being a fighter and that worked in 2016 when they wanted a disruptor to go in there. And they still want a disruptor, but they don't want someone who is a complete asshole. And so, you have to turn on the other thing you do very well, which is to woo people. And I think that's what this election is about. And you know, my concern is that in some ways you become a captive of the Beltway in that you have all these self-anointed spokespeople for your base who come and tell you what they want. They are drowning you in their needs."

Barr was thinking of some of these interest groups who had an open door to the West Wing—the gun groups, the Judicial Watch leader going after liberals inside the federal bureaucracy, Fox News personalities.

"The other basic theme," Barr said, "and I know this is self-serving because I know you're impatient about the work we're doing over at the department. But I actually think that the people, the mom and pops up in Wisconsin and Pennsylvania and Michigan, they don't give a shit." Don't care about prosecuting former FBI director James Comey and others for their handling of the Russia investigation.

"Your base cares about seeing Comey and the rest of these guys held accountable, but these other people don't. They don't care about your fucking grievances. And it just seems that every time you're out there, you're talking about your goddamn grievances. They're worried about their future. They're worried about the economy now with Covid and stuff like that.

"You should be talking about what you did pre-Covid, how you're the guy to bring the country back after Covid, that you have a demonstrated track record and then give them a vision of where you're going to take the country. And that's all you should be talking about, not all this other shit, not every grievance you have."

"Bill," Trump responded, "these people are vicious. I've got to fight. I need my base. My base wants me to be strong. These are my people."

"Here's my assessment, Mr. President," Barr said. "I think you were able to pull it off at the last minute, after 'grab them by the pussy' last time, because that sobered you up and you realized you didn't know everything, and you started actually listening to people like Kellyanne and others. And so, you behaved yourself for about one month. And that was just enough because the electorate was fluid. I'm afraid there are two things that are different this time, and this is why I'm talking to you now.

"The electorate is not as fluid. Last time, they didn't know you as a public figure and they were willing to give you a chance. Now, a lot of people have made up their minds about you. They think they know who you are. So, they're not as fluid. And the other thing that's different, and I think the thing that's the main problem, is you think you're a fucking genius, politically.

"You think you're a genius and so you're not going to listen to anybody. You think you know what they want. And I think you're wrong. I have yet to meet one of your supporters who hasn't said that to me. And these are people who do like you and they actually tolerate your bullshit. But it's toleration. They don't support you because you act that way. And I think unless you, you know, unless you sort of go on a charm offensive and start trying to patch up some of the damage that's happened in some of these suburbs, I think you're going to lose."

"I need to be a fighter," Trump said. "I've gotten where I am because I'm willing to fight. They like that I'm willing to fight. I have to fight." His advisers, he said, told him if he got 65 million votes, he would win.

Barr believed that meant the advisers thought Trump could win by stoking the base and getting new registrations in rural areas. "It's not a static playing field," Barr warned. "The other side is working, too."

SEVENTEEN

Despite Barr's pleas, Trump would not change.

Trump convened a meeting in the Roosevelt Room on May 4, 2020, with his top policy and legal advisers on the Affordable Care Act, the health care law better known as Obamacare.

The Supreme Court had taken up a challenge to the health care measure that provided medical coverage to more than 20 million Americans.

"Mr. President," Barr said jumping in, "this case is not going to win. You're going to be lucky to get anything better than 9–0 on this."

Obamacare had already survived two Supreme Court challenges. Trump wanted the federal government to join a case against Obamacare brought by Texas and 17 other attorneys general in GOP-led states.

No, no, no, no, Barr said.

"Mr. President, this is an election year. The liberals on the Supreme Court voted to hear this case because they realize this is a fucking loser for you. We're in the middle of a Covid epidemic. And you are now creating uncertainty as to people's medical coverage. And you haven't put up a substitute and we're going to lose the case. We knocked out the mandate."

In 2017, the Republican-controlled Congress successfully nullified one of the ACA's core provisions, the individual mandate, so there was no longer a tax penalty on individuals who failed to purchase it.

"That's the victory," Barr argued. "Declare victory and say you're going to put up a better bill next time. But why should we be doing this? We're not going to win. It's just political downside."

"We need to be with Texas," Trump said. "That is my base."

"The attorney general of Texas is not the president of the United States," Barr said. "He has his constituency. You have your constituency. I don't see outsourcing our policy to the fucking state of Texas."

"Well, I'll think about it," Trump said. He again invoked his base.

"Mr. President," Kellyanne Conway said, "I think I know a little bit about your base. I've been a pollster for the Republican Party for decades. This is a loser. This doesn't help you. The health care issue is the reason we lost seats in 2018, Mr. President. Why are we teeing it up again for the other side?" It was unseemly for the president of the United States to be part of a legal crusade to take away health insurance from 20 million Americans.

White House counsel Pat Cipollone backstopped and said he agreed but did not offer any additional arguments.

It went back to Barr. "Mr. President, this case sucks," he said. "It's hard not to laugh at our argument."

Texas and the 17 other Republican-led states were arguing that because Congress had repealed the individual mandate penalty, the entire health law, its coverage and protections, should be struck down.

"Let's cut our losses on this one," Barr said. "No one's going to strike that statute down." Barr pushed Trump to take a more targeted approach, consider preserving parts of the law.

Other Republicans also shook their heads at the challenge. "The Justice Department argument in the Texas case is as far-fetched as any I've ever heard," Senator Lamar Alexander, Republican of Tennessee, said.

As Barr predicted, the Supreme Court later rejected the Trump administration's argument and upheld the law on a 7 to 2 vote on June 17, 2021.

"When are you going to get this order on birthright citizenship?" Trump asked Barr and Cipollone one day. It had become his constant refrain with them in the spring of 2020 as he slipped in the polls.

Barr shook his head and didn't smile. Trump never stopped. Barr called it "Groundhog Day," his version of the 1993 Bill Murray movie about being trapped in an endless and torturous time loop of the same day.

Birthright citizenship is rooted in the 14th Amendment, adopted in 1868, designating that all persons born or naturalized in the United States "are citizens of the United States."

Trump wanted an executive order that would deny citizenship to people born in the United States whose parents were in the country illegally. The U.S. would then not issue citizenship documents to them.

Such an order would turn political and constitutional history on its head. Week after week, Barr and Cipollone told the president it was a complicated legal matter. There was an argument to be made, Barr said. But the way to do it is to ask Congress to pass legislation. Congress would have the power to fine-tune it, refine the definition of a constitutional amendment. But if you do it by executive order, it's not going to work. It's going to get slapped down. It would not survive a court test, the attorney general said.

"And what you'll be doing in an election year is calling into question the citizenship of 10 million American people or more," Barr said.

"I won't make it retroactive," Trump said. The order would only apply to future children of illegal immigrants.

"But you can't say you won't make it retroactive," Barr said. "You're basically saying that they're not citizens. Okay? The premise would be that all these other people in the past are not citizens. So how are you going to give them comfort at that point?"

Trump didn't want to give them comfort at all. These people were mostly Democrats, Trump believed, and if they didn't have citizenship, they couldn't vote.

"There are all kinds of statutes that require people to be citizens for holding certain licenses and other things," Barr said, including voting.

Trump seemed to like the *Groundhog Day* quality to this. He continued to push and push and push and push. At one point, he wore Cipollone down.

"Bill," Cipollone said to Barr in private, "you know, we've been stepping on landmines. Do you think you could see your way clear on this?" After all the resistance, shouldn't they give the president something? It certainly would not stand a court test.

Barr had previously been head of the powerful Office of Legal Counsel in the Justice Department that gives legal advice to the president and all executive departments and agencies. He held the post early in the Bush senior administration and as a 39-year-old lawyer became steeped in the constitutional issues of presidential power.

"No, we're not doing it," Barr said. "I'll take the heat on this."

On the morning of May 14, Trump told Fox News that former Justice and FBI officials deserved prosecution.

"If I were a Democrat instead of a Republican, I think everybody would've been in jail a long time ago" with 50-year sentences, he said. "People should be going to jail for this stuff. . . . This was all Obama. This was all Biden." He was referring to the investigation being run by Connecticut U.S. Attorney John

Durham, who was probing how the FBI handled its look into the Trump campaign and alleged Russian collusion.

For Barr, this was a dramatic overreach by Trump. He had told him he needed to be patient about the Durham probe, especially as the pandemic slowed down operations across the department. Let Durham be.

Barr prepared a little speech to give at a press conference the next day. He said he was tired of politicians using the "justice system as a political weapon." By raising Biden and Obama as targets, Trump was effectively discrediting Durham's work. Barr knew if Trump kept it up, Durham would quit.

"I know people want accountability and we're working on that, but it's not going to be, we're not doing this politically and it's not going to be tit for tat," Barr told Trump. And he reminded the president that the Supreme Court had recently ruled that not everything considered an abuse of power legally equates to a crime. Trump said he hated that answer.

EIGHTEEN

"Deep in the heart of Delaware, Joe Biden sits in the heart of his basement. Alone. Hiding. Diminished," declared one Trump ad. "Punxsutawney Joe," was another barb, referring to the Pennsylvania groundhog, Phil, who emerges from his underground burrow once a year to predict the length of the winter. And Trump's campaign tweeted daily about how many days had passed since Biden's last news conference.

Democrats, too, were worried about Biden's months-long disappearance from the campaign trail. He was a candidate known for engaging voters at town halls and with handshakes. His six-point lead in March 2020 was smaller than Hillary Clinton's at that same marker in 2016.

But the strategy of letting Trump run against himself seemed to be working. Biden's lead widened to double digits as the president continued to mismanage the pandemic. At a press conference on April 23, 2020, Trump mused about injecting bleach to fight the virus.

Meanwhile, Biden, who could be a gaffe-machine himself, was using the isolation as an unexpected gift. Normally, candidates barely have a moment's rest from their campaign travels.

Unknown to the public and media, Biden was receiving daily briefings on the virus from two of the country's top medical experts: Dr. Vivek Murthy, Obama's former surgeon general, and Dr. David Kessler, former commissioner of the Food and Drug Administration, known for his war against tobacco.

Each day, Murthy and Kessler prepared a written Covid-19 report for Biden based on the most up-to-date information, gleaned from their hours of research on the phone with government and industry experts around the country and supplemented with data provided by a small team of confidential volunteers who scoured public and private information. Initially, the daily report ran up to 80 pages with maps, charts and diagrams.

Scheduled for 45 minutes on the phone or Zoom, the oral briefings routinely extended to an hour and a half. Kessler and Murthy were both deeply alarmed by Trump's attitude and failure to comprehend what he and the world were facing.

"I wanted to always play it down," Trump told Woodward in a March 2020 interview. "I still like playing it down, because I don't want to create a panic."

Trump had tweeted earlier that month about his view: "So last year 37,000 Americans died from the common Flu. It averages between 27,000 and 70,000 per year. Nothing is shut down, life & the economy go on. At this moment there are 546 confirmed cases of CoronaVirus, with 22 deaths. Think about that!"

Trump shut down the country a week later, but almost immediately began talking about opening it back up. "Our country wasn't built to be shut down. This is not a country that was built for this," Trump said on March 23, during a White House press briefing. "America will again and soon be open for business."

Murthy knew Trump had it all wrong. A coronavirus was like an iceberg. So few reported cases of an airborne, highly contagious virus and limited testing meant that there were many, many, more undetected cases. It was already here in the United States, and would soon spread.

Biden dove into the science with Murthy and Kessler, seeking a daily tutorial. He was a question machine. He asked, how does the virus attack the body?

Droplets from an infected person's cough or sneeze, or even normal breath, enter the nose and throat and attach to the plentiful cell-surface receptors called ACE2, taking over the cell and multiplying, they told him. Since the lungs are like a respiratory tree ending in small air sacs, also rich in the ACE2 receptors, the virus moves there and can destroy the lung cells.

They also described how the virus can attack different cell types and tissues, including blood vessels and the heart.

How about the vaccines being developed? Biden asked.

There are two types, the doctors said. The first was an adenovirus-based vaccine that enables the cells to produce spike proteins that build up antibodies, effectively soldiers, to defend against the virus.

The second was the mRNA—the "m" is for messenger. This vaccine activates immune responses by giving cells the instructions to produce a spike protein. It's like a recipe of your DNA. The body then remembers how to fight off the virus if later infected. The mRNA formulation can be changed in the vaccine if a variant of the virus pops up. Viruses often mutate.

"That's not detailed enough," Biden said at one point. "That doesn't make sense" at another. "Why?" or "How does the science work?"

During an interview with Trump on March 19, Woodward asked the president if he ever sat down with Dr. Anthony Fauci, the director of the National Institute of Allergy and Infectious Diseases, to get a tutorial on the science behind the virus.

"Yes, I guess," Trump said, "but honestly there's not a lot of time for that, Bob. This is a busy White House. We've got a lot of things happening. And then this came up."

Woodward asked, was there a moment where you said to yourself, this is the leadership test of a lifetime? "No," Trump said.

Murthy was surprised at the level of detail Biden wanted. He picked through their explanations with more questions. Why does the virus affect people of color, Black Americans and Brown Americans, more severely?

The doctors explained that entrenched inequities in health

care, education and financial resources made already vulnerable populations more vulnerable. Black and Brown people were exceedingly more likely to be hospitalized or die from the virus.

If a vaccine could be created, equitable distribution would be essential, Biden said.

"If we are blessed to have the chance to lead," he said, "we all have to figure out how to execute together, and how to take on this pandemic and turn it around together." They began to develop a detailed virus response plan.

Murthy was sure their daily briefings would soon come to an end. They were taking too much campaign time. Instead, the briefings grew longer and more detailed.

"Sir," Murthy said, "you know we're coming to the end of our time. We're happy to hold some of this over until tomorrow."

"No, no, no," Biden said. Let's talk this through.

Do you want us to try to pull these back, curtail them? Murthy asked Jake Sullivan, the Biden campaign's policy director.

He drives the boat on this, Sullivan said. He wants to get into this. He cares deeply about it. So let him drive.

Murthy could see that candidate Biden seemed to understand that the virus was going to define not just his campaign, but if he won, his presidency.

Murthy was "Mr. Bedside Manner," with a soothing voice. As a practicing physician, he had learned to spend abundant time listening to patients because he found they often gave an accurate self-diagnosis.

Before Biden had announced his decision to run for president a third time, Murthy had visited him in Wilmington. He would write a book, *Together: The Healing Power of Human Connection in a Sometimes Lonely World*, and discussed with Biden how loneliness and isolation affects mental and physical health.

In their virus briefing sessions, Biden alluded frequently to friends who were calling him to chat—he had a habit of giving his cell number to people he spoke to on the campaign trail. It was evident, he said, the virus was isolating people and affecting their mental health. Children missed the social contact in classrooms, as did office workers. The pandemic was eating away at the social fabric, Biden said.

NINETEEN

In late May, angry protests erupted in more than 140 cities across the country. Minneapolis police officer Derek Chauvin had been caught on video pressing his knee on the neck of George Floyd, a 46-year-old Black man, for seven minutes and 46 seconds, killing him.

Some of the protests escalated into violent clashes with police and looting as darkness fell each evening. The scenes replayed endlessly on cable news.

In an interview at the time, Trump told Woodward, "These are arsonists, they're thugs, they're anarchists and they're bad people. Very dangerous people.

"These are very well-organized. Antifa's leading it," Trump said, pointing his finger at the anti-fascist movement that had confronted white supremacists and others.

Stephen Miller, the 34-year-old director of White House speechwriting and one of Trump's most conservative senior advisers, was a hardliner on the unrest. Several colleagues believed he was responsible for stoking and spinning up the president about the violence.

Articulate and harsh, and known for his fitted suits and skinny ties, Miller had helped draft Trump's "American carnage" inaugural address and had been the architect of the controversial travel ban for Muslim-majority countries. He seemed to forever be lingering in the Oval Office, waiting for an opportunity to push his agenda.

If there were ever a modern-day Rasputin, Joint Chiefs chairman Milley had concluded it was Miller.

Milley had his staff prepare a daily, classified SECRET report, "Domestic Unrest National Overview." The report tracked the latest violence in American cities with a population over 100,000 people.

Less than a week after Floyd's murder, Milley was walking through the report with Trump in the Oval Office.

"Mr. President," Miller said, piping up from one of the Oval Office couches, "they are burning America down. Antifa, Black Lives Matter, they're burning it down. You have an insurrection on your hands. Barbarians are at the gate."

Milley spun around from his seat in front of the Resolute Desk. "Shut the fuck up, Steve.

"Mr. President," Milley said turning back to Trump, "they are not burning it down." His extended hands were flat in front of him, and he raised them up to his shoulders and slowly lowered them in a calming motion. He cited information from the daily SECRET report.

"Mr. President, there are about 276 cities in America with over 100,000 people. There were two cities in the last 24 hours that had major protests," he said. "Elsewhere, it was 20 protesters to 300." While images of burning and violence had been on television, many of the protests were peaceful—about 93 percent of them, according to a later nonpartisan report.

"They used spray paint, Mr. President," Milley said. "That's not insurrection. That guy up there." He pointed to the portrait of Abraham Lincoln on the wall in the Oval Office. "That guy up there, Lincoln, had an insurrection." Milley cited the militia bombardment of the U.S. Army's Fort Sumter in 1861 that started the Civil War.

"That was an insurrection," Milley said.

"We're a country of 330 million people. You've got these penny packet protests," Milley said, saying the situation was not even close to being as threatening as the 1968 riots in Washington, D.C., and elsewhere after the assassination of Rev. Martin Luther King Jr.

Barr, who also attended the meeting, understood Milley's frustration with Miller. He had also once told Miller to shut the fuck up. And Milley had been calling Barr regularly in recent weeks, asking him to weigh in during Oval Office meetings as a heat shield and protection for the military.

"Look, Steve," Barr said, "you don't have operational experience to be talking about this stuff, okay? These things are very delicate. For every time you have a success, you have Waco," referring to the 1993 FBI siege and assault of the Branch Davidian religious sect that led to the death of 76 sect members, including 25 children and pregnant women.

"You have to be careful," Barr said. "You have to know what you're doing. Stop mouthing that kind of stuff. Getting that kind of confrontation going, we can do it. But using the military isn't required right now. I'm not willing to roll the dice on that." He said bringing in the military was only a "break-glass option," a last resort.

Milley turned to retired Army General Keith Kellogg, Pence's national security adviser and a Trump loyalist, who was also sitting on a couch.

"Keith," Milley said, "this is nothing like 1968. You were Lieutenant Kellogg in 1968 sitting on top of one of these buildings collocated with the commanding general of the 82nd Airborne." President Lyndon B. Johnson had deployed combat troops into Washington.

"This isn't even on the same level of the 1968 stuff when tens of thousands of protesters and rioters are going through Detroit and Chicago and L.A."

"That's right, Mr. President," Kellogg said.

The protests should be monitored, Milley said. "We should

pay attention to it. It's important." But it was an issue for local police and local law enforcement, mayors and governors.

"It is not an issue for the United States military to deploy forces on the streets of America, Mr. President."

Milley then carefully broached the issue of systemic racism and policing with Trump.

"That's pent up in communities that have been experiencing what they perceive to be police brutality," he said.

Trump didn't say anything.

By June 1, 2020, Trump was furious.

The protests had continued to grow in size and intensity across the country. Trump had agitated all weekend about the loud protests at the White House gates. A pedestrian area off 16th Street, leading up to the White House, which would soon be renamed "Black Lives Matter Plaza," had become a focal point for different groups, with an increasing police presence.

The previous evening, May 31, a fire had been lit in the basement nursery of the historic St. John's Episcopal Church, barely 1,000 feet from the White House and often called the Church of Presidents. At one point, the Secret Service had taken Trump to the underground bunker.

Boarded up and charred, the church and the sprawling scene outside brought the racial unrest convulsing the country to Trump's front door.

Trump called his top officials to the Oval Office for a meeting on June 1 around 10:30 a.m.

Trump told them he wanted a law-and-order crackdown—10,000 active-duty, regular troops in the city. He asked about the Insurrection Act, an 1807 law which gave the president the authority to use active-duty troops domestically by simply declaring an insurrection.

"We look weak," Trump said angrily. "We don't look strong." He was sitting with his arms folded at the Resolute Desk.

Secretary of Defense Mark Esper was fielding most of Trump's questions. Esper knew that Trump's "we" meant "he."

Esper, 56, square-jawed and with thin spectacles, could have been an extra on the television program *Mad Men* about 1960s advertising executives. He also kept a low profile. But he was one of the most experienced defense appointees in modern times, having graduated from West Point in 1986 and then serving 21 years in the Army. He had deployed with the 101st Airborne "Screaming Eagles" as an infantry officer for the 1991 Gulf War, winning a Bronze Star. He later served in the National Guard and earned a master's degree from the Kennedy School at Harvard, and a doctorate in public administration.

Esper had worked in Congress as an aide, and as a Raytheon lobbyist before Trump made him Army secretary, then acting deputy secretary and then, finally, secretary.

"Mr. President, there is no need to call up the Insurrection Act," Esper said. "The National Guard is on the ground and more suited." The National Guard, comprised of volunteer reservists, often helped with national disasters.

Barr interjected and said they could bring in additional law enforcement, which was the traditional way to handle domestic protests. Barr had the FBI and the U.S. attorneys working together to pull everything together on what was happening in the various cities, and he was talking near daily with Milley.

"Mr. President," Barr said, "if it comes to keeping law and order on the streets, I would not hesitate to use regular troops, believe me, if we had to. But we don't have to. They're not necessary," he said. "You got a lot of stuff going on in different cities, but they're manageable, if the cities step up. They have the adequate resources to do it, especially if they use their National Guard or their state police.

"It looks like a lot because of the way the media is covering it. But some of these cities are like 300 people on a street corner and a burning car in the background. You don't need the 82nd Airborne Division."

But Trump was adamant: He wanted the storied 82nd Airborne, stationed at Fort Bragg, North Carolina, the military's elite crisis responder, to arrive in Washington before sunset when a protest was planned in Lafayette Square, the seven-acre park between the White House and St. John's Church.

Esper explained to Trump the 82nd was trained to take the fight to the enemy with the biggest, most modern weapons. They were not trained in crowd control and civil unrest. They were exactly the wrong troops for the job.

The president was getting increasingly contentious, and Esper worried that if he didn't put something on the table, Trump might formally order him to bring the 82nd to D.C. He needed the president to calm down.

"Mr. President," Esper said, "let's do this. We will alert the troops and start moving them north from Fort Bragg. But we're not going to bring them into the city. We can get the Guard here in time. If we can't, if it gets out of control, we have these other forces."

Milley agreed with Esper's approach. Neither he nor Esper wanted a potentially bloody, unpredictable street confrontation between Black Lives Matter protesters and highly lethal, combat-trained U.S. military forces.

Trump sat there. His arms were still folded. He started to yell, his face heating up. Esper could sense Trump's wheels moving. Esper stayed still.

An aide hurried in: "Mr. President, the governors are on the phone for your conference call."

Trump got up and strode down to the Situation Room. On the call, he told the governors they should forcefully crack down on their demonstrators. There was none of his usual cajoling. His tone was belligerent.

"You have to dominate," Trump told them, almost issuing a command. "If you don't dominate, you're wasting your time. They're going to run over you. You're going to look like a bunch of jerks. You have to dominate, and you have to arrest people, and you have to try people and they have to go to jail for long periods of time."

"Law enforcement response is not going to work unless we dominate the streets as the president said," Attorney General Barr told the governors, adopting the same language. "We have to control the streets."

Esper then echoed them. "I agree, we need to dominate the battlespace," he said on the call.

Milley left the White House and headed downtown to visit the FBI command post monitoring the demonstrations. Expecting a late night, he changed into his uniform of camouflage fatigues to be more comfortable.

TWENTY

Esper left and called the director of the National Guard, General Joe Lengyel, who was the chief of the nearly 460,000 Army and Air National Guard.

"Joe, we need to get Guardsmen into the city, ASAP," Esper said. "Who do I start calling?"

Esper called the governors of Maryland, Virginia and Pennsylvania. Eventually, he and Lengyel convinced at least ten states to send Guard units.

Esper did not tell them that Trump wanted to flood the city with active-duty forces if they did not move quickly.

Near 6 p.m., Esper headed to the FBI command center to meet up with Milley. They planned to visit the Guard in the streets, thank them, and get a feel for what was happening on the ground. Go to the scene, find out for themselves.

But on his way to the FBI, a call came in to Esper: "The president wants you at the White House."

Once he arrived in the West Wing, Esper asked, "Where's the meeting?"

Sir, there is no meeting.

What do you mean there is no meeting?

So Esper waited.

Around 6:30 p.m., U.S. Park Police led a group of law enforcement officers, in riot gear and on horseback, into the crowd, and began forcefully clearing protesters from Lafayette Square. While the push was planned days earlier with the intent of building a fence around the park, it quickly unraveled into a chaotic scene.

Washington, D.C., police officers used riot control devices, creating loud explosions, sparks and smoke. "Pepper balls" that irritate the eyes and nose were shot at protesters. Some officers pushed protesters to the ground. Others on horseback herded people away.

At 6:48 p.m., after the protesters were dispersed, Trump spoke for seven minutes in the Rose Garden at the White House. "I will fight to protect you. I am your president of law and order and an ally of all peaceful protesters," he said, pledging to control the "riots and lawlessness that has spread throughout our country.

"If a city or state refuses to take the actions that are necessary to defend the life and property of their residents," he said, "then I will deploy the United States military and quickly solve the problem for them.

"As we speak, I am dispatching thousands and thousands of heavily armed soldiers, military personnel and law enforcement officers to stop the rioting, looting, vandalism, assaults and the wanton destruction of property."

One of Trump's low-level White House aides turned to Esper and other senior officials who had attended Trump's speech and said, "Line up."

"Line up for what?" Esper asked.

Well, sir, we are going to walk across Lafayette Square, the aide said. The president wants to go through the park and see St. John's Church. He wants you all, he wants his cabinet members, to join him.

Milley had arrived in his camouflage uniform.

"We're going to the church," Trump told them.

Almost everyone at the White House that evening seemed to join in: Esper and Milley, National Security Adviser Robert O'Brien and Barr, senior advisers, family members Jared Kushner and Ivanka Trump, Trump aide Hope Hicks and White House chief of staff Mark Meadows.

It was one of the most photographed and videotaped parades of the Trump presidency.

Esper suddenly felt sick as he saw a crowd of reporters and cameras rush by, filming and flashing as the parade hustled through the park. Trump kept moving, pulling everything toward him like a magnet.

"We've been duped," Esper said to Milley as they walked to the church. "We're being used."

Milley agreed completely.

Milley turned to his personal security chief and said, "This is fucked up and this is a political event and I'm out of here. We're getting the fuck out of here. I'm fucking done with this shit."

Milley peeled off from the group.

But it was too late for Milley to escape notice. He was photographed in his camouflages, looking dressed for battle. He also took a phone call that some interpreted as a call to coordinate the push against the protesters. It instead was to his wife, Hollyanne.

"What's going on?" she asked. She had seen the scene on television. "Are you okay?"

Milley said he was fine, but he was not.

In 45 seconds, Milley realized he had made a mistake that threatened to compromise his most prized possession, forged over decades: his integrity and independence as the senior military officer in the United States of America.

Walking with Trump when he was on a political mission, even for a split second, was utterly wrong. This is my Road to Damascus moment, Milley thought, feeling as if he was looking into a personal abyss.

Milley was not at the church when Trump stood for about two minutes, holding a Bible uncomfortably and waving it around. But it did not matter. The damage was done.

The president had misused him and politicized the U.S military. They had become Trump's pawns.

Esper, who recognized his political antennae were less sensitive than Milley's, would have to deal with the inevitable fallout from standing and walking alongside the president as thousands of Americans gathered by the church, chanting and pleading for policing reforms.

But Esper was more worried the most highly regarded institution in the country, the finely tuned and proudly nonpartisan military machine, was in jeopardy of being swept into a political storm. The republic seemed a little wobbly. How could he calm things down? How could he break what could only be described as a fever?

"Bill! Bill! Bill!" Trump had yelled over at Barr at one point on the walk. "Come here!"

At that moment, Barr felt like he could sink into concrete. Unlike Milley, he was a political appointee who wanted to see Trump get some good press and win. But he knew this spectacle, which he had been told earlier would be a simple "outing" by the president, was utterly ridiculous. There was no other way to describe it.

He had a feeling for why Trump did it: He still felt embarrassment about going down into the White House bunker. He wanted to show strength.

To cap it off, Barr hesitated as he watched Trump walk back into the White House. He saw the uniformed branch of the Secret Service line up, in two straight lines, holding their shields. It looked like an honor guard, all the trappings of a showy military operation.

"I'm not going to walk through this fucking guard of honor," Barr muttered.

Later that evening, Esper and Milley finally toured the city to check on the rest of the Guard. Dozens of National Guard troops in body armor—with their faces almost completely covered with gray masks and dark sunglasses—were later photographed on the Lincoln Memorial steps. They looked menacing, a militarized version of Trump's law-and-order declaration.

"We've got to ratchet it down," Milley said to Esper.

Esper could not agree more. He had brought a battalion, about 600 regular combat troops from the 82nd Airborne, to Joint Base Andrews in Maryland outside Washington. He was intentionally keeping them outside the city. But for how long would it hold? Trump's fuse was lit—and he had already manipulated them once.

The next day, June 2, Milley issued a one-page memo, "SUBJECT: Message to the Joint Force," to the chiefs of all the military services and top combatant commands.

It was a reminder to the military of their duty, and a recentering for himself, one day after the chaos alongside Trump in Lafayette Square.

Near his signature, Milley scrawled out an additional message in longhand: "We all committed our lives to the idea that is America—we will stay true to that oath and the American people."

UNCLASSIFIED

CHAIRMAN OF THE JOINT CHIEFS OF STAFF
WASHINGTON, DC 20318-9999

2 June 2020

MEMORANDUM FOR CHIEF OF STAFF OF THE ARMY
COMMANDANT OF THE MARINE CORPS
CHIEF OF NAVAL OPERATIONS
CHIEF OF STAFF OF THE AIR FORCE
CHIEF OF THE NATIONAL GUARD BUREAU
COMMANDANT OF THE COAST GUARD
CHIEF OF SPACE OPERATIONS
COMMANDERS OF THE COMBATANT COMMANDS

SUBJECT: Message to the Joint Force

1. Every member of the U.S. military swears an oath to support and defend the Constitution and the values embedded within it. This document is founded on the essential principle that all men and women are born free and equal, and should be treated with respect and dignity. It also gives Americans the right to freedom of speech and peaceful assembly. We in uniform – all branches, all components, and all ranks – remain committed to our national values and principles embedded in the Constitution.

2. During this current crisis, the National Guard is operating under the authority of state governors to protect lives and property, preserve peace, and ensure public safety.

3. As members of the Joint Force – comprised of all races, colors, and creeds – you embody the ideals of our Constitution. Please remind all of our troops and leaders that we will uphold the values of our nation, and operate consistent with national laws and our own high standards of conduct at all times.

We all committed our lives to the idea that is America — we will stay true to that oath and the American People.

Mark Milley

MARK A. MILLEY
General, U.S. Army

cc:
Secretary of Defense
Deputy Secretary of Defense
Vice Chairman of the Joint Chiefs of Staff
Director, Joint Staff

UNCLASSIFIED

TWENTY-ONE

"We must be vigilant about the violence that's being done by the incumbent president to our democracy and to the pursuit of justice," Biden said during a speech in Philadelphia's City Hall on June 2. Several American flags were behind him. It was his first speech before a live audience since March and the start of the pandemic.

The message: presidential. The lone campaign sign was the one on his lectern. After George Floyd's death, Biden showed a new readiness and resolve to step up and to be more aggressive. Many of his advisers saw it as a turning point for him to remind voters of the stakes.

"We can't leave this moment thinking we can once again turn away and do nothing. We can't," Biden told the crowd in Philadelphia. "The moment has come for our nation to deal with systemic racism. To deal with the growing economic inequality in our nation. And to deal with the denial of the promise of this nation to so many."

Esper was flustered on June 3. With protests continuing in Washington, Trump still wanted 10,000 active-duty troops deployed to the city.

As with Milley, Esper was acutely aware of what that could mean. The 1968 riots erupted amid similar plagues of urban poverty, racism and anger over police brutality. Putting active-duty military in the streets, in an age of social media and global television, could provoke a human tragedy.

Esper decided that he had to act before things further deteriorated with Trump. But his private counsel only meant so much. This was a president who traced political capital through public statements and media hits. Esper decided he would declare publicly and unequivocally that he saw no reason to invoke the Insurrection Act.

He suggested Milley stand next to him.

"I shouldn't do that," Milley said. "You're about to make a significant political statement of policy and I shouldn't be there in uniform. But, you know, this is one of those moments."

Esper stood before the Pentagon press corps alone. Milley listened from the back of the room.

"I've always believed and continue to believe that the National Guard is best suited for performing domestic support to civil authorities, in support of local law enforcement," Esper said. "I say this not only as a secretary of defense, but also as a former soldier and a former member of the National Guard.

"The option to use active-duty forces in a law enforcement role should only be used as a matter of last resort, and only in the most urgent and dire of situations. We are not in one of those situations now. I do not support invoking the Insurrection Act."

Milley thought Esper should be forever thanked for drawing a bright line. It was an important moment.

Their phones started to blow up.

"The president is really pissed," Mark Meadows, the White house chief of staff, said within minutes to Esper. "And really mad. He is going to rip your face off."

Esper and Milley were due at the White House at 10 a.m. for a National Security Council meeting about plans for withdrawing U.S. troops from Afghanistan. General Frank McKenzie, the Central Commander who oversaw the 19-year war, was in Washington to brief the president.

"Can you just go do the briefing?" Esper asked Milley. "You and Frank by yourselves because this is going to be ugly."

"We can do that for sure," Milley said. "But we shouldn't. You need to go."

Esper exhaled loudly. "It's going to be really bad. Going to get screamed at and yelled at."

"Yep," Milley said. They knew each other well. They had worked closely before taking the top military jobs in the United States government. Esper had been secretary of the Army, and Milley the Army chief of staff for 18 months.

"That's true," Milley said, "but you've got to face down the dragon sometimes. Just pretend you're back on The Plain"—the parade field—"at West Point and you're just getting your ass whipped."

When they walked into the Oval Office, almost everyone there had their head down, looking at their shoes.

Something bad must be happening, Milley thought. Ambush.

Chairs were arranged in a half-circle facing the Resolute Desk where Trump sat with his arms folded. Pence occupied one. Meadows another. The center chair was reserved for Esper. Another for Milley.

A group of Trump's staff sat on the couches and in other chairs. Trump sat ramrod straight. His face was red. He glared at Esper, who glared back.

"What did you do?" Trump yelled. "Why did you do that?"

"Mr. President, I told you," Esper said. "What I said before is I do not believe that this situation calls for invocation of the Insurrection Act. I think it would be terrible for the country and terrible for the military."

"You took away my authority!" Trump screamed.

"Mr. President, I did not take away your authority. That is your authority. I offered my views on it and whether or not I would support it."

Trump retorted fiercely, quoting some garbled version of Esper's comments to the media earlier in the day.

Esper pulled a transcript of his press conference from his binder. He had highlighted his comments on the Act and slapped it on the Resolute Desk. He pushed it toward the president.

"That's what I said!"

Trump glanced at it. "I don't care a fuck about your fucking transcript."

Esper wasn't sure Trump read the comments but felt he had at least called the president on it. Trump's face steadily grew redder and Esper believed the president thought his ability to invoke the Insurrection Act was over. Esper was fine with that. Trump had been contained.

"Who do you think you are?" Trump screamed at Esper. "You took away my authorities. You're not the president! I'm the god damn president."

Milley, sitting silently next to Esper, watched Trump carefully. He believed the escalation and rage he was witnessing firsthand was disturbing, another face-off that reminded him of *Full Metal Jacket*.

An avalanche of invective kept coming. When the president had fully vented to Esper, he turned to the others sitting in the Oval Office. "You're all fucked up," he yelled at them. "Everybody. You're all fucked. Every one of you is fucked up!"

"Robert," Milley whispered to O'Brien, "I think we probably need to be briefing the president on Afghanistan." The meeting was supposed to start soon.

"All right," Trump finally said, as if he were abruptly changing the television channel. "Get out of here. Everybody, get out of here."

Milley liked to think he and Esper had not subverted the authority of the president but fulfilled their duty to provide him with the best, unvarnished advice. They had a constitutional obligation to ensure the president was fully informed on his options. But once Trump decided and issued an order, they were required to execute it.

The only exception was an illegal, immoral or unethical order. That would be the point at which someone might consider resigning, Milley reasoned. But Milley could not recall a time in history when a cabinet officer, one as essential as the secretary of defense, had angrily slapped a paper down on the Resolute Desk.

"We checkmated him," Milley thought with tentative relief. They had tied Trump's hands, outplayed him, and that was what made him so enraged.

On the way over to the Situation Room, Milley said to Esper, "You just sit there. Don't say anything. Let me and Frank handle this."

Minutes later in the Situation Room, the president took his seat at the head of the table.

General McKenzie, a Marine with vast command experience, began to review the options for withdrawing from Afghanistan, one of Trump's central campaign promises. The generals kept arguing they wanted to fight the terrorists in Afghanistan and not in the homeland. They regularly invoked the memory of the September 11 plot, which had originated in Afghanistan, and argued that the U.S. troop presence was an insurance policy against another 9/11 attack.

This discussion started very calm and rational, with no noticeable spillover from the "Full Metal Jacket" fireworks in the Oval Office.

Then someone brought up the threat from Iran.

"Okay," Trump said, "tell me about Iran. Tell me what plans you've got, options you've got for Iran."

Iran was under General McKenzie's Central Command, which had responsibility for the Middle East and Afghanistan. Iran, however, was not on the agenda. But McKenzie knew the strike and war plans cold.

"Frank, go ahead," Milley said, "brief the president on what we've got for Iran."

McKenzie reeled off an array of options—air strikes, sea strikes, sabotage, cyberattacks, infiltration, and land invasion if necessary.

"Oh, wow," Trump responded, "how long will it take to do that?"

In the course of being responsive, McKenzie made some of the options sound enticing. "Oh, yes, sir," McKenzie said, "we can do this."

"Whoa, whoa, whoa," Milley said putting his hand in the air. "Frank, tell him the rest of the story."

Milley then rattled off, rapid-fire, a list of statements and questions, all of them meant to raise doubts about launching an attack on Iran.

"Tell him the cost."

"Tell him casualties."

"Tell him how much time."

"How many ships get sunk?"'

"And how many troops die?"

"How many pilots get shot down?"

"How many civilian casualties?"

"And what about the families in Bahrain?" That was the home-port for the U.S. Navy's Fifth Fleet.

"How long do you think this is going to take?"

"Is it 30 days or 30 years?"

"Is this going to be another war?"

The president kept looking back and forth between Milley and McKenzie. The answers telegraphed unknown consequences and outcomes.

One of the hawks on Iran was O'Brien, the national security adviser. If Iran struck U.S. military targets, retribution should be swift and massive, he said.

"Let's hit 'em hard, Mr. President," O'Brien said several times. "Hit 'em hard."

"It's easy to get into a war," Milley interjected, using one of his and Esper's favorite lines. "But it's hard to get out of a war."

Over the years, Milley had studied World War I. The trigger had been the assassination of the Archduke Franz Ferdinand in Sarajevo in 1914.

Yet there were many assassinations that year in global politics. Why had that one been the trigger? It was a question that stayed with Milley. Historians tried to answer it, but at the time, no one could have predicted the global ramifications. With any strike, you could have a plan, but outcomes were never certain. And a great powers war was always possible if the U.S. was not careful.

Milley knew that Meadows had told the president that a war would be bad news for Trump's reelection campaign. Meadows also told him that firing another secretary of defense would not serve Trump politically.

"You don't want a war," Milley told Trump at a previous meeting. And even now, sitting in the Situation Room, Milley didn't think the president was seeking a war. But a strike seemed to always be on the table. His curiosity had to be managed.

Striking Iran or some other action became less and less appealing as the session ended.

TWENTY-TWO

Milley continued to be hounded by the events of June 1. His critics were everywhere: on cable news channels, on social media, and on op-ed pages.

Milley understood the ridicule. He had been photographed in battle fatigues alongside a president who was intent on politicizing the military. It was a fiasco.

He called many of his predecessors to seek advice.

"Should I resign?" he asked Colin Powell, who had been the chairman of the Joint Chiefs of Staff from 1989 to 1993 under President George H. W. Bush.

"Fuck no!" Powell said. "I told you never to take the job. You never should have taken the job. Trump's a fucking maniac."

Milley received similar, though less colorful, advice from a dozen former secretaries of defense and former chairmen.

Milley decided to apologize publicly but did not give Trump advance warning.

On June 11, at a videotaped talk at the National Defense University graduation, Milley said, "As senior leaders, everything you do will be closely watched, and I am not immune.

"As many of you saw, the result of the photograph of me at Lafayette Square last week, that sparked a national debate about the role of the military in civil society," he said. "I should not have been there. My presence in that moment and that environment created a perception of the military involved in domestic politics. As a commissioned uniformed officer, it was a mistake that I've learned from, and I sincerely hope we all can learn from it.

"Embrace the Constitution, keep it close to your heart. It is our North Star."

Several days later, Trump stopped Milley after a routine meeting in the Oval Office.

"Hey, aren't you proud of walking with your president?" Trump asked.

"To the church?" Milley asked.

Yes, Trump said. "Why did you apologize?"

"Mr. President, it's got nothing to do with you actually."

Trump looked skeptical.

"It had to do with me," Milley said. "It had to do with this uniform. Had to do with the traditions of the United States military and that we are an apolitical organization.

"You're a politician," Milley said. "You're a political actor. For you to do it, that's your call. But I cannot be part of political events, Mr. President. It's one of our long-standing traditions."

"Why did you apologize?" the president asked again. "That's a sign of weakness."

"Mr. President," he said, looking directly at Trump, "not where I come from." He was a Boston-area native. "Where I was born and how I was raised is when you make a mistake, you admit it."

Trump tilted his head to the side like the Victrola Dog, the small dog famously pictured staring at a windup phonograph and long used by RCA Records as a mascot.

"Hmm," he said. "Okay."

Trump later called Milley twice to inquire about how the military should deal with the issue of Confederate flags, statues and military bases named after Confederate generals. Milley said he favored making changes.

During an Oval Office meeting, Trump returned to the issue. He said he did not want a change. "We're not going to ban Confederate flags. It's Southern pride and heritage."

Meadows said that the Confederate flags could not be banned. It was a freedom of speech issue, and the Pentagon lawyers agreed with him.

Trump asked Milley, what do you think?

"I've already told you twice, Mr. President. Are you sure you want to hear it again?"

Yeah, go ahead, Trump said.

"Mr. President," Milley said, "I think you should ban the flags, change the names of bases, and take down the statues."

He continued, "I'm from Boston, these guys were traitors."

Someone asked, what about the Confederate dead buried at Arlington National Cemetery?

"Interestingly," Milley said of the nearly 500 Confederate soldiers buried there, "they're arranged in a circle and the names on the gravestones are facing inward, and that symbolizes that they turned their back on the Union. They were traitors at the time, they are traitors today, and they're traitors in death for all of eternity. Change the names, Mr. President."

There was brief silence in the Oval Office.

Pence, who almost always took the super-serious path supporting Trump, half-joked, "I just think I found my Union self."

Pat Cipollone, the White House counsel, added, "I'm a Yankee, too!"

Without saying anything, Trump jumped to the next topic that came to mind.

David Urban, the lobbyist and Trump ally close to Esper, later tried another approach to Trump. "If you don't do this," he said, encouraging the name changes, "the Democrats are going to rename them."

Urban asked, are you familiar with the USNS *Harvey Milk*?

"What's that?" Trump asked.

"It's a U.S. Navy ship named after a gay city councilman in San Francisco" who was assassinated in 1978. "Do you think Democrats or Republicans did that?"

"Okay. All right," Trump grunted. "Let me think about it."

Urban suggested renaming the bases after Medal of Honor recipients. "Celebrate the best of America."

When Trump kept stalling, Urban blamed Meadows. Another mistake during a tough campaign.

"This is a fucking layup," Urban told Esper. "Did Meadows get like 800 dudes from the South to call the president and say they're all heroes?"

Milley decided he needed to develop a game plan for the run-up to the election and beyond.

Trump's curiosity and comments about a possible attack on Iran had stayed with Milley, and so did Trump's rage, seemingly ever ready to emerge. Milley had to hold firm, be a bulwark. He had to be ready for anything, including a sudden breakdown in Trump's conduct and the order inside the West Wing.

"This is how I see the next period of time," Milley said in a private meeting. "My obligation to the American people is to make sure that we don't have an unnecessary war overseas. And that we don't have the unlawful use of American force on the streets of America. We're not going to turn our guns on the American people and we're not going to have a 'Wag the Dog' scenario overseas."

Wag the Dog was a 1997 movie about a president using war to distract from a scandal.

Milley believed staying on gave him leverage with Trump because Trump effectively could not fire him.

If Trump did not like Milley's advice, he could just ignore it. But the symbolic power of the office carried weight. To fire a chairman would be a political earthquake—and Milley had been confirmed by the Senate 89 to 1, suggesting near unanimous bipartisan support.

In the Tank, the hallowed JCS meeting room in the Pentagon

where military leaders can speak frankly, Milley outlined his plan for the chiefs.

"Phase 1 is from now until the election, November 3," Milley said. "Phase 2 is the night of the election through certification," when Congress formally certified the election on January 6, 2021. "Phase 3 is certification through the inauguration on January 20. And Phase 4 is the first hundred days of whoever wins the election.

"We're going to take it step by step. We're going to be in constant contact. We're going to work our way through this. I'll be on point. JCS, you guys, I just need you to stand shoulder to shoulder—everybody.

"And the watchword of the day is steady in the saddle. We're going to keep our eye on the horizon. And we're going to do what's right for the country, no matter what the cost is to ourselves."

TWENTY-THREE

By late June 2020, coronavirus cases were surging. But Trump was determined to revive his trademark arena rallies, teeming with cheering supporters in red hats and carrying signs. He dearly missed them.

A large rally at Tulsa, Oklahoma's 19,000-seat BOK Center was scheduled for June 20, his first in 60 days. City health officials, however, worried about a "super-spreader event," and urged him to cancel it.

A day before, Trump told Woodward in an interview the rally would be a huge success.

"I have a rally tomorrow night in Oklahoma," Trump said. "Over 1.2 million people have signed up. We can only take about 50, 60 thousand. Because, you know, it's a big arena, right? But we can take 22,000 in one arena, 40,000 in another. We're going to have two arenas loaded. But think of that. Nobody ever had rallies like that."

At the rally, the arena was only about half-filled, if that, with a sea of empty blue seats facing Trump, partly the result of a social media prank organized by teenage Trump critics. Thousands of them registered for a ticket, never intending to show up.

Trump later erupted about his campaign manager, Brad Parscale. At 6-foot-8 and bearded, Parscale looked like a professional wrestler in a suit. He had gained national notice for his digital efforts and for organizing Trump supporters on social media platforms like Facebook.

"Biggest fucking mistake," Trump said at a meeting in the Oval Office. "I shouldn't have ever done that fucking, fucking rally," calling Parscale a "fucking moron."

Parscale was fired as campaign manager July 15 and demoted to senior adviser.

Not long after, at another July meeting in the Oval Office, his pollster, Tony Fabrizio, said that voters, especially independents, were emotionally drained.

"Well, to be honest, Mr. President," Fabrizio said, "the voters are just fatigued. They're tired of the chaos. They're tired of the tumult."

Normally solicitous with Fabrizio, who had helped his 2016 campaign, Trump snapped his head around.

"Oh, they're tired?" Trump said loudly and in a rage. "They're fucking tired? Well, I'm fucking fatigued and tired, too."

The Oval Office went dead silent.

Then Fabrizio raised Biden, and Trump was immediately dismissive. "He's old," Trump said. "He's not up to it. You know, he can't even string together a sentence."

"You can't make him into a crazy liberal," Fabrizio said. "I don't think people will buy it."

Fabrizio knew he had broken his pick with Trump, but the president continued to look for something, or someone, to shore up his flagging campaign.

The White House and campaign reached into every corner, consulting with former House speaker Newt Gingrich and even with Dick Morris, a discredited Bill Clinton campaign adviser.

"If you are perceived as having failed during a time of crisis, you cannot come back. Think Neville Chamberlain or Herbert Hoover," Morris wrote in one summer email to Trump's senior advisers, referring to the British prime minister known for his disastrous meetings with Hitler and the president remembered for the Great Depression.

Trump remained defiant amid the worldwide health crisis. On August 7, he decided on an apparent whim to hold a news conference at his New Jersey golf club.

The pandemic "is disappearing," he insisted. "It's going to disappear." Cases in the U.S. had reached nearly 4.9 million confirmed cases—and over 160,000 deaths. Schools were, for the most part, not scheduled to reopen.

"The deep state," Trump tweeted two weeks later, "or whoever, over at the FDA, is making it very difficult for drug companies to get people in order to test the vaccines and therapeutics. Obviously, they are hoping to delay the answer until after November 3rd. Must focus on speed and saving lives!"

The "whoever" was Dr. Stephen Hahn, 60, the commissioner of the Food and Drug Administration.

A Trump appointee, Hahn had been the prestigious chief medical executive of the MD Anderson Cancer Center at the University of Texas and had published more than 220 peer-reviewed articles during his medical career. He also was a regular donor to Republican candidates.

A skilled political player from his years in the sharp-elbowed world of academic medicine, Hahn had a strained relationship with Meadows, who was under pressure from Trump to expedite the process.

"He definitely wanted me to speed up, and he wanted the data. He wanted information so that he could talk to the president," Hahn said to a colleague.

"When I talked to him about the process we were using, he would mention that he worked for some consulting firm and was experienced in, you know, process and process improvement. And that we had gotten it all wrong and we had too many steps involved in this analysis.

"He didn't bother to ask questions about why certain steps were needed. He didn't see that there was any validity to what I was saying with respect to our process."

After Trump's "deep state" tweet, Hahn immediately called the president.

"I want to reiterate that no one is blocking anything," Hahn said. Producing a vaccine is a complicated procedure governed by laws, and the vaccine manufacturers and government agencies were already fast-tracking the process at record speed, working in partnership with the Trump administration's "Operation Warp Speed" initiative.

"We are not slowing down enrollment of the trials. We're trying our best in terms of getting data and information," he said. This has nothing to do with politics. He tried to explain the clinical trial process to Trump.

The FDA is a regulator and follows strict guidelines to determine whether and when a vaccine is safe and efficacious for use by the general public in the U.S. It does not produce the vaccine. A typical vaccine usually takes around 10 to 15 years to create. The mumps vaccine, the fastest ever developed, took four years.

"Look," Hahn said. "These clinical trials are set up by companies, by the NIH," the National Institutes of Health.

The vaccine was being developed by companies like Pfizer-BioNTech, Johnson & Johnson, and Moderna. They conducted the scientific study, including laboratory research and nonclinical trials in animals before then applying to the FDA for permission to begin multiphased clinical human trials.

"While FDA has oversight over clinical research, it does not conduct the trials," Hahn said again. Its role is to evaluate the data submitted by the companies to determine safety and efficacy.

"I'm proud of you," Trump said, changing tune completely and putting an end to the conversation. He seemed embarrassed and didn't talk about his tweet.

Hahn realized the president had no idea how the FDA operated and had made no effort to find out before sending the tweet. It was a classic tweet-burst, ignorant and disruptive. Trump did not understand the power of his words. Public faith in safety procedures was critical to convincing people to get vaccinated.

Hahn did not ask the president whether he ever considered what thousands of FDA workers might think when they read the statements attacking their work from the president of the United States.

TWENTY-FOUR

Jim Clyburn continued to have unique standing with Biden, who would always remember the South Carolina primary win. Biden had beaten the runner-up, Bernie Sanders, by nearly 30 percentage points after Clyburn offered his heartfelt, momentous endorsement. It had saved his candidacy.

In March, Biden had publicly pledged to pick a woman as his running mate. Clyburn was careful to never demand Biden put a Black woman on the ticket. Picking a Black woman would be a "plus not a must," a phrase he repeated often in private with Biden and others. He had already made his deal with Biden for a Supreme Court seat, with Biden promising to nominate a Black woman to the high court.

But Clyburn knew a Black woman could be a big advantage in the Democratic Party and carried its own logic. He had several Black women on his short list, including two distinguished House members and one senator.

Clyburn did not know Senator Kamala Harris as well as his House colleagues. But one thing about Harris stood out: She was an alumna of Howard University in Washington, one of the most prominent HBCUs—historically Black colleges and universities. And she was a member of one of the nation's oldest, historically Black sororities—Alpha Kappa Alpha.

When Biden brought up Harris in a summer phone call, Clyburn said, "She's an HBCU graduate."

Clyburn, who also had graduated from a historically Black

university, South Carolina State, explained to Biden the significance.

"That means something to HBCU people," he said.

While high-achieving Black Americans now went to Ivy League schools, Clyburn said, "People tend to forget that these people, their parents went to HBCUs, their grandparents went to HBCUs. When it comes to their grandparents, very few of them could have gone anywhere else."

Harris's diploma was more than a degree. It carried political weight with the exact people Biden needed to show up to vote, Clyburn said.

"That's one of the things I think people miss, they don't think about the history of all of this," he said. "It's all, you know, 'I went to Yale, I went to Harvard.' Well, a lot of us came along at a time when those opportunities were not there. It was South Carolina State, North Carolina A&T, whatever it is."

Clyburn had held this view for years. For him, the HBCUs were the nucleus of identity and power in the Black community, beyond education. He felt most Americans tended not to recognize how, when most of his generation was coming along, Black men and women were not privy to civic participation in Rotary Clubs, Lions Clubs and other groups. Black people looked at fraternities and sororities as one of the rare places where they could contribute.

One other question was at the heart of Biden's decision: What would his late son, Beau Biden, recommend?

He confided to others that the answer would almost certainly be Kamala Harris.

Kamala and Beau had served together as state attorneys general, Harris for California and Biden for Delaware. During the housing crisis and economic recession a decade earlier, the pair collaborated on an investigation into the biggest banks. "We had each other's backs," Harris wrote in her 2019 memoir, *The Truths We Hold*.

When Beau died in 2015, Harris attended the memorial service. She posted a picture on Instagram on June 8, 2015, and called the service a "moving tribute" for "my dear friend."

In 2016, Joe Biden endorsed Harris to fill retiring Senator Barbara Boxer's California seat. "Beau always supported her," he wrote in a statement. She became the first Black person elected to represent California in the Senate.

Harris was the daughter of an Indian mother, Shyamala, and a Jamaican father, Donald, who had immigrated to the United States before Harris was born. They met as fellow civil rights activists in Berkeley—Donald an economist, Shyamala a scientist.

Harris projected an inner gutsiness, a fighting spirit that had fueled the glass-shattering trajectory of her career. She had been the first woman to serve as San Francisco's district attorney and first Black person and first woman to serve as state attorney general.

While her voting record was unabashedly liberal, in a party where Bernie Sanders now represented the left wing, she seemed more to the center. She remained close to President Obama and was an early supporter of his 2008 bid.

Her presidential campaign, which kicked off in Oakland before 20,000 supporters, had failed. But since Biden had dropped out of two presidential races, he told others he did not view Harris's decision to withdraw as a flaw. It was part of the road you walked to reach the presidency.

As a former chairman of the Senate Judiciary Committee, he also admired how she had made an early mark as a high-profile voice on that committee. Her direct questions during the Kavanaugh confirmation hearings in 2018 had brought new attention.

And while her hits had stung during the campaign, he knew she was not all cold business. She was confident and athletic, with an easy laugh, and wore sporty and classic Converse sneakers on the campaign trail over flats or heels.

Biden told former Connecticut senator Chris Dodd, who headed the vice presidential search committee, he was over any hurt from the 2019 debate where Harris had attacked his record on busing policy. Dodd then told the vetting committee that if Biden could get over it, everyone else should, too.

At a campaign event in Wilmington, Delaware, on July 28, Biden's note card was photographed.

"Kamala Harris," the card read. "Do not hold grudges. Campaigned with me & Jill. Talented. Great help to campaign. Great respect for her."

After Clyburn spoke to Biden by phone during the final week of the vice presidential search, he walked away feeling it was her spot to lose.

Protests calling for fundamental policy changes to address systemic racism were sweeping the country after George Floyd's murder. Calls on Biden to choose a woman of color were growing louder. Even Harris's rivals, including Senator Elizabeth Warren and Michigan governor Gretchen Whitmer, both contenders for the pick, said as much. That passion was shared by many others in the party who wanted to recognize the power and vitality of Black women not only in the party, but in American politics.

The logic of picking Harris was evident.

On August 11, Biden sat in front of his laptop at his desk in Wilmington, readying himself to call Senator Harris on Zoom. On his desk rested a framed greeting card, a gift from his own father, with the comic strip character Hagar the Horrible. Hagar was screaming at the stormy skies, "Why Me?!" The sky replies, "Why not?"

"You ready to go to work?" Biden asked Harris.

Harris paused.

"Oh my God. I am so ready to go to work."

Harris's husband, lawyer Doug Emhoff, joined Harris on-screen and Jill popped in alongside Biden. "We're going to have fun," Dr. Biden said.

Shortly after the call, Biden formally announced Harris as his running mate.

The pick was covered as a historic American moment and a savvy political move, potentially bringing new voters to the Democratic coalition. There were about 10 million more women than men registered to vote. Harris would also bring prosecutorial energy when she met Vice President Mike Pence at their debate.

Harris polled popularly across the board. The campaign raised $48 million in the 48 hours following the announcement and a record-breaking $365.4 million in August, more than any single month's fundraising total in previous presidential elections.

On August 12, Harris and Biden appeared in Delaware together. "Joe likes to say that character is on the ballot and it's true," she said. "When he saw what happened in Charlottesville three years ago today, he knew we were in a battle for the soul of our nation."

TWENTY-FIVE

Trump had seethed for weeks over news coverage of his retreat into the White House's bunker. His rage flashed again on August 10, when he was in the White House briefing room answering questions.

A Secret Service agent interrupted Trump and pulled him out of the room, into a waiting area for the White House press office.

"There were shots fired outside," the agent told the president.

Trump scowled.

"I'm not going in the fucking bunker," he said.

A day later, shortly after Biden's vice presidential announcement, Trump tweeted. "Kamala Harris started strong in the Democrat Primaries, and finished weak, ultimately fleeing the race with almost zero support. That's the kind of opponent everyone dreams of!"

The Trump campaign followed up with a video—"Slow Joe and Phony Kamala," a narrator's voice said. "Perfect together, wrong for America."

Outside Trump adviser Dick Morris later emailed the president's pollsters and campaign officials. He wondered if the Harris pick could be weaponized.

"Is Biden easy to manipulate? We know he is weak and feeble, but does it follow that he can be unduly influenced by staff, consultants, and donors? Can we say that he chose Harris because the black leaders told him to do so? Can we cite his embrace of the radical agenda as a successful manipulation by Bernie's people?"

Inside the Trump campaign, which was now being run by veteran New Jersey political operative Bill Stepien after Brad Parscale was demoted, there was mounting frustration. Trump's numbers were sagging. Outsiders like Dick Morris and Sean Hannity had too much influence, feeding him ideas and advice that cut against poll-tested strategy.

On Wednesday, September 23, at 8:20 a.m., Trump adviser Jason Miller emailed Stepien and the campaign's pollsters, John McLaughlin and Tony Fabrizio. The subject line: "Was this new poll shared with Dick Morris???"

Fabrizio responded at 11:23 a.m., writing "the President had told me to share numbers with him."

Miller responded three minutes later.

> *Well, that was a fuck up.*
>
> *Now he's "threatening" to tell the President our numbers have "tanked."*
>
> *I don't want anybody talking to Dick Morris about anything ever.*

In late September, the FDA submitted guidelines on its process for emergency approval of the coronavirus vaccines to the White House. For over two weeks, they waited for a sign-off. The holdup was Mark Meadows. He was concerned there were too many unnecessary steps in the FDA authorization process. It would take too long.

For Hahn, it was another intervention by Meadows, the brash former North Carolina businessman, weighing in as a supposed expert on FDA process, even though he was not a doctor.

The guidelines called for Phase 3 studies to include a two-month follow-up period to see whether participants reported any serious side effects.

Peter Marks, the director of the Center for Biologics Evaluation and Research at the FDA, had a PhD in cell and molecular biology and was working arm in arm with Hahn on the approval process.

"It was stunning to me that Mark Meadows thought he knew more than Peter Marks, with respect to how to evaluate the safety and efficacy of a vaccine," Hahn told others. "He thinks he knows things that he doesn't know and has expertise that he doesn't have."

Seven former FDA commissioners published an op-ed in *The Washington Post* on September 29 asking the White House to let the FDA do its job: "The White House has said it might try to influence the scientific standards for vaccine approval put forward by the FDA.

"This pronouncement came just after key leaders at the FDA, the Centers for Disease Control and Prevention and the National Institutes of Health all publicly supported the guidance," they wrote. "Drug makers have also pledged to use the FDA's scientific standards."

Later that same evening, at the first presidential debate, held in Cleveland, Trump said, "I've spoken to Pfizer, I've spoken to all of the people that you have to speak to, Moderna, Johnson & Johnson, and others."

"We're weeks away from a vaccine," Trump claimed, insisting the companies "can go faster." Despite all his rhetoric playing down the virus, Trump knew a vaccine before the election could help him politically.

Pfizer's chief executive Albert Bourla joined the chorus of voices in the scientific community trying to shift the president's tactics and tone.

"Once more, I was disappointed that the prevention for a

deadly disease was discussed in political terms rather than scientific facts," Bourla said in an open letter to colleagues.

During a debate prep session in the fall, Biden asked Ron Klain, "Have you thought about what you want to do after the campaign is over?"

"If you win," Klain said, "I would be interested in coming back and serving."

"Would you think about being my chief of staff?"

"I'm honored, flattered you would think of me," Klain said. "I think we're going to have a real mess on our hands if you win. I'd love to be part of it."

"Look, I'm superstitious," Biden said, keeping all the options for himself. "I'm not going to offer anybody any jobs until after I'm elected. But it's important to me to have in my mind that you would do this."

"Yes," Klain said. "You know if you offer me that job, I will accept."

Klain's prediction months earlier, during that private meeting in Delaware, came true at the first Trump-Biden debate. Nothing was out of bounds, including Biden's family.

Trump was aggressive and angry—needling and interrupting Biden. "Will you shut up, man?" Biden asked with exasperation. It was the line of the night.

President Trump's hospitalization with the coronavirus, late Friday, October 2, briefly ruptured his campaign's final stretch, with Trump helicoptered to Walter Reed National Military Medical Center in Bethesda, Maryland.

Trump had resisted going. But when his blood oxygen levels plummeted into the 80s range, a potentially fatal zone, and the president had trouble breathing, his physician had to give him oxygen. Several aides warned he would have to be taken out in a wheelchair or worse if he did not go. He agreed to board Marine One and head over to Bethesda.

Once hospitalized, Trump's condition stabilized. Trump was given what his doctors called an "antibody cocktail," including Regeneron, an antibody treatment that was still in its clinical trial phase. U.S. health officials went into a frenzy to secure FDA approval for Trump's use of the drug and debated whether it was appropriate for him, with his obesity at age 74, to take the cocktail, according to the *Washington Post*'s Yasmeen Abutaleb and Damian Paletta.

"Enjoy your hospital food," Kellyanne Conway told Trump on the phone during his three-night stint at the hospital.

Months earlier, when Conway was in a home-based quarantine after contracting the virus, Trump had buoyed her spirits.

"You have zero percent body fat, honey," Trump said. "Honey, if you have zero percent body fat, you're fine."

He was released on October 5, theatrically removing his mask from the White House balcony, then flashing thumbs-up and saluting at Marine One.

The White House remained a hot zone for infection. Meadows and other senior staffers eschewed masks and low-level staffers felt the office culture seemed to encourage ignoring public health guidelines. They sat through meeting after meeting where missives from Fauci and others were derided by Trump and his aides as preachy and liberal. At least "34 White House staffers and other contacts" had contracted the virus, noted an internal memo from FEMA, the Federal Emergency Management Agency, in October.

Senate Majority Leader Mitch McConnell kept watch on Biden's understated general election campaign. He thought the Biden campaign was clever in styling him as a moderate—the calm grandfather from Delaware versus a wild Republican incumbent. Almost any Democrat was certain to be elected after voters observed Trump's behavior.

"Being Donald Trump," McConnell told others, was enough for Trump to lose in November. "Trump's personality was his biggest problem and from a personality point of view, Joe was the opposite of Trump."

McConnell saw the dynamic as a Republican tragedy. They had passed tax reform. Pedal to the metal on filling federal judgeships with conservatives. The economy was humming before the pandemic took hold in March. None of it was an accident. Trump's hand was in all of it.

"We had a hell of a good four years," McConnell said.

But it was now all personality. All Trump.

Biden, who had never won more than 1 percent of the vote in his two previous presidential outings, had luck and a perfect matchup.

"I'm not saying it was all just good luck, but he did have good luck," McConnell said.

As for Trump, McConnell did not want a public war with the president. But he did not hold out any hope that Trump could change.

For nearly four years, McConnell had had what he called a "brotherhood" with cabinet officials like former secretary of defense James Mattis and former White House chief of staff John Kelly, and now with Attorney General William Barr. They tried to push Trump toward normal.

It was routinely a losing exercise. Futile. And by this final lap, the so-called brotherhood had seen many of its members exit the stage.

Inside the Republican cloakroom, one joke McConnell enjoyed telling was about Trump's former secretary of state Rex Tillerson, a cabinet member he had liked.

In 2017, the State Department had strongly denied Tillerson called Trump a "moron."

"Do you know why Tillerson was able to say he didn't call the president a 'moron'?" McConnell would dryly ask colleagues in his Kentucky drawl.

"Because he called him a 'fucking moron.'"

TWENTY-SIX

On Friday, October 30, four days before the election, Chairman Milley examined the latest sensitive intelligence. What he read was alarming: The Chinese believed the United States was going to attack them.

Milley knew it was untrue. But the Chinese were on high alert, and whenever a superpower is on high alert, the risk of war escalates. Asian media reports were filled with rumors and talk of tensions between the two countries over the Freedom of Navigation exercises in the South China Sea, where the U.S. Navy routinely sails ships in areas to challenge maritime claims by the Chinese and promote freedom of the seas.

There were suggestions that Trump might want to manufacture a "Wag the Dog" war before the election so he could rally the voters and beat Biden.

Miscommunications were often the seeds of war. In 1987, Admiral William J. Crowe, chairman of the Joints Chiefs under President Ronald Reagan, had established a back-channel relationship with the head of the Soviet Union's military, to avoid an accidental war. Crowe had not informed President Reagan about his decision to take national security into his own hands and work directly with Marshal Sergei Akhromeyev, the chief of the Soviet General Staff.

Milley was aware his immediate predecessors, Generals Martin Dempsey and Joseph Dunford, had set up similar back-channel arrangements with the heads of the military in Russia and China.

And in a time of crisis, Milley knew he could dial up Russian General Valery Gerasimov or General Li Zuocheng of the People's Liberation Army.

This was such a moment. While he often put a hold on or stopped various tactical and routine U.S. military exercises that could look provocative to the other side or be misinterpreted, this was not a time for just a hold. He arranged a call with General Li.

Trump was attacking China on the campaign trail at every turn, blaming them for the coronavirus. "I beat this crazy, horrible China virus," he told Fox News on October 11. Milley knew the Chinese might not know where the politics ended and possible action began.

To give the call with Li a more routine flavor, Milley first raised mundane issues like the staff-to-staff communications and methods for making sure they could always rapidly reach each other.

Finally, getting to the point, Milley said, "General Li, I want to assure you that the American government is stable and everything is going to be okay. We are not going to attack or conduct any kinetic operations against you.

"General Li, you and I have known each other for now five years. If we're going to attack, I'm going to call you ahead of time. It's not going to be a surprise. It's not going to be a bolt out of the blue.

"If there was a war or some kind of kinetic action between the United States and China, there's going to be a buildup, just like there has been always in history.

"And there's going to be tension. And I'm going to be communicating with you pretty regularly," Milley said. "So this is not one of those times. It's going to be okay. We're not going to have a fight."

"Okay," General Li said, "I take you at your word."

Milley instantly realized how valuable and important a channel he had. In a few minutes, he had been able to deescalate and avoid miscommunication that could lead to an incident or even a war between the U.S. and China.

Milley could see the Lincoln Memorial from Quarters 6, his home. Arlington National Cemetery was nearby.

"I've buried 242 kids up here," he later told others one Saturday morning. "I'm not really interested in having a war with anybody.

"I'll defend the country if it's necessary. But war, the military instrument, must be a last resort, not a first resort."

He did not tell Trump about his call with General Li.

Just before the election, Milley reminded the chiefs that the post-election period—what he had labeled "Phase 2" in the Tank months earlier—would be the most dangerous period for the country, with an unnerving wait between the election and the January 6 certification of the results.

"If President Trump wins, then the street's going to explode with riots and civil unrest. If President Trump loses, there's going to be significant issues there about a contested election," Milley said at a meeting.

There were hints of coming tumult in the streets. On social media, Trump's campaign was pumping the idea of a military-style political clash. Mail-in ballots, which many states were using due to the pandemic, were being cast as fraudulent and the tools of conspiracy.

"We need you to join ARMY FOR TRUMP's election security operation!" read one official Trump campaign post at the end of September, with Donald Trump Jr. imploring "every able-bodied man, woman" to enlist in the president's "security" effort.

"Don't let them steal it," Trump Jr. said. "Enlist today."

TWENTY-SEVEN

Election night at the Trump White House began like other Trump parties over the previous four years: with fast food orders. Pizzas and bags of Chick-fil-A piled up in the Roosevelt Room. The Map Room, where Franklin Roosevelt tracked battles during World War II, was set up as the nerve center.

Trump's family members and senior aides moved anxiously in and out, with Fox News playing on television screens set up around the West Wing.

In the months before the election, Trump systematically claimed the outcome would be rigged. If he didn't win, the election would be stolen. It was his unless there was massive fraud.

On June 22, he had tweeted: "MILLIONS OF MAIL-IN BALLOTS WILL BE PRINTED BY FOREIGN COUNTRIES, AND OTHERS. IT WILL BE THE SCANDAL OF OUR TIMES!"

In his own Republican National Convention speech on August 27, Trump declared, "the only way they can take this election away from us is if this is a rigged election."

Early in the evening on November 3, Trump's allies were buoyant. Trump won a host of red states by 8 p.m.—Kentucky, West Virginia and Tennessee, among others. By 11 p.m., he had picked up Missouri and Utah. Then, 19 minutes after midnight, the Associated Press called Ohio for Trump. Then Iowa, then Florida and Texas. Cheers went up in the East Room, where hundreds of supporters were gathered.

James Clyburn was nervous as he watched television from

home. When Biden called to check in, Clyburn said he did not like what he was watching.

Biden was upbeat. He said his advisers knew that many states were behind on counting mail-in ballots. The Biden campaign had encouraged mail-ins, while Trump had been pushing in-person voting, he said, so the early numbers were always likely to lean toward the president.

"I think we're going to be fine," Biden said.

The mood in the Map Room was beginning to darken.

Three of Trump's children—Donald Trump Jr., Eric Trump and Ivanka Trump, his senior adviser—kept showing up and pestering aides. Eric asked for data his father could cite in a speech. He grew frustrated when told the numbers would continue to change. States were still counting.

Fox News's decision desk called Arizona for Biden shortly before 11:30 p.m., stunning Trump's crowd. Trump pressed his family members and advisers to tell the network to pull the call back. Fox refused, enraging the president, who said Fox News was now in on the steal.

Biden started to pile up wins. The Associated Press called Wisconsin and Michigan for him. Pennsylvania and Georgia, two of the night's prizes, were too close to call. At 12:26 a.m., November 4, the electoral count was Biden 214, Trump 210, with both men likely hours away from nearing the necessary 270 electoral votes to win the election.

Shortly before 12:45 a.m., Biden took the stage in Wilmington. He predicted victory but did not declare it outright. The crowd was mostly parked in cars outside the Chase Center due to the social distancing rules. Drivers honked their horns.

"Your patience is commendable," Biden said. "But look, we feel good about where we are. We really do. I'm here to tell you tonight, we believe we're on track to win this election." He urged patience as they waited for the mail-in vote and for every ballot to be counted.

At 2:30 a.m., November 4, as his leads in other states were slipping away, President Trump strode to a lectern in the East Room. He wore a dark suit, with a blue silk tie and flag lapel. The first lady, Melania Trump, and Vice President Pence were at his side. "Hail to the Chief" played loudly before he began his remarks in front of a wall of American flags and a crowd that had expected a celebration.

"This is a fraud on the American public," he said. Trump's tone was dismissive, indignant. "This is an embarrassment to our country. We were getting ready to win this election. Frankly, we did win this election." He added, "So we'll be going to the U.S. Supreme Court."

"How the hell did we lose the vote to Joe Biden?" Trump asked Kellyanne Conway a few hours later, November 4. Conway, the veteran pollster, had left the White House in August but remained close to Trump.

Trump was refusing to concede publicly, but he seemed ready, at least privately, to acknowledge defeat.

It was the mail-in ballots, she said. Covid. Your campaign running out of money. The debates.

"Yeah, yeah," he said, upset. "It just doesn't make any sense. It's terrible."

There were two ways to look at the returns. On one hand, Biden had won by 7 million votes—81 million to Trump's 74 million. On the other, a switch of 44,000 votes in Arizona, Wisconsin and Georgia would have given Trump and Biden a tie in the Electoral College.

A *Washington Post* analysis noted Biden ended up doing what Hillary Clinton could not in 2016: pick up some support from working-class Americans who rarely participated in politics.

Some previously voted for Trump. In addition, Biden had generated strong turnout among traditional Democrats nationwide.

"These Trump-to-Biden voters were overwhelmingly concerned about covid-19, with about 82 percent rating it as a 'major factor' in their presidential pick," the analysis concluded, based on exit polls.

Advisers tried to keep him positive.

Brian Jack, Trump's 32-year-old political director from Georgia, who kept him updated on every member of Congress, briefed the president in his private dining room on November 5.

House Republicans had won a net of 10 seats, flipping 13 Democratic seats, and losing just three GOP seats, Jack said, running through the numbers. A record number of Republican women had been elected, bringing the total number of GOP women to over 25 in the House.

You helped them with tele-town halls, tweeted for them, Jack said. Trump was downbeat.

"Were they grateful?" he asked. "Were they thankful?"

Jack assured him they were.

Trump made dozens more phone calls in the following days, with many allies fervently insisting he had won. It was stolen right from you, many told him. We're hearing crazy stories out of Pennsylvania and Michigan.

Some longtime allies then went on Fox News and kept up the drumbeat. Rigged. Fraud.

One of them was Rudy Giuliani, the former New York mayor and Trump's personal lawyer. Once the hero of the Big Apple after the 9/11 attacks, he was now a combative regular in Trump's orbit who regularly smoked cigars. He told the president that he needed a better strategy. He offered to help.

Trump stopped privately saying he lost the vote. And he gave Giuliani his blessing to start poking around.

TWENTY-EIGHT

Giuliani arrived at the Trump campaign headquarters in Arlington on November 6, and headed to a conference room, surrounded by friends and assistants.

Nearby, the campaign's general counsel, Matt Morgan, was watching them. Morgan had worked with Pence and shared much of Pence's personality. Quiet, deeply conservative, careful.

Morgan asked what Giuliani was doing there. His legal team had a plan. They were already filing lawsuits in states and working with several outside law firms. The campaign's post-election strategy had been in place for months with the president's approval.

Giuliani's friends and Trump campaign officials were chatting excitedly, a frenzy of paper and memos and iPhones. Giuliani started in, speaking confidently about massive, late dumps of votes in Democratic states and blue cities. The numbers are impossible, he insisted. It had to be stolen.

Morgan was silent. Any seasoned election lawyer knew some counties were infamous, decades-long late reporters of their results. Nothing new.

Giuliani said the Trump campaign's observers were barred from tabulation rooms. "They kicked them out because they were cheating! This is all part of a coordinated effort by the Democrats."

He held up a sheaf of papers. "I have eight affidavits," he said. "I have eight affidavits that say observers were kept out of Michigan. Bad things are happening."

That same day, Trump summoned the Giuliani group and his lawyers to the Oval Office, where they were joined by the White House's lawyers. Giuliani again launched into his connect-the-dots conspiracy theory.

Trump asked, how do we get these abuses that Rudy is talking about before the court? It would not be easy, the lawyers replied. You need standing, a legal threshold demonstrating a party's right to sue. Being upset is not legal grounds.

"Well, why don't we just get up to the Supreme Court directly?" Trump wondered. "Like, why can't we just go there right away?" There was a legal process to follow, the lawyers repeated.

Go figure this out for me, now, Trump told them. The group wandered across the hall to the Roosevelt Room.

Inside, Trump's campaign lawyers and White House counselors had a tense, basic, law school 101 discussion about what they should tell Trump. They knew they could never go straight to the Supreme Court. Trump would have to file in district courts, then get a federal appeals court to hear the case, then file for the Supreme Court. It would take time.

Giuliani came in. He was yelling.

"I have 27 affidavits!" Giuliani said, rattling off election claims in various states. Strange, Morgan thought. Just an hour earlier, Giuliani had claimed he had only eight affidavits.

Trump soon called everyone back to the Oval Office. The group circled the president. Giuliani kept yelling, slamming Michigan about supposed fraud.

Giuliani raised his hand. "If you just put me in charge," he told Trump, we could fix this.

"I have 80 affidavits," Giuliani said with certainty.

On Saturday, November 7, the Associated Press declared Biden the winner at 11:25 a.m., after they concluded that Biden had won Pennsylvania and its 20 electoral votes, pushing him over the 270-vote threshold necessary to win the White House.

"Joe Biden is Elected the 46th President of the United States," read the headline on the *New York Times* website. Even though all the votes had not yet been counted in some states, the rest of the national media, which usually followed the AP in reporting election results, began to say the same, a commonsense conclusion based on the available data.

Inside the majority leader's inner circle on Capitol Hill, McConnell was the least surprised. And McConnell had seen it all, up close. "There were so many Maalox moments during the four years," he told his staff.

With Trump brashly contesting the results, McConnell said he would give Trump room to let off steam and not publicly recognize Biden as president-elect. He still needed to have a working relationship with Trump, and, more importantly, McConnell worried Trump might react negatively and upend the upcoming, hotly contested runoff Senate elections in Georgia. Those seats were necessary to keep the Republican majority—and McConnell as majority leader.

He also said he did not want Biden, a serial telephone user, to call him. Any call from Biden was sure to infuriate Trump and set off unwanted calls from him, asking if he believed Biden had won the presidency. Better to keep the line dead.

McConnell tasked Senator John Cornyn—Republican of Texas, his former deputy in the leadership and a close friend—to speak privately with Senator Chris Coons, Biden's close ally from Delaware. Coons had reached out to McConnell after the election and offered to be a back channel if McConnell wanted to reach Biden.

Tell Coons to tell Biden not to call him—a firm request.

McConnell wanted his strategy kept confidential. He did not

want a blizzard of news stories saying he would not take Biden's phone call. Biden would understand. They were two seasoned political hands who understood the long game.

"We're in a delicate situation," Cornyn told Coons. "I recognize that your guy is probably the duly elected next president of the United States. And we both know he and the majority leader have had a long, close relationship. And the majority leader doesn't want the vice president to take any offense at his not calling directly.

"But it won't help things if the vice president is calling the majority leader. President Trump will somehow assume that they're cutting a deal behind his back to cut him out, and it'll make him even more irrational."

Coons relayed the message to Biden.

Biden addressed supporters in Wilmington on the evening of November 7. Once again in a parking lot outside the Chase Center, with lines of honking cars instead of crowds. But even with the drive-in-movie look, it was an unequivocal victory gathering.

Biden's top campaign aides told Biden he needed to be resolute and clear: It's over.

"Folks, the people of this nation have spoken. They've delivered us a clear victory, a convincing victory," Biden said, smiling in a dark suit and powder blue tie. He thanked the Black voters who had lifted him all year. "The African American community stood up again for me. You've always had my back, and I'll have yours."

Adopting a theme Gerald Ford used 46 years earlier when he assumed the presidency in August 1974 after Nixon's resignation, Biden said, "This is the time to heal in America."

"Let this grim era of demonization in America begin to end here and now," he said, reading from a text Mike Donilon and Jon Meacham, the keepers of the soul theme, had shaped with suggestions. "For all those of you who voted for President Trump, I understand the disappointment tonight. I've lost a couple times myself. But now, let's give each other a chance."

"(Your Love Keeps Lifting Me) Higher and Higher," the classic Jackie Wilson R&B song, started playing as the cars started honking again. Supporters jumped into the back of pickup trucks and onto trunks, waving flags and signs. Fireworks exploded in the dark sky.

The Biden family embraced onstage. Jill Biden. Hunter Biden. Ashley Biden. The grandchildren. Kamala Harris and her family joined in. They all looked to the sky, the glow of the colored sparks on their faces.

Margaret Aitken, who had been Biden's Senate press secretary for 10 years, was in the audience. She remained a close friend of the president-elect and was a clearinghouse for a vast number of the Biden Delaware connections, still one of the centers of his life.

Aitken had sent a text message to Biden: Elaine Manlove, who had been Delaware's elections commissioner for 12 years, and her husband, Wayne, had been killed in an automobile accident the previous week, just after celebrating their 51st wedding anniversary. They had stopped in their Chevrolet Equinox at a red light on Route 13 when a tractor-trailer, whose driver had fallen asleep, hit and killed them.

Aitken told Biden a funeral Mass would be held on November 9 at St. Elizabeth, Wilmington's largest Catholic church.

Elaine had worked on Biden's first Senate campaign in 1972 and always called Biden "My Senator." She was an institution in the state. She had lived at the beach in Sussex County in Delaware, a Republican enclave. Every time somebody in her neighborhood put up a Trump sign, she put up another Biden sign in her lawn. She eventually had 17 Biden signs. Biden ultimately won his home state, which has a population of less than one million, by 19 points and the state's three electoral votes.

On Sunday, November 8, in his first full day as president-elect, Biden called Aitken.

"I saw you last night," Biden said.

"You did?" Aitken said.

"I was waving at you."

"I thought you were just waving at the crowd."

"I can't go to Elaine's funeral," Biden said. "There are so many restrictions. People around me have to be tested for Covid. I have to be very careful. There is the whole Secret Service thing. I can't interrupt something like a funeral."

Aitken said everyone would understand.

Elaine had a son, Biden recalled. What is his phone number?

Aitken gave him Matthew Manlove's phone number. That night, Biden called Matt's cell phone. Matt, 42, noticed an incoming call about 7 p.m. from an unknown number. Given the upcoming funeral, he answered.

"Hey, Matt, this is Joe Biden."

"Joe," Matt said, suddenly catching himself realizing he was talking to the president-elect. He asked permission to put his phone on speaker so his two brothers, Joseph, 39, and Michael, 35, could join in.

I am so sorry about your mother and father, Biden said. Your mother, who I knew so well, was such a force for good and honor in politics. A loyal servant of Delaware. She was so generous to me and everyone. I thought the world of her.

I am so sorry for such a loss, he said. This must be the worst time for all of you. Nearly 50 years ago in 1972, I lost my wife and daughter in an automobile accident. I can relate to what you are going through. The greatest grief. Everything going wrong in your lives. But I can tell you, I know, each day it gets a little bit better. You will get through it.

Biden went on. He did not seem rushed.

I planned to attend your parents' funeral tomorrow, but I cannot because of Covid, he said. My doctors are not allowing me within 100 feet of a crowd. Everyone would have to be tested. Then there is the Secret Service thing. I am sorry I can't be there. But I will be with you in spirit. Bless you and your parents forever.

Biden then said he wanted to recite some of his favorite lines from the great Irish poet Seamus Heaney. He considered it a prayer and quoted it often, most recently to close out his acceptance speech for the Democratic nomination in August.

"History says, don't hope
On this side of the grave.
But then, once in a lifetime
The longed-for tidal wave
Of Justice can rise up.
And hope and history rhyme."

Thank you, President Biden, the three boys each said.

Matt thought it had been an amazing call for several minutes but looked at the timer on his phone. Biden had talked for nearly 20 minutes. He felt an explosion of emotions. The first person he thought of calling to explain they had heard from President Biden was his mother. Biden later sent the three boys a personal letter.

TWENTY-NINE

"I'm the dog who caught the car," Biden joked on the phone with his old friend, Senator Lindsey Graham, in the days after the election.

Graham laughed hard.

"We used to be friends," Biden said.

"Joe, we're still friends," Graham said. "You know, I'll help you any way I can."

Graham expected to support several of Biden's cabinet nominees, especially for top national security posts.

A dozen years earlier Biden, while vice president, had told President Obama, "Lindsey Graham has the best instincts in the Senate." Obama agreed, and Graham, the bachelor-lawyer colonel in the Air Force Reserve, and Biden had traveled the world on various diplomatic and military missions during Obama's presidency. It was a real bipartisan bond.

The friendship had unraveled during Trump's presidency due to Graham's support for Trump's attacks on Hunter Biden and his business dealings.

Graham made no apologies.

In the phone call with Biden, he said, "I've got no problem with you. But Joe, if Mike Pence's son or a Trump person did what Hunter did, it'd be game, set, match."

For Biden, anything relating to family was deeply personal. Graham, who had no children, had crossed a red line.

Biden and Graham would not talk again for months—and if

Biden had anything to do with it, they likely would never talk again.

Hope Hicks, a former model who in 2017 had become Trump's White House director of strategic communications at age 28 and was the closest aide to Trump during the 2016 campaign, had rejoined the White House in February 2020, after a stint as Fox's chief of communications.

Due to their history and close working relationship, Hicks felt she could be candid. Unlike most other aides, she had no agenda.

On November 7, the day media outlets called the election for Biden, Hicks met with Trump's son-in-law and senior adviser Jared Kushner and several other Trump campaign advisers that morning at the Arlington campaign headquarters. Trump was playing golf at his nearby club in Virginia.

Who is going to tell the president the race is over after he finishes golf? No one volunteered.

Kushner, thin and with a soft voice, who served as the president's confidant, spoke up. "There is a time for a doctor and a time for a priest," he said. He looked at several senior campaign aides. Perhaps they could be the doctor and give the president the tough diagnosis.

Last political rites, if they ever came, would be left to the family, Kushner indicated.

"The family will go in when the family needs to go in," Kushner said. "But it's not time for that."

Others argued the legal fight was only beginning. Maybe Trump could score a few wins. But no one was confident Trump could claim the presidency.

Hicks spoke up. "Why don't we just tell him the truth?" she asked.

"He can make the best of a bad outcome. This wasn't a blowout.

This wasn't a repudiation," Hicks said, pointing to the more than a dozen pickups in the House. The Democrats' 232-seat majority had shrunk to just a handful of seats above 218, the bare minimum for holding power in the chamber.

"This was an embrace of his policies, if not him personally, and sometimes things just go a different way," she said.

Hicks said there was a way to shutter things with dignity, or something close to it. The book deals, comeback rallies, splashy television shows and paid speeches could maybe make it a little easier for Trump to accept he lost. He could be the king of Palm Beach, running the GOP.

Several other senior campaign officials agreed to speak with Trump that afternoon, including communications adviser Jason Miller and campaign manager Bill Stepien, who had ascended as pivotal figures after Parscale was demoted.

Trump brushed away any talk of conceding.

Rudy Giuliani held a news conference in Northeast, a blue-collar Philadelphia neighborhood known for its auto shops and fair-priced cheesesteaks, in the parking lot of Four Seasons Total Landscaping.

Photographs of Giuliani and serious-looking Trump advisers standing in a random parking lot soon ricocheted around Twitter and news outlets.

Standing outside the small company's garage and a building with faded green paint, and next to a self-proclaimed poll watcher who news reports later identified as a convicted sex offender, Giuliani rambled at length, with conspiratorial claims and one-liners.

"Joe Frazier is still voting here—kind of hard, since he died five years ago," Giuliani joked, referring to the late boxing legend. "But Joe continues to vote. If I recall correctly, Joe was a

Republican. So maybe I shouldn't complain. But we should go see if Joe is voting Republican or Democrat now, from the grave."

He also claimed actor Will Smith's father, who died in 2016, had voted twice since he died. "I don't know how he votes, because his vote is secret. In Philadelphia, they keep the votes of dead people secret."

When a reporter told Giuliani the election had been called for Biden, he laughed. "Come on, don't be ridiculous," he said. "Networks don't get to decide elections. Courts do."

That evening, up in the White House residence, Trump told a group of allies and advisers that he was not pleased with Giuliani's performance or the low-rent location, which was being mocked on cable news. He thought Rudy was going to be at the luxury Four Seasons hotel.

The media coverage of Biden's victory and Four Seasons Total Landscaping seemed to make Trump more determined to push forward. He asked, what's the plan? What's our plan in each state? What are our options?

He was focused on how to pick up just tens of thousands of voters in several states. That would give him a second term, another four years.

"You know, this is going to be hard," Trump's outside political adviser, David Bossie, told him. "We need to do this the right way, methodically, and work hard at it. But we can fight this and win."

But, Bossie emphasized, "it's going to be difficult. It's going to be an uphill battle."

Bossie, a seasoned political knife-fighter, had been Trump's deputy campaign manager in 2016.

"Oh?" Trump asked him. "Are you not thinking we should fight?"

"No," Bossie said. "We have to fight for every legal ballot."

Residence staff brought in plates of meatballs and pigs in a blanket. Trump had his usual Diet Coke.

"How do we find the 10,000 votes that we need in Arizona? How do we find the 12,000 that we need in Georgia?" Trump asked. "What about the military ballots? Are they all in?"

The next morning, November 8, Trump summoned Bossie back to the White House. Maybe Bossie could be in charge and let Rudy do Rudy. Bossie could keep the trains running. That was his skill.

When Bossie arrived that afternoon, he was tested for the coronavirus, then walked toward the residence. But before he headed upstairs to see Trump, a White House official abruptly pulled Bossie aside. He needed to head back to the medical unit. His test was back.

"Fuck, fuck, fuck, fuck," Bossie thought as he entered the medical office. His coronavirus test was positive, joining a long list of Trump White House aides and Trump loyalists who had contracted the virus.

Bossie took a few more tests, just to make sure. He sat on the steps of the Old Executive Office Building and hung out with Peter Navarro, Trump's hardline trade adviser, talking politics on a sleepy Sunday.

Bossie was angry. He knew Trump was about to give him the reins of the election fight. It would be a huge public role. But he now had to isolate and leave the White House grounds. Those were the rules.

From the steps, as dusk fell, he saw Giuliani and Sidney Powell. Powell, a stern, right-wing lawyer, had once been a well-regarded attorney. But she had recently been making bizarre claims about voting machines being rigged.

Speaking to Fox Business host Lou Dobbs, who Trump watched

regularly, on November 6, Powell asserted a "likelihood that 3 percent of the total vote was changed in the pre-election, voting ballots that were collected digitally.

"That would have amounted to a massive change in the vote that would have gone across the country," she said, and "explains a lot of what we're seeing." She claimed hundreds of thousands of ballots were appearing out of nowhere to illegally give Biden the presidency.

Bossie watched Powell and Giuliani walk into the White House together. A panic rose.

Powell was a peddler of "concocted bullshit," he thought. And he could not stop her. She and Giuliani were now the ones inside the room.

THIRTY

On November 9, Meadows called Esper in the afternoon to say Trump was going to fire him.

"You serve at the pleasure of the president. You haven't supported him enough," Meadows said, making no apologies for the summary judgment.

Esper had always set his own course and had recently written a classified letter opposing the withdrawal of U.S. troops from Afghanistan. In Meadows's view, Esper had not learned how to play the necessary politics that went with the job of being Trump's secretary of defense.

"My oath is to the Constitution," Esper replied. "I recognize that the president has this authority."

About eight seconds later at 12:54 p.m., Trump tweeted that "Mark Esper has been terminated" as secretary of defense. "I would like to thank him for his service," Trump wrote.

Esper was surprised he had lasted this long, knowing he was walking on a tightrope and telling people all summer he might be fired any day.

In anticipation of being fired sooner or later, he had told the *Military Times* in an interview, "Who's going to come in behind me? It's going to be a real 'yes man.' And then God help us."

Trump appointed Chris Miller, the head of the Counterterrorism Center, as acting secretary of defense.

"Chris will do a GREAT job!" Trump wrote.

David Urban, who was Esper's close friend, called Jared Kushner. He was irate.

"Jared, what the fuck? This is unhinged shit."

Kushner said he had nothing to do with it. "I'm not the one driving the bus," he said.

"Then who is?"

Kushner did not answer.

"This is really shitty what he did to Esper." Urban reminded Kushner that Esper had always been willing to resign upon request. "He's a soldier!"

I know, Kushner said.

Urban ended the call. He told others that Miller and his allies would surely begin to try to assert more influence over national security policy. People he knew and trusted were no longer in position.

"That was the day the fucking music died for me," he said.

Esper's firing was overshadowed that day by a sudden breakthrough on a vaccine. Pfizer announced its vaccine trials were 90 percent effective in preventing the virus, calling it "a historical moment."

Kathrin Jansen, head of vaccine research and development at Pfizer, told *The New York Times* she learned of the results the day before, Sunday, at 1 p.m., and maintained the election had no influence on the release of the information. "We have always said that science is driving how we conduct ourselves," she said, "no politics."

But Trump refused to believe it. "The @US_FDA and the Democrats didn't want to have me get a Vaccine WIN, prior to the election," he later tweeted, "so instead it came out five days later – As I've said all along!"

Pfizer went to work on its FDA application for Emergency Use

Authorization to distribute the vaccine to the general public, a rigorous process.

Vice President Mike Pence, ever a team player, also refused to publicly accept that Biden had won. He had banked his political future on being embraced by Trump's voters as the president's reverent second in command and most logical successor.

"It ain't over til it's over," Pence tweeted on November 9, "and this AIN'T over!"

But Pence's team did not want to see him get swept into Trump's election fight.

"Get him the hell out of D.C., the hell out of Crazytown," Pence's veteran political adviser, Marty Obst, advised Marc Short, now Pence's chief of staff.

Short—an intense conservative with deep ties in the business and congressional realms, who had a closely shaved head—started planning day trips for Pence. The vice president, who still headed the White House's coronavirus task force, would travel to vaccine development sites and manufacturing plants.

Pompeo, heavy and gregarious, with little tolerance for liberals, was always thought to be one of Trump's staunchest supporters in the cabinet. He came to see Milley at Quarters 6 on the evening of November 9 for a one-on-one kitchen table session with the chairman.

"The crazies are taking over," Pompeo said. He was increasingly worried as he watched Trump meet with Giuliani's traveling circus act. Now Sidney Powell, Michael Flynn and the My Pillow Guy—Mike Lindell, the outspoken former drug addict and millionaire CEO of My Pillow, a mattress and pillow company—had Oval Office access.

First in his class, West Point 1986, Pompeo was as military as Milley. He was a classmate of Esper's and was upset at the handling of the firing by Trump. It was cruel and unfair. Firing the secretary of defense was symbolically different than firing any other cabinet secretary because of the vast military power and weaponry.

Milley vividly recalled a statement that Trump had made to *Breitbart News* in March of 2019: "I can tell you I have the support of the police, the support of the military, the support of the bikers for Trump. I have the tough people, but they don't play it tough until they go to a certain point, and then it would be very bad, very bad."

It seemed to be a warning. Milley thought of the military, the police, the FBI, the CIA and the other intelligence agencies as the power ministries. These power centers had often been the tools used by despots.

As they sat in the Quarters 6 kitchen, Milley confided that he believed Trump was in a mental decline. Anyone who sought the presidency already had a large ego. Trump's ego was even more outsized, he noted. And Trump had just suffered the most painful rejection possible. It's got to hurt in ways others will never fully understand.

"You know," Pompeo replied, "he's in a very dark place right now."

"I don't know that," Milley said vaguely. He said his focus was on stability. Transition.

For Milley, the firing of Esper in the cauldron of the election upheaval was a turning point. The danger to the country was accelerating, a mindless march into more and more disorder.

Pompeo said it was turning in a direction that was perilous for the republic.

"We've got to stand shoulder to shoulder," Pompeo said. "We're the last of the Mohicans."

The next day, at a public State Department session with reporters, Pompeo was asked about the Biden transition.

"There will be a smooth transition to a second Trump administration," Pompeo said. He then smiled and added with a smirk, "Right."

On November 10, at 8:10 a.m., Central Intelligence Agency director Gina Haspel, the first woman to head the CIA on a permanent basis, called Milley.

Haspel, who had served 35 years in the CIA, was a trained case officer, tough and skilled at monitoring unstable leaders abroad. She was upset about the dismissal of Esper, and believed Trump wanted to fire her.

"Yesterday was appalling," Haspel told Milley. "We are on the way to a right-wing coup. The whole thing is insanity. He is acting out like a six-year-old with a tantrum."

"We're going to be steady," Milley repeated his mantra. "Steady as a rock. We're going to keep our eye on the horizon. Keep alert to any risks, dangers. Keep the channels open."

What else could they do? Trump was still president, and they were subordinates, constitutionally and legally.

That Tuesday afternoon, Hope Hicks visited Trump in the Oval Office.

"There are opportunities," she said, brightly, suggesting a laying down of political arms as an opening for the future.

"You have a huge amount of goodwill and you can capitalize on it in lots of different ways," she said. "We can't squander it."

Trump did not want to hear about anything that inched close to a concession. He glared at her and frowned, showing disappointment but not surprise. He had appeared to sense her reserve for days.

"It's not who I am to give up," Trump told her. "It's not in me to do that."

The president continued, "I don't care about my legacy. My legacy doesn't matter. If I lose, that will be my legacy.

"My people expect me to fight, and if I don't, I'll lose 'em," Trump said.

"I know this is hard," Hicks said. "It's really hard. I don't like to lose. Nobody likes to lose. But there is so much to be gained by moving forward."

THIRTY-ONE

Milley, Pompeo and Meadows began regularly conferring at 8 a.m. most November mornings on a secure phone line, just the three of them, to assess the international diplomatic and military situation.

The call's purpose was to preserve stability during a period of potential instability, and to avoid anything untoward or provocative.

Chris Miller was not invited to join. Milley was also suspicious of Meadows, who seemed to be part of the group supporting Trump's claims that the election was stolen.

"We've got to land this plane," Milley said cautiously on one of the early calls of the new power troika. "We've got to make sure there's a peaceful transfer of power."

Milley arranged to speak at a Veterans Day celebration at the Army Museum on November 11.

"We do not take an oath to a king, or a queen," Milley told the crowd, "to a tyrant or a dictator. We do not take an oath to an individual. No, we do not take an oath to a country, a tribe, or a religion. We take an oath to the Constitution." He added, "Each of us will protect and defend that document, regardless of personal price."

After his speech, Secretary of the Army Ryan McCarthy said, "You've got about five hours" until Trump finds out and fires you.

Hollyanne, Milley's wife, assumed the same. "And we haven't even bought a home yet!"

But apparently Trump didn't learn about the remarks. He did not say anything to Milley and took no action.

Later that day, Milley walked upstairs to Acting Secretary Miller's office about 1 p.m. and sat down. They were joined by Miller's chief of staff, Kash Patel, an attorney and a little known but highly controversial former congressional intelligence aide to California congressman Devin Nunes, one of Trump's staunchest defenders.

Columnist David Ignatius called Patel "almost a 'Zelig' figure" in the ranks of the Trump administration who believed a "deep state" was operating against the president. After working with Nunes, Patel had joined Trump's National Security Council and later took another top intelligence post before winding up as Miller's chief.

Once, while talking with Barr, Mark Meadows floated the idea of having Trump name Patel deputy FBI director. Meadows, who was a fierce critic of the Russia probe and the FBI's handling of it, felt Patel could be an ally inside a bureau whose leadership he believed was corrupt.

"Over my dead body," Barr said.

"You have to understand something," he added. "Everyone in that building is an *agent*. They've all been through the academy. They've all been running cities, they've been doing counterterrorism, crime. They all have the same background. The only person who is not an agent is the director."

Barr asked Meadows, "Do you think that son of a bitch is going to go over there and command respect from these guys? They'll eat him alive."

Meadows persisted in trying to force Patel into the FBI post. But this was Barr's world and he would not give. Meadows eventually dropped the subject. Meadows next tried to insert Patel into the CIA.

CIA director Gina Haspel told Barr that Meadows, apparently the de facto chief job placement officer for Patel, directed her to fire her current deputy, Vaughn Bishop, to make way for her new deputy. It was a fait accompli.

She described her White House meeting with Meadows.

"Okay, I need to go down the hall," she told him.

"Why?" asked Meadows.

"I have to tell the president that I'm not going to tolerate that," she said. "I would leave."

Meadows then backed off for the second time.

On November 11, Patel slid a one-page memo across the table—*whoosh*—to Milley.

It read: "November 11, 2020 Memorandum for the Acting Secretary of Defense: Withdrawal from Somalia and Afghanistan."

"I hereby direct you to withdraw all U.S. forces from the Federal Republic of Somalia no later than 31 December 2020 and from the Islamic Republic of Afghanistan no later than 15 January 2021. Inform all allied and partner forces of the directives. Please confirm receipt of this order."

It was signed "Donald Trump," with large, thick strokes of his celebrated black marker.

"Did you have something to do with this?" Milley asked Patel.

"No, no," Patel said. "I just saw this, Chairman."

"Are you the one behind this?" Milley asked the acting secretary of defense.

"No, no, no," Miller said.

Trump had been trying to get a full withdrawal from Afghanistan his whole presidency. The military had resisted year after year. Now, in his last five months, Trump was going to order it—if the memorandum was genuine.

On one hand, it was suspect because the format was wrong and not in the style of a traditional "NSM"—National Security Memorandum—which were often long and formal. On the other hand, Milley doubted that he would be presented with a forgery in the office of the secretary of defense, even though Miller was new and only the acting secretary of defense.

"Well, I'm putting my uniform on," Milley said because he was just wearing camouflage. "I'm going to see the president since he signed something that concerns military operations, and he did so without all the due diligence and military advice that I'm supposed to give him by law.

"This is really fucked up and I'm going to go see the president. I'm heading over. You guys can come or not."

They chose to accompany him. Once Milley changed into his regular uniform, all three were driven by security to the White House for an unusual, no-notice appearance.

"Robert, what the fuck is this?" Milley said after he, Miller and Patel walked into National Security Adviser O'Brien's corner office in the West Wing. Keith Kellogg, Pence's national security adviser and a Trump ally, was also there.

Milley handed the copy of the order to O'Brien, who stood at his desk.

"How did this happen?" Milley asked. "Was there any process here at all? How does a president do this?"

O'Brien looked at the memo and read.

"I have no idea," he said.

"What do you mean you have no idea? You're the national security adviser to the president. You're telling me you didn't know about this?"

"No, I didn't know about this," O'Brien said.

"And the secretary of defense didn't know about this? And the chief of staff to the secretary of defense didn't know about this? The chairman didn't know? How the hell does this happen?"

"Let me have that," Kellogg, a retired lieutenant general, said. He took it and scanned it.

"This is fucked up," Kellogg said. "The header is wrong. This wasn't done right. This wasn't the president."

"Keith," Milley said to Kellogg, "are you telling me someone forged the president of the United States' signature on a military directive?"

"I don't know," Kellogg said. "I don't know."

Let me have that, O'Brien said. "I'll be right back."

He left for several minutes. As best O'Brien could tell, the National Security Council, the staff secretary and the White House counsel had not been involved or consulted.

"Mr. President, you've got to have a meeting with the principals," O'Brien said. The president did not say the signature was a forgery. He had signed it. But he agreed to have a Principals Meeting before any formal policy decision was finalized.

"All right," O'Brien said returning to his office, "we've already taken care of this. It was a mistake. The memo was nullified." It was effectively a rogue memo and had no standing. The president would later meet with the principals to render a decision on Afghanistan troops.

"Okay, fine," Milley said, accepting the assurances. He, Miller and Patel then left, never having seen the president.

Case closed.

Jonathan Swan and Zachary Basu of Axios later established in May 2021 that John McEntee, the president's former body man and a former college quarterback now running personnel, and retired Army Colonel Douglas Macgregor, a senior adviser to Miller, played roles in the drafting and signing of the memo.

The next day, Thursday, November 12, election security groups, including from the Department of Homeland Security's Cybersecurity and Infrastructure Security Agency (CISA) and the National Association of State Election Directors, released a joint statement that said, "The November 3rd election was the most secure in American history.

"All of the states with close results in the 2020 presidential race have paper records of each vote, allowing the ability to go back and count each ballot if necessary. This is an added benefit for security and resilience. This process allows for the identification and correction of any mistakes or errors." In bold it added, "There is no evidence that any voting system deleted or lost votes, changed votes, or was in any way compromised."

Trump soon fired Department of Homeland Security's cyber chief, Chris Krebs, by tweet.

At 5 p.m. on November 12, Trump summoned his national security team to another meeting on Iran.

The International Atomic Energy Agency had just reported the day before that Iran had stockpiled 5,385 pounds of low-enriched uranium, 12 times the amount allowed under Obama's nuclear deal with Iran, which Trump had abandoned.

That was enough uranium eventually to produce two nuclear bombs, but it would take months for Iran to further enrich the uranium to bomb-grade.

CIA director Haspel confirmed that their intelligence showed Iran was many months from having a nuclear weapon.

Milley reviewed the standard list of options, from increased cyberattacks to the use of U.S. ground forces.

Here are the costs in casualties and dollars, he said. High and not certain at all. Here are the risks: Very high and uncertain. And here are the likely outcomes.

Military strikes inside Iran means war, Milley said. "It means you're going to war. You're on an escalation ladder you're not going to get off. You're not necessarily in control of the outcome and the ending."

Milley realized one of the permanent variables was that he, perhaps no one, knew any president's trigger point. Maybe the president, especially Trump, did not know himself.

I recommend you reject all the options, Milley said. Too risky and unnecessary.

Milley turned to Pompeo. "What do you think, Mike?" Pompeo had long been an advocate of military action against Iran.

"Mr. President," Pompeo said, "the risk isn't worth it."

Pompeo and Milley went back and forth like a tag team underscoring the reasons not to take any military action.

Vice President Pence and Acting Defense Secretary Miller, in office just three days, seemed to agree that no military action should be taken.

Okay, thanks, Trump said. He wouldn't say "do it," he wouldn't say "don't do it." The decision was left hanging, a maddening and inconclusive pattern particularly given the experience with the nullified Afghanistan memo. As Milley once said to an adviser, "The whole Iran thing comes and goes and comes and goes and comes and goes."

Haspel was worried about the lack of a clear decision and called Milley, "This is a highly dangerous situation. We are going to lash out for his ego?"

Later that night, Pompeo called Milley and thanked him for arguing against a strike and emphasizing the downsides.

"We're all good," Milley said, emphasizing the importance of calm and piling on the metaphors. "Just steady. Breathe through our noses. Steady as a rock. We're going to land this plane safely. We've got a plane with four engines and three of them are out. We've got no landing gear. But we're going to land this plane and we're going to land it safely."

Milley added, "Climb Suribachi," a reference to the 554-foot mountain on Iwo Jima where Marines raised an American flag in 1945, depicted in an iconic photograph. Nearly 7,000 Marines died and 20,000 were wounded in the celebrated battle.

Pompeo said the time for military action had passed.

"We're too late," he said. "We can't strike Iran now. Leave it to the next person. I never want to talk about fucking Iran again."

THIRTY-TWO

Rudy Giuliani, through his assistant, asked the Trump campaign for compensation. In a letter, the assistant wrote he and his team would need $20,000 per day.

Several campaign officials went to Trump and asked, what do you want us to do?

"No, no, no, no," Trump told them. "Rudy bets on the win," he said, using language from his days running the Trump Plaza casino in Atlantic City. He said it was all a contingency exercise. If Trump ended up winning, Rudy gets paid. The campaign told Giuliani it would reimburse him for expenses.

Trump and Graham continued to talk on the phone. Graham was trying to ease Trump toward acceptance of defeat even while voicing understanding for Trump's legal fight.

On November 18, in an early morning call, Graham told him, "Mr. President, working with Biden helps you, drives the left crazy.

"You've expanded the Republican Party," Graham told him. "You got more minority votes. You've got a lot to be proud of, in terms of accomplishments. You're going to be a force in American politics for a long time. And the best way to maintain that power is to wind this thing down in a fashion that gives you a second act, right?"

Trump resisted the advice. Graham found him angry, disappointed and occasionally nostalgic.

The next day, November 19, Rudy Giuliani and Sidney Powell held a press conference at the Republican National Committee headquarters in Washington.

Giuliani was sweating and seemed almost like a cartoon caricature. "Did you all watch *My Cousin Vinny*?" he asked reporters, tying a legal reference to the 1992 comedy.

At one point, a dark brown liquid mixed with beads of sweat rolled down his cheek. The headline in *Vanity Fair*: "Rudy Giuliani's hair dye melting off his face was the least crazy part of his batshit-crazy press conference."

Powell, wearing a leopard print cardigan, went even further than Giuliani, insisting the voting machines made by Dominion, a company headquartered in Toronto and Denver, were part of a global communist conspiracy.

"What we are really dealing with here," Powell said, "and uncovering more by the day, is the massive influence of communist money through Venezuela, Cuba, and likely China in the interference in our elections."

Over at Fox News, prime-time anchor Tucker Carlson watched Powell.

"If Sidney Powell has that information, if she has that evidence of fraud, we give her the whole week of shows. We'd give her the whole hour," Carlson told his producers. "That would be the biggest story ever in American politics." Watergate 2.0. But, he added, let's first see if she has the goods.

It soon became clear she did not. Carlson texted Powell and she was vague and evasive. Carlson noticed she was directing people to her website, where you could donate money.

"When we kept pressing, she got angry," Carlson wrote in a post for FoxNews.com, "and told us to stop contacting her."

Powell's stumbles did little to calm the fervor. That evening, Graham said the media had a double standard for election challenges. "When Stacey Abrams challenged her election, she was a patriot. Trump's challenging his, he is a dictator."

Abrams, the first Black woman to be her party's nominee for governor in Georgia, refused to concede to Republican Brian Kemp in 2018, accusing him of voter suppression and saying her campaign had "well-documented" evidence. Her refusal irritated Republicans, though she eventually acknowledged Kemp would be certified as the winner.

Still, Graham said, the Rudy and Sidney show was a turning point. "They were just beyond bizarre. And I think it took a lot of the air out of the balloon that the challenges are so unfocused, haphazard and conspiratorial." The news conference "accelerated the beginning of the end."

Trump shrugged off calls of concern.

"Yeah," Trump told advisers, speaking about Giuliani, "he's crazy. He says crazy shit. I get it. But none of the sane lawyers can represent me because they've been pressured. The actual lawyers have been told they cannot represent my campaign."

Inside the White House press office, inquiries about Powell and Giuliani piled up. A new refrain among junior staffers: Don't let Rudy in the building. Don't let Sidney in the building.

But the laughs faded. John McEntee made it clear to many Trump aides that no one should start looking for new jobs. A second term was coming, he vowed. No smile.

McEntee was known as Trump's favorite enforcer—and had the look. He was tall, fit, and could pass as a Secret Service agent. He had lost his White House job in 2018 for a security reason, which was later found to be concerns over his gambling habit, often betting tens of thousands of dollars at a time.

But when Trump brought back Hicks in February 2020, he brought back McEntee, too. He wanted his core loyalists around.

White House communications director Alyssa Farah grew

weary of the charade and McEntee's pressure. She was happy to sell Trump's agenda, but the West Wing was hurtling toward a strange new reality. A fantasy.

"I felt like we were lying to the public," Farah said to an acquaintance. "Good, hardworking, salt of the earth people that supported the president, who don't have a lot of time or money or energy to invest in politics, are being sold a bill of goods."

Farah, youthful and conservative, had been Pence's press secretary and had worked for Esper. She had been friends with Hicks and had been one of Meadows's first hires as White House chief. Trump was no longer listening.

"You can have all sorts of structures and reporting mechanisms in place," she said. "But at the end of the day, he's going to call people up from his dining room. He's going to bring in who he wants to. Or he's going to have them at the residence, and you won't even know until you get alerted by Secret Service."

It was all too much. She resigned.

Barr took a call from Cipollone on November 23.

"Bill," Cipollone said, "it's getting a little awkward. He's asking about you. You haven't shown up."

Barr went to the White House.

"Mr. President," he said, "you did a great job there at the end, and it's too bad it worked out the way it did."

"Well, we won. We won by a lot. And, you know, it's fraud. Bill, we can't let them get away with this. This is stealing the election. I hear that you guys are hanging back. You're not—somehow you don't think it's your role to look at this."

"No, Mr. President, that's not correct. You know, it's not our role to take sides. The Justice Department can't take sides, as you know, between you and the other candidate. That's what we have elections to decide.

"But if there's a crime of sufficient magnitude, of specific and credible information indicating potential fraud on a scale that could affect the outcome, I'm willing to take a look.

"By the way," Barr said, "a lot of the people at Justice don't think we should. And I've overruled that. And I said on a case-by-case basis, we will."

In five states where the numbers were close, he had asked the U.S. attorneys to look at the big-ticket items, when someone made an allegation of systematic fraud that could affect the outcome. Those states were Arizona, Wisconsin, Michigan, Georgia and Pennsylvania. He had directed them not to open a full-fledged investigation but a preliminary analysis or assessment. If there was anything there and sufficient grounds, they should talk to him.

"But the problem is this stuff about the voting machines is just bullshit," Barr said.

A week earlier, on November 16, Barr said he and FBI director Chris Wray set up a meeting with computer experts at the FBI and Department of Homeland Security. They had two meetings, with the experts walking them through the operations of the machines and how microchips and methods made cheating all but impossible.

"It's all bullshit," Barr said. "The allegations were not panning out."

"Did you see what they did in Detroit and in Milwaukee?" Trump asked. "These dumps in the early morning of all these votes." He then pulled out some charts and other materials he had been accumulating from advisers and friends. "I'm going to give you these charts."

"Well, okay, Mr. President, I'll take a look at the charts. But you know that is the normal pattern in those states. I think that happens all the time. But I'll look at it."

Barr brought up a version of his message from April, when he had stopped by the Oval Office's dining room. Trump should focus on what matters.

"Mr. President the best way to protect your legacy is for you to remind the American people of all the great things you've accomplished, okay? Be positive. And then go down to Georgia and make sure the Republicans hold the Senate. That's the way to preserve your legacy."

Barr soon spoke with Meadows and Kushner.

"How long is this going to go on?" Barr asked. "This is getting out of hand."

They said Trump was aware and monitoring the situation. They said they thought he was going to start laying the groundwork for a graceful exit and that he realized he could take it too far. And later that day, Trump authorized proceeding with the transition to Biden. It seemed like a sign he might start accepting defeat.

But then Trump started calling Pennsylvania legislators, and state legislative leaders in Michigan and officials in Georgia. There was no sign he was letting up. To Barr, it seemed like an escalation.

Barr next spoke with McConnell, who said, "Bill, you know we have these elections coming up in Georgia. I can't afford a big frontal attack on the president at this point. I have to be gentle."

Trump kept going on Fox News saying the election was stolen. The election was rigged. The Justice Department was missing in action.

"These fucking nuts," Barr said. Giuliani, Powell and the rest of them. "Clown car."

Vice President-elect Harris called James Clyburn's cell phone one November weekend when he was on the golf course.

Do me a favor, he asked, talk to my golfing buddies. They kept him up to date on the political gossip in Charleston or over in Holly Hill and Orangeburg.

Clyburn handed over his cell phone to his "barber shop," as he called them, and Harris happily chatted.

Later, Clyburn successfully encouraged Biden to name South Carolina's Jaime Harrison, a Black ally, chairman of the Democratic National Committee. Harrison had lost his Senate race to Lindsey Graham by 10 points but spent a record $130 million and built a national profile.

On a phone call, Clyburn got into the weeds like an old ward boss. He told Biden to make sure Harrison was not paid less than the prior DNC chairman.

Clyburn said Biden would not want a headline saying the Black chairman was being paid less than outgoing DNC chair, Tom Perez, who is Latino.

"You're absolutely right," Biden told Clyburn. "I don't know what it is, but I promise you, it won't be less."

"Look, I've been Black a long time, I know what the headline is going to be," Clyburn explained to others. "Don't argue with me about things you don't know. I've lived this."

Harrison's salary was the same as Perez's.

Now that he had come so far, Clyburn was not going to ease up. He complained publicly about the lack of Black appointees to cabinet positions. "So far, it's not good," Clyburn told *The Hill* newspaper on November 25.

In the end, Biden picked five Black Americans for top positions or cabinet posts. Retired four-star Army General Lloyd Austin became the first Black secretary of defense.

Clyburn told Biden to think hard about President Harry S Truman, not just FDR. Truman was a better friend of Black Americans, he said. FDR's New Deal programs had discriminated against Blacks and given preferences to whites, he said, while Truman desegregated the military.

"Now the man from Delaware can be just like the man from Missouri," Clyburn told Biden.

THIRTY-THREE

Barr called Mike Balsamo, the Associated Press Justice reporter, over for lunch on December 1. Trump's rhetoric was veering into overdrive. The president was listening to lawyers who were feeding him conspiracies.

"To date," Barr told him, "we have not seen fraud on a scale that could have effected a different outcome of the election." Balsamo filed the story soon after, with Barr's comments going global.

Later that day, when he was at the White House for a 3 p.m. meeting on the administration's agenda for the next month, Barr got a message that the president wanted to see him in his private dining room. Barr went and found the president sitting at his standard seat at the head of the table.

Cipollone and his deputy, Pat Philbin, and Meadows were sitting three abreast on one side of the table. Eric Herschmann, another White House lawyer, stood at the side, as did Will Levi, Barr's chief of staff.

Barr did not sit down. He put his hands on the back of the chair facing the three from the White House. The large TV on the wall, off to Barr's right, was tuned into some hearing or discussion of election fraud on OAN, the far-right, pro-Trump network One America News.

"Did you say this?" the president asked, holding a report of Barr's remarks on finding no election fraud.

"Yes."

"Why?"

"Because it's true. We haven't seen it, Mr. President."

"You didn't have to say that. You could have just said no comment."

"During the weekend you were there saying that the Justice Department was 'missing in action' and that you know the election was stolen. And I think the reporter asked me what we'd found, and I told him what we found, which is, so far, nothing."

Trump said to Barr, "*You must have said that because you hate Trump, you must really hate Trump.*"

"No, Mr. President, I don't hate you. I think you know that at some significant personal sacrifice to myself, I came in to help this administration and I've tried to serve it honorably. Let me tell you why you are where you are right now. There are only five or six weeks after an election to resolve any of these issues because the Electoral College is a hard-and-fast date.

"What you needed was a team of crackerjack lawyers ready to go who could quickly formulate a strategy that would actually be able to say, 'We're going for these votes here, these votes here, and here's our argument here,' and execute. Instead, you have wheeled out a clown car.

"Every self-respecting lawyer in the country has run for the hills. Your team is a bunch of clowns.

"They are unconscionable in the firmness and detail they present as if it is unquestionable fact. It is not. You have wasted four weeks on the one theory that is demonstrably crazy, which is these machines."

"Well, what do you mean?"

"Mr. President, these machines are like adding machines. They're tabulators. If you take a stack of 20-dollar bills and you run them through a machine that counts them, it comes up and then it puts a band around every thousand dollars.

"Now, guess what? The law requires that the actual ballots be saved, just like the banded money would be saved. So, if you say the machine hasn't counted right, you just go to the money and see if that's a thousand dollars. And if it's a thousand dollars and the machine says it's a thousand dollars, I don't want to hear all this stuff about, you know, how this functionality was this and this.

"Show me where there's been a miscount. And so far, every place has shown no discrepancy. This is crazy."

"How about the votes that came in in Detroit?" Trump asked. "You know, I'm ahead by so many thousand. And then all these votes come out at four o'clock in the morning or whenever it was." His lead was wiped out.

"Mr. President, did you go and check that against what happened last time in 2016? You actually ran stronger this year than you did in Detroit last time. The margins were the same, except you ran better and Biden ran a little worse in Detroit."

"Well, there were boxes," Trump said. "People saw the boxes," flooding in hours after the polls closed.

"Mr. President, there are 503 precincts in Detroit. In Michigan, it is the only county where the votes are not counted in the precincts. Every other county, they're counted in the precincts. In Detroit, however, they go to a central counting station. And so, all night these boxes are being moved in. And so, the fact that boxes are going into the counting station in the early morning hours is not suspicious. That's what they do. The votes always come in at that time and the ratio of votes is the same as it was last time. There's no indication of a sudden surge of extra Biden votes."

What about Fulton County, Georgia?

"We're looking into that. But so far, the word is, you know, that those were legitimate ballots. Mr. President, we're looking into this stuff, but these things aren't panning out."

Trump shifted to other deficiencies. "When is Durham going to come to a conclusion?" Trump could not let go of U.S. Attorney John Durham's investigation into the FBI's conduct during the Russian probe.

"I don't know, Mr. President. You know, this is not the kind of thing that you can just say, deliver the product." Barr snapped his fingers. "It has its own pace depending on what the evidence is. So, I can't say. But I would imagine it would be in the first part of the Biden administration, hopefully maybe in the first six months."

Trump shouted, "*First part of the Biden administration!*"

Oh, shit, Barr thought. Trump was steaming. Barr had never seen Trump in such a fury. If a human being can have flames come out of his ears, this was it. Barr imagined the flames. He had never seen Trump madder. But Trump was obviously trying to control himself. Tamping himself down and then flaming.

At another point, Trump said, "Bill, I don't know if you've noticed, but I have not been calling." Trump said it as if Barr was really missing out not getting regular calls. Thank God, Barr thought. He could not help but think of the character in the 1964 dark comedy *Dr. Strangelove* who ruminates about withholding his "essence" from women.

"Comey! You didn't indict Comey when you could have," Trump shouted. "You declined."

"I told you a hundred times, Mr. President, there was no case there."

But the Justice Department's inspector general, Trump said, sent a referral about Comey giving two memos to his New York lawyer that contained classified information. The memos were then given to the media.

Comey had gone through the memos and taken out the classified material, Barr reminded the president. There was a dispute. A few sentences that were arguably confidential.

"That's classified information," the president said.

"I'm sorry, Mr. President, I'm not going to prosecute. We're not going to prosecute that case."

"The inspector general recommended he be prosecuted, and you overruled it," Trump said.

"No," Barr replied, "that's not what happens. The IG doesn't recommend prosecution." He sends his investigative findings over to the criminal division to see what they want to do, and as attorney general, Barr had the final say.

"Is there anything that the criminal people want to do?" Trump asked.

No, Barr said. He then said he had to leave. He had a dinner with Pompeo.

"I think we can see a way through this," Meadows said in a call with Barr after the December 1 blowup with Trump.

"Oh, yeah?" Barr replied skeptically.

"You know, he doesn't like people quitting on him," Meadows said. "He'll do a preemptive strike. He's worried, people are worried you might just pull out unexpectedly between now and January 20th. So, will you stay? Will you commit to stay?"

Barr faced a choice: Commit or likely be fired. He told Meadows, "Number one, I wouldn't blindside anybody. I would not leave without telling you in advance. And number two, I'll stay as long as I'm needed."

Barr, ever the lawyer, felt he gave himself a little wiggle room because he didn't say exactly who would judge the need.

"Okay, okay," Meadows said seeming to accept the terms. There would be no surprise resignation.

Barr immediately regretted saying he would stay. Nothing changed. Trump was not listening to him, and the attorney general was now a figurehead at best.

Barr had complicated feelings about his role in the Trump presidency. On the one hand, he strongly supported conservative principles—a strong executive, lower taxes, less regulation, and an aversion to the progressives. He also believed Trump's critics had transformed and hardened Trump. The Democrats, the media and the Mueller investigation had "pulled a Clarence Thomas on

Trump," referring to the belief among many conservatives like Barr that the searing 1991 Supreme Court confirmation hearings had pushed Thomas to the hard right.

In this view, shared by Thomas's close friends and family, Thomas was more moderate before Anita Hill lodged her sexual harassment charges, forever hardening Thomas.

"When the left was done with Thomas, he moved," Barr said. He believed Trump would also have been more pragmatic except for the relentless attacks. The same might be said of Barr, who had left his first tour as attorney general with a strong reputation but had come under blistering attacks for protecting Trump and dug in as a staunch ally for the president.

Barr continued to be fiercely criticized for protecting Trump. During the 2020 presidential campaign, Barr actively supported and amplified Trump's push against mail-in ballots. Republicans did not like mail-ins and neither did Barr. And he said so publicly, claiming that the fraud potential was "obvious" and "common sense," but neither he nor anyone else provided any proof.

When Chairman Milley heard Barr might resign, he quickly called.

"Man, you can't leave," Milley told him. "You know you can't leave. We need you."

"You know what?" Trump asked his aides on Air Force One on the ride back to Washington on December 5 from a campaign rally in Valdosta, Georgia. "That was perfect. I don't think we need to go back."

Trump was bored by the two runoff Senate elections that would be held in Georgia on January 5. He told aides that Republican senators Kelly Loeffler and David Perdue were business Republicans, not tough enough. He would campaign for them, but not go overboard. He had other things to do.

His legal team was falling apart. He was losing cases. And on December 6, Giuliani was hospitalized at Georgetown University Hospital with the coronavirus.

The next day, Trump stewed alone in the Oval Office as a White House holiday party was about to begin down the hall. Few attendees wore masks as they mingled by a huge Fraser fir Christmas tree in the Blue Room, even though cases were spiking, including at the White House.

"Amazing time," Donald Trump Jr. wrote on an Instagram post, posing with his girlfriend, former Fox News personality Kimberly Guilfoyle. Both were unmasked.

Conservative commentator Steve Cortes, a Chicago investor who had become a constant presence in Trump's election fight effort, was invited to visit the president. Cortes's Twitter profile described himself as a "Voice of the Deplorables. Hispanic. Born for a storm." The "deplorables" was a phrase Hillary Clinton used when describing some Trump supporters in 2016.

No one else was around. Cortes later told others he was struck by the emptiness of the West Wing as he walked up to the Oval Office to find Trump alone.

When Cortes walked in, Trump was screaming at Rudy Giuliani on a video call. He was heated, yelling again about the election being stolen and his campaign's legal challenges.

"Ah. Cortes is here. I've got to go." He shut off the video.

"You can still resurrect it," Cortes said, reassuringly. He had come to keep Trump from backing off. "But it's going to take a lot of allies. It's going to take a lot of fighting and money raising."

Trump agreed. This seemed to be what he wanted to hear. Someone who saw hope.

Cortes said Trump needed to hit the road.

"You've been dark since the election," Cortes said.

"No, I haven't."

"Yes, you have."

Trump grew loud. He was furious.

"I've been tweeting a lot!"

"Tweeting doesn't count. Tweeting from the residence is not being the public president of the United States."

Cortes kept at it. He wanted to get under Trump's skin. The deplorables were yearning for Trump to go wild on the establishment.

"Go do CNN, do Brian Williams" on MSNBC, Cortes said. "The facts are on our side. Let's have Lester Holt in here. Stand up and make your case."

Trump dismissed the idea. They were fake news, he said. Never. He turned to Fox News and started yelling again. They had called Arizona for Biden. They were in on the rigging as much as anyone. They were terrible, he said.

"We have to fight," Cortes said. "We need to pressure the legislatures publicly. We need to put them on the hot seat."

Trump talked about Giuliani, the court cases.

"No judge in the country wants to rule on this stuff, least of all the Supreme Court," Cortes said. "It's the court of public opinion that matters."

THIRTY-FOUR

McConnell remained laser-focused on the Georgia Senate races. He was troubled by polls showing the two Democratic candidates holding steady near or above 50 percent.

His ally, Senator Todd Young of Indiana, who ran the GOP's Senate campaign arm, recruited veteran George W. Bush adviser Karl Rove to head up a special joint fundraising operation for both Perdue and Loeffler. Rove called up almost every major Republican donor, asking them to pony up thousands.

Rove heard through the grapevine that Trump and the White House were not happy to see a person so linked to George W. Bush, whom Trump loathed and mocked, running the Georgia races. Rove was also publicly dismissive of Trump's "Stop the Steal" rally cry, and the headline of his November 11 column in *The Wall Street Journal* was, "This Election Result Won't Be Overturned."

Rove called Jared Kushner and asked if Trump was unhappy with his involvement. Kushner told him to continue. I don't know what the hell you're talking about, Kushner said.

But the Rove-McConnell axis was not driving the message in Georgia, despite coordinating the spending. Instead, a brash lawyer named Lin Wood, who had deeply conspiratorial views on the election, was becoming a key figure. He was prominent at rallies and on social media, railing against Biden's win as illegal. Astonishingly, at an early December rally with Sidney Powell, he told Georgia Republicans to stay home.

"They have not earned your vote," Wood said of the two GOP

senators. "Don't you give it to them. Why would you go back and vote in another rigged election for God's sake? Fix it!"

Rove was stunned. The president's lawyer and Lin Wood were depressing the GOP vote. On purpose.

"You have Sidney Powell and Lin Wood out there slinging these outrageous accusations of Dominion voting machines being a Hugo Chávez created firm," Rove complained, referring to the dead Venezuelan president. He was unnerved by a looming disaster for the Republican Party.

Rove had lengthy experience crusading against voter fraud. It just did not apply here. The machines were reliable and safe, he repeated to others as questions mounted.

"They're not connected on the internet and they tabulate the votes by taking a thumb drive, encoded to a specific machine in a specific precinct, and taking that to a central location to transfer the votes and count them."

Trump was losing everywhere.

"Trump and the GOP have now lost more than 50 post-election lawsuits," read the headline in *Forbes* on December 8, after the Supreme Court threw out an effort by his ally, Pennsylvania congressman Mike Kelly, to block the state from certifying the election for Biden.

The high court's rejection, from one of the court's most conservative justices, Samuel Alito, was one sentence: "The application for injunctive relief presented to Justice Alito and by him referred to the Court is denied."

Frustrated, Trump called Senator Ted Cruz, the outspoken Texas Republican. Cruz, a Harvard Law graduate, had clerked for Chief Justice William H. Rehnquist from 1996 to 1997.

The pair had been enemies during the 2016 Republican presidential primary race, and on Twitter, Trump had crudely compared the attractiveness of Cruz's wife, Heidi, to the glamorous Melania.

"A picture is worth a thousand words," Trump's tweet read, retweeting a line from a supporter. Then, below the text, were two pictures. One was of Melania, looking like a supermodel in a perfectly lit studio. The other was Heidi Cruz, seeming to sneer and in a harshly lit room.

Trump later told *New York Times* columnist Maureen Dowd he regretted it, one of the only times he ever apologized for a tweet. He had also accused Cruz's father of associating with Lee Harvey Oswald, JFK's assassin.

Trump and Cruz had put that past aside and built a transactional alliance during Trump's presidency—two politicians who could use each other.

Cruz was at a steakhouse, in the middle of dinner, when the president called.

"I'm frustrated, too," Cruz said.

"But are you surprised?"

"No," Cruz said. "There are lots of institutional reasons why they would decline to take the case. There's real risk to taking the case." Cruz had publicly supported taking the case to the Supreme Court, but privately recognized it was a long shot.

Well, Trump said, another case from Texas has been filed with the Supreme Court that day. Would you be willing to argue it?

Sure, Cruz said. Happy to help. "But they might not take it," he added.

"Why? Why? Why would they not take it?"

Cruz said if the Supreme Court would not take the Pennsylvania case, it was very likely they would reject the Texas case, too.

Three days later, December 11, Trump gathered a large group of his campaign's lawyers in the Oval Office. He went around the room, asking for their latest tidbits on the cases and the counts.

"What do you think of Nevada?

"What do you think of Pennsylvania?"

The answers were measured, careful.

He then suggested a photograph with him. Smiles were forced.

Matt Morgan and Justin Clark, another top campaign lawyer, hung back after others left.

Trump asked them about Pennsylvania. He asked them about the case in Texas. Cruz might argue it. What do you think? What are our chances of getting legal challenges in those states heard before the Supreme Court?

"I think it's a huge uphill climb," Morgan said. I don't think you have the votes on the court.

"They don't have courage," Trump said.

The outlook was bleak. Trump ended the meeting and sent them out. He had other lawyers. They were telling him he could win the White House again, the court be damned.

Barr believed Trump had acquired the worst possible team of attorneys to challenge the election. Rudy Giuliani was in ascension, along with the likes of conservative lawyer Jenna Ellis, whom Barr believed was a moron. And he thought Sidney Powell was certifiable. But Giuliani was the worst—"a fucking idiot" who had gotten Trump impeached, Barr said. Giuliani was "drinking too much and was desperate for money, representing lowlifes and creeps like Lev Parnas," the Ukrainian-born American businessman involved in various efforts to assist Trump.

"Sitting around with their shirts open and gold hanging out in the Trump Hotel," Barr summarized.

The weekend after December 1, Barr wrote a resignation letter to have it ready. He knew all the buttons on Trump's psychological console. Kill him with flattery: "Your record is all the more historic because you accomplished it in the face of relentless, implacable resistance." While voter fraud allegations would continue to be pursued, your Operation Warp Speed and the development of vaccines "will undoubtedly save millions of lives." The crackdown on violent crime domestically in the U.S., and internationally on trade with China, were singular Trump achievements.

He went to see Trump privately on December 14 with the letter in hand.

"I know you're disappointed with me," Barr began. "I know you're upset at a number of things I've done. You've made that clear. And we had gotten off to a good start. I think you know that I've tried hard to serve you honorably as an attorney general. And you know, we had a good relationship for a while, but we're now butting heads pretty severely. And I don't think this is going to end. And so I'd like to leave and try to leave on an amicable basis. I don't want to do anything that embarrasses you or hurts you. But by the same token, I think I've served my purposes here. There's nothing more I can do positively."

Barr said he wanted to leave December 23 so he could spend the Christmas holidays with his family. Trump accepted the resignation and tweeted, "Our relationship has been a very good one, he has done an outstanding job."

On December 14, the electors in all 50 states and Washington, D.C., formally cast their ballots, giving Biden 306 electoral votes, Trump 232. But due to Trump's various legal and legislative challenges, the final outcome had to wait for three weeks, until a joint session on January 6, when Congress would formally count the electoral votes that would certify the constitutional result.

Trump was still exhorting Congress to reject certification. Many Republicans were signing on to his fight. Days before the electors cast their ballots, nearly two-thirds of the House GOP, including House minority leader Kevin McCarthy, said they supported a "friend of the court" brief backing a lawsuit in Texas seeking to have the Supreme Court block the electoral votes from Pennsylvania, Michigan, Wisconsin and Georgia from being counted for Biden.

But Lindsey Graham believed the fever pitch in the House did not correspond to the political will in the Senate GOP. Based on his personal whip count, interest in overturning the Electoral College seemed nonexistent and he hoped Republican senators would resist being pulled in. He and other Senate Republicans kept that view away from Trump and tried to keep his anger from erupting even further.

In a call with Trump, Graham stoked Trump's ego, saying, "Nobody in American history is going to leave office as powerful as you are. You're a shadow president. Mr. President, you're sitting on top of a money-making machine. You've raised hundreds of millions in the last five or six weeks. You've locked down the Republican Party nomination if you want it.

"Repair the damage with college-educated women," Graham recommended—an unlikely prospect.

The Electoral College vote was enough for McConnell, who called Mark Meadows on the morning of December 15.

"Give the president a heads-up that I'm going to acknowledge that Biden won," McConnell told him.

McConnell soon went to the Senate floor.

"Many millions of us had hoped that the presidential election would yield a different result. But our system of government has processes to determine who will be sworn in on January the 20th," he said. "The Electoral College has spoken. So today, I want to congratulate President-elect Joe Biden."

Trump called McConnell immediately and spewed expletives.

"Mr. President," McConnell told Trump, "the Electoral College has spoken. That's the way we pick a president in this country."

Trump cursed McConnell. Disloyal! Weak! He claimed McConnell had won his reelection bid in Kentucky, months ago, because of Trump's support.

"And this is the thanks I got?" Trump asked. He was furious. Incredulous. "You never really got me. You don't understand me."

McConnell was silent. But Trump's claim of carrying him was absurd. He noted to aides that in 2014, when Trump was still hosting *The Apprentice* reality show on NBC, he had won in Kentucky by a 15-point margin, just like in 2020.

On the phone, McConnell's final remark to Trump was a short statement of fact.

"You lost the election," he said, "the Electoral College has spoken." He hung up.

McConnell hoped it would be the final time he and Trump would ever speak to each other.

Biden called McConnell.

"Mr. President," McConnell said intentionally, even though Biden was still only president-elect. The two had a congenial but inconclusive talk.

McConnell and Biden had been friendly for years. McConnell admired him as a first-rate, equal-opportunity eulogist. He had even spoken at the funeral of Strom Thurmond, the late senator who once was a segregationist. Biden was a man who got along with his colleagues, who formed bonds, even if their political views did not align.

The two had worked closely together to cut budget deals during the Obama years. Biden had visited the McConnell Center at the University of Louisville in 2011. It was the closest a Senate leader could get to a presidential-library-style archive and gathering place. Biden said the crowd had come because they wanted to "see whether or not a Republican and a Democrat really like one another."

"We do," Biden said as McConnell looked on and smiled.

THIRTY-FIVE

Meadows called FDA commissioner Stephen Hahn one morning in mid-December and accused him and Peter Marks, his deputy in charge of the vaccine, of not doing enough to expedite the approval process for vaccines. They were not taking it seriously and not putting enough resources into it.

The average citizen doesn't care if the FDA used this process or that process, Meadows said. It had nothing to do with vaccine confidence.

Hahn was shocked. He had been on calls, sometimes three times a week, with the president and Meadows.

"It's like saying, we didn't have enough brain surgeons, so I'm going to put a physician's assistant in to do your craniotomy to remove your brain tumor," Hahn later said to others. "You can't do that."

You don't know what you're doing, Meadows yelled at Hahn.

Mark, I totally disagree with you, Hahn said. "You are wrong." Meadows then mumbled something about resignation.

"Excuse me, what did you say?" Hahn asked.

"Nothing. I didn't say anything," Meadows said. "I'll handle this." Meadows hung up, then called back 30 minutes later and apologized.

But Trump soon sent off a tweet: "While my pushing the money drenched but heavily bureaucratic FDA saved five years in the approval of NUMEROUS great new vaccines, it is still a big, old, slow turtle. Get the dam vaccines out NOW, Dr. Hahn. Stop playing games and start saving lives!!!"

Pfizer-BioNTech was authorized later that day for use on individuals 16 years of age and older in the U.S. One week later, Moderna's vaccine was authorized for individuals 18 years of age and older. The development of two highly effective vaccines in record time was an unprecedented achievement.

But distribution lagged.

For Ron Klain, the incoming chief of staff, work soon accelerated almost nonstop. This was what Klain considered the prose of governing amid crises. They had to get it right.

Coronavirus infections and deaths had been rising since November and on pace to hit record numbers. On December 2, hospitalizations hit an all-time high—over 100,000—and at least 2,760 deaths were recorded on that one day, outpacing the previous record for one day—2,752 deaths on April 15.

While the vaccine had been developed at unmatched speed, unless it started getting into enough people's arms, the impact would be blunted.

Klain watched as the first vaccinations began on December 14 with 3,913 frontline health workers receiving the jab. Around 2.9 million doses were distributed to the states, and 12.4 million by December 30—well short of an initial 20-million target. Most Americans were not expected to be vaccinated until 2021. The delivery system was key, and inadequate. Could they fix it?

And how could they ignite the flat-on-its-back economy? The economy, which had started to recover in May, was now buckling. More than 140,000 Americans would lose their jobs in December, with restaurants and bar employees enduring sweeping layoffs as few Americans went out to eat and drink.

Klain had spent hours with Biden discussing the important lessons learned from his time as Obama's Ebola czar in 2014. Separate the science from the policy. Keep everyone in their lane.

These things are like forest fires, Klain told Biden, and even if only five embers remain, the trees will burn down again. You have got to ride this all the way to the bottom.

As Ebola czar, Klain reminded Biden he decided to build 17 Ebola treatment units in West Africa, in every potential site where it might flare up. Of the 17 units, he said, nine were never used. I got whacked later for wasting money. But since they took two months to build, it would have been too late if they had waited to see if they were needed. That is the way epidemics work. You must stay in front.

Scaling up, Klain said, was now critical on all fronts. Scale up and be prepared. Buy everything the United States could need, or risk it not being available when it counts. The early shortages—of masks, protective equipment for health workers, ventilators—had certainly been a factor in the virulent spread of the airborne virus in the first months of the pandemic.

Biden absorbed Klain's lessons and repeatedly instructed his team to go big. Biden flashed frustration whenever he heard about operational hiccups.

"How many doses of the vaccine might be needed?" Biden asked. "How many people need to be hired to give the shots in the arm?" He wanted to hear everything, he said.

"Look," Biden said in one transition meeting, "don't underestimate it. Overestimate it. If we wind up with too much vaccine, if we wind up with too many vaccination sites, if we wind up with too much of everything, I'll take heat for that. But what I don't want to take the heat for is coming up short."

In early December, Biden had named his 54-year-old transition chair, Jeff Zients, to be the White House coronavirus response coordinator.

Zients was not a doctor or a scientist, but a management guru who also had held top economic posts in the Obama White

House, including acting Office of Management and Budget (OMB) director.

Among his previous assignments was straightening out the calamitous breakdown of the Healthcare.gov website used to sign up for Obamacare. Then vice president, Biden had pulled him aside.

"This is stressful," Biden said, "and it may or may not work. Just always tell us the unvarnished truth and we can deal with anything."

Zients knew coordinating the response to Covid-19 was orders of magnitude more complicated and significant.

As a businessman, Zients's philosophy was to overwhelm a problem, plan like hell, commit assets, reevaluate and readjust daily if necessary, and then recommit. The approach had earned him a personal fortune of at least $100 million.

Zients and his team immediately set to work developing Biden's national virus response strategy and any executive orders needed to speed up its execution. They needed to hit the ground running at noon on January 20. The plan grew to 200 pages.

Natalie Quillian, a national security expert and former senior adviser to the White House and Pentagon, was named Zients's deputy. The two spent weeks trying to understand how Trump planned to actually get shots in arms, but cooperation and information from the Trump administration had been spotty and insufficient. Worse, the Trump team did not seem to have a comprehensive vaccine distribution plan.

But given the magnitude of the problem, Zients and Klain assumed there must be a secret plan the Trump team did not want to share. Eventually, they concluded there was simply nothing to share, public or secret.

Klain updated Biden. "They fucked it up completely," Klain said.

To build their national strategy, Quillian then divided their task into three baskets.

One, increasing vaccine production and supply. Two, getting enough vaccinators to give the shots. Three, acquiring the sites, clinics or stations for people to get the shot.

The Trump administration had encouraged and helped develop the vaccine, a remarkable achievement in record time, but intended to drop-ship the vials to the states and let each state come up with a distribution plan.

"That was the worst possible decision," Dr. Anthony Fauci told Zients's team on a Zoom call. It put the states on their own.

Fauci was the face of the medical side of the U.S. coronavirus response. Biden had offered the 80-year-old scientist the job of chief medical adviser.

Fauci said their big challenge would be getting anywhere from 70 to 85 percent of the population vaccinated to achieve "herd immunity," a marker for when infections began to rapidly diminish in number without taking additional, drastic action to stop the spread. It would require several months of efficient vaccination to reach that goal. He warned about a "surge upon a surge" after the holidays, with hospitals potentially overwhelmed.

What we need to do is get the federal government working in partnership with the states, Fauci said.

"Don't just tell the states: Here's the money, go do it on your own," he said. "They often need direction. They need resources."

What levers would Biden have at his disposal to bring a federal response into communities and help on the ground? Zients's team put together a comprehensive spreadsheet of all the federal agencies and subagencies.

FEMA! It was a big "aha" moment, Zients told his team. The Federal Emergency Management Agency was set up to respond to emergencies just like the pandemic. While Trump had tapped FEMA and its funding pool with executive orders earlier in the year, Zients was convinced it was being underutilized.

He contacted Tim Manning, who had worked as a deputy administrator of FEMA during the eight years of the Obama administration. Zients asked Manning, is it possible that FEMA could help stand up and operate mass community vaccination sites across the country?

FEMA could do it, Manning said. He soon became Zients's supply coordinator.

During the transition period, Zients and Quillian knew they couldn't direct FEMA to begin preparations. Instead, they began submitting question after question to FEMA, signaling the plan FEMA would operationalize at noon on January 20.

They also planned to use the Defense Production Act, which gives the president broad emergency powers to mobilize the resources and manufacturing capabilities of U.S. private companies, to boost vaccine production, testing and equipment. Trump had used this authority to increase the production of ventilators.

January 20 would be launch day for a new national virus response plan. "Fairness and equity," that was Biden's mantra. He wanted it at the center of his plan, along with efficiency.

They could use the 1,385 community health centers across the country, Zients told Biden. These are state and locally run organizations that deliver affordable, quality primary health care to about 30 million Americans in the hardest-hit and most difficult-to-reach communities.

More than 91 percent of their patients live below the poverty line and more than 60 percent are racial or ethnic minorities, he said. The federal government could partner with health centers to facilitate direct access to vaccine supply, funding and personnel.

Biden's team soon presented him with their first estimates for the priorities he wanted in his initial spending package: more than $150 billion to buy vaccines, another $150 billion to vaccinate, and $150 billion to reopen shuttered schools.

Brian Deese, who helped lead Obama's rescue of the automobile industry in 2009 when he was just 31, was now the designated head of the White House Economic Council. He was bearded and deep-voiced, professor-like.

Deese said the administration also needed to extend unemployment benefits. The economy was battered, with millions sinking into poverty since the summer and another hiring slowdown in November. That cost could run $350 billion. More than $400 billion would be needed to give millions of Americans stimulus checks. More money was needed to feed people with a nutrition program.

After Congress passed a $900 billion stimulus in December, Trump sounded like a Democrat when he railed against the bill's new $600 stimulus checks as a "disgrace" and "ridiculously low." He said checks should be "$2,000 or $4,000 for a couple."

Biden and Klain welcomed it, even if Trump's stance was driven, more than anything, by his fury with McConnell's refusal to echo his claims about a rigged election. Senate Minority Leader Chuck Schumer of New York, whose long-standing dream was to oust McConnell and serve as majority leader for the first time in his career, argued the checks could help rally voters ahead of the two runoff elections for Senate in Georgia.

As it stood, Democrats had 48 seats in the Senate. But if Democrats Jon Ossoff and Reverend Raphael Warnock could both win in Georgia on January 5, they would have 50 seats.

And after January 20, under the Constitution, Vice President Kamala Harris would be able to break 50–50 ties. It would be razor thin. But they would control the floor and the committees.

Biden and Schumer agreed to weaponize Trump's words and make $2,000 checks the keystone of the Georgia campaigns. The only way to guarantee those checks is a Democratic Senate majority, they argued.

THIRTY-SIX

Kevin McCarthy, the highest-ranked Republican in the House of Representatives and the minority leader, held court in his Capitol suite with a stream of lawmakers and aides on the evening of December 16.

As he sat in a high-backed chair in front of a log fire, McCarthy, 55, cracked jokes and swapped stories. The mood felt celebratory, even victorious. Biden might have big plans, but McCarthy and House Republicans had reduced Pelosi's majority. Thirteen Democratic seats flipped! A historic number of Republican women.

"What mandate?" McCarthy asked the group, dismissing Biden's 2020 showing.

"He's yesterday, we're the future," McCarthy said of the president-elect—a title he had so far been reluctant to utter. "He's bringing everybody back from the past. He's misreading this election.

"People are going to be bored with him," he continued. McCarthy mocked Biden, saying that when some voters describe a Biden campaign rally, "They say circles. Not circles of people but circles where people should stand in," to maintain social distance.

A Bakersfield, California, native with tufts of silver hair, and the son of an assistant fire chief, McCarthy had spent his entire adult life in politics. He was particularly proud of the four pickups in his home state, which *The New York Times* later called a "stinging setback" and a "warning for Democrats."

"I won four seats in California," McCarthy told those gathered around him. "When everybody said I would lose 15 seats, we didn't lose one seat." He rattled off a list of winners.

This was the next incarnation of the Republican Party in the House, on private display: defiant and empowered. McCarthy had been majority leader from 2014 to 2019. He believed he would rise again, this time as speaker.

McCarthy made sure to credit Trump. His alliance with him had brought him within spitting distance of regaining the majority.

McCarthy's eye was already on 2022. Hold on for two years and then win the speakership.

"The majority," McCarthy flatly told anyone when asked about his priority.

To get there, McCarthy envisioned a partial revival of the now defunct Tea Party's slash-government-spending ethos, alarm over the debt, culture warfare, and pitches to voters fed up with politically correct politics. He would have Trump hold rallies for House candidates.

"I think the debt is going to become a bigger issue than people think because it's the hangover afterwards, like, 'Whoa,'" McCarthy said. "I think people are going to wake up.

"You know who I'm going to recruit? Small business owners," he added. "They are going to have a passion; they can see what abuse government can do to your own life.

"We're the party of the working people. They're now the elitists who tell us where to eat, how to eat, what to drink, what to think, what we can read, what's news and not," he said. "That doesn't sell at the end of the day."

McCarthy was pessimistic about any relationship with Biden. "He's a Senate man. He's always going to go to the Senate."

Biden had not called him yet, McCarthy noted, although several allies told him his refusal to acknowledge Biden as president-elect was the reason. Nothing personal.

THIRTY-SEVEN

Sidney Powell had a new idea to expand the power of the presidency: Trump could issue a presidential order to take control of the vote count. The states were rigged, the media was rigged. Trump had to act.

Powell laid out her strategy to Trump on the evening of December 18. She was joined by her former client and former national security adviser, Michael Flynn, who had just been pardoned by Trump, and former Overstock.com chief executive Patrick Byrne. The meeting was unplanned, with the three of them stopping by the White House that night for a supposed tour given by a low-level staffer they knew, only to be waved into the Oval Office by Trump.

Byrne, a business gadfly with a shock of red hair, had resigned from his company in 2019 after he acknowledged a romantic relationship with a woman later imprisoned in the U.S. for acting as an unregistered Russian agent.

He also claimed in a statement that the FBI had used him to engage in "political espionage" against Hillary Clinton and Donald Trump during the 2016 election.

"You have any idea how easy it would be for me just to leave on January 20th and get in Marine One and fly away?" Trump asked them. He seemed tired. "I've got my golf courses. I've got my friends. I've had a really good life." But he said the presidency was stolen so he would fight.

The trio pitched the president on appointing Powell to be a

special counsel to investigate the election, perhaps inside the White House counsel's office or even inside the Justice Department.

Trump nodded. He seemed to take the idea seriously. He called in other advisers. Meadows and White House counsel Pat Cipollone discouraged the suggestion, as did other Trump campaign lawyers. They privately thought Powell's ideas were insane, dangerous, and that she drew out the worst in Trump.

Trump did not close the door on the idea. He wanted action. Powell said he could seize voting machines. She said it was necessary since the machines had been manipulated by corrupt, anti-Trump forces.

Several lawyers heatedly said Trump could not do that. Eric Herschmann, an attorney and senior adviser in the West Wing, warned the president not to throw his political capital Powell's way. It would be a waste.

"Sidney Powell promises and never delivers," Herschmann said, looking at Powell, prompting Flynn and others to disagree.

"Lawyers," Trump sighed, "I have nothing but lawyers that stop me on everything."

"I'm very embarrassed by my lawyers and the Justice Department," he added.

Trump looked at Powell. "At least she's giving me a chance." The siren song of declarative presidential action.

Trump called Meadows on speakerphone. Make Powell a special counsel, he said. Meadows dodged, showing support for Trump's fight but making no promises.

"You got to do it the right way. You got to run it through the Department of Justice," he said. "You can't, you can't just kind of order this up tonight."

"I care about getting these machines," Trump told the group. "I want to get these machines and I have the right to do so under the Act," a reference to the National Emergencies Act, which formalizes emergency presidential powers.

FDR had used the act to address the Great Depression, and Truman had tried to use it as a means of countering a steel strike during the Korean War, but the Supreme Court eventually told Truman in a landmark case, *Youngstown Sheet & Tube Co. v. Sawyer*, that a president could not seize the steel mills, or any private property.

Trump's campaign lawyers and White House counsel lawyers glared at each other. Seizing voting machines through executive action could have drastic consequences. How would you do it? With the military? In an interview with Newsmax the previous day, Flynn had floated "martial law" as an option.

Trump fumed. "I need lawyers on TV. I need people who go on TV. Sidney goes on TV. Rudy goes on TV.

"Get Rudy on the phone."

Herschmann, Powell and Flynn began arguing.

Trump directed the White House operator to call Giuliani.

"Everyone should calm down!" Giuliani said on the speakerphone. He heard the yelling match.

There was a loud clanking and noise in the background. Trump asked Rudy about the noise. "Rudy? Is that you?"

Giuliani told his associates on his side of the call to quiet down. "I'm on a call.

"Do you want me to come over to the White House?"

Trump said yes. "Are you close?"

"Well, I'm in Georgetown." He was having dinner at an Italian restaurant. "I can be over there in like 15 minutes. I've got a driver."

"All right," Trump said. "Come over."

Trump turned back to the group in the Oval Office. Giuliani remained on the line. Trump looked at Powell. "Love her on TV," he said. "She'll make a good argument for us." He spoke to Meadows, who was also calling in.

"I'm making Sidney a special counsel to the president. Mark, you get her the forms," Trump said. "Give her the forms to onboard her."

When Giuliani heard Trump's instruction, he spoke up immediately. He took pride in being Trump's main lawyer. What was this special counsel business? He did not like it.

"I'm on my way," Giuliani said.

Trump said okay, then told the room the meeting would continue in the residence in about 30 minutes. Before he went upstairs, Trump turned to the trio. For this to work, he said, you've got to work well with Rudy.

After others left, Powell, Flynn and Byrne waited in the Cabinet Room for Giuliani to arrive before they joined Trump. When Giuliani was on speakerphone, Byrne could sense the former mayor was not happy about Powell trying to take charge. He was the legal boss. Byrne was hoping they could now have a conversation and figure out how to work together.

Once Giuliani arrived, still putting on his tie, it was apparent there would be no harmony. Giuliani gruffly told Powell she had to start looping him into her legal work. No more surprises. She was sharp in response: *You* never get back to me when I do. Read *your* texts.

Giuliani shook his head. Not true, he said. You're the one keeping me in the dark!

"Don't you talk down to me, Rudy Giuliani!" Powell said, nearly shouting.

The meeting in the residence never clicked. Giuliani and Powell would barely acknowledge each other. Powell was never made a special counsel.

That Monday, December 21, Attorney General Barr, who had announced a week earlier he would resign and leave in late December, told reporters there was no need for a special counsel, and that he saw no evidence of "systemic or broad-based" fraud during the election.

"If I thought a special counsel at this stage was the right tool and was appropriate, I would name one, but I haven't, and I'm not going to," Barr said, adding he would not appoint a special counsel to investigate Hunter Biden, either. Hunter Biden had revealed in December he was being investigated by federal prosecutors in Delaware.

Trump was irate. Don't worry, Giuliani and others assured him, we still have another play.

Mike Pence.

THIRTY-EIGHT

In late December, Pence phoned former vice president Dan Quayle. At 74, the once boyish looking Quayle was living the private, golf-playing life he loved in Arizona.

The two men shared a unique profile: Indiana Republicans who had become vice president.

Pence wanted advice. Despite the Electoral College casting its ballots for Biden on December 14, Trump was convinced that Pence could throw the election to Trump on January 6, when Congress certified the final count.

Pence explained to his fellow Indianan that Trump was pressuring him to intervene to ensure Biden would not secure the needed 270 votes during the certification and push the election to a vote in the House of Representatives.

If thrown to the House, there was a twist. And Trump was fixated on the twist, Pence said. It was the provision that could keep Trump in power.

While the Democrats held the current House majority, the 12th Amendment of the Constitution stated the voting on a contested election would *not* be done by a simple majority vote.

Instead, the amendment states that the election vote would be counted in blocs of *state delegations,* with one vote per state:

> *If no person have such majority . . . the House of Representatives shall choose immediately, by ballot, the President. But in choosing the President, the votes shall be taken by states, the representation from each state having one vote.*

Republicans now controlled more delegations in the House of Representatives, meaning Trump would likely win if the chamber ended up deciding the victor.

Quayle thought Trump's suggestion was preposterous and dangerous. He recalled his own January 6—January 6, 1993—28 years earlier. As vice president and president of the Senate, he had to certify the victory of Bill Clinton and Al Gore, who had trounced Bush and Quayle.

He had researched his duties. He had read and reread the 12th Amendment. All he had to do was count the votes.

The President of the Senate shall, in the presence of the Senate and House of Representatives, open all the certificates and the votes shall then be counted.

That was it.

Trump's effort to cajole Pence was a dark, Rube Goldberg–like fantasy, Quayle believed, and could precipitate a constitutional crisis.

"Mike, you have no flexibility on this. None. Zero. Forget it. Put it away," Quayle said.

"I know, that's what I've been trying to tell Trump," Pence said. "But he really thinks he can. And there are other guys in there saying I've got this power. I've—"

Quayle interrupted him.

"You don't, just stop it," he said.

Pence pressed again. It was easy for Quayle to make a blanket statement from political winter. He wanted to know, veep to veep, whether there was even a glimmer of light, legally and constitutionally, to perhaps put a pause on the certification if there were ongoing court cases and legal challenges.

"Forget it," Quayle repeated.

Pence finally agreed acting to overturn the election would be antithetical to his traditional view of conservatism. One man could not effectively throw the election to the House of Representatives.

Quayle told Pence to let it go.

"Mike, don't even talk about it," he said.

Pence paused.

"You don't know the position I'm in," he said.

"I do know the position you're in," Quayle said. "I also know what the law is. You listen to the parliamentarian. That's all you do. You have no power. So just forget it."

Pence told Quayle that he had studied the video from January 6, 1993. It was on the C-SPAN website's archive. Many of the people in the footage were now dead, including then House Speaker Tom Foley, a Democrat who shook Quayle's hand as the vice president opened the session.

"Mine was pretty simple," Quayle chuckled. "You announce it, and you go on."

Quayle turned to Trump's assertion that the election had been stolen from him. He told Pence those statements were ridiculous and eroded public trust.

"There's no evidence," Quayle said.

"Well, there's some stuff out in Arizona," Pence said, updating Quayle on the Trump campaign's legal efforts there. There was a lawsuit in federal court to compel Arizona's governor to "decertify" Biden's win in the state, which had enraged Trump ever since Fox News called Arizona for Biden at 11:20 p.m. on election night.

"Mike, I live in Arizona," Quayle said. "There's nothing out here."

Quayle sensed that Pence knew that, but Pence was careful to offer a few lines straight from Trump's talking points about how the process needed to unfold in the courts. Quayle suspected Pence had a marathon of Trump conversations ahead.

Still, Quayle said, it is nonsense to say the election was stolen, and to even entertain the idea of blocking Biden in January.

They soon turned to rosier topics, such as what life is like for a former vice president.

Glancing outside, not far from Scottsdale's gleaming green golf courses and the cliffs of the McDowell Mountain Range, Quayle assured Pence that things would be fine. They were conservatives. Just follow the Constitution.

During that same period in December, Senator Mike Lee of Utah spoke with Leader McConnell and summarized what he had been telling his colleagues for weeks about attempts to not certify the election results: "We have no more authority than the Queen of England. None."

"I agree with you," McConnell said. "I agree."

One of the most conservative senators, Lee had chosen to sit at the Senate desk once used by Senator Barry Goldwater of Arizona, who became the conscience of the Republican Party during Watergate, one of the prime movers in persuading Nixon to resign.

Lee was one of Trump's most reliable GOP supporters, but he was also a legal wonk and a former Supreme Court law clerk for Justice Samuel Alito. He had appeared on Trump's short list for Supreme Court nominations and had an impeccable legal pedigree. His father, Rex Lee, was solicitor general in the Reagan administration and was the founding dean at the law school at Brigham Young University.

He considered himself a strict constructionist, meaning he believed the Constitution designated specific powers to Congress, but no more than stated in the original language.

Before Christmas, Lee went to see Ted Cruz. They were two former Supreme Court law clerks, two strict constructionists—"law nerds" as Lee called them. They loved this stuff—who had the power and why?

In a long discussion, Lee felt they came to the exact same conclusion that the Congress had no role.

But Cruz believed he could find an alternative way of stopping a certification. He was listening to Trump allies like Congressman Mo Brooks of Alabama, who was pleading with fellow conservatives to object on January 6. They needed just one senator.

If a single senator formally objected to the certification, all 100 senators were going to have to vote on that certification. Instead of a routine certification, finished within a few hours, the exercise could mushroom into a political nightmare, forcing Senate Republicans to choose between the Constitution and Trump.

Cruz asked his staff to begin researching the counting of electors, the history of the Electoral Count Act. He was hearing from people back home. They did not trust the election outcome. But McConnell and others in the leadership were leaning hard on members. Don't object.

Lee never wavered. He kept saying throughout December, with growing intensity to Mark Meadows and anybody who asked for his view, "The president should never pretend that the Congress itself can fix this. We don't have that power.

"You need to realize that you've basically lost this unless something really extraordinary happens," Lee said, referring to an unlikely phenomenon or ballot scandal, "something that would be itself eyebrow raising and very, very troubling."

But based on the facts and evidence, he would add, I'm just not seeing that.

Lee went back to Utah for Christmas. Just as Cruz had, he began hearing from friends, neighbors, family members about the election being stolen. He saw the extent of Trump's power to persuade.

People who would not be regarded as being on the fringe of society—mayors, city council men, county commissioners, sheriffs—said they were expecting him to go back to Washington and "stop the steal." Text messages, social media posts, people who got his phone number wanting to know what was going on. How was the election stolen? What are you going to do?

Lee was directed to John Eastman, another Trump lawyer. The two spoke with each other.

"There's a memo about to be developed," Eastman said. "I'll get it to you as soon as I can."

THIRTY-NINE

Trump played golf in Florida with Lindsey Graham on Christmas Day.

"Mr. President," Graham said, "there's no doubt in my mind that there's a lot of shenanigans going on in Georgia and other places but it's just not going to rise to the level of overturning the election."

Graham's strategy was now not to try to convince Trump he lost—he had lost that battle—but to convince him he could not change the outcome.

Trump persisted. He could not understand how he won 74 million votes and lost. His pollsters and campaign staff told him if he won 74 million votes, he had to win. That was more votes than any presidential candidate in history—except Joe Biden. Trump had won many bellwether counties. He had won Ohio and Florida.

"Mr. President, you lost a close election. You need to be thinking about 'The Great American Comeback.' "

"Why won't you let me play it out?" Trump asked Graham twice during the round.

"I'm going to let you play it out," Graham said after the second time. "There's certain things I can't do, and you know what they are. But let's play this out. Keep shining a light on election processes that you think were tainted."

Graham said he, too, believed some mail-in-ballots were suspect. "Keep fighting" in the courts, he said, but do not go to the extreme.

After 18 holes, Trump and a Russian-born golf prodigy were tied with Graham and the club pro.

"Let's keep playing," Trump said.

They kept tying for several holes. At a par 4, the wind was howling at 30 miles an hour.

On the second shot, Trump said to his partner, "Make sure you hit it there. Make sure you're using enough club."

The young man plunked his ball in the water before the green.

Graham thought that the kid was going to cut his wrists for having let the president down.

"Oh, that's okay," Trump said. "You're a great player. Make sure you think next time. That's life."

Graham thought he would remember Trump's comment for the rest of his life. Graham almost said, "I couldn't say that any better—make sure you think next time."

But Trump couldn't get that 74 million out of his head and kept coming back to it. He didn't believe that Biden got 81 million—7 million more.

Graham toggled between support and tough love, friendship and realism.

"Mr. President," Graham said, "I'm not going to argue with you. When you win 19 out of 20 bellwether counties. Win Florida and Ohio. When you get 74 million votes and you lose, that's got to be hard to take."

"You better believe it's hard to take!"

"It is what it is," Graham said. "That's life."

Pence's chief of staff, Marc Short, and his taciturn counsel, Greg Jacob, told Pence there was no legal or constitutional basis for him to do anything to disrupt the counting of the electoral votes. Lawmakers, not the vice president, could object. But they felt their boss was in a corner. Pence was only 61 years old and harbored presidential ambitions. He could not sever his relationship with Trump.

The risk became real when Senator Josh Hawley of Missouri,

a Yale Law–educated freshman and former Supreme Court law clerk for Chief Justice John Roberts, announced on December 30 that he would object to the Electoral College certification on January 6, becoming the first senator to do so.

"At the very least, Congress should investigate allegations of voter fraud and adopt measures to secure the integrity of our elections. But Congress has so far failed to act," Hawley said.

Down in Houston, after watching Hawley garner attention for his plan to challenge the count, Cruz grabbed his laptop and began to sketch out his own idea: an electoral commission created by Congress to investigate the result. He kept typing as he took his seat on a Southwest Airlines flight back to Washington.

Maybe I'll do it solo, maybe others will sign on, Cruz told his staff on a conference call. Once back in Washington, he mentioned the commission idea to Senator John Kennedy of Louisiana. He signed on. Cruz kept moving down the line of conservatives.

Senator Lee, his closest friend in the Senate, did not sign on. When Lee said a commission was not viable, Cruz said they would agree to disagree.

There was no out. Pence would now be forced to emcee his own defeat, and Trump's, on national television, as rivals and allies pounded lecterns.

"JANUARY SIXTH, SEE YOU IN DC!" Trump tweeted on December 30 from Mar-a-Lago, where he was spending the holiday.

His allies, led by a group called "Women for America First," had filed a National Park Service permit for January 22 and 23 in Washington. But they amended their permit application for a rally and instead reserved space at Freedom Plaza near the White House for January 6.

If Trump had any hesitation, it was erased by his supporters on television and on the right-wing websites he tracked on Twitter.

The deplorables, the MAGA crowd, "my people" were all about the fight.

Former White House chief strategist Steve Bannon was on the second floor of his townhouse on Capitol Hill on December 30, talking with Trump by phone.

Trump and Bannon had had a falling out two years earlier over Bannon's high profile but had rekindled their relationship despite Bannon's current legal troubles.

In August, Bannon had been charged in a federal Manhattan court for defrauding donors on a private project called "We Build the Wall," an attempt to sidestep the government and build Trump's wall along the U.S.-Mexico border. Trump did not seem to care. Maybe Bannon would get a pardon.

Trump ranted about how Republicans were not doing enough to keep him in power.

"You've got to return to Washington and make a dramatic return today," Bannon told him.

Bannon's gray hair was shaggy, and he wore heavy layers, black on black. His eyes were sunken and bloodshot from staying up until nearly dawn on many days, making phone calls and plotting with friends around the world, or writing out notes for his right-wing podcast.

"You've got to call Pence off the fucking ski slopes and get him back here today. This is a crisis," Bannon said, referring to the vice president, who was vacationing in Vail, Colorado.

Bannon told Trump to focus on January 6. That was the moment for a reckoning.

"People are going to go, 'What the fuck is going on here?'" Bannon believed. "We're going to bury Biden on January 6th, fucking bury him."

If Republicans could cast enough of a shadow on Biden's victory on January 6, Bannon said, it would be hard for Biden to govern. Millions of Americans would consider him illegitimate.

They would ignore him. They would dismiss him and wait for Trump to run again.

"We are going to kill it in the crib. Kill the Biden presidency in the crib," he said.

On December 31, Trump returned early from Florida, cutting his trip short and skipping the New Year's Eve gala at Mar-a-Lago. Stepping off Marine One, Trump, in a heavy black winter coat and bright red tie, stared over at reporters. He did not take questions.

FORTY

In early January, Lee and Graham began separate, personal investigations into the president's election fraud allegations. If there were any truth to them, there would be evidence, they concluded.

Lee received a two-page memo from the White House on Saturday, January 2, authored by legal scholar John Eastman, who was working with Trump.

> **PRIVILEGED AND CONFIDENTIAL**
>
> January 6 scenario
>
> 7 states have transmitted dual slates of electors to the President of the Senate.

Lee was shocked. He had heard nothing about alternative slates of electors.

In the arcane process set out in the Constitution, electors cast the final votes for president, as they had done on December 14. And in four days, the Senate was required to formally count those votes to certify the election.

The possibility of alternate or dueling slates would be national news. Yet there had been no such news.

For weeks, Lee knew some Trump allies in various states had been putting themselves forward as "alternate electors." But those efforts were more of a social media campaign—an amateur push with no legal standing.

There had also been calls from Trump supporters to release

electors pledged to Biden, so that they could vote for someone else. But that 11th-hour push was also complicated by the law, with most states prohibiting so-called "faithless" electors from switching their votes.

Trump adviser Stephen Miller had nonetheless stoked the possibility of a coming election upheaval. On Fox News in December, he claimed "an alternate slate of electors in the contested states is going to vote and we're going to send those results up to Congress."

In private, Eastman was insisting that groups of people in the states who sought to be electors should be considered as legitimate by Congress. They were organized and determined, he told others, and there was a precedent for recognizing a second slate. Hawaii had sent in two competing slates during the 1960 election, following a dispute between the Republican governor and state Democrats.

But unlike in 1960, this time there was no formal attempt to offer dueling slates gaining any traction at the state legislative level. Calls to governors for special sessions on the vote went unheeded. It was just an outcry—mostly Trump supporters in various states who wanted another group of electors recognized by Congress.

By January 2, Lee knew nothing had happened. It had all been talk, mere noise on the matter, which was rigorously spelled out in the Constitution.

"What is this?" Lee wondered as he glanced down at Eastman's document.

Lee also knew any attempt to make the vice president the critical player in the certification would be a deliberate warping of the Constitution.

Lee had kept telling Mark Meadows and others in the White House and GOP that the vice president was a counting clerk, period. No other role. It was power concisely articulated and capped by those seven words in the 12th Amendment: "and the votes shall then be counted."

Eastman's two-page memo turned the standard counting process on its head. Lee was surprised it came from Eastman, a law school professor who had clerked for Supreme Court Justice Clarence Thomas.

Lee read on. "Here's the scenario we propose." The memo set out six potential steps for the vice president. The third item jumped out at the senator.

3. At the end, he announces that because of the ongoing disputes in the 7 States, there are no electors that can be deemed validly appointed in those States. That means the total number of "electors appointed" – the language of the 12th Amendment -- is 454. This reading of the 12th Amendment has also been advanced by Harvard Law Professor Laurence Tribe (here). A "majority of the electors appointed" would therefore be 228. There are at this point 232 votes for Trump, 222 votes for Biden. Pence then gavels President Trump as re-elected.

He read it again, just to make sure. Pence "announces that because of the ongoing disputes in the 7 States, there are no electors that can be deemed validly appointed in those States." So, Pence would cut the number of states whose votes would be counted in the election to only 43 states, leaving 454 electors left to decide who wins.

"There are at this point 232 votes for Trump, 222 votes for Biden," Eastman wrote of such a scenario. "Pence then gavels President Trump as re-elected."

A procedural action by the vice president to throw out tens of millions of legally cast votes and declare a new winner? Lee's head was spinning. No such procedure existed in the Constitution, any law or past practice. Eastman apparently had drawn it out of thin air.

Eastman had also thought ahead to the certain outrage and worry of a coup.

4. Howls, of course, from the Democrats, who now claim, contrary to Tribe's prior position, that 270 is required. So Pence says, fine. Pursuant to the 12th Amendment, no candidate has achieved the necessary majority. That sends the matter to the House, where the "the votes shall be taken by states, the representation from each state having one vote . . . ." Republicans currently control 26 of the state delegations, the bare majority needed to win that vote. President Trump is re-elected there as well.

That was their ballgame. Either have Pence declare Trump the winner, or make sure it is thrown to the House where Trump is guaranteed to win.

The House had decided the presidential election only twice before in American history. Lee absorbed the rest of Eastman's memo, which also asserted "Pence should do this without asking for permission."

"The fact is that the Constitution assigns the power to the Vice President as the ultimate arbiter," it stated.

Nothing could be further from the truth, Lee knew. The vice president was not the "ultimate arbiter." Like Quayle, he had memorized the line of the 12th Amendment that said the president of the Senate simply opens "all the certificates and the votes shall then be counted."

What a mess. Lee had spent nearly two months trying to impress upon Trump and Meadows that they could pursue legal remedies, audits, recounts or other claims. They could file dozens of lawsuits. But their time was limited. "Just remember you've got a shot clock," he said.

If none of that panned out, Pence only could count the votes. That was it.

Mark Meadows grew up as a self-described "fat nerd" who was an outsider. By age 61, he had slimmed down a bit to husky, and prided himself as the Trump insider. He had become the person Trump called early or late. Colleagues privately remarked how happy he was talking about calls from "POTUS," his way of describing the president.

Meadows also worked in whispers, loving pull-asides and closed meetings. But he was not reserved. If anything, some Trump aides found him too emotional. He openly cried in the West Wing on several occasions when dealing with tricky personnel and political decisions.

Meadows called a meeting in his White House office on Saturday, January 2, so Giuliani and his team could brief Graham, in his capacity as a lawyer and chairman of the Senate Judiciary Committee, on the voting problems and fraud they claimed they had found.

The findings were sufficient to turn the election in Trump's favor, Giuliani said, citing evidence that had been given to him.

Giuliani offered a computer expert who presented a mathematical formula that demonstrated the near impossibility of a Biden win. Several states had recorded more votes for Biden than previous votes for Obama in 2008 and 2012. Since polling showed that Obama had been more popular in these states, it was almost mathematically impossible for Biden to outpace Obama in raw numbers during the 2020 presidential election, Giuliani's expert maintained.

Too abstract, Graham said. A presidential election would not be turned based on some theory. While he was suspicious of the mainstream media, which was asserting categorically that claims by Trump were false, he wanted more. Show me some hard evidence, Graham said.

Giuliani and his team said they had overwhelming, irrefutable proof of the dead, young people under the age of 18, and felons in jail voting in massive numbers.

Graham said he was sure some of this was true, but he needed proof.

"I'm a simple guy," he said. "If you're dead, you're not supposed to vote. If you're under 18, you're not supposed to vote. If you're in jail, you're not supposed to vote. Let's focus on those three things."

Some 8,000 felons voted in Arizona, they said.

"Give me some names," Graham asked.

They said they had 789 dead people who had voted in Georgia.

Names, Graham said. They promised to get names to him by Monday. They said they had found 66,000 individuals under the age of 18 who illegally voted in Georgia.

Do you know how hard it is to get somebody who's 18 to vote? You've got 66,000 under 18 who voted, right?

Right.

"Give me some names. You need to put it in writing. You need to show me the evidence."

They promised by Monday.

"You're losing in the courts," Graham said.

Trump's lawyers had now lost nearly 60 challenges. By the end, about 90 judges, including Trump appointees, would end up ruling against Trump-backed challenges.

Vice President Pence walked into his office near the Senate chamber to meet privately with the Senate parliamentarian, Elizabeth MacDonough, late Sunday evening, January 3, after swearing in new members of the Senate.

McConnell and his chief of staff, Sharon Soderstrom, a master of policy and procedure, had encouraged Pence to do so. They did not want any surprises and believed even the scripted Pence should practice.

Sitting with his chief of staff, Marc Short, and his counsel, Greg Jacob, Pence asked MacDonough to walk him through the plan for January 6. Let me know how this will go. He took notes as MacDonough outlined how challenges could be handled and his options while presiding.

Pence peppered her with hypotheticals: What happens if this objection is made? How does this go? What are the scripts I am required to recite versus the scripts where I might have some latitude?

Short and Pence had discussed for weeks whether it was possible for Pence to avoid a made-for-TV moment announcing Trump's defeat to the world. Instant fodder for a Pence rival in 2024.

"Can I perhaps express sympathy with some of the complaints?" Pence asked.

MacDonough was curt, professional. Stick to the script, she advised. You are a vote counter. Pence agreed.

FORTY-ONE

Graham was at the White House on Monday, January 4, where he received some memos supporting Trump's claims. He sent his driver to take them to Lee Holmes, Graham's chief counsel on the Judiciary Committee, who had been with Graham for seven years.

The first memo from Giuliani to Graham contained 20 pages of 39 names each, plus nine additional names. It looked impressive.

Holmes read that a team of accountants had identified "789 dead people who voted in Georgia in the 2020 General Election." The analysis was of mail-in and absentee ballots.

MEMORANDUM

TO	**CHAIRMAN LINDSEY GRAHAM**
FROM:	**MAYOR RUDY GIULIANI, TRUMP LEGAL DEFENSE TEAM**
DATE:	**4 JANUARY 2021**
RE:	**DECEASED PEOPLE WHO VOTED IN THE 2021 ELECTION IN GA**

Overview
Many independent interest groups have undertaken analyses to review the mail-in and absentee ballots that were reported by various Secretaries of State to determine if deceased voters had ballots requested, cast and counted in their name. While there are many reports across the country that show significant numbers of dead voters participating in various states, the number that we are absolutely certain of, is that provided by an independent firm run by Bryan Geels and Alex Kaufman, who are based in Georgia.

Georgia – Margin - 11,779
They have identified 789 dead people who voted in Georgia in the 2020 General Election. Their team did a comprehensive analysis of mail-in and absentee ballot voter names and obituaries, which showed these as definitive numbers. A comprehensive list of those voters is attached herewith.

To Holmes, it was not clear how anyone could get such a massive list of people who died and meaningfully match it to their recent voting history. But perhaps several of the names on Giuliani's list had voted fraudulently.

In any event, once Holmes started checking on hundreds of names, he found no credible evidence of fraud.

Robert Drakeford, for example, was 88 years old, and got a ballot on September 18. The ballot was returned five days later. He died on November 2, according to the document. Another old person had voted and died, proving nothing even if the document was accurate.

But Giuliani had said in his memo to Graham that the data was "definitive." It was a reckless claim.

Holmes was stunned at the blatant discrepancies in Giuliani's submission. As best he could tell, nearly all of the 789 dead people who allegedly voted in Georgia had properly received their ballots before they died. The sourcing was unclear. He could not figure out which government documents might have been used.

Some people in Georgia no doubt voted and then died. This proved nothing. It was laughable. Holmes could see why the Georgia courts had rejected Trump's claims.

A second Giuliani memo on Georgia read:

To: Senator Lindsey Graham (R-SC)
From: Rudolph Giuliani
Re: Voting Irregularities, Impossibilities, and Illegalities in the 2020 General Election
Date: January 4, 2020

Introduction
The 2020 U.S. General Election had several abnormalities that contributed to multiple irregularities, which raises concerns about the integrity of the election. The concerns span multiple states, and have consistent patterns seen in each of the states. United States laws, as well as the laws of each of the states, set specific standards for who is eligible to vote, and how and when votes may be legally cast. The information below details proven fallacies that invalidate the vote count and outcome of the each of the respective states. Per your request, this memorandum is limited to traditional voter fraud in a sample of the contested states and does not discuss machines, algorithms, or technological manipulation.

The detailed information provided in this memorandum is a simple snapshot of the verifiable information available. Per your request, we limited the number of names and identities provided to a small sample, and this memo is intended to exemplify the fact that the illegal votes are provable, documented, and identifiable.

Georgia (Tally Spread = 11,779)
In Georgia, 66,248 individuals under the age of 18 registered to vote and illegally voted in the 2020 general election, or more likely, someone illegally voted in their name. Evidence suggests that10,315 dead people voted in Georgia, and 2,560 felons with incomplete sentences registered to vote and cast their votes. 4,502 unregistered voters cast ballots. 2,506 convicted felons voted in Georgia.

Turning to a PowerPoint printout sent by Giuliani, Holmes read, "Independent analysis conducted by expert CPAs and Ivy League statisticians show a sufficient number of illegal votes . . . . there were at least 27,713 illegal votes cast and counted in Georgia's election."

Holmes wondered, who were these unnamed brainiac experts? That total was more than twice the 11,779-vote margin that gave Biden the state.

The memo's "confidential" analysis also said that 18,325 voters had "registered at a residential address which is marked vacant per the USPS," the United States Postal Service.

How could anyone, or even a team of Ivy League statisticians, go through 7.6 million registered voters and correlate that with the postal records to find 18,325 registered at vacant addresses?

Holmes was a hound on the internet and clicked away at the massive number of public records on voters that were publicly available. He could find nothing that would allow someone access to information that would make such a search possible. Yet the Giuliani memos said all the information was in public records.

The Giuliani analysis also said there were "305,701" instances in which "absentee ballot applications date precedes earliest date permitted under Georgia law."

But that would again mean examining 7.6 million voter files. As best Holmes could tell, the information on absentee ballot applications might only be available in some Georgia counties. It would be a near impossible task to try to apply this to 7.6 million voters.

And another "confidential" memo said that "4,502" people voted, "yet do not appear on the State's own voter registration rolls." How could unregistered people cast a vote? And how could anyone find out?

Holmes received an email from a team of veteran conservative lawyers working with Giuliani in Georgia. The email read:

Georgia Election Official's Numbers Don't Add Up

Caught – Either Lying or Profoundly Ignorant of the Election Data

Georgia's election officials announced on Monday, January 4, that the election was valid because it had a small margin of error and that those contesting the election were all wrong. In doing so, they either lied to the public or betrayed a profound ignorance of the election data. Below is a chart that describes the official position of the Georgia Secretary of State vs the truth.

Holmes backtracked to the Giuliani memos and found much of the latest data could be traced to investigative work done by Christina Bobb of the One America News Network, a pro-Trump television network that touted conspiracies about "voting machines" being "notorious" for fraud. He believed the number of alleged underaged voters in Georgia was exceptionally large.

Turning to Nevada, the memo said that "42,284 registered voters voted more than once."

Holmes wondered how this was possible. In multiple precincts? The same precincts? Voting twice was clearly illegal, but who exactly would track and register that in what Giuliani said were public records?

In Nevada, the memo also said, "2,468 voters had moved out of the state of Nevada 30 days prior to the election and were therefore ineligible to vote." And 1,506 were listed as "deceased by the Social Security Administration Master Death File, Consumer Data Vendors, Public Obituary Data Matches, Credit Bureau Deceased Data."

"8,111 voters had registered with non-existent addresses," the memo stated. "15,164 out-of-state voters voted."

Holmes could find no public records that would even allow someone to reach these conclusions.

On Arizona, the memo said, "there were 36,473 individuals who could not establish citizenship, but whose ballots were accepted and counted."

Holmes knew that citizenship checks were not required or even permitted in federal elections. He found a 2013 Supreme Court case, *Arizona v. Inter Tribal Council*, that held the National Voting Registration Act of 1993 mandated that states could not require proof of citizenship in federal elections. Holmes called election officials in Arizona, who said they did not require citizenship proof and abided by the definitive Supreme Court case.

It was another number with no basis, and, most importantly, no names.

The real deception was a claim that there had been 11,676 overvotes in Arizona. "Overvotes" are when a voter votes for more than the number of candidates allowed. It was based on a five-page memo that listed overvotes for 220 state races, including appeals court judge, constable, county assessor, Phoenix council member, and Phoenix mayor. The memo then added all these up cumulatively to get the 11,676 total.

But the so-called "overvotes" in the presidential election were only 180—the only ones that would count in the Trump-Biden contest. It was the only field that was relevant. The 180 was not going to change the election in Arizona because Biden had won, according to the latest count, by 10,457 votes.

In Wisconsin, the memo claimed 226,000 people who may have been "indefinitely confined" voted, and another "170,140 individuals voted with an absentee ballot without having registered for absentee voting."

The memo said that in Pennsylvania, "682,777 mail in ballots were processed in the middle of the night on November 3–4 in violation of states laws," requiring that counting be monitored by representatives of both parties. The claim was based on one poll watcher's sworn statement.

"All the fraudulent votes must be deducted," the memo said. Holmes was again astonished at the overreach. Fraudulent? There was no evidence.

The memo continued, "If you deduct just this number, President Trump wins the state by hundreds of thousands."

Holmes found the sloppiness, the overbearing tone of certainty, and the inconsistencies disqualifying. The three memos added up to nothing.

Yet as one of the memos to Graham said, "The detailed information provided in this memorandum is a simple snapshot of the verifiable information available. Per your request, we limited the number of names and identities provided to a small sample, and this memo is intended to exemplify the fact that the illegal votes are provable, documented, and identifiable."

Holmes reported to Graham that the data in the memos were a concoction, with a bullying tone and eighth grade writing.

Graham looked over the memos.

"Third grade," he said. Holmes said part of the claim was based on an affidavit.

Graham said, "I can get an affidavit tomorrow saying the world is flat."

Although Trump continued to be irate about Arizona's and Fox News's decision to call it for Biden early on election night, Graham was convinced that Arizona governor Doug Ducey, a Republican, ran a fair election and had an effective system to verify signatures.

Graham told Trump that he lost Arizona because of his attacks on the late John McCain, who remained popular in his home state. His widow, Cindy, had endorsed Biden, who was a good friend and spoke at McCain's funeral.

"I think the reason you fell short in Arizona is you started beating on a dead guy," Graham said.

Senator Lee and his wife, Sharon, flew to Georgia to attend Trump's January 4 rally for Republican Senators Loeffler and Perdue ahead of their respective elections.

Lee met with Trump's Georgia legal team challenging the state's presidential result. They were zealous, arguing they had abundant evidence that many mail-in ballots had been sent to addresses that were not residential addresses—and not legitimate addresses for a voter in Georgia. They said enough votes were improperly cast for Biden that the election should now be called for Trump.

"If you are right," Lee said, "why aren't you in court at this moment arguing for a temporary restraining order? Or a preliminary injunction? Or making this pitch to the election officials in Georgia? To the secretary of state? To the governor or the attorney general or your legislature?"

The state legislature had all the authority. He asked, "Why are you making it to me?

"You might as well make your case to Queen Elizabeth II. Congress can't do this. You're wasting your time."

The lawyers indicated that a court or the state legislature might still act.

"I'm sure that will be big news," Lee said, "and I will be made aware of it."

FORTY-TWO

Retired Lieutenant General Keith Kellogg had been drawn to Trump since working on his 2016 campaign. Trump took him seriously and paid attention to him. With his broad shoulders and straight jaw, and his gruff manner of speaking, Kellogg had the kind of look Trump liked for his generals.

But in recent years, Kellogg was torn between two worlds: Pence World, where he was the vice president's national security adviser, and Trump World.

"I make no bones about it. I'm a Trump loyalist," Kellogg told others. Yet he worked directly for Pence, in a job he accepted after briefly acting as Trump's national security adviser following the resignation of Michael Flynn.

"I had my own personal nicknames for both of them," Kellogg said. "Fire and Ice."

Trump felt comfortable with Kellogg. He could curse around him and not worry.

"I'm dealing with a fucking lunatic," Trump said in one meeting with Kellogg, referring to his engagement with North Korean dictator Kim Jong-un.

Pence was the total opposite of Trump. Pence had an open Bible on his desk and prayed daily. He held Bible study meetings with friends and kept things tight with Marc Short and his wife, Karen Pence, with few others in the know. In four years of being around Pence, Kellogg had never heard him curse—and Kellogg did not curse around him.

Since November, Kellogg had felt pained as he watched Pence suffer silently under Trump's pressure to contest the election. On one trip on Air Force Two to watch a rocket launch, Kellogg pulled him aside.

"Sir, you got to end this and here's how you end it," Kellogg advised. "Walk in there and say, 'I ain't going to do it.' Not just that you can't do it, you won't do it."

He said for Trump, there was no greater quality than being tough. Tough was his language.

Pence did not respond.

Pence had flown to Georgia to campaign for the two GOP senators on January 4. The White House had planned a political doubleheader: Pence would go there early in the day, and then Trump would come to the state late at night. Separate trips.

After long talks with aides, Pence leaned into the idea that the election had problems, but he avoided the words "rigged" and "fraud." It was his way of staying in Trump's good graces without going full Giuliani.

"I know we all, we all got our doubts about the last election," Pence told the crowd in Milner, Georgia, standing before an enormous American flag, "and I want to assure you, I share the concerns of the millions of Americans about the voting irregularities.

"And I promise you, come this Wednesday," he said. The crowd began to stir at those words. "We'll have our day in Congress." Attendees began to roar.

"We'll hear the objections. We'll hear the evidence. But tomorrow is Georgia's day."

On his flight back to Washington, Pence and his advisers worked on drafting the letter he wanted to release on January 6, explaining his decision to properly count the electoral vote.

Short did not love the idea and suggested at one point that

Pence could move forward without issuing a letter at all. Why would you create a target? But Pence wanted a letter.

Sitting in his Air Force Two cabin, they decided not to use the word "fraud" anywhere. Instead, like in his speech, it would be "irregularities." Fox News was playing on low volume, running a segment on Pence.

"There's going to be people that aren't happy about this," his senior adviser, Marty Obst, said, playing out the conservative response should Pence stick with his plan to not meddle with the count. "But there's a lot less people than you think." Obst was trying to buck him up.

"I'm not so sure about that," Pence said.

Obst later took Pence aside on the flight. He was worried about his longtime boss.

"I'm in a good place," Pence assured him. "I think there'll be blowback. We'll figure it out."

Pence eyed Obst. He knew Obst, stocky and fast-talking, could get hot. He might be itching to be an attack dog on Pence's behalf in the coming days.

"You'll be tempted to engage," Pence said, but avoid the temptation. "That's not helpful."

Back in Washington, Trump was waiting for Pence to return. He told his aides he would not head to Georgia that night, for his late election eve rally, until he had a chance to talk with the vice president.

Once he landed at Joint Base Andrews, Pence was informed the president wanted to see him. Short called Meadows and said they would swing by, but he asked for the number of attendees to be small so the discussion would not drift. Meadows agreed.

When Pence stepped into the Oval Office with Short and Jacob, Trump and Eastman were waiting for them.

Trump was fired up. He went on for minutes about Eastman's credentials as one of the nation's best scholars. He made it clear that Pence could act. Eastman spoke up and said it was all sound: Pence could act.

"I've been getting guidance that says I can't," Pence said, glancing at his counselor, Greg Jacob.

"Well, you can," Eastman said. His January 2 memo to Lee had since expanded into a six-page memo. Its gist: Have Pence pause the process in Congress so Republicans in state legislatures could try to hold special sessions and consider sending another slate of electors.

It also still asserted there were dueling slates and offered a scenario where "VP Pence opens the ballots" and "determines on his own which is valid." But Eastman acknowledged those alternative slates remained goals, not something that was legally tangible.

"You really need to listen to John. He's a respected constitutional scholar. Hear him out," Trump said. "Listen. Listen to John."

Marine One was humming steps away outside, ready to go. Jacob and Eastman then quickly agreed to meet, one-on-one, the following day.

Pence thanked Trump for going to Georgia and told him it was important to do so—a trip critical for keeping the Senate. Trump shrugged.

That night in Georgia, Trump tore into the Democrats and indulged conspiracies about the election in a nearly 90-minute speech. He barely mentioned the Senate races and focused on his own hopes of keeping the presidency.

"They're not taking this White House. We're going to fight like hell, I'll tell you right now," Trump told the crowd of thousands packed into grandstands, with cranes hoisting huge American flags.

Lee attended the rally. "Mike Lee is here, too," Trump said. "But I'm a little angry at him today. I just want Mike Lee to listen to what we're talking about, because you know what, we need his vote."

Trump launched a salvo at Pence. His meeting with him hours earlier resolved nothing.

"I hope Mike Pence comes through for us. I have to tell you," Trump said.

"He's a great guy," he added. "Of course, if he doesn't come through, I won't like him quite as much." He slapped the side of the lectern as the crowd laughed.

Mike Lee went to bed that night with a deep feeling of frustration and bewilderment. Was there something he was not seeing? Or was it as strange as it seemed?

Meanwhile, people he did not know continued to call his cell phone, urging him to "stop the steal." The callers were from states where people suggested the courts or state legislatures were about to spring into action.

Was it possible? Lee wondered. He could see plainly the strategy all hinged on Trump lawyer John Eastman's claim that "7 states have transmitted dual slates of electors." He had heard nothing from anyone else. Nothing was in the news. Was there even one state doing it? I've got to find out if this was true, Lee concluded.

Over the next 48 hours, Lee tracked down the phone numbers of elected officials in Georgia, Pennsylvania, Michigan and Wisconsin—and through third parties, he sought out information on Arizona.

They all had Republican legislatures. He talked with their leaders. A U.S. senator could get almost anyone on the phone. Lee made dozens of calls.

Every single person he contacted told him the same: Not a chance you would get a majority in either statehouse of any of these states to say that the election had failed, or to decertify their slate of electors. Not one house chamber in any of these states.

Lee soon grew tired of being told the same thing over and over.

FORTY-THREE

On the evening of January 5, as he waited for Pence to arrive from a coronavirus task force meeting, an aide informed Trump his supporters were gathering near the White House on Freedom Plaza near Pennsylvania Avenue.

Despite the bitter cold, the supporters were cheering loudly and chanting his name. They were waving "Make America Great Again" flags.

When Pence arrived, Trump told him about the thousands of supporters. They love me, he said.

Pence nodded. "Of course, they're here to support you," he said. "They love you, Mr. President.

"But," Pence added, "they also love our Constitution."

Trump grimaced.

That may be, Trump said, but they agree with him regardless: Pence could and should throw Biden's electors out. Make it fair. Take it back.

That is all I want you to do, Mike, Trump said. Let the House decide the election.

Trump was not ready to give up, especially to a man he maligned as "Sleepy Joe."

"What do you think, Mike?" Trump asked.

Pence returned to his mantra: He did not have the authority to do anything other than count the electoral votes.

"Well, what if these people say you do?" Trump asked, gesturing beyond the White House to the crowds outside. Raucous cheering and blasting bullhorns could be heard through the Oval Office windows.

"If these people say you had the power, wouldn't you want to?" Trump asked.

"I wouldn't want any one person to have that authority," Pence said.

"But wouldn't it almost be cool to have that power?" Trump asked.

"No," Pence said. "Look, I've read this, and I don't see a way to do it.

"We've exhausted every option. I've done everything I could and then some to find a way around this. It's simply not possible. My interpretation is: No.

"I've met with all of these people," Pence said, "they're all on the same page. I personally believe these are the limits to what I can do. So, if you have a strategy for the 6th, it really shouldn't involve me because I'm just there to open the envelopes. You should be talking to the House and Senate. Your team should be talking to them about what kind of evidence they're going to present."

"No, no, no!" Trump shouted.

"You don't understand, Mike. You *can* do this. I don't want to be your friend anymore if you don't do this."

"You're not going to be sworn in on the 20th. There is not a scenario in which you can be sworn in on the 20th," Pence said. "We need to figure out how to deal with it, how we want to handle it. How we want to talk about it."

Trump seemed furious. The man who had acceded to Trump's every request, who had never publicly disagreed or criticized him once he became vice president, would not do him this final favor. The power he held over Pence for four years, the loyalty that seemed like an inherent character trait, seemed now to slip away by the second.

Trump's voice grew louder. You are weak. You lack courage.

"You've betrayed us. I made you. You were nothing," Trump said. "Your career is over if you do this."

Pence did not budge.

A Pence adviser, Tom Rose, saw Pence leave the Oval Office. One of Pence's closest friends, Rose later told others that Pence looked chalk white, like someone who had received terrible news at a hospital.

Rose, a conservative Jewish former talk radio host from Indiana, who wore a kippa to work and shared Pence's politics and passion for the Midwest, said his heart sank. He loved Mike Pence. He did not deserve this humiliation.

Pence, who joked to aides he was "at a 9" out of 10 when he was stressed, looked to be at level 15.

"I left it all on the field," Pence told the handful of aides when he arrived back in his West Wing office. "I made my case. I gave it my all in there."

The room remained quiet. There was little to say. As the vice president walked to his motorcade, he told Marc Short he did not waver. He did not break.

Pence ducked into his waiting vehicle.

Once Pence left, Trump opened a door near the Resolute Desk. A rush of cold air blasted the room.

The temperature was around 31 degrees Fahrenheit outside, with the wind making it feel even colder. Trump stood there, still, and listened.

Through the din of police sirens and the whir of a city, he could hear his people. They sounded joyful. He breathed in the cold air and smiled.

Trump left the door open, the muffled soundtrack of excited screams and yells from his supporters filling the room.

Trump called his press secretary, Kayleigh McEnany, and her

deputies into the office. His director of social media and former manager of his golf club in Westchester, New York, Dan Scavino, sat on a couch near the president.

As staffers filed in, some began to shiver. Still, Trump did not close the door. A couple whispered they were freezing as they stood at attention.

The noise outside grew louder, almost like a party.

"Isn't that great?" Trump exclaimed. "Tomorrow is going to be a big day.

"It's so cold and they're out there by the thousands," Trump said.

Judd Deere, Trump's loyal deputy press secretary, spoke up. "They are excited to hear from you, Mr. President," he said.

Another staffer offered they hoped Wednesday was peaceful. Others nodded and said they agreed.

Trump looked over and said, "Yes, but there is a lot of anger out there right now."

Trump went around the room, asking for advice about congressional Republicans. "How do we get them to do the right thing?" he asked.

No one offered an answer that satisfied him.

"Republicans and the RINOs," Republicans in name only, "are weak," Trump fumed.

"They need courage," Trump said. "Courage.

"The vice president, the members of Congress, all of them should do the right thing!" Trump said. He warned he would support primary challenges to those in Congress who supported Biden's certification.

Trump repeated his question: "How do we get them to do the right thing?" He asked for suggestions on what he could tweet, and Scavino had his laptop open, ready to type.

Those there looked awkwardly at each other, some with hands stuffed in their pockets for warmth. A few offered their encouragement.

McEnany turned to her team and asked if they would like to take a picture with the president. They scooted over toward him, stood, and smiled as a picture was taken.

Trump later called Senator Ted Cruz of Texas. He wanted to hear the latest. Were Republicans going to come through and object to everything?

Cruz and ten other Senate Republicans were pushing for a congressional commission to investigate the election. It was his rationale for supporting the objection to the electoral count. Arizona, Pennsylvania, and Georgia were expected to come up the next day. But Cruz had not planned to offer wholesale objections to every state's count.

You need to object to all the states that could be raised by the House, Trump said.

"Mr. President, my focus is on keeping this group of eleven together and the consensus of the group is not to do that."

Trump asked, do you object to one or two then?

Cruz said his group would object to the first state brought up, Arizona, and have a debate over his proposed commission as part of that process.

Trump was unhappy hearing this plan. Object anyway, he said. He was not interested in Cruz's commission. He wanted aggression, objection to all the states that come up.

No, Cruz said.

Marc Short stayed at the White House until around 10 p.m. Pence had to pull himself together for a scheduled dinner, with corporate CEOs and supporters at the Naval Observatory. He was supposed to be there at 6:30 p.m., but he was nearly an hour late.

Obst was with Second Lady Karen Pence, entertaining the guests as they waited for the vice president to arrive. Obst was also fielding text messages from Giuliani associate Boris Epshteyn, a close friend of Eric Trump, who was urging Obst to help him work Pence.

Next to Freedom Plaza, upstairs in a suite at the famed Willard Hotel, Epshteyn was with Rudy Giuliani and Steve Bannon, prodding Republicans in Congress by phone to join forces with Trump on January 6 and block Biden's certification.

As midnight approached, crowds outside were becoming rowdier. Police officers clashed with far-right militia-type activists and the so-called Proud Boys who roamed the otherwise empty streets of the capital. Food debris piled to the brim of trash cans. Metropolitan Police arrested five people on assault and weapons possession charges.

People in the streets were yelling, delighted and almost euphoric about Trump possibly taking back the election on Wednesday. They waited to see Giuliani and other Trump World stars emerge from the Willard. They nodded warmly at others in red hats, a movement in total solidarity.

Epshteyn told Obst that Giuliani would be happy to come over to Pence's residence and have a discussion. For Obst, the suggestion felt straight out of a bad mafia movie.

When Pence arrived home, he looked exhausted. The former local radio and television personality put on a smile and launched into a warm welcome and thanked the wealthy executives for their support. He did not mention the events of the coming day. He stuck to happy talk.

Obst approached as the dinner ended.

"You good?"

"I'm good," Pence said. "I'm good."

Late Tuesday evening, January 5, as word dripped out in the press that Pence was holding, Trump directed his campaign to issue a statement claiming that he and Pence were in "total agreement that the Vice President has the power to act."

Short was stunned. The president had just issued a statement speaking on the vice president's behalf without consulting with the vice president or his office. It also asserted the exact opposite of Pence's position.

Short called Jason Miller, who was with Bannon and Giuliani at the Willard.

"This breaks protocol," Short said tersely.

Miller refused to retract a word.

"The vice president has the ability to do this, he needs to be loyal," Miller said.

Trump soon called Giuliani, and then called Steve Bannon, who was also at the Willard with the former New York City mayor. Trump brought up his meeting with Pence. He said the vice president's whole demeanor had changed—Pence was not the same man he had long known.

"He was very arrogant," Trump said.

Bannon agreed. Trump's four words were sobering. It was Trump explaining away a deal gone bad. Pence was not going to break. If Mike Pence was arrogant, that meant Trump's push was dead.

"Very arrogant," Trump repeated.

Trump kept tweeting into the night.

At 1:00 a.m., the president tweeted: "If Vice President @Mike_Pence comes through for us, we will win the Presidency. Many States want to decertify the mistake they made in certifying incorrect & even fraudulent numbers in a process NOT approved by their State Legislatures (which it must be). Mike can send it back!"

Trump had promised a "wild" protest on January 6, and in the weeks leading up to the certification, the Pentagon and law enforcement agencies began looking for any hints of violence. The FBI created a unit to monitor intelligence reports.

Twitter and social media posts lit up with virulence: I'm going to kill this person. Shoot this person. Hang this guy. Blow this up. The FBI tracked and followed up the threats, but none seemed credible. Welcome to America, 2021.

Ken Rapuano, the Pentagon civilian coordinating security for the day, checked in regularly with more than a dozen police and security units in the Washington area with interagency conference calls.

He asked, does anyone need any National Guard? A crowd of 10 to 20 thousand was expected, not small but also not huge. The mantra in response: We have it under control. The representatives maintained they handled crowds of that size all the time. Only the Washington, D.C., Metropolitan Police asked for a small supplement of 340 National Guard soldiers, mostly to man traffic points around the Ellipse and the White House.

Their uniform would be commensurate with their duties: orange vests and soft caps. No helmets, no riot gear, no weapons. A small, 40-person quick reaction force, called QRF, also was called up, as was a contingency of Army and Air National Guard F-16 mechanics. Not exactly SWAT teams.

The message was blunt: No repeat of the use of force at Lafayette Square. No troops with guns. No militarization. No helicopter or satellite or radar operations.

"To be clear," Washington, D.C., Mayor Muriel Bowser wrote January 5 to Acting Attorney General Jeffrey Rosen and top Pentagon officials, "the District of Columbia is not requesting other federal law enforcement personnel and discourages any additional deployment without immediate notification to, and consultation with" the Metropolitan Police Department.

But as January 6 neared, ominous signs appeared, including a potential mini version of the September 11 terrorist attack. The

FBI received a report of a potential air threat to the national capital region by a privately owned, fixed wing aircraft.

General Milley asked Christopher Miller, the acting defense secretary, to order a snap NOBLE EAGLE exercise, a flight training exercise featuring fighter jets and flyovers that was developed after September 11 to practice responses to any similar attack.

Be ready for anything, Milley said. Have the practice run, NOBLE EAGLE, with F-16s and other air defenses. "Given the intel, we ought to just shake out the cobwebs here."

Milley told Miller he had the authority to shoot down an aircraft threatening the Washington region. And if Miller was unavailable, the generals at the North American Aerospace Defense Command had the authority to shoot.

FORTY-FOUR

Trump woke up early on January 6, tweeting and demanding Pence reject the electoral votes.

"All Mike Pence has to do is send them back to the States, AND WE WIN," Trump tweeted at 8:17 a.m. "Do it Mike, this is a time for extreme courage!"

Marc Short and Greg Jacob joined Pence that morning at 9 a.m. to finalize the letter.

Jacob had worked on the letter for weeks. A former partner in O'Melveny & Myers's Washington office, he was a Federalist Society member and steeped in conservative legal doctrine.

Early in the process, Jacob had reached out to conservative lawyer John Yoo at the University of California, Berkeley, where he taught. Yoo had sterling credentials in conservative legal circles. An alum of George W. Bush's Justice Department, he was the author of the "torture memos," which provided a legal basis for torturing detainees in the war on terror and had also been a Supreme Court law clerk for Justice Clarence Thomas.

"My view is that Vice President Pence has no discretion anymore. It's not something to worry about or even think about," Yoo told Jacob. "I feel bad for your boss because he's going to have an angry employer" in Trump.

Jacob kept seeking out advice. He called Richard Cullen, a former United States attorney in Virginia, who had signed on as Pence's personal lawyer in 2017 during the probes into Russian election interference. He agreed with Yoo.

At dawn on January 6, Cullen called J. Michael Luttig, a retired former federal judge popular on the right. Years ago, Luttig had hired John Eastman as his law clerk. His opinion could be a powerful tool for the vice president.

"Today is the day," Cullen said. "I've been asked to ask you, 'Is there any way you can help?' "

"When does he need something?" Luttig asked.

"Immediately," Cullen said.

"You can tell the vice president that I believe he has to certify the Electoral College vote today," Luttig said. He then started to type out a statement on his iPhone, sitting in his den in the dark.

Luttig sent it to Cullen, and it went straight into Pence's letter.

Cabinet officers held a Principals Meeting without President Trump for 30 minutes at 9:30 a.m. on January 6. New and sensitive intelligence reporting from overseas that morning seemed to be worrisome, but once it was run down, tensions eased in the room.

Cabinet members were briefed on Trump's scheduled rally at the Ellipse. Traffic points to control the crowds were set up. The Guard, in orange vests and no helmets, would augment the Metropolitan Police.

Milley said he expected a routine day, at least in terms of security threats. Trump had held countless rallies that were rowdy, but never crises.

President Trump called Pence around 10 a.m. on January 6 as Pence met with Short and Jacob. Pence excused himself to take the call upstairs, alone.

"I'm heading to the Capitol soon," Pence told Trump. "I told you I'd sleep on it, I'd take a look with my team. We'll hear any objections and evidence. But when I go to the Capitol, I'll do my job."

"Mike, this is not right!" Trump said, calling from the Oval Office. "Mike, you can do this. I'm counting on you to do it. If you don't do it, I picked the wrong man four years ago."

As Trump kept pushing Pence, the president's body man, Nick Luna, entered and handed the president a note. They were ready for him at the rally outside. His people were waiting.

"You're going to wimp out!" Trump said. His anger was visible to others in the Oval Office, including his daughter Ivanka.

She turned to Keith Kellogg.

"Mike Pence is a good man," Ivanka Trump said to Kellogg.

"I know that," Kellogg said.

He later worked hard to make sure Ivanka's sympathy for Pence was widely reported.

Before Trump took the stage on January 6, Giuliani used militaristic language in his own rally remarks.

"Let's have trial by combat," he said, as the crowd hooted their approval.

They were bundled up in heavy coats, but ecstatic. Homemade signs. Red Trump caps. "Save America March" read the screens onstage. Trump's family members and aides were gathered backstage, giddy.

"This is incredible," President Trump said shortly before noon, as he looked out at thousands.

"Media will not show the magnitude of this crowd," Trump said. "Turn your cameras please and show what's really happening out here because these people are not going to take it any longer. They're not going to take it any longer."

Like Giuliani, he was all fight.

"You'll never take back our country with weakness. You have

to show strength and you have to be strong," he said. "We have come to demand that Congress do the right thing and only count the electors who have been lawfully slated, lawfully slated.

"I know that everyone here will soon be marching over to the Capitol building to peacefully and patriotically make your voices heard."

Just before 1 p.m., Trump made one last try for Pence to submit and do his bidding.

"Mike Pence, I hope you're going to stand up for the good of our Constitution and for the good of our country. And if you're not, I'm going to be very disappointed in you. I will tell you right now. I'm not hearing good stories."

Pence released his two-page letter shortly before 1 p.m., and then tweeted it at 1:02 p.m. He and his team did not share it with Meadows or White House counsel Pat Cipollone beforehand.

"As a student of history who loves the Constitution and reveres its Framers, I do not believe that the Founders of our country intended to invest the Vice President with unilateral authority to decide which electoral votes should be counted during the Joint Session of Congress, and no Vice President in American history has ever asserted such authority," Pence wrote.

The letter finished with a short oath: "So Help Me God."

Following Trump's hour-long speech, thousands of attendees took his advice. They marched down Pennsylvania Avenue toward the Capitol, and when they arrived, they found small groups of Capitol Police officers gathered near waist-height barriers and bike-rack-like fencing.

They jumped over the racks and surged closer and closer to the Capitol, despite pleas from the officers.

By 1:30 p.m., parts of the crowd had become a mob, pounding on the doors and demanding entry. At 1:50 p.m., Robert Glover, the Metropolitan Police's on-scene commander, declared a riot. Possible pipe bombs had just been found nearby.

Shortly after 2 p.m., windows at the Capitol began to shatter. They were in. Many were looking for Mike Pence. "Hang Mike Pence!" they chanted as they roamed the halls. "Bring out Mike Pence! Where is Pence? Find him!" Outside, a makeshift gallows had been erected.

When Capitol Police approached Speaker Pelosi in the House chamber, she initially dismissed their attempt to pull her away. She was in charge. She was prepared to sit through a long afternoon of listening to Republican gripes. It would be embarrassing for the nation, political theater, but it was her duty to endure it.

The building has been breached, they told her. We need to get you out of here.

"No, I want to be here."

"You have to leave."

"No, I'm not leaving."

"No, you must leave."

She finally agreed.

Nearby, inside the House chamber, Capitol Police officers were leaning down and whispering the same to Jim Clyburn. He couldn't believe it. He flashed a dubious look at his agents: Wasn't the House floor supposed to be the safest place in America?

Surrounding her in a protective hive, Pelosi's security detail rushed her off the floor. So did Clyburn's detail, which whisked him out a door where Capitol rioter and Air Force veteran Ashli Babbitt would soon be shot and killed by a police officer. They hustled Clyburn down more steps. He had been in Congress since 1993 and was the third-ranking House member, but he had never known this area existed. They helped him into his SUV, his "truck," as he called it.

"We can't take you home," an agent told him. "We've been instructed to take you to this undisclosed location."

After a five-minute drive, Pelosi and Clyburn, traveling separately, arrived at Fort Lesley J. McNair, a small, secure U.S. Army post a few blocks from the Washington Nationals' baseball stadium. A caravan of black vehicles. It was raining. They stepped out and went inside.

Pelosi thought of her colleagues and staff—and her late father, who had served in the House decades ago representing Baltimore. He had watched Winston Churchill speak in the chamber. She knew he would have been horrified by the scene. It was un-American.

She called her staff. They were hiding and crouched under tables. They barricaded the door and turned out the lights and were silent in the dark.

Rioters eventually made their way into her office, stealing her papers and other personal items. They ransacked her second-floor workspace, gleefully taking pictures on their phones and putting their feet on her desk.

"Where's the speaker?" some screamed. "Find her!"

Clyburn called his staff. They were in his private office with heavy furniture pushed in front of the door. There are people attempting to force themselves into the office, the terrified aides said.

Clyburn was alarmed. Was he being targeted? Was this an inside job? His private office was all but unmarked. Why hadn't the rioters gone to his public office that had his name plate on the door? How do they know this location?

The rioters broke more windows and a mirror. Shards of glass littered the floor.

"This was an act of violence," Pelosi told others at McNair. "Not just troublemakers picketing. An act of violence."

McConnell was listening to Senator James Lankford of Oklahoma speak when he noticed security piling into the Senate chamber. Within moments, an agent with an assault rifle was next to him. He, too, headed to McNair.

McConnell called Milley.

"We need the Guard in. Now," he said.

He spoke with Pence, who also had been guided out of the Senate chamber.

"We are looking for help. We need help in securing the building," McConnell said, "and we need to get these clowns out of the place."

McConnell found the law enforcement response disturbingly slow.

Meadows called McConnell several times, promising to be helpful, and gave the Department of Defense the leader's cell phone number so McConnell could be in direct contact.

At McNair, McConnell instructed his chief of staff, Sharon Soderstrom, to find the Democrats. Democrats and Republicans were in separate areas. He was worried that the rattled Capitol Police might try to delay their return to the Capitol after it was cleared.

"Find out where they are and tell them no matter what," McConnell said. "We are coming in tonight. I want to do it in prime time, so the country sees us back and we're going to finish the counting of the electoral votes.

"It's important that the public, in prime time, know the assault had failed," he said.

McConnell had grown up in the Capitol. In the summer of 1964, he interned in the Senate. He loved the place. This was his office. His home.

FORTY-FIVE

Pence, who arrived at the Capitol wearing a navy blue mask, had been presiding over the joint session of Congress when he was removed from the Senate floor at 2:13 p.m. by Secret Service agents. They moved him into the vice presidential office near the Senate on the second floor, where he was joined by his wife, Karen, and his daughter, Charlotte, who had come with him to the Capitol.

As word came that rioters were swarming the building and running through the hallways toward the Senate chamber, Tim Giebels, one of the Secret Service agents on his detail that day, told him he needed to move to a secure location downstairs, near the vice president's motorcade. Once there, Giebels kept hearing more updates. The rioters were everywhere in the Capitol. No one was in control.

"I'm not leaving," Pence said. He knew the Secret Service would whisk him away if he stepped inside his vehicle. It would look like he was fleeing.

"We've got to go now!" Giebels said, and suggested Pence sit in the vehicle.

"I'm not getting in," Pence said. He said he would stand there and make calls with the motorcade humming, ready to go if the crisis worsened.

Pence spoke by phone with McConnell and other leaders who said they needed the National Guard to move faster. The Capitol needed to be secured. McConnell asked, where were the troops?

"I will call them and call you back," Pence said.

Keith Kellogg, in the West Wing as the riot unfolded, noticed the president watching television in his private dining room next to the Oval Office.

Images of the Capitol rioters were beginning to appear on the screen. They were not just wandering around inside the building. They were climbing walls, clashing with police, and screaming threats in the marble hallways. This was no longer a protest. It was being called an insurrection by some lawmakers and others there.

Holy shit, Kellogg thought. *What is happening?*

As rioters stormed throughout the Capitol, many of them were checking their phones, and keeping tabs on Trump. The crowds inside were swelling. More windows were broken.

Trump tweeted at 2:24 p.m. He slammed Pence for not having "the courage to do what should have been done to protect our Country and our Constitution."

Kellogg went to see Trump in the president's dining room. He had just traded notes with Pence's team at the Capitol.

"Sir, the vice president is secure," Kellogg told Trump.

"Where's Mike?" Trump asked.

"The Secret Service has him. They're down in the basement. They're okay and he's not going to get in the vehicle.

"He knows," Kellogg said, "that if they put your ass in the vehicle, they're going to take you somewhere.

"Mr. President," he added, "you really should do a tweet." On Capitol Hill, "nobody's carrying a TV on their shoulder. You need to get a tweet out real quick, help control the crowd up there. This is out of control.

"They're not going to be able to control this. Sir, they're not prepared for it. Once a mob starts turning like that, you've lost it," he said.

"Yeah," Trump said.

Trump blinked and kept watching television.

Kellogg looked around and realized the West Wing was nearly empty. Meadows was in his office, but Trump was essentially alone. National Security Adviser Robert O'Brien was in Florida. Kushner was not there.

Kellogg went to find Ivanka Trump.

Police officers had weapons drawn inside the House of Representatives, pointed at the doors as protesters banged on the heavy wood, screaming loudly.

Congressman Joe Neguse, a 36-year-old Democrat from Colorado, texted his wife, Andrea. She told him the mob was in Statuary Hall, steps way. He told her he loved her, loved their daughter, everything would be fine.

But Neguse and others around him, crouched on the floor, were not so sure. The chamber was in lockdown. Police told lawmakers to retrieve gas masks and shouted out instructions. Get down. Masks on!

As members opened the gas mask packages, they made a blaring noise. A ringing. A cacophony of rings and yelling filled the House chamber.

"Prepare to take cover!"

Neguse could hear the rioters banging on the doors.

Officers swept over to several groups of House members. Head out! Follow us!

They were evacuated to a secure location.

Paul Ryan, the former House speaker, was alone at his home office in the Washington area. His television was on. He had a pile of work on his desk. These days, he was on boards, teaching. Zoom calls.

He eyed the screen. A riot? At the Capitol? He turned up the volume. He immediately recognized the faces of the Capitol Police officers. Oh my God, he thought. I know these guys. Not just from his former detail, but from his decades as a staffer turned congressman, beginning in 1992 and ending in 2018.

He saw a bearded rioter take a plexiglass police shield and hoist it in the air, then smash it into a window of the Capitol. Glass shattered. Another smash. More shards. Another smash. The window was now broken open. Rioters roared menacingly and jumped up, then climbed inside.

I assumed Trump's fight was an act, Ryan thought. Trump would have his rally and tell his supporters he didn't lose. It would be post-election spin. I didn't think it would go this far.

But it was happening. He kept seeing the faces of cops he knew. It was hard to absorb. He called up friends who were House members and staffers. Some of them told him they were fending off rioters in stairwells. Statuary Hall, which he crossed ten times a day as speaker, was being overrun.

"I hope you're safe," Ryan told them. He said he felt guilty about not being there.

"Donald Trump fomented this, he revved them up," Ryan angrily told several friends. "He sent them up there. He filled their heads with this. He chose to believe crackpot advisers. He could have listened to Pat Cipollone or Bill Barr but listens to Rudy Giuliani."

Ryan later sat down at his computer. He typed out an email to a small group of Capitol Police officers who were part of his security detail. He said he and his wife, Janna, "were sickened and distraught" over the violence toward officers and the desecration of the Capitol.

Ryan looked up at the television again and watched the scene. He rubbed his eyes. My God, he said, catching himself by surprise.

The rioters kept shouting, climbing. Police officers were being hit with metal poles.

Ryan began to bawl.

He called his assistant and told her to cancel his meetings for the rest of the day. "I don't have the bandwidth for anything else," he said.

"Where is the president?"

House Minority Leader Kevin McCarthy was calling into the White House, asking aides to connect him with the president.

McCarthy's office on the second floor of the Capitol was being vandalized. His office windows were shattered. His detail had rushed him out.

Trump came on the line.

"You got to get out and tell these people to stop. I am out of the Capitol. We've been run over," McCarthy said. He was intense. "Someone just got shot."

McCarthy had heard a shot fired. At 2:44 p.m., Air Force veteran Ashli Babbitt was shot and killed by a police officer inside the Capitol as she and others tried to breach a door near lawmakers.

"I'll put a tweet out," Trump said.

"I've never seen anything like this," McCarthy said. "You've got to tell them to stop. You've got to get them out of here. Get them out of here. Now."

Trump did not seem to grasp the gravity of the situation. He never asked about McCarthy's safety. And one remark stood out: *"Well, Kevin, I guess these people are more upset about the election than you are."*

Kellogg found Ivanka Trump. I need you to go talk to your dad about the riot at the Capitol, he said. She could reach her father in ways others could not. She could talk to him as a daughter.

Ivanka went into the Oval. When she came out a few minutes later, Kellogg immediately recognized the look on her face. He had seen it with his own daughter. She had just had a tough conversation.

For weeks, Ivanka Trump and her husband, Jared Kushner, had watched as Trump indulged in the legal theories and congressional plots offered by his allies. They had used a light touch with Trump, with Kushner telling aides that it was Trump's presidency, and he alone should be the one to decide how to finish it.

Kushner did not want to be the point person for an intervention. He told others to respect Trump and give him space. Kushner had traveled to the Middle East in November, and again in late December.

As Kellogg and others watched, Ivanka went in two more times to see her father.

"Let this thing go," she told him.

"Let it go," she said.

Trump never called Pence that day.

Marc Short, who was with Pence, later called Meadows to provide a clipped status report.

"The vice president is working with the leadership to make sure we get back to vote," Short said.

"Probably the right thing to do," Meadows said. "Anything else we can do for you?"

Short was deeply frustrated with Meadows. "Anything else we can do for you?" Was he kidding? Where was the urgency?

At 3:13 p.m., Trump sent out a tweet: "I am asking for everyone at the U.S. Capitol to remain peaceful. No violence! Remember, WE are the Party of Law & Order—respect the Law and our great men and women in Blue. Thank you!"

Inside the White House press office, Trump adviser Sarah

Matthews cringed. She and other Trump aides had been glued to their computers, knowing the president was down the hall being told to tweet. But when she read it, she told colleagues his tweet would do little to stop the riot. It was a gentle wave-off, not a demand.

"The situation is out of control," Matthews said. She walked down to the lower press office, closer to the briefing room. "This is really bad."

Congresswoman Elissa Slotkin, a 44-year-old Michigan Democrat, reached Chairman Milley by phone at 3:29 p.m. Before her election to Congress, Slotkin had been a CIA analyst who worked in Iraq for three tours and later been a top Pentagon official during the Obama years.

Slotkin knew Milley well. They had a bond of trust, of familiarity.

"Mark, you need to get the Guard down here," she said sharply. She was agitated and alert. Baghdad mode. The Capitol was under siege, and she and her congressional colleagues were hiding in their offices.

"I know it," Milley said. "We're working on it."

"I know I was yelling at you for what happened in June," Slotkin said, referring to the Lafayette Square episode. "But now, we need you and we need you here now. And we need you here with the military. And get everything you can down here right now."

"Elissa, I get it."

"I know how hypocritical this sounds," she said. She had decried the military's involvement with the Floyd protests in Lafayette Square.

"You're right," Milley said. "It does a little bit. But we'll be there."

"You're in a ridiculous spot," she said.

"Congresswoman, we're going to get there with as much stuff as we can as fast as we can."

"Is it true Trump said no?" Slotkin asked. Had the president refused to send in the National Guard? That possibility was flying around Capitol Hill.

"I purposely did not go to Trump," Milley told her. "I went to Pence. I informed Pence we were sending the Guard. Pence welcomed that."

"It was smart you didn't involve Trump," Slotkin said. "Good on you for not involving Trump."

"I don't think Trump would necessarily say no," Milley said.

"Why not?" Slotkin asked.

Milley explained that several days earlier, at an unrelated national security meeting, he had told Trump they were going to be sending some Guard to support the Capitol Police and Washington, D.C., police on January 6. And Trump had been supportive saying, "Good, good, do what you need to do."

But Milley told Slotkin, "I think he wanted this. I think that he likes this. I think that he wants that chaos. He wants his supporters to be fighting to the bitter end."

Milley then quickly qualified that judgment by adding, "I don't know."

Biden shelved plans to talk about the economy that day and put together a short speech. He took the stage at his transition site in Wilmington at 4:05 p.m. Huge blue screens were behind him, digitally projecting "Office of the President Elect" in white letters. His voice was hushed, almost a whisper, as he began to speak.

"At this hour, our democracy is under unprecedented assault," he said, "unlike anything we've seen in modern times. An assault on the citadel of liberty, the Capitol itself.

"This is not dissent. It's disorder." His voice began to rise, angry. "It's chaos. It borders on sedition."

Biden pleaded with Trump to "go on national television now" and "fulfill his oath and defend the Constitution and demand an end to this siege."

After he finished, he turned and walked toward the backstage area, away from the bright lights shining on his lectern. A reporter shouted, "Are you concerned about your inauguration, sir?" Another reporter yelled out, "Have you spoken to McConnell today?"

Standing in the shadows near the back, Biden turned and raised his right hand to make a point. His face was barely visible on screen. His voice was loud.

"I am not concerned about my safety, security, or the inauguration," he said. "The American people are going to stand up. Now." He paused.

"Enough is enough is enough!" Biden said, seeming to punch the air, his binder in hand. He turned around again, dipped his head, and left the room.

FORTY-SIX

Shortly after 4 p.m., as the rioters kept coming inside the Capitol and overwhelming the Capitol police force, Pence called Christopher Miller, the acting defense secretary, and said, "Clear the Capitol."

Miller assured Pence he was on it and things were moving.

At the White House, Kellogg stayed close to the president, who remained inside the Oval. Meadows hovered nearby.

Deputy National Security Adviser Matthew Pottinger, a former journalist who was a key adviser to Trump on China and the pandemic, came by.

Meadows unloaded on Pottinger. The National Guard was moving too slowly.

"God dammit," Meadows said. He said he had told Miller to hurry up. "Where's the Guard?"

Pottinger, who was in touch with contacts at the Pentagon and at related agencies, said Miller was wary of aggressively using the Guard to put down the riot. It seemed too militarized to Miller, too in-your-face.

Meadows did not want to hear the excuse.

I told him to get the Guard moving. Get out there and get it done, Meadows said. He told Pottinger to call Miller and push him.

Kellogg tried to pitch in, and called Miller's chief of staff, Kash Patel.

"What the hell are you guys doing?" Kellogg asked him. "Meadows is furious that the Guard is not moving."

"Oh, they're moving now, they're moving now," Patel said.

Anthony Ornato, a Secret Service official who had become Trump's White House chief of operations, reminded Kellogg about another option.

"We've got 2,000 marshals that we can call up right now and put them out there," Ornato said.

"That's probably pretty smart, put them out there, too," Kellogg said.

More and more people kept coming by the Oval Office. Damage control ideas were flying. Type out more tweets. Do a video. Hold a news conference.

"That's probably the dumbest thing he could do right now," Kellogg said. "If you go to a news conference that means somebody will ask more questions and you've got no control of it. You make sure you control the situation."

Meadows and Kellogg, and other aides, went in to see the president. They decided on a video. It was soon taped outside the White House, Trump speaking to a single camera. No apologies, no concession. It posted at 4:17 p.m.

"This was a fraudulent election, but we can't play into the hands of these people," Trump said. "We have to have peace. So go home. We love you. You're very special."

Seven minutes later, the U.S. Marshals Service issued a tweet: "The U.S. Marshals Service is joining with other law enforcement agencies in supporting the U.S. Capitol Police during operations in Washington, D.C."

In a cavernous room inside one of the Senate office buildings, senators in both parties were being told to stay put, with Capitol Police guarding the door. There was little food and senators grumbled they were hungry. As they scrolled through updates on their phones, and broke into small groups, tensions flared.

Senator Sherrod Brown of Ohio, a Democrat, at one point told Lindsey Graham to shut up.

No one spoke to Senator Hawley, who many of them blamed for instigating the riot by announcing his opposition to the certification a week earlier.

A photo of Hawley, his fist raised and clenched outside the Capitol, as if in solidarity with the Trump supporters, was ricocheting across the internet. He was becoming the face of Trump's bloc in the Senate.

Eventually, senators watched Senator Cruz walk over to Hawley. "What are you going to do?" Cruz asked.

Nearly a dozen Senate Republicans had been planning to object to Arizona's electoral vote. But with the riot ongoing, some GOP senators, including defeated Georgia senator Kelly Loeffler, were ready to just end the drama and approve the certification of Biden's victory.

McConnell told several senators he wanted to move faster. Reconvene and be done with Arizona, move on. But he knew if Hawley continued, and objected to Pennsylvania's count, moving fast would be impossible. According to the Senate rules, any objection would trigger more debate.

Hawley said little to Cruz and to Senator Roy Blunt, his fellow Missouri Republican, who also approached him and asked for a status update.

Eventually, even with the carnage and push from some colleagues to stand down, Hawley decided he would keep his objection to both Arizona and Pennsylvania. He would remain in lockstep with Trump.

When told of Hawley's decision, many of his Republican colleagues groaned. What they saw as a political pageant, all for a president who could not accept defeat, was now going to go past midnight. Other Republicans would surely stick with Hawley, fearful of being seen as out of step with Trump's voters.

As evening neared, Trump kept tweeting as police and troops worked to secure the Capitol. Violent militia extremists and white supremacists, later identified by the FBI, broke glass and ripped signs as they went through the hallways. Office equipment was strewn across floors. Colorful flags reading "TRUMP" and "AMERICA FIRST" were raised next to busts of vice presidents near the Senate.

National Guard troops, which had arrived, patrolled the premises, clearing people out as police made arrests. There were screams. Defiant chants.

"These are the things and events that happen when a sacred landslide election victory is so unceremoniously & viciously stripped away from great patriots who have been badly & unfairly treated for so long," Trump tweeted at 6:01 p.m. "Go home with love & in peace. Remember this day forever!"

Shortly after 8 p.m., the Senate returned to its chamber.

Senator Tim Scott of South Carolina, the Senate's lone Black Republican, approached Pence.

"I feel in a moment like this, I wish I could pray," Scott said.

"Well, go ahead," Pence said. "Let's do it." Senator Steve Daines of Montana, another Republican, joined them.

When Arizona came up for a vote, 93 senators rejected the objections of Hawley and five others—Cruz, plus Senators Cindy Hyde-Smith of Mississippi, Tommy Tuberville of Alabama, Roger Marshall of Kansas, and John Kennedy of Louisiana.

Senator Loeffler did not join them.

"When I arrived in Washington this morning, I fully intended to object to the certification of the electoral votes," she said, glancing down. "However, the events that have transpired today have forced me to reconsider and I cannot now, in good conscience, object."

But Hawley still objected to Pennsylvania's electoral votes, prompting hours of additional debate. Senator Romney's death stare at Hawley, while sitting behind the 41-year-old senator, caught the eye of millions watching the broadcast of the proceedings.

As the debate continued, senators took the floor. Many looked exhausted, rumpled.

Senator Mike Lee was solemn, but firm. "We each have to remember that we have sworn an oath to uphold, protect, and defend this document," Lee said, holding up a copy of the Constitution.

"The Vice President of the United States shall open the ballots and the votes shall then be counted. It is those words that confine, define and constrain every scrap of authority that we have in this process. Our job is to open and then count. That's it. That's all there is.

"I have spent an enormous amount of time reaching out to state government officials in those states, but in none of the contested states—no, not even one—did I discover any indication that there was any chance that any state legislature, or secretary of state, or governor or lieutenant governor, that had any intention to alter the slate of electors."

"Our job is to convene, to open the ballots, and to count them. That's it."

Lindsey Graham's turn on the floor was a stream of consciousness of personal distress and political realism.

"Trump and I, we've had a hell of a journey. I hate it to end this way. Oh my God, I hate it. From my point of view, he's been a consequential president, but today, first thing that you'll see" in his obituary. January 6 would be etched forever into Trump's legacy.

"All I can say is, 'Count me out,'" Graham said. "Enough is enough.

"They said there's 66,000 people in Georgia under 18 voted. How many people believe that? I asked, 'Give me ten,' and they had one. They said 8,000 felons in prison in Arizona voted. 'Give me 10.' I hadn't gotten one.

"We've got to end it," he said.

"Mike, Mr. Vice President," he added, "just hang in there.

"You got a son who flies F-35s. You've got a son-in-law who flies F-18s. They're out there flying so that we get it right here.

"Joe Biden, I've traveled the world with Joe. I hoped he lost. I prayed he would lose. He won."

As with Arizona, the Senate rejected the objection to Pennsylvania's electoral votes, this time with a 92 to 7 vote. The House rejection on Pennsylvania was 282 to 138.

Shortly after 3:40 a.m. on Thursday, January 7, Pence announced that Biden had been certified the winner.

Pence headed out to his motorcade. Short texted the vice president: "2 Timothy 4:7."

Pence knew it well.

"I have fought a good fight, I have finished my course, I have kept the faith," the verse reads in the King James Bible.

FORTY-SEVEN

Pelosi and Schumer jointly called Pence the morning of January 7 to urge him to invoke the 25th Amendment, which allows for "the Vice President and a majority of either the principal officers of the executive departments" to issue a declaration to Congress that "the President is unable to discharge the powers and duties of his office." Such action would enable the vice president to "immediately assume the powers and duties of the office as Acting President."

"I don't think he's coming to the phone. Somebody's not telling him," Pelosi told her aides. She thought his likely unwillingness to talk punctuated his weakness.

Pence did not take the call. Short instead called Schumer's chief of staff, Michael Lynch, to ask why they were calling. Short wanted to insulate Pence from any attempt to remove Trump from office.

"What's the context here? How can I be helpful?" Short asked Lynch as the leaders of congressional Democrats remained on hold.

"They kept us on hold for 25 minutes and then said the vice president wouldn't come on the phone," Schumer said later.

"If the VP takes the call, then they go to the sticks," Short told colleagues, referring to the microphones inside the Capitol, "and say we've spoken with the vice president about invoking the 25th, putting the VP in an incredibly awkward position."

Pence never considered resigning or invoking the 25th Amendment to remove Trump from office. Greg Jacob advised him that the 25th Amendment was designed to be used if a president was incapacitated and this situation, however bad, did not meet that criterion. Pence agreed.

Pence worked the entire day from his residence and did not go to the White House. He did not speak with Trump, who was facing resignation calls from some Republicans and even the conservative editorial board of *The Wall Street Journal*.

Trump's secretary of transportation, Elaine Chao, the wife of Mitch McConnell, resigned, saying she was "deeply troubled" by the events of January 6. Barr said in a statement that Trump orchestrated a "mob to pressure Congress" and called his conduct a "betrayal of his office and supporters."

Later Thursday, Pence called his lawyer, Richard Cullen, and thanked him for his guidance. He said he was sitting at the residence with Mrs. Pence.

"What was it like?" Cullen asked.

Cullen could hear Pence turn to his wife. "Honey, were we scared?" He could not hear her answer.

"I'm praying for the president," Pence said.*

Graham saw that revenge was a very hard thing for Trump to give up. For Trump's sake, and everyone's, Graham hoped the difference with Pence would not keep consuming the president.

Later, at the airport, Graham was shouted at and trailed by Trump supporters. "Traitor! Traitor!" they screamed at Graham as he walked through the terminal, staring down at his phone.

"Did you take an oath?" one man shouted.

"I did," Graham said.

---

* See Prologue for more on Milley's role on January 8, 2021, pages xiii-xxviii.

“I have to speak out on this,” Biden told Mike Donilon in August 2017 as Biden watched television reports of the white supremacist march in Charlottesville, Virginia. “This is different. This is darker. It is more dangerous. This is really a fundamental threat to the country.” Weeks later, Biden published an article in *The Atlantic* with the headline, “We Are Living Through a Battle for the Soul of This Nation.” It became the theme of his eventual campaign.

“Look, you’ve got to run on who you are,” Mike Donilon, pictured left, told Biden in early 2019, as Biden contemplated launching a third presidential campaign. “And you try to change it, you may as well go home. Don’t bother.” For decades, “Mike D.,” as Biden calls him, has been Biden’s confidant, wordsmith, and political strategist, who helped forge the concept of “soul” at the heart of Biden’s 2020 campaign. Donilon, Ron Klain, pictured center, and Anita Dunn, right, are key members of Biden’s inner circle.

"You're not in the foxhole with me!" Trump screamed in an August 2017 phone call with House Speaker Paul Ryan. The Wisconsin Republican had just assailed Trump for blaming "both sides" of protesters for the white supremacist march in Charlottesville. Ryan shot back, "Are you finished? May I have some time now? You're the president of the United States. You have a moral obligation to get this right and not declare there is a moral equivalency here."

"Do you know why [Rex] Tillerson was able to say he didn't call the president a 'moron'?" Senate Majority Leader Mitch McConnell would dryly ask his Republican colleagues in his Kentucky drawl about the former Trump secretary of state. "Because he called him a 'fucking moron.' "

"Mr. President, I think you're on a trajectory to lose the election," Attorney General William Barr told Trump in a private conversation in April 2020. "You pride yourself in being a fighter and that worked in 2016 when they wanted a disruptor to go in there. And they still want a disruptor, but they don't want someone who is a complete asshole."

"Oh, they're tired?" Trump loudly asked veteran pollster Tony Fabrizio in July 2020 during his reelection campaign. He was raging in the Oval Office over new polling data that showed independent voters were emotionally drained by Trump's handling of the pandemic. "They're fucking tired? Well, I'm fucking fatigued and tired, too."

"We've been duped," Secretary of Defense Mark Esper, center, told JCS chairman Mark Milley, right, as they trailed Trump across Lafayette Square on June 1, 2020. Milley, clad in combat fatigues, agreed. "This is fucked up and this is a political event and I'm out of here." The parade of the president and military officials coincided with law enforcement officers forcibly clearing the square of mostly peaceful protesters. Front from left: President Trump is trailed by Attorney General William Barr, Secretary of Defense Mark Esper, and Joint Chiefs of Staff chairman Mark Milley. Also in the back are senior advisers Jared Kushner and Ivanka Trump, and Trump's chief of staff, Mark Meadows.

"I do not believe this situation calls for invocation of the Insurrection Act," Secretary of Defense Mark Esper told Trump on June 3, 2020, soon after Esper publicly opposed putting active-duty military in the streets of Washington amid racial unrest and ongoing protests. "You took away my authority!" Trump screamed at him.

Senator Kamala Harris was selected by Biden as his running mate on August 11, 2020. She had been a force on the Senate Judiciary Committee, where Biden had once served as chairman, and brought governing experience and political capital to the ticket. While serving as California's attorney general, she developed a bond with Biden's son, the late Beau Biden, who had served as Delaware's attorney general. On January 20, 2021, she became the first woman, Black American, and person of South Asian descent to serve as vice president of the United States.

"You're not going to be sworn in on the 20th. There is not a scenario in which you can be sworn in on the 20th," Vice President Mike Pence told Trump in the Oval Office on January 5, 2021. Trump was stunned by Pence's refusal to do his bidding, following weeks of relentlessly pressuring him to thwart the congressional certification of Biden's victory.

Capitol Police officers were overwhelmed on January 6, 2021, by swelling mobs and rioters who climbed the walls and shattered windows. Some officers were beaten with metal poles and their own shields. Once inside, rioters breached the Senate chamber. Over in the House, officers drew their firearms as Trump supporters banged on the doors. Officers shouted at lawmakers to get down and take cover.

"Hang Mike Pence!" Trump supporters chanted as they roamed the Capitol's marble halls and waved huge blue Trump flags from balconies. "Bring out Mike Pence! Where is Pence? Find him!" Nearby, a makeshift gallows had been erected for Pence. Rioters also ransacked House Speaker Nancy Pelosi's office. "Where's the speaker?" some screamed. "Find her!"

"I think that he likes this," General Mark Milley, chairman of the Joint Chiefs of Staff, confided in a phone call with a House member as a mob stormed the Capitol on January 6, 2021. "He wants his supporters to be fighting to the bitter end." Two days later, Milley confronted his fear that the riot could be a precursor to what he called a "Reichstag moment," a Trump version of when Adolf Hitler manufactured crisis in 1933 and cemented his absolute power in Germany.

On February 4, 2020, House Speaker Nancy Pelosi ripped up a copy of Trump's State of the Union address after the president delivered his remarks. Nearly a year later, after Trump supporters rioted at the Capitol, she called Chairman Milley and said, "It's a sad state of affairs for our country that we've been taken over by a dictator." She added, "He should have been arrested on the spot."

"They, the most important people in my life, want me to run," Biden said in February 2019. His wife, Jill, was at his side for three grueling presidential campaigns and during repeated family crises and tragedies that nearly stopped the Bidens from returning to national politics. Shown here, the president and first lady embrace as they arrive at the North Portico of the White House on January 20, 2021.

“If we cannot deliver, authoritarianism may be on the march,” Senator Bernie Sanders told Biden on February 3, 2021. His raspy voice and urgent Brooklyn accent filled the Oval Office. Long a political outsider and Biden’s foil during the 2020 primary campaign, Sanders is now a central Biden ally, helping shepherd his $1.9 trillion rescue plan to passage and keeping Biden tuned into progressives.

“They act like they’re going to shove it down my throat,” Senator Joe Manchin told Biden in a phone call on March 5, 2021. “They can kiss my ass.” Manchin, a West Virginia moderate, was furious with fellow Democrats’ last-minute changes to Biden’s $1.9 trillion rescue bill. Manchin finally voted for it after hours of negotiation. “You’re going to come out of this looking like you’re the dealmaker,” Biden told him.

“Mr. President,” Secretary of State Tony Blinken told Biden in April 2021, “this was an incredibly hard decision.” It was done in the presidential style. “I admire the fact that you made it.” As Biden deliberated on Afghanistan, Blinken served as a liaison to NATO allies and as a trusted arbiter of policy options. It is a role he has played for Biden for more than 20 years, going back to Biden’s Senate days.

Secretary of Defense Lloyd Austin has deliberately kept a low public profile. But behind the scenes, he was a pivotal figure during Biden’s discussions on Afghanistan. He asked colleagues to consider what he called a slow, “gated” withdrawal of U.S. troops, where a staged exit with three or four parts might provide leverage for negotiations. Biden said it reminded him of the old “conditions based” approach and Austin eventually backed off from his proposal.

"I have trouble these days even showing up at a cemetery and not thinking of my son Beau," Biden said as he walked among the rows of white marble tombstones in Section 60 at Arlington National Cemetery, where the dead from the wars in Afghanistan and Iraq are buried. Earlier in the day Biden had announced his decision to withdraw U.S. troops from Afghanistan. Biden turned to the hundreds of tombstones and said in anguish, "Look at them all."

"Give me your word as a Biden," Beau Biden told his father in May 2015, shortly before Beau died of brain cancer. "No matter what happens, you're going to be all right." Beau Biden's life, which included a Bronze Star for military service in Iraq, continues to deeply shape his father, from the president's lingering grief and sense of fate to his decision to withdraw U.S. troops from Afghanistan.

"Being the president of the United States and making a decision like this, you have to stare in the face the human and potential human costs of your decision," National Security Adviser Jake Sullivan said as Biden mulled whether to withdraw U.S. troops from Afghanistan. In meetings, Biden almost always asks, "Jake, what do you think?"

"Now he comes into the office, every day, kind of in a mid-range emotional space," White House chief of staff Ron Klain once said privately of Biden. "There is no news I can walk in and give him in the morning that is worse than the news he's been given many other times in his life." Klain knew the president missed Delaware. "He is not comfortable living in the White House."

“Yeah, the buck really does stop here,” Biden told Secretary of State Blinken and National Security Adviser Jake Sullivan in April 2021. It was a nod to how his decision to withdraw U.S. troops from Afghanistan had quickly become a political target for his critics, both Republicans and Democrats who dreaded a possible breakdown of the Afghan government and brutal abuses of human rights by the Taliban.

“Democracy is on fire and the Senate is fiddling!” House Majority Whip James Clyburn said as Democrats struggled to enact their overhaul of voting rights legislation in 2021. A year earlier, when Biden’s primary campaign was on the brink of collapse, the South Carolina kingmaker struck a deal with him: Clyburn would endorse him if Biden agreed to nominate a Black woman to the Supreme Court.

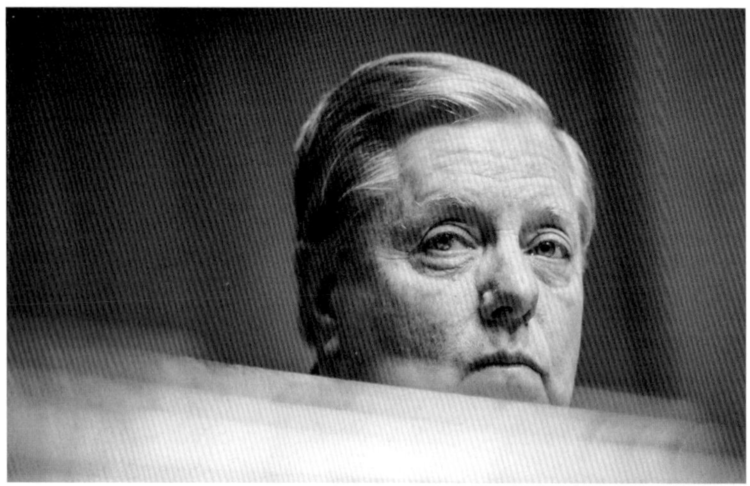

“You fucked your presidency up,” Senator Lindsey Graham told Trump in the summer of 2021. Trump abruptly hung up the phone. “Listen, I don’t blame you,” Graham told him a day later. “I would have hung up, too!” But he again urged Trump to move on from election grievances and focus on the 2022 elections. Graham was now like an addiction counselor to Trump, trying to keep his patient from taking one more drink of an imagined 2020 reelection victory.

“Trump 2020 resembled Hillary 2016. You had too much money, too much time, too much ego,” Kellyanne Conway, Trump’s longtime strategist, told him in the summer of 2021. His 2020 campaign, which raised over $1 billion, had been riven by acrimony among Trump’s staffers and allies. “What you didn’t have this time was the hunger and the swagger,” she said, unlike his low-maintenance campaign operation in 2016.

"We will not bend," Trump proclaimed on June 26, 2021, in Wellington, Ohio. He was back on the stage, holding massive rallies before thousands of enthralled supporters and stoking talk of a possible 2024 comeback. "We will not break. We will not yield. We will never give in. We will never give up. We will never back down. We will never, ever surrender." It was a war speech.

In a phone call on July 9, 2021, President Biden warned Russian president Vladimir Putin he must crack down on Russian-based criminals launching ransomware cyberattacks. "If you can't or won't, I will," he said. At the very end of the conversation, Biden added, "You know, Mr. President, great countries have great responsibilities. They also have great vulnerabilities." U.S. offensive cyber capability was formidable, as Putin knew. Biden left it at that. It was as close as he came to threatening Putin.

"Well, you pissed on that oath."

Security took him to a holding room where Pence called to thank him for his kind words on the Senate floor about the vice president's son and son-in-law.

Graham believed Trump's treatment of Pence was one of the worst things Trump had done. Any sensible Democrat, Graham believed, now understood Trump had inflicted a lot of damage to himself and the best strategy was to get out of the way as Trump mowed down those closest to him.

Graham told Trump, "This has made every critic more right than wrong." He later observed, "I don't think he realizes to this day the effect of his words."

I just had the most unbelievable, unsettling experience, Congressman Adam Smith said in an 11:30 a.m. call on January 8 to Chairman Milley.

Smith, the chairman of the House Armed Services Committee, was a 24-year congressional veteran from Washington State. A moderate Democrat, little known and no headline grabber. But in military and Pentagon circles, he was a powerful, behind-the-scenes lawmaker.

Smith, 55, described sitting in the aisle seat in row 26 on the Alaska Airlines 5 p.m. flight out of Washington Reagan National Airport to Seattle on the day after the insurrection at the Capitol. He was surrounded by what looked like nearly 100 MAGA hat–wearing Trump supporters.

A regular on the nearly six-hour flight returning home on weekends or congressional recesses, Smith had noticed the plane had been mostly empty during the last year due to the pandemic. But this time he was lucky to get a seat. As the crowd grew loud, no one seemed to realize this man who looked like a friendly business traveler was a congressman.

Ugly talk about conspiracies to steal the election from Trump filled the plane. So did chatter about the QAnon group, which passengers said with confidence was a bulwark against a cabal of cannibalistic, anti-Trump pedophiles who worship Satan and run a global child-sex-trafficking ring.

Several passengers also mentioned "6MWE." Smith did not know what they were talking about. He was horrified to learn, listening as some passengers explained and discussed openly that it meant "6 million weren't enough," a reference to the 6 million Jews exterminated in Nazi concentration camps.

They voiced deep disappointment that the riot had not overturned the presidential election. This was the final struggle for a new order. Heads nodded.

Smith, sitting silent with a mask, felt it was like being in the losing locker room after a game. They voiced such dejection that they made Smith, momentarily, feel good. The country's just gone to hell, they said, it's horrible, a terrible place.

America was so bad, so lost, one young man said, "I'm just going to move to South Korea."

South Korea? Smith thought to himself, confused. Why? The young man answered Smith's unvoiced question, telling other passengers, "South Korea is 90 percent Christian." In actuality, South Korea is 29 percent Christian.

"You should move to Idaho," suggested one woman.

"I just don't think they have decent seafood in Idaho," the young man replied.

Smith thought that this young man wanted a fascist takeover of the United States, but at the end of the day, if he couldn't get decent sushi, it just might not be worth it.

The rioters at the Capitol the day before had to come from somewhere, but he was surprised that so many were returning to his traditionally blue state.

Smith, who had just had his first vaccine shot, sat with his mask on, not saying a word as the raw chatter continued. If I'm ever going to catch the coronavirus, he thought, this would be the time.

In the middle seat next to him a small woman, about 50 years old and decked out in Trump paraphernalia, clearly had the same thought. She was intensely wiping down her seat area.

As Armed Services chairman, a number of members had come to him, since January 6, voicing concern about the security of the top secret nuclear launch codes. Trump had them. Was there some way to contain the president? Smith had passed along those concerns to Speaker Pelosi.

One member of Congress said he was worried that Trump was going to steal Air Force One in his last days, fly it to Moscow and sell U.S. secrets to Putin. Another concern from members was that the Capitol would come under attack during Biden's inauguration. How could they make sure Trump didn't stop law enforcement forces from protecting Biden?

As the flight progressed across the country, white supremacist and anti-Semitic talk continued unabated. It was one thing to read about and talk about something all day, but another to sit there for hours in the middle of it. The experience was jarring, like the riot itself. Smith was convinced many on this flight, and at the Capitol, absolutely tried to overturn the election of a legitimately elected president. No doubt.

But Smith also felt the riot had an element of reality being suspended. It was like someone tried to kick a 90-yard field goal in football. Is such an unrealistic play an attempted field goal? You could call it that, sure, but it was impossible. Trump and his supporters weren't going to overturn a legitimate election, but that didn't mean they wouldn't try. Hail Mary.

Smith liked to think of Donald Trump as a hundred-year flood in American democracy. But he told colleagues there was nothing Congress could put into law to protect the country if a lunatic wound up in the White House. The war-making power was ceded to the president as commander in chief. The only power Congress had, in a practical sense, was to cut off the money. He believed the system for controlling the use of nuclear weapons was vulnerable.

"The focus needs to be making sure that we don't let a lunatic back into the White House," Smith said. "Two hundred years of history teaches us the president of the United States uses the military the way he wants.

"Trump is mentally unstable," he said. "He's a narcissistic psychopath. The great fear was that he would use the Pentagon and the Department of Defense basically to stage a coup."

It was a conclusion, startling and grim, that ricocheted around Congress on January 8. A day before, Trump had issued a video saying, "a new administration will be inaugurated on January 20th," and said he wanted a "smooth, orderly and seamless transition of power." But the video was muted, flat, and insincere. It reassured few members.

"My fear with Trump was always that he was going to engineer a fascist takeover of the country," Smith said. "I never really worried that he would start a war. He's a coward. He doesn't want that level of responsibility."

FORTY-EIGHT

Karen Pence had been working for days on goodie bags for staffers in her husband's office, packing them with champagne flutes, honey from their beehive at the Naval Observatory, and cutting boards with the vice presidential seal. She also dropped in a print of her painting of the Naval Observatory, a nod toward her work to bring attention to art therapy, a mental health initiative she had promoted for years.

And despite the horror of January 6, Karen Pence was adamant about going forward with a staff farewell party 4 p.m. on Friday, January 8, in the sprawling vice president's office in the Eisenhower Executive Office Building.

When she and Pence entered the vice president's office that Friday afternoon for the party, about 70 staffers erupted in applause. She began to cry.

Mike Pence's eyes welled up and his face grew red, with a smile clenched as the staffers kept applauding for minutes. This was a world where feelings about Trump were always left unspoken, where angst was packed away. The applause said everything they wanted to say to Pence, and he seemed to know it.

"It has been an emotional week," Pence began, looking over at Karen. He thanked her and his family for their support.

"She's the best second lady in history, and has been with me through thick and thin," Pence said, looking at his wife. "She is always at my side."

Karen Pence wept some more.

The room fell silent as the Pences gathered themselves.

Pence pivoted to a short farewell speech. He said nothing specific about Trump or about the Capitol riot. He addressed it in his own way. He asked them to define their time with him, and their time in government, with no remorse or loathing.

"I hope you all take pride in having served this administration. There is a lot to be proud of," Pence said. "I hope that you will consider public service in other parts of your career. There is no greater honor than serving the public.

"I never had the honor of working in a White House as a young man," Pence said. "And when you're working every day here, sometimes you don't stop and think what an incredible opportunity that is."

Pence looked at Short, whose stoicism was a defining trait. He described how Short had texted him with the Timothy verse after Biden was certified. Pence said Short was the deepest kind of friend, something close to a brother. Short's eyes, too, welled up.

"It meant a lot to me and my family in that moment," Pence said. "This office has fought the good fight. We have kept the faith."

"Now, let's finish the race in these last two weeks," Pence said, "and finish it well, with an orderly transition to the Harris team."

Pence joked that he and Karen might relax that evening after a long week.

"We might go crazy and have pizza and O'Doul's," a nonalcoholic beer, Pence said. The staffers groaned since Pence loved to make this comment almost every Friday afternoon and kept it in speeches to his speechwriters' chagrin.

Short informed Pence the whole staff had pitched in and bought him his cabinet chair. It cost $1,200 to buy it from the federal government.

Short noted that years ago, when he worked for Pence in the House and Pence was conference chairman, Pence put his core principles on the wall of the office: Glorify God, have fun, and promote all House Republicans.

"Well, we stopped that last one after the Louie Gohmert lawsuit," Short said, referring to Texas congressman Louie Gohmert's unsuccessful efforts to sue Pence in December to try to overturn the presidential election by rejecting states' electors.

"We all got you a goodie bag as a thank-you," Karen Pence chimed in, showing them all the items she had included. The staff lightened up.

Mike Pence then signed the inside of his desk drawer, a vice presidential tradition upon leaving. Biden signed in 2017. He scrawled his name inches from Biden's, from Dan Quayle's, Nelson Rockefeller and George H. W. Bush.

Marty Obst relaxed with Pence and Mrs. Pence after the farewell party ended. They exchanged small talk and smiles. But Obst felt both simmering fury and sadness. The goodie bags, the unspoken effort to make this goodbye feel normal, provided the thinnest possible sheen to a tragedy.

Obst turned to a colleague and confided that this moment was a consequence of the "toxicity of power."

Can you imagine, Obst asked, if Trump had reacted to defeat with a touch of grace and then bowed out, with an eye on 2024?

"The guy would have a complete stranglehold on the Republican Party," Obst said. "It would be completely galvanized. And the vice president would be the first to say, 'I'm out. How do I work for you for four years, to make sure you're president again?' "

FORTY-NINE

Ron Klain had been in his hotel room in Wilmington when the final results came in from Georgia officials on January 6, shortly after 4 p.m. Ossoff and Warnock had both won. Senate Democrats were in control.

Biden, who had been watching television coverage of the Capitol with horror, was cheered when Klain dropped by with the update. This obviously changes things, Biden said. The president-elect soon called Warnock and Ossoff to congratulate them. The two senators-elect had one message: Now we've got to get people those checks.

Biden laughed. Yes, we do, he said. The $600 checks had started going out to Americans in December, after Congress passed its spending bill. Now it was time to make sure an additional $1,400 check was sent out. $2,000 total for millions of Americans in need.

The checks would pour much needed cash into the economy but Klain also thought they were a symbol of Democrats having taken control in Washington. The people had given the party enormous power. Go deliver. Georgia erased any hesitation.

Biden convened a senior staff meeting from his home in Wilmington on Friday, January 8.

Before Georgia, his initial rescue plan had a price tag of around $1.4 trillion—a staggering number coming right after December's $900 billion infusion into the national economy. Biden now wanted to hear from his aides about going even higher.

Klain was the only transition staff member physically present with Biden. The others were on a video conference call.

Deese, slated to be Biden's National Economic Council director, presented a deck of slides, and Klain started to feel a bigger plan falling into place. He told Biden they would put together a more formal plan for review the next day.

Deese made another presentation that Saturday. Options ranging from the $1.4 trillion to something closer to $2 trillion were floated.

Biden peppered them with questions.

"Do we really think we can get something this big done?" he asked.

Biden had been a Senate lifer and knew a one-vote majority guaranteed little. He did not want to get bogged down for months.

"Is this going to consume my entire first 100 days, my entire first year?" he asked. "How long will this take? 50-50 in the Senate? And with a very narrow margin in the House?"

Biden added, "This is clearly what we need to do to beat this virus and get the economy off its back. But, you know, can we really do this?"

"We really have no choice," Klain answered.

Klain recalled the Obama experience in 2009, when Republicans opposed the Obama administration's stimulus plan during a global recession, which had caused Obama to ultimately accept a $787 billion package, a number lower than his economists believed was needed to kick-start the economy. This time around, he said they needed an economic boom.

"Rather than negotiate with ourselves, rather than ask what's possible, rather than sit here and scope the thing back through some political screen, let's put on the table what we think we really need," Klain said. "And if Congress rejects that, well, then that's just the way it'll be."

Democrats should not trim their sails out of some sense of

what was politically feasible or what was politically possible, Klain said.

Several Biden advisers raised concerns, making two sharp points in response. First, Anita Dunn said, there is a risk that if we ask too much, we are just kind of dead-on-arrival. You shock the system. "Holy shit," and even some Democratic lawmakers shut down.

The second point, she said, was if they asked for too much, the Republicans had an easy out, crying out about deficit spending, inflation, and passing on a burden to our grandchildren.

Dunn already had a target on her back with progressives, but she decided Biden needed to hear the risks.

Biden took it all in. The country was in a crisis. Some 4,000 people were now dying every day from the coronavirus, the deadliest month of the pandemic in the United States. The country could be heading toward a million Americans dead by the end of the year, and two years of a devastating pandemic. The economy was sputtering, losing 140,000 jobs in December and earning Trump the distinction of being the first president since Herbert Hoover to lose jobs on his watch.

Biden said the crisis was genuine and had to be treated like one.

Biden finally signed off on a $1.6 trillion package. "We're going to go in there with our best recommendation to the country, to the Congress, of what we really need."

Biden had spent decades in the Senate and the vice presidency, stymied by the limits of those roles. He had told his friend and later Delaware senator, Ted Kaufman, he always believed that the presidency, and only that, offered a chance at securing transformational change.

He now had the presidency, and more than enough experience with fate.

"I could get hit by a bus this afternoon and it'd be over. So, I'm going to do as much as I can as fast as I can," Biden said.

"You guys go try to start to sell it to the Democrats on the Hill and I'll give a speech to the country, you know, laying this out," Biden told his advisers.

To underscore the seriousness, Biden advisers discussed the possibility of the president-elect addressing the nation on January 14, just days before his inauguration.

On one level, a pre-inauguration speech seemed to be a serious breach of protocol. Biden was not yet president. Most presidents-elect engaged in ceremonial, pre-inaugural rituals at that point in mid-January. Traditionally, it was a time to bury partisan rancor.

But Trump was still arguing that the election was stolen. Co-operation on the transition was spotty at best, even obstructionist.

Biden was uncertain but did not dismiss the idea. Would a big speech seem tone-deaf? Grasping for power before his time?

His aides looked at the calendar. In the days after the inauguration, the schedule was packed with other events. He could do it on January 14 or January 25. Those were the slots.

Biden eventually came down on the side of urgency. Waiting would send the wrong message, he said. He chose January 14.

Klain deployed everyone—Deese, incoming White House legislative director Louisa Terrell, Ricchetti and Dunn, among others—to go see Pelosi, Schumer and all the other senior Democrats in the House and Senate. Time to listen.

The response was positive but prodding. After scoring the wins in Georgia, Democratic leaders felt they had the political capital to do more. They pushed Biden and his advisers to add in two more central components: another $100 to $200 billion allotted for state and local aid, and a significant increase of the child tax credit.

An expansion of the child tax credit—essentially cash for families with children—was a safety net that could pull millions of kids out of poverty. If passed, nearly 40 million American families would qualify for monthly federal payments—$300 for each child under six years old, and $250 for each child six or older. Right into the family bank account.

Congresswoman Rosa DeLauro of Connecticut and Senator Patty Murray of Washington were two of the biggest Democratic proponents of the program on Capitol Hill. It was transformational, they said, knowing that framing could catch Biden's interest. Both women also led the all-important appropriation committees in their respective chambers, which direct federal spending.

DeLauro, who had been in Congress for nearly 30 years, representing New Haven, was a founding member of the Progressive Caucus and long an outspoken advocate for children.

"This is the moment," she said in a call to Klain on January 12. "You have to do this."

Biden added $100 billion to his proposal.

Now, Biden's emerging plan was $1.7 trillion, with another $200 billion for state and local aid that Schumer was championing.

The new total: $1.9 trillion.

Biden told his aides that was it. A hair beneath $2 trillion. Bold enough for progressives, but something he felt he could sell broadly. He implored them to stay at it, to keep pushing not just on the legislation but on the virus. One hundred million vaccinations in 100 days and passing the rescue plan—those were his priorities.

FIFTY

On January 9, one day after his fraught calls with General Li of China and Speaker Pelosi, Chairman Milley jotted some thoughts in his daily notebook.

It came almost like a brainstorm.

On the January 6 riot, he wrote, "What is this amorphous thing that just happened on the 6th? Who are these people?"

He jotted rapidly:

"6MWE"

"Extreme Tea Party"

"QAnon," he added, taking note of the fully discredited conspiracy theory.

"Patriot Movement," a far-right militia.

"We the People Movement"

"Nazis"

"Proud Boys"

"The Oath Keepers"

"Newsmax," the conservative news website, which had been friendly toward Trump for a long time.

"Epoch," referring to the *The Epoch Times*, a far-right publication that was critical of the Chinese Communist Party.

Milley summarized and scribbled.

"Big Threat: domestic terrorism."

Some were the new Brown Shirts, a U.S. version, Milley concluded, of the paramilitary wing of the Nazi Party that supported Hitler. It was a planned revolution. Steve Bannon's vision coming to life. Bring it all down, blow it up, burn it, and emerge with power.

Milley began to draft a public memo to the military. "January 6, 2021 was a direct assault on the U.S. Congress, the Capitol building, and our Constitutional process." He added, "On January 20, 2021 . . . President-elect Biden will be inaugurated and will become our 46th Commander in Chief."

It was not traditionally the job of the chairman to make such declarations.

Milley took a draft to a confidential Tank meeting at the Pentagon. He handed out copies to the joint chiefs.

"You don't have to sign it," he said. "I can sign it by myself for myself as chairman on behalf of the chiefs. Or we can all sign it. Take a look and tell me what you think."

They all read it, and all said they would sign the letter. It went out January 12.

Media coverage of Milley's letter was scant, but *Vox* reported it was a "remarkable statement" and "it looks as though America's top military officials won't tolerate another thing: the attempted overthrow of American democracy by force."

Still, Milley remained worried. He thought back to how Trump engaged with U.S. allies. There was no one in the global leadership who could connect with him, hold him back.

He recalled other Oval Office outbursts.

"That bitch kraut, Merkel!" Trump had shouted in one meeting about the German chancellor, Angela Merkel. Trump turned to Milley and others.

"I was raised by the biggest kraut of them all, Fred Trump," he said. He wheeled around in his chair and pointed to the picture of his father that sat on the table behind the Resolute Desk.

Others in the room were speechless.

Even his family was not off-limits.

"You know," Trump joked in another meeting, mocking his son-in-law, Jared Kushner, who was raised in a modern Orthodox Jewish family and was working on Middle East peace, "Jared's more loyal to Israel than the United States."

On January 15, with Secret Service cooperation, Milley called the heads of all departments or their deputies for a rehearsal of the Biden inauguration. They met in Conmy Hall at Joint Base Myer-Henderson Hall. The space was historic, a massive former indoor equestrian facility long used by the military. But it had been transformed in recent years into a modern space with a 144-foot by 14-foot screen and rows of lights that made it look like a Hollywood movie set.

The Department of Homeland Security had initially designated the Biden inaugural as a National Special Security Event from January 19 to 21. But after January 6, the special event designation was reset to begin January 13. That meant the Secret Service, the lead agency, would have more time to ensure the city was locked down.

Using an overhead projector, Milley had a bright map of the entire city beamed onto the floor, showing all the roads and bridges, monuments and other buildings, including the Capitol and the White House.

"What happened on January 6th is not happening again," Milley told the group. "We are going to make sure we are going to have a peaceful transfer of power. This city is going to have layer upon layer of security. Joe Biden is going to be the president of the United States at 12 noon and it's going to be done peacefully."

Milley began to conduct what is known as a "ROC drill" in the military, a rehearsal of concepts and responsibilities.

The National Guard would have 25,000 troops in the city and

every police and law enforcement agency was going to be there. No one was going to be able to move.

"The Proud Boys are coming across the 14th Street Bridge," Milley said. He asked each key leader from the departments, "What do you do?"

"Is there an airplane threat? What would you do? Who would be responsible?

"How about a car-bomb threat?

"Unmanned aerial vehicle? A drone?

"A threat against a specific monument?"

Some had answers, some did not.

"I hope there's an attorney in here because I'm going to caveat my answers," one FBI deputy director said at one point. Rehearsing law enforcement decisions was difficult, the FBI official said. "It's not a perfect science. We're doing the best we can." Others agreed.

A Capitol Police official asked, "What about armed protests before the inauguration?"

Books, maps and pages of data were shuffled and exchanged as the discussion continued. Milley told them to focus on who makes decisions. This operation demanded coherence. "Where's the one command post?" he asked. After a round of answers, they agreed on a classified spot.

What kind of weapons would the Guard use?

M4 carbine, the primary infantry weapon.

Someone asked, "If a guy shows up with horns, a painted face, wearing bear skin and tries to take your weapons, what do our soldiers do?"

"We've trained for that," a one-star general replied.

Milley's projection showed two security lines around the Capitol: a green-dotted line was the first and would be manned by National Guard. The second was a red-dotted line, one block further inside.

"You could have 200, 300 guys, the Boogaloo Boys, with Nazi shirts and flying Confederate flags, saying, 'We're headed to tear down the Martin Luther King monument.' Do you want troops or law enforcement?"

The answer was law enforcement officers who could make arrests. Park Police said they'd have roaming golf carts on the National Mall starting at 8 a.m. on January 20, keeping watch of the monuments and museums.

As the meeting stretched on, there were grumbles and more long, multipart questions. The room was full of uncertainty and discomfort. There was no playbook for securing a post-insurrection inauguration. There were so many stakeholders, so many federal agencies.

"Pain of preparation is much less than the pain of regret," Milley said. And for emphasis, he repeated the mission.

"There's a huge amount at stake. On the 20th, at 12:01, Joe Biden will be sworn in. We're going to make that happen."

FIFTY-ONE

Over at the White House, Keith Kellogg went to see Ivanka Trump in her office. The retired lieutenant general wanted to offer an after-action report.

He also sought some closure. Unlike others in Pence's circle, he remained convinced Trump was a decent man, a president who had let a situation spin out of control. He did not want his years at Trump's side to now be scarred.

"I believe in the president of the United States. I'm a deep believer. I always have been," Kellogg told her. "When I support Donald J. Trump as a loyalist, I take him for the good and bad. I have made that decision.

"I just wish the calmer heads had prevailed," he said. "There were some voices that I wish weren't in the room."

"You know he's a very stubborn person," Ivanka replied.

"It runs in the family," Kellogg said, appreciating her willingness to confront her father on January 6.

She was calm, controlled and business-like. She kept her responses short.

Kellogg would later suggest to Ivanka and Jared Kushner that Pence should be awarded the Presidential Medal of Freedom as a way of smoothing out the relationship.

Their response: Nice idea, but we need to let some time go by. Let's see what happens.

Former vice president Dan Quayle called Pence in the days after the riot.

"Congratulations," Quayle said. "You absolutely did the right thing."

Pence was thankful but muted.

"How's your relationship with Trump?" Quayle asked.

"Well, I don't know," he said.

Trump and Pence met in the Oval Office at the White House on Monday, January 11, their first conversation since January 6.

Trump had been bitter all morning, lashing out at the Professional Golfers' Association of America for canceling its plans to hold a future major tournament at his New Jersey golf club. Trump seemed to take the news harder than the various cabinet resignations over January 6, venting about how hard he had worked for years to secure a major golf tournament.

Another blow came when New England Patriots football coach Bill Belichick decided against traveling to Washington to accept the Presidential Medal of Freedom from Trump. "The tragic events of last week occurred, and the decision has been made not to move forward with the award," Belichick said in a statement.

Trump hated all of it. His favorite coach, the PGA, the companies—they were all deserting him because of January 6. He said it was a disgrace.

In the Oval Office, Trump did not apologize to Pence. They kept their discussion limited, with curt and vague statements about how they would serve out their term together. Pence mostly listened. It lasted for about an hour.

"I just want you to know, I'm still praying for you, Mr. President," Pence said.

"We've all been through a lot, it's been a trying time for all of us, but I haven't stopped."

"Thanks, Mike," Trump said.

The next day, the House formally called on Pence to invoke the 25th Amendment to remove Trump from office. Pence, in an unusually emotional letter, rejected the request.

"Last week, I did not yield to pressure to exert power beyond my constitutional authority to determine the outcome of the election, and I will not now yield to efforts in the House of Representatives to play political games at a time so serious in the life of our Nation," Pence wrote.

"The Bible says that 'for everything there is a season, and a time for every purpose under heaven . . . a time to heal . . . and a time to build up.' That time is now."

The second move against Trump was filed on January 11 as "H. Res. 24," "Impeaching Donald John Trump, President of the United States, for high crimes and misdemeanors." The charge: "incitement of insurrection."

"He must go," Speaker Pelosi said on January 13 ahead of the House's impeachment vote. "He is a clear and present danger to the nation that we all love."

House Democratic leaders expected impeachment to gain traction after their overtures to Pence failed.

"There was a general view that if we can force a resignation or compel the cabinet secretaries and Mike Pence to invoke the 25th Amendment, that's the faster course of action," Congressman Hakeem Jeffries of New York, a member of the leadership, said privately. He was close with Pelosi and seen as her possible successor.

"But in order to be able to do it, we had to be prepared to move forward with impeachment." Create an environment for action, either within the Trump administration, or at least within Congress.

GOP fissures appeared during the House impeachment vote. Ten House Republicans joined with Democrats, including

Congresswoman Liz Cheney of Wyoming, the No. 3 leader in the chamber and the daughter of Bush Vice President Dick Cheney.

Trump was impeached by a 232 to 197 vote, becoming the first president ever to be impeached twice. All 222 Democrats were joined by the 10 Republicans.

McConnell would not say whether he would vote to convict Trump in the Senate. "I have not made a final decision on how I will vote, and I intend to listen to the legal arguments when they are presented to the Senate," he said in a letter to Republican senators.

Pence met with Short, Obst and other former aides, including former chiefs of staff Nick Ayers and Josh Pitcock, in Pence's West Wing office on January 13.

Emotions were still frayed. They found it off-putting that Meadows and Kushner seemed to be ignoring the gravity of what had happened, and of how poorly Trump had treated Pence.

Ayers, who had nearly accepted an offer to be Trump's White House chief of staff in December 2018, had flown to Washington from his home in Georgia for the meeting. He was angry and unhappy with Pence's response, which he felt was too soft and too ready to move on. He told Pence he was not interested in going over to see Trump.

Jared Kushner soon popped his head into Pence's office and said he would like to chat with Pence about encouraging the president to issue a statement affirming his commitment to governing in the final days of the administration, and to an orderly transition.

"Can you help me convince the president to do this?" Kushner asked.

Sure, Pence said, smiling and nodding. He said he would stop by Kushner's office.

Once Kushner left, Pence turned to his inner circle and said it was nice of Jared to bring him into that process. His aides' faces were blank.

"Is this a joke?" Ayers asked Pence. "Is that what you called us here for?

"Sir," Ayers said, "these are transactional people. They made it very clear what they think of you. How many calls did they make when you were at the Capitol?"

Obst then dismissed Kushner's efforts as "propaganda" and an attempt for Kushner to spiff up his own image following January 6 by seeming to be a broker of a peace with Pence.

"This is about their personal financial situation, this isn't about the country," Obst told his colleagues. He said Kushner was probably worried about being linked to the riot once he rejoined the private sector.

Pence nevertheless later walked down to Kushner's office and offered some thoughts. That evening, the White House released a video of Trump sitting at the Resolute Desk, his hands clasped. Several aides who worked with Trump on the video recalled he seemed nervous as he talked about the impeachment proceedings. He said he could not trust the Senate Republicans. They could convict him.

That is why it's important for you to tape this video, the aides told him. You need to give the Republicans something useful, a talking point.

"My fellow Americans," Trump said in the January 13 video, "I want to be very clear. I unequivocally condemn the violence that we saw last week. Violence and vandalism have absolutely no place in our country and no place in our movement."

He added, "Like all of you, I was shocked and deeply saddened by the calamity at the Capitol last week. I want to thank the hundreds of millions of incredible American citizens who have responded to this moment with calm, moderation, and grace. We will get through this challenge, just like we always do."

Before ending, Trump took a shot at "the efforts to censor, cancel, and blacklist our fellow citizens."

It seemed to be a wink to his supporters that even though he was reading this stiff presidential statement, he was with them in spirit.

FIFTY-TWO

Biden laid out his $1.9 trillion plan on January 14 to the country. He couched it as an emergency response to a crisis, with a touch of soul.

"We not only have an economic imperative to act now, I believe we have a moral obligation," Biden said. "In this pandemic in America, we cannot let people go hungry. We cannot let people get evicted. We cannot watch nurses, educators and others lose their jobs."

The plan's core components included:

- $1,400 checks for millions of Americans
- An additional $400 a week in federal unemployment insurance available through September, a bump up from the $300 benefit scheduled to expire in March
- $400 billion for the pandemic response
- $350 billion in state and local aid
- An extension of the expanded federal food stamps program through September
- $30 billion to help Americans with home rental issues and utility bills
- A vast expansion of the child tax credit

Klain was heartened by the response—and gave credit to Anita Dunn for captaining the efforts on communications and on lining up support from the business community, Democrats on the Hill and governors. It was taken seriously, and Republicans seemed distracted by the January 6 fallout, with their fiscal hawk tactics also rusty after four years of boosting Trump.

"I think we might have even underestimated how much the country was looking for someone, him, to say, this is what we need to do," Klain said. "Yes, it's big. Yes, it's bold. Yes, it's all these things. But you know what? We're kind of tired of half-assed measures. We're kind of tired of not being told it straight, you know?"

But the coverage was far less rapturous on some MSNBC panels and in corners of Twitter where progressives tracked every Biden move. Some House members criticized the $1,400 checks as falling short of the $2,000 Trump had suggested. Others liked that Biden was talking big, but could he pull it through? Was he just putting a marker down before he cut a deal with Mitch McConnell?

When McConnell watched Biden's January 14 speech, he thought Biden was smart to get out there early to sell it.

"They want to do as much as they can as fast as they can," McConnell said privately, "because political capital is always fleeting." If he were in Biden's shoes, he probably would have done the same thing.

But despite understanding Biden's approach, McConnell reminded colleagues that his own 2016 memoir was titled *The Long Game*. That approach would continue to be his guide. Sit. Wait.

During the Obama years, McConnell and Biden usually only cut deals with each other when both sides were "between the 40-yard lines," as McConnell called the sweet spot.

While there were many magazine profiles and newspaper stories about the two of them working on deals, McConnell knew they were not grand bargainers. At best, they were closers. Political realists.

Sitting idle while Biden pursued his big spending bill would be fine with McConnell. He had been in Congress long enough to watch Obama, George W. Bush, Bill Clinton and others get elected president and be aggressive, only to be rebuked by voters in the midterm elections.

"The old Joe will only come back when he has to, and that will depend upon whether or not he can succeed in running the table with Democrats only," McConnell said. "If he can't, then we'll be back in the game."

On a private, January 14 conference call with some of the party's biggest donors, Karl Rove lamented the lack of Republican turnout in certain areas of Georgia. It was a disaster, but worse, it was a disaster that seemed destined to be repeated if Trump and his allies kept sowing doubt about the integrity of the vote.

"Essentially, I chalk it up to hardcore Trump supporters, who became convinced it wasn't worth turning out because the election in November had been rigged and it wasn't going to be any different in the runoff," Rove told them. "The second problem was that the other side did its job. Black turnout was a bigger share of the overall vote."

Near the end of the call, a donor pressed Rove for guidance on the future of the Republican Party, particularly for "old-line" Republicans like himself, following the Trump years and the events of January 6.

"What are your thoughts about how deep the rift is and what the last couple of months have meant?" the donor asked.

"I think there are deep divisions in our party," Rove said. But inside the GOP's grass roots, he worried that "a large number of Americans believe that the election was stolen." It was a different reality.

"Look, I've been through a couple of presidential elections. But the president was given over 50 times to make this case in court. And I've gone and tried to be, you know, I've read the pleadings. And the pleadings don't match up with the rhetoric," he said. "But we have a large number of people who believe that it was stolen from him and that's their first touch point."

Moving forward, Rove said, "the question is going to be, are there people whose lives depend upon division and dissension and disruption in the party, who fight for the sake of fighting? Who say, 'You know what, you can't disagree with me unless—if you're not with me, you're a zero and I'm going to punish you.' And I think that's very problematic.

"I don't have a good answer."

Trump kept up his election claims, continuing to meet with allies who believed it was stolen.

On January 15, *Washington Post* photographer Jabin Botsford took a picture of Mike Lindell, the conservative Trump ally and CEO of MyPillow, heading into the West Wing to meet with Trump. Lindell was a fixture on Fox News and other networks, proclaiming election fraud in state after state.

"Insurrection Act *now*," part of the memo in Lindell's hand read, as captured by Botsford. "Martial law if necessary."

Trump's mood on the eve of Biden's inauguration was flat. His aides had watched him, through the open door of the Oval Office, writing a letter to Biden, longhand, around 7 p.m. on January 19. He had asked some of them for suggestions. They encouraged him to be positive. But Trump had kept its contents private. He wrote it out alone.

Trump spoke with Kevin McCarthy, the House minority leader, by phone around 10 p.m.

"I just finished the letter."

McCarthy said he was glad to hear it. He had been telling Trump to write it for weeks.

McCarthy grew emotional. Trump was not going to be attending the inauguration. It was a far cry from their sessions at Mar-a-Lago and on Air Force One, where they traded political stories and ate Starbursts, Trump's favorite candy.

"I don't know what happened to you in the last two months," McCarthy said. "You're not the same as you were for the last four years.

"You've done good things and you want that to be your legacy. Call Joe Biden."

Trump dismissed the idea. McCarthy told him it was important for the country for some sort of conversation to take place. Make the transition real.

"Do it for me."

McCarthy was upset.

"You've got to call him. Call Joe Biden."

No, Trump said.

"Call Joe Biden."

No.

"Call Joe Biden!"

No.

Trump changed the subject.

There had been reports that Trump was thinking about bolting the GOP.

"I'm not going to leave the party. I'm going to help you," he said. He then gave McCarthy his new Florida phone number.

Trump never called Biden.

Later that night, Trump was busy at the White House, debating who should be given a pardon. The biggest question, though, was whether he should get one.

As various investigations, especially in New York, seemed to expand in January, Trump told Graham, "They're trying to destroy my family." Pardons for everyone in the family were possible. Trump asked Graham if he should pardon himself.

"A self-pardon would be a bad idea," Graham said, "a bad idea for the presidency, bad idea for you."

A self-pardon also would not be a cure-all for Trump's legal troubles, his lawyers said. The Manhattan district attorney, Cyrus Vance, looking into the Trump Organization's business practices, could continue to probe. A presidential pardon only applied to violations of federal, not state laws.

Trump resisted the self-pardon but plowed ahead with others during his final and frenzied hours in office. Over 140 people were granted clemency with a stroke of Trump's pen near midnight on January 19, including Bannon, rapper Lil Wayne, former Detroit mayor Kwame Kilpatrick, and countless other allies in politics and business.

Biden's inaugural eve was more subdued. Standing at the Major Joseph R. "Beau" Biden III National Guard Reserve Center in New Castle on January 19, the president-elect said he only had one regret: "He's not here."

"We should be introducing him as president," Biden said.

For a split second, Biden's voice cracked sharply and rose. His face scrunched in agony.

A second later, he carried on with his speech. The glint of the lights near the stage showed tears running down his cheeks.

FIFTY-THREE

Trump, with First Lady Melania Trump, came down from the residence early on January 20. The staff of the White House—the cooks and butlers and housekeepers—waited for them shortly before 8 a.m. in the Diplomatic Reception Room.

As the first couple entered, staff clapped and some shed tears as the president thanked them for their service and shook their hands. A White House usher presented the president and first lady with the American flag that had flown over the White House the day they arrived four years earlier and a gleaming cherrywood set for it.

Trump spotted Robert O'Brien and Pat Cipollone and waved them over for a picture.

Melania wore sunglasses. Those who spoke with her and leaned in to bid farewell could see a hint of tears.

"Give my love to Lo-Mari and the two girls," Melania told O'Brien.

The Trumps then went outside, into the cold morning light, and boarded Marine One.

Over at Andrews Air Force Base, Trump's family waited for them to arrive. In a reception room near the tarmac and Air Force One, Trump's youngest daughter, Tiffany, snapped a picture on her phone of the television showing the helicopter taking off.

Other Trump children watched Marine One take off in silence. Everyone in the room was watching the same TV. Spellbound. Taking in the moment.

It was full circle from January 20, 2017. That day, Trump and President Obama rode together from the White House to the

Capitol. Senator Roy Blunt, one of the senators responsible for inaugural planning, rode with them.

During the ride, Trump turned to Obama.

"What was your biggest mistake?" Trump asked.

Obama paused and glanced at Trump.

"I can't think of anything," he said.

Trump changed the subject.

"Is this the car you use all the time?"

Mark Meadows, the outgoing Trump chief of staff, invited Klain to meet him in his White House office on January 20 for the handover. Klain was not going to attend the inauguration and instead would monitor real-time intelligence and law enforcement reporting from the White House. Tens of thousands of National Guard troops remained in Washington, wearing camouflage and helmets, carrying rifles. They had flooded much of downtown, which was barricaded by metal fences.

Violence and the threat of violence was now part of an inauguration—and American politics.

A clash on the streets or even a single gunshot could mar, and under the worst circumstances, define the inauguration. Klain was anxious, tense.

Klain arrived at the White House about 10:30 a.m. He had worked in the White House five times and never seen the West Wing so deserted. It was eerie. Few Trump people were there. The well-known offices and elegant hallways were filled with cleaning crews.

He walked to the chief of staff's office. The door was closed. He knocked. No answer. He turned the knob. Locked. He stood outside the second most important office in Washington, soon to be his, barred from entering, and waited.

A Trump aide eventually approached and said, "Mr. Meadows is on the phone." Klain put the phone to his ear.

I'm running late, Meadows said. He had accompanied Trump to his departure and he would be there soon.

When Meadows arrived, he took Klain in.

Our meeting will have to be briefer than I intended, Meadows said. Trump had unexpectedly signed a final pardon for Al Pirro, the ex-husband of Fox News host and Trump ally Jeanine Pirro. Meadows had to run it to the Justice Department before noon so it could be legally registered.

Meadows asked if Klain had been briefed on various continuity of government programs, top secret codeword plans for ensuring presidential succession and continuation of government in any conceivable emergency—bombings, air strikes, cyberattacks, even invasions.

Yes, Klain said. Two days before he had met with Brigadier General Jonathan Howerton, who headed the White House military office of more than 2,500 employees, for a complete briefing.

Have you been briefed on the confidential capacities at the White House for security and communications? Meadows asked.

Klain said he had been fully briefed on those as well.

"I wish you all the luck in the world," Meadows said graciously. "I wish you success. I'll be rooting for you. I'll be praying for you."

Klain thanked him. Meadows left.

It was about 11:15 a.m., 45 minutes before Klain could do anything, even sign on to his computers. He was idle.

He walked down to the Oval Office where a crew was setting up Biden's office, installing artwork. There were busts of Robert Kennedy, Martin Luther King Jr., Cesar Chavez and Rosa Parks. A massive portrait of Franklin D. Roosevelt. And *Avenue in the Rain*, an impressionistic early-20th-century painting of American flags by Childe Hassam, also hung by Clinton and Obama.

Out went a portrait of Andrew Jackson, the owner of hundreds of slaves and who had waged a brutal campaign against Native Americans.

Biden's friends said it was total Biden and Donilon. Soul interior decorating.

In the days after the election, O'Brien had started preparing for the transition to a Biden presidency. He also said so publicly. Trump was not happy but did not order him to stop his work.

On January 20, O'Brien had prepared 40 or 50 binders of documents, some 4,000 pages. On the desk, soon to be Jake Sullivan's, he placed a personal letter with a memo on highly classified covert actions and special access, codeword programs. He pulled out the various identification cards he carried, passwords for different contingencies, and placed them on top of his letter.

Anything you need, O'Brien told Sullivan, you let me know.

A photographer snapped a photo of the two of them, one with mask on, one with no mask.

"God bless," O'Brien said to Sullivan. The authority was passed to the new team.

Down Pennsylvania Avenue, Pence was not planning to speak with Biden on Inauguration Day, but their Secret Service details crossed paths in the Capitol. Biden smiled broadly and approached him.

"Thanks for being here!" Biden said. "I'm glad you're here." They had met years ago at the vice presidential residence after Pence was elected. Pence recalled the meeting several times to others, calling Biden a friendly man who went out of his way to welcome Pence's family.

Former president Bill Clinton made a point to wander to the front and greet Pence.

"Thank you for what you did. You did the right thing," Clinton said.

Harris was escorted to her seat by Eugene Goodman, the Black

Capitol Police officer who acted valiantly on January 6. Biden was in a heavy black winter coat and powder blue tie. Members of the Senate and House sat behind him, masked.

Harris had two Bibles at the ceremony. One belonged to the late Supreme Court justice Thurgood Marshall, the first Black justice, and the other to Regina Shelton, her second mother during her childhood. She wore her signature white pearls, a symbol of her sorority, as did other Democratic women in homage to her new place in history.

Although massive security precautions were in place to protect the transfer of power, extreme worry remained inside the West Wing and at the classified command center monitoring the entire capital. Bridges, monuments and cars were being watched. Soldiers patrolled the Capitol with their M4 firearms. Police officers made their rounds.

Milley was on the inaugural platform. Being there was part of the job, but he thought he might be one of the happiest people up there. Not because it was President Biden, but because Trump was out of the presidency and it looked like another peaceful transfer of power.

Ahead of the inaugural, as he had reviewed war plans and the authorities for nuclear weapons command and control, Biden had thanked Milley personally, though he was vague about what exactly he was referencing.

Milley had not shared his decision to "pull a Schlesinger" outside the tightest possible circle.

"We know what you went through," Biden said. "We know what you did."

At the Capitol and on the dais, Vice President Harris and various incoming cabinet members gave versions of the same thank-you. Milley did not know the extent of what they knew about his struggles with Trump, but he suspected they did. That was Washington with its flow of sensitive, inside information—sometimes wrong, but in this case right.

At one point, Pence walked by.

Milley nodded and said, "Thanks for your leadership, Mr. Vice President."

Pence nodded and moved on. The moment went quickly, almost instantly.

Milley noticed the silence.

Clyburn circulated, kingmaker-style. President George W. Bush waved him over.

"You know, you're the savior," Bush told Clyburn. "If you had not endorsed Joe Biden, we would not be having this transfer of power today."

Joe Biden is the only one who could have defeated Trump, Bush said.

Five minutes earlier, Bill Clinton had used the same word—"savior"—when chatting with Clyburn.

"I guess you overheard Bill Clinton," Clyburn told Bush as they took selfies with attendees.

The conversation with Hillary Clinton was more serious. "It is very important to the future of the country for accountability to be had, as it relates to January 6th," Clyburn told her.

Biden's thin white hair, longer than usual, fluffed up with the wind as he sat up front. He watched intently as Amanda Gorman, a young Black woman and Harvard graduate, delivered her poem, "The Hill We Climb."

"We've braved the belly of the beast," Gorman said to millions, wearing a bright yellow coat. "We've learned that quiet isn't always peace.

"Somehow," she said, "we've weathered and witnessed a nation that isn't broken, but simply unfinished."

Klain walked over to the national security adviser's office where Jake Sullivan was moving in. They had known each other for 15 years, since 2006, when Klain was a partner at the law firm of O'Melveny & Myers. Sullivan, a summer associate, worked directly for Klain. Klain later had helped Sullivan get a job on Obama's 2008 campaign.

The pattern was typical of Biden's White House, where so many had grown up together from low-level jobs to now.

Before noon, Klain and Sullivan headed over to the Situation Room. They had arranged for a secure video conference to get updates on threats from all the security and law enforcement leaders: NSA, Homeland Security, FBI, CIA and other intelligence agencies.

Security was the only thing on their mind as they settled into their seats. A video feed of Biden's inaugural was on one screen in the room. The sound was purposely off so they could concentrate solely on seeing anything out of the ordinary. They had both offered ideas and knew the final version of Biden's inaugural address.

They watched on a nearby television as Biden placed his hand on a family Bible with Celtic cross, a nod to his Irish heritage and the same Bible he used at his boys' hospital bedside in 1973 to be sworn into the Senate, following the death of his wife and daughter. He became the nation's second ever Catholic president, following in the steps of the hero of his youth, JFK.

Biden's 2,552-word speech, which Donilon and Meacham and others had helped to shape, was an ode to bipartisanship, as well as to democracy.

"This is democracy's day," Biden began. "A day of history and hope. Of renewal and resolve. Through a crucible for the ages America has been tested anew and America has risen to the challenge. Today, we celebrate the triumph not of a candidate, but of a cause, the cause of democracy.

"We will press forward with speed and urgency, for we have much to do in this winter of peril and significant possibilities," he told the small, socially distant crowd in Washington.

Lawmakers clapped. Small flags fluttered on the Mall in lieu of spectators—191,500 of them, planted by the Presidential Inaugural Committee as a memorial for those whose lives had been lost during the pandemic, and as a stand-in for the thousands who could not attend.

Breakfast of southern-style steak and eggs and grits was served on Trump's final flight to Florida. Once landed, a few thousand people lined the streets to watch Trump's motorcade head to Mar-a-Lago. It was a slow crawl, with Trump waving and giving a thumbs-up through the tinted glass.

When Trump's motorcade entered his property, he went straight to his residence, joined by Melania. He had ten minutes left as president.

At 11:59 a.m., January 20, Trump was in his apartment. No tweets. No speeches.

At 12:01 p.m., several Secret Service agents began reducing their setup around the estate. Trump was no longer president. No more access to the nuclear "football." The security footprint shrunk in an instant.

After the inaugural ended, Vice President Harris and her husband, Doug Emhoff, escorted Pence and Karen Pence to the bottom of the Capitol steps. The Pences headed to Andrews Air Force Base to fly to Columbus, Indiana, with family members and the family's dogs, cat and rabbit on board.

It was a bright afternoon when the plane landed. Two fire trucks held a large American flag from their raised ladders and the lectern on the tarmac read: "BACK HOME AGAIN." The upbeat 1970 rocker, "All Right Now" by Free, played as Pence and his family walked toward a small stage.

"You know, we have a tradition on Air Force Two: We always invite someone to sit in the jump seat, in the cockpit, as a guest," Karen Pence told the crowd of friends and family.

Sitting up front, she said, gives you "perspective," since you can "kind of see where everything is and you kind of get a feel for where you are going.

"In the jump seat today was Mike," she said. She began to cry.

FIFTY-FOUR

Security held in a seemingly fortified Washington. The planning, preparations and worry, from the session at Conmy Hall to the troops and officers on the streets, had apparently deterred any of the threatened violence.

Klain and Sullivan, along with several other aides, including Elizabeth Sherwood-Randall, Biden's homeland security adviser, stayed in the Situation Room for over an hour on January 20, monitoring it all.

When Biden arrived at the Oval Office after 4 p.m., he greeted his team and asked Klain what he had for him to sign. Where was the work? Let's go, he said.

Biden signed 15 executive actions and two agency directives, which press secretary Jen Psaki later noted were far more than Trump's two orders on Day One.

Many strokes peeled back some of Trump's signature agenda items. Requiring people to wear masks on federal property. Nixing the permit for the Keystone XL pipeline. Reestablishing ties with the World Health Organization and the Paris climate pact. Ending the national emergency Trump used to secure funds for his border wall. Repealing the travel ban on some Muslim-majority nations.

Inside a drawer in the Resolute Desk, Trump had left his letter for Biden. He put it in his pocket and did not share it with his advisers.

His attention turned to the virus.

As Biden had headed to the Capitol earlier on January 20, Sonya Bernstein, 30, one of Jeff Zients's deputies, was preparing to launch the president's coronavirus response plan as soon as the clocks struck noon.

Bernstein, formerly executive assistant to budget director Sylvia Burwell, had spent nearly every day for months working from her English basement apartment in Mount Pleasant, D.C. The operational command center, she joked. In her prior job, she worked in New York City's public hospital system as cases surged in the nation's first big nightmare of an outbreak, overwhelming hospitals and staff.

Each day, she would wake up thinking of the lives lost and hoping tomorrow would be better, but the number of deaths had climbed and climbed. She had found it crushing and jumped at the chance to help Biden change the trajectory.

Bernstein joined a video meeting on inauguration morning. They had an elaborate to-do list, plus their spreadsheet listing all of the federal agencies and subagencies. They tracked their top questions and actions. They had to go from zero to a hundred in just a few days.

An organized Covid testing infrastructure had to be built fast. Funding, personnel and equipment for getting vaccines, vaccinators and sites had to be found. Vaccines were not being given from retail pharmacies, and Zients wanted a pharmacy program built. Teachers had to be given vaccine priority as Biden wanted schools reopened. Supply chains had to be improved.

Representatives from Homeland Security, Defense and Health and Human Services joined the video call. They seemed eager to have a seat at the Zoom table.

Bernstein could almost feel the vaccines going into people's arms.

On Monday afternoon, January 25, Zients met with Biden and Vice President Harris in the Oval Office to talk about vaccine supply.

The Trump team had a prolonged negotiation with Pfizer for a second 100 million vaccine doses but had not ordered them.

"Mr. President," Zients said, "I think that we have the opportunity here, if we move quickly, to get more supply delivered across the summer and we should make a commitment." The total cost was $4 billion for 100 million additional Pfizer doses.

It's wartime, Biden said, embracing the recommendation instantly. "The worst-case scenario here is not a bad scenario at all," Biden said, "which is we have excess supply."

Zients agreed. "You never run to the top of the hill," he said, "you run beyond the top of the hill, right?" Overwhelm the problem.

"How confident are you that they can deliver?" Biden asked.

"Stuff can always go wrong," Zients said, "but we're going to monitor it really close. We're going to use every one of your authorities, including the Defense Production Act to support them in getting this done on time or faster. If we can expedite it, we'll expedite it."

"Sounds to me like the right decision for sure," Biden said, "not a close call."

Biden decided to announce the additional 100 million Pfizer doses the next day. He also agreed to buy 100 million more Moderna doses, and the 200 million additional doses were added to the 400 million already ordered, giving the U.S. 600 million doses—enough for 300 million Americans with the two-shot regimen.

He had more questions for Zients. "Is there anything we can do to make it faster? How do we know they are going to be able to deliver on time?

"How are we doing on getting the masking orders in place?"

Biden had announced he wanted all Americans to "mask up" for his first 100 days. Mask wearing was the fastest and easiest way to save lives but had become intensely politicized following mixed messages from the Trump White House on whether it was necessary.

"What are we doing to stand up mass vaccination sites?" Biden asked Zients.

FEMA is making progress, Zients said. They would have 21 mass vaccination sites up and running by the end of March with the ability to deliver a total of 71,000 shots per day at full capacity.

"Are they all big stadiums?"

No.

"Mobile vaccination units?"

It was an umbrella term describing efforts to bring vaccination services into communities and reach specific population groups.

"How are we going to deploy those in rural areas and hard-to-reach areas and make sure the vaccine is done in an equitable way?" Biden asked.

Some data showed it was not yet being handled equitably, Zients said.

Biden said they had to focus on equity. He said he wanted to be sure all the assets and capabilities of the federal government were being used.

"Let's do what we can to get people masked up," he said. "Let's do what we can to push supply as hard as we possibly can. Let's do what we can to create more places where people can get vaccinated, more vaccinators, more needles in arms."

FIFTY-FIVE

"Hey, did you leak this lunch?"

President Trump, in a dark suit and yellow tie, was grinning at Kevin McCarthy, the House minority leader, who had come to visit him at Mar-a-Lago on January 28.

"No," McCarthy said, stepping toward Trump past a vase of yellow roses and gold drapes. "Your staff must have, right? I never told my staff."

"You think my staff did it?"

"No. I don't think your staff did it."

"Well, who do you think did it?"

"You," McCarthy said.

McCarthy's visit to the former president was all over the news. The former president did not deny leaking the story. He seemed very eager to be back in the headlines, back in the action. Having the top House Republican come for lunch was not something to keep secret.

The leaders of the Republican Party were still coming to him. McCarthy, in particular, was a wild card after he said on January 13 that Trump "bears responsibility" for the Capitol riot, a remark that enraged Trump. Now, McCarthy was visiting him, seeking his input and advice.

"You know, Melania said this has more press than when I met Putin," Trump said. There were news helicopters nearby, he said, and lots of media interest.

"You know it's good for you and me, right?"

"All right," McCarthy said.

McCarthy came with the hope of keeping Trump involved with the House GOP so he could retake the majority in 2022. He needed to steer Trump away from unnecessary primary fights and to lend his name to winnable seats. They sat down for lunch.

"You want a cheeseburger and fries?"

"I'll have a cheeseburger, but I'm fat," McCarthy said. "No fries. Salad. Take the bun out."

"That really works?" Trump asked, looking over at McCarthy's plate. Trump took the bun off his own burger.

"You want some ice cream?"

"I'll have some fruit."

Trump ordered ice cream for himself.

"You know, being off Twitter has kind of helped me."

"Oh, really?"

"Yeah, a lot of people would say they liked my policy, didn't like my tweets."

"Yeah, like everybody."

"My numbers have kind of gone up."

Trump asked about the upcoming Senate impeachment trial.

"I don't think it's going anywhere," McCarthy said.

Graham spoke with Trump again on January 31, just 11 days after Biden was sworn in. The Senate trial was scheduled to begin in early February. A day earlier, Trump had shaken up his legal team for the trial, lurching from one group of little-known lawyers to another.

Trump's calls with attorneys and his aides about the trial were haphazard. Trump was distracted and intent on relitigating the election and his claims of fraud. It was the same loud, angry refrain, every call, to the point where even his closest aides were exhausted.

Most of our guys, the Senate Republicans, Graham assured Trump on his call, will vote to acquit you, on the grounds that it is unconstitutional to try a former president who is already out of office.

Trump, however, seemed more excited about the support of Congresswoman Marjorie Taylor Greene, the freshman Georgia Republican and far-right lawmaker whose extremist politics were at the core of her political image. Greene had supported Trump's efforts to overturn the election and had filed articles of impeachment against Biden the day after his inauguration.

Greene had also promoted QAnon conspiracies on social media. "Q is a patriot," Greene once wrote in one video post. "He's on the same page as us, and he is very pro-Trump."

"Be careful," Graham warned him, "don't let her draw you into quicksand here."

"She says nice things about me," Trump said.

Graham sighed. This was how it was going to be in Trump's post–White House world.

He would do his best, guiding Trump where he could. He would still be the senator Trump could call for a read on Congress, or a round of golf.

But there was no changing him. You just kept the conversation going.

FIFTY-SIX

Senator Susan Collins, the Maine Republican and moderate, was being driven to the Bangor airport by her husband, Tom Daffron, on Sunday, January 31, when President Biden phoned.

"Just got your letter," Biden said in his instantly recognizable chipper and encouraging voice.

Collins, now beginning her fifth term in the Senate, had orchestrated a letter to Biden from 10 Republican senators. They had sent it to the White House earlier in the day with a counteroffer to Biden's $1.9 trillion rescue plan. The Republicans proposed less than one third of what Biden had outlined—$618 billion.

She instantly recognized the old Joe on the phone, engaged and unhurried. He wanted to update and chat. They knew each other very well. They had overlapped during her first 12 years in the Senate and another eight when Biden was vice president and president of the Senate.

Collins did not want to cut off the new president, but she also did not want to miss her flight to Washington. She asked her husband to keep circling the airport.

"I really have to catch my plane," she finally said.

Biden said he would be happy to meet as the Republicans had requested in their letter. How about tomorrow?

"May I inform the other nine Republicans?"

Please wait until you have landed in Washington, Biden said. Collins thought the request unusual, but she realized he probably wanted to inform his staff. Biden had long been a compulsive phone addict, always anxious to pick up the phone to reach out or meet when he saw a problem, especially an opportunity to negotiate. Collins had just sent the letter hours earlier to the White House, which might not have been fully staffed on a Sunday.

When Ron Klain saw the letter, he was flabbergasted. One third of Biden's $1.9 trillion plan was a staggeringly low number, certainly not serious.

The letter was filled with optimism and appeals to bipartisan action, beginning, "As you proclaimed in your Inaugural Address, overcoming the challenges facing our nation 'requires the most elusive of things in a democracy: Unity.'"

The letter also said, "In the spirit of bipartisanship and unity, we have developed a COVID-19 relief framework that builds on prior COVID assistance laws, all of which passed with bipartisan support." But the opening bid did not seem to match the professed comity.

Biden, however, told Klain he would not reject the proposal. That did not mean he would embrace it. He just wanted to hear more. Perhaps these Republicans were willing to move on from Trump and cut a deal with him. Perhaps the number in the letter was fluid. He would have them over. His style, of course, was to listen. Do not let one letter define everything. It was an overture.

Once back in Washington, Collins was informed the White House had reached out. Biden would see them at 5 p.m. the next day, Monday, February 1. She called up the nine other Republicans in her group, from Senator Lisa Murkowski of Alaska to Senator Todd Young of Indiana to Senator Bill Cassidy of Louisiana.

Collins whipped them into gear, playing assignment editor. Each senator was to present and focus on a key part of the rescue plan. They were going to show Biden he was proposing far too much too soon, with too much unnecessary spending.

Collins informed Leader Mitch McConnell about the coming meeting with Biden. He gave his blessing but told her he did not want to be directly involved at this point. Ten of them going over to see Biden could serve as McConnell's trial balloon, his chance to take Biden's measure. He would watch how Biden, his newly empowered former colleague, handled a big-money, big-stakes negotiation. He would also get a better sense of where the president might be heading.

McConnell also knew Collins had long been a member of a broader group of about 20 Republican and Democratic senators who liked to meet privately to discuss bipartisan ideas. They often got together for dinners and hush-hush meetings. McConnell tracked those discussions but rarely fretted about them. They talked a lot but there was little evidence they went anywhere.

Politics was ruthlessly partisan, McConnell believed. Bipartisanship was fine—if it was the only way to achieve something concrete that he could not get any other way, and without giving up too much in a deal with the Democrats.

Biden had learned over the decades that meetings—particularly long meetings—could be useful to move people off their talking points. Most senators only knew the short version of proposed legislation, which could run hundreds of pages. A long discussion might eventually open some areas for compromise. But it took time. As Obama's vice president, he had led a marathon of 11 working-group meetings with Republicans from May 5 to June 22, 2011, on a long-term resolution to the federal debt. The talks broke down, he knew all too well. But they had come close.

The context for the upcoming meeting was important. Biden's rescue plan was a tax-and-budget bill. If the Democrats chose, they could invoke a Senate rule called "reconciliation." Under arcane Senate rules for legislation involving budgets, only a majority vote was required. It would also not be subject to the filibuster, which effectively required 60 votes for passage. With the 50-50 Senate and Vice President Harris's tie-breaking vote, the rescue plan could pass, 51 to 50, if Biden could keep all 50 Democrats in line—a big, uncertain task. But maybe a possibility.

A masked President Biden entered the Oval Office at 5 p.m. on Monday, February 1, on the 12th day of his presidency. He took the presidential seat with his back to the fireplace.

He was friendly but this was not entirely the old Joe strolling in, all laughs and smiles, catching up with pals and talking about a sports team. He seemed to be saying this is business time. He had a stack of memos in his hand and a notebook in his lap.

One light touch: his dark socks with small blue dogs poking out of his pant legs.

Vice President Harris was to his right in the other chair. Collins, sitting upright in a hunter green dress, was to Biden's left on the couch nearest to him. All were wearing masks and seated far apart.

"Thanks for coming down," Biden said softly as he looked around the room. They thanked him profusely. "Thank you, Mr. President."

"No, no, no," Biden said, "I'm anxious to talk." He paused. "I feel like I'm back in the Senate, which I liked the best of everything I did."

The nine Senate Republicans in the room chuckled. They also came armed with folders and notebooks. The 10th, Senator Mike Rounds of South Dakota, joined by speakerphone. Klain, Ricchetti and other aides sat in the back.

The good news, Collins began, was they agreed with Biden's $160 billion proposal for vaccine distribution and testing as a direct, necessary response to the pandemic.

But then she and other Senate Republicans addressed the core of their objections to the $1.9 trillion. They did not believe the economy was in dire straits. The $900 billion aid package just passed by Congress in December was more than enough.

"Now," Biden told them, "let's go through where we're in disagreement." He wanted the details, to get to the "granularity," the word he used more and more in meetings.

The Republicans seemed to speak with one voice. Biden was proposing $465 billion for direct payments or stimulus checks of $1,400 to individuals. The Republican proposal was for $220 billion, less than half. Instead of the additional $1,400 check in his plan, which came on top of the $600 checks already in the December package, why not shrink the new check to $900? Maybe $800 or $700? They piled on.

Senator Murkowski of Alaska suggested $1,000.

Biden was listening but he did not give any ground.

Klain began shaking his head. No. If there had been one winner for Biden on politics and policy, it was the $1,400 check. Added to the $600 sent out in the previous stimulus plan in December, it amounted to $2,000.

The $2,000 was a promise made by the two new Democratic senators from Georgia. They had both won in a long-standing red state by telling crowd after crowd they needed to vote for them to get the extra $1,400. Biden had been right there with them. The result was a 50-50 Senate.

Klain shook his head again.

Collins looked over at Klain. Who was this random man in the back making a spectacle? Rudely shaking his head? She did not recognize him behind his mask. She turned to Senator Rob Portman of Ohio. "Do you know who that guy is?"

Ron Klain, Portman whispered.

Senator Mitt Romney of Utah, a fiscal conservative who had been the lone Republican senator in the upper chamber to vote to convict Trump at his first impeachment trial, also noticed Klain's head shakes. A former member of corporate boards, Romney knew the power of little gestures.

"I think Ron thinks this a nonstarter," Romney said, turning to the room.

Some Senate Republicans and Biden aides laughed uneasily. Klain did not answer. It was crazy, in his view, to want to discuss how Biden might not do the one thing he made clear he would do.

Klain later realized he was perhaps shaking his head a little more vigorously than he had intended. He had not meant to be venal or dismissive. But he thought the Senate Republicans' position was ridiculous, a flat-out denial of a major Biden win.

Biden brought up what Klain had been thinking about: Georgia.

"We won the elections in Georgia on this issue," Biden said.

The room fell quiet for a moment. No Old Joe. He was playing and talking practical politics.

Romney, sitting across from Biden and Collins on another couch, kept the discussion moving. He brought out some charts he had carried in. He proceeded to argue, CEO-style, that some states did not need money at this point in the pandemic, even if some struggling cities did. He started to explain his formula for how aid for states and cities should be allocated.

Romney said nearly half of the states had seen their revenues increase, so why give them more? And others, he said, had not yet spent the money Trump and Congress had passed and allocated last year.

Romney's argument perplexed Klain. He knew the Republican proposal included no state or local aid. Biden's proposal was a whopping $350 billion. Why was Romney talking about a formula? Zero times anything is still zero. The idea that these people were lecturing them about a formula, when they had put nothing on the table. It was bullshit, Klain thought.

He shook his head again.

Portman, a former Office of Management and Budget director and U.S. trade representative during George W. Bush's presidency, weighed in. Like Romney, he was known as a calm, business-minded Republican who remained close to the Bush family. Unlike Romney, Portman was far less antagonistic toward Trump, who was still beloved by Ohio Republicans.

Portman also had reason to hope Biden might be willing to deal. He had announced a week earlier he would not seek a third Senate term in 2022. Biden had called him. The conversation had gone well.

But he was also realistic. Days earlier, Portman had spoken with Steve Ricchetti by phone, urging him to tell the president he was starting off on the wrong foot if they were going to plow ahead without looping in Senate moderates, along with the Problem Solvers Caucus in the House.

Ricchetti had disagreed. He said President Biden and Senate Republicans did not see this crisis the same way. They were looking at different data, talking to different experts. The president was determined to go big. He could never be convinced to sit on his hands in his first few months.

Portman urged Ricchetti to have Biden think hard about that position. Whatever Biden did in the coming weeks could define his presidency.

"This is a Sister Souljah moment for Biden," Portman had told Ricchetti, a reference to Bill Clinton's rebuke, in 1992, to the Black female activist's call for Black people to kill white people for a week instead of killing Black people. It was widely seen as an attempt by Clinton to define himself as a centrist and to court suburban voters.

Portman had told Ricchetti, "Take the microphone and say, 'You know what? We sent this package up there. It's our campaign agenda. We believe in it. But we're all going to take a deep breath and we're going to stop.'" He said Biden could easily start over and do something bipartisan and smaller. Unite the country. Ricchetti was polite but they were speaking different languages.

In other meetings and calls with Senate Republicans in late January, Brian Deese and Jeff Zients also had not given any indication Biden might back down. Ricchetti was part of a White House chorus.

Sitting in the Oval Office on February 1, Portman tried again, this time directly addressing Biden, to pull him back from his left-leaning temptations. He told Biden he was not enthralled by parts of the rescue plan he believed had nothing to do with the pandemic. That included the child tax credit, he said, and he noted the Internal Revenue Service had told him and others it would probably take a long time to implement it.

Passing the child tax credit will not immediately help families dealing with the virus, Portman said. He said the economy was improving, with the nation's gross domestic product poised to bounce back.

We have worked together in the past, Biden said.

I know that, sir, Portman said.

Biden would not back off his approach or his numbers.

Klain vehemently disagreed with Portman's characterization of the child tax credit. Would implementing it be hard? Of course. Asking the IRS to do anything was a challenge. But it was doable. He started to shake his head again.

Collins glared at Klain.

White House aides perked up when Senator Shelley Moore Capito of West Virginia began to speak. Capito, though a Republican, was close to Joe Manchin, her state's Democratic senator. Manchin was the critical Democratic vote. Whatever she said could be an indicator of what Manchin might want.

Capito said Biden should consider a shorter time frame for the $400 unemployment insurance benefit that was part of the president's plan, which was in addition to the $1,400 checks. Biden's plan called for the $400 to be paid through September 2021. The Senate Republicans called for the $400 to be paid only through July.

Capito said keeping that benefit on a tight leash was her paramount concern. If it went on too long, she worried too many people in West Virginia would decide against returning to work. In her state, the weekly unemployment payment would amount to $724—or about $19 an hour, which was more than twice the $8.75 minimum wage in West Virginia.

Biden said he was happy to discuss Capito's suggestion. He then declared, "I'm definitely sticking with September."

Let's get back to areas of agreement, Biden said turning to Collins. "You have a way of doing small business in your bill." He knew aid to shuttered businesses was one of her core issues. She had been a regional director for the Small Business Administration in George H. W. Bush's administration before being elected to the Senate.

"I have a way of doing small business. They're roughly the same size," Biden said. Both had plans for $50 billion. "You know what? I will put aside mine and I'll do it your way. We could replace my small business plan with your small business plan. We can do that."

Collins was receptive. "Good," she said. "Our goals are the same."

The discussion continued—civil and circular. Biden stuck to his $1.9 trillion, frequently looking down at one of his memos or his notebook. The Republicans stuck to $618 billion.

Biden adjourned the meeting. He said his staff would follow up with them. "Brian Deese will be in touch with you," he said. "Right, Brian?"

Klain believed Biden had handled the meeting well.

Some of the Republicans later told others they began to wonder if this was all show. Was Biden just having a meeting as cover to say he tried? It would be hard to believe. Joe was not that type of guy to lead them on and then bolt, right? And he had given them an hour more than scheduled.

FIFTY-SEVEN

As Biden mingled with departing senators in the Oval Office, Senator Portman approached Steve Ricchetti. This was a good, constructive, meeting, Portman said. Ricchetti, who rarely uses email and is uber-careful in any setting, was curt in reply. Portman then turned to Ron Klain.

"This was a good meeting," Portman said. "Thank you for inviting us down." If we can move forward on this, he said, that would be a turn in the right direction.

"But if you go forward on reconciliation, that will just set a bad tone."

"Senator Portman, look," Klain said, "we spent a lot of time thinking about this package and I'm not going to tell you that every single dollar in here is life or death. But I am going to tell you that something very close to what we proposed is absolutely needed to beat this virus and save this economy.

"This isn't just some giant ask," Klain said. "This is a plan we've put together. And at $600 billion, really $500 billion, if you count the real money in it, we are miles and miles apart.

"You guys came in here and gave us a take-it-or-leave-it offer. That's not a good meeting."

"Ron," Portman said, "that's not at all what happened here. It's not take it or leave it." We heard you make your case. You heard us. We could come back together again, keep this discussion going.

"Okay," Klain said. "Okay."

Portman believed Klain was misreading the entire meeting. Republicans were feeling Biden out, not presenting an ultimatum. This was a gang of 10 senators, moderate in temperament, not McConnell or the hardline conservative Freedom Caucus.

Klain took Portman's remark, that this was not a take-it-or-leave-it gambit, as a potential opening down the line. Portman was close to McConnell and a veteran fiscal negotiator. As trade representative he had negotiated with 30 countries and gone toe-to-toe with China. Portman would not express an openness to more talks unless he meant it.

Collins was delighted. "It was a very good exchange of views," Collins told reporters, standing in her winter coat outside the White House that night. "I wouldn't say we came together on a package tonight. No one expected that in a two-hour meeting.

"What we did agree to do is follow up and talk further," she said.

"I practically gushed," she later said in a private meeting, "and I meant it because the president had given us two hours! He listened carefully to us. It was an excellent, productive meeting from my perspective."

Later, *The Washington Post* asked the White House press office if Biden's socks with blue dogs were telegraphing something about his politics. Blue dogs are the mascot for moderate Democrats.

"It is extremely unlikely that was done with any subtle purpose in mind," an adviser told the *Post*, requesting anonymity to discuss the socks.

"I'm almost positive," the adviser said. "It's interesting. But accidental, I think."

Unbeknown to the Republican senators leaving the White House on February 1, Biden had invited Manchin, probably the most conservative member of the Democratic Party in the Senate, for his own private Oval Office meeting that same evening.

Manchin had been waiting on the ground floor of the White House as the Republican meeting had dragged on an hour over schedule. He was almost hiding so that he would not be seen by reporters or by the Republicans.

Manchin previously served as West Virginia's governor from 2005 to 2010, when he was elected to the Senate. At 6-foot-3 with broad shoulders, he had the confident air of a former college athlete. He won a football scholarship to West Virginia University and was a childhood friend of fellow Farmington, West Virginian, Nick Saban, the legendary football coach at the University of Alabama.

Manchin was also a notorious wild card in Democratic ranks. He was gregarious with his colleagues but relished a lone-wolf style of politics. He lived on a houseboat, *Almost Heaven*, docked at the Washington Channel of the Potomac River, when the Senate was in session. His good-old-boy manner helped him survive in West Virginia, where he was the only Democrat to hold statewide office. Trump had won the state in 2020 by 39 points.

Manchin bragged that he had such good relations with the other party that he had never campaigned against a Republican.

In a 50-50 Senate, Manchin's independence gave him immense power. Lose him and any vote would be at risk of falling apart. Biden would have to find a Republican to get a bill back to 50 so Harris could break the tie. But with McConnell holding an iron grip on the Senate GOP, that was always a long shot.

Manchin and Biden knew each other when they worked together during Manchin's early years in the Senate and Biden's time as vice president. "Joe, I get it," Biden had said to Manchin about being a Democrat in a conservative state. Delaware was widely considered the most business-friendly state in the country. "Tell me what I can do. I can be for you or against you, whatever helps you the most."

Biden knew it would be hard to persuade Manchin, even if West Virginia was slated to receive lots of money. You had to win him, not buy him.

Manchin's mantra was, "If I can go home and explain it, I'll vote for it. If I can't explain it, I can't vote for it." But he was also stubborn and if he started as a "no," he often stayed a "no."

In declining to join a party-line vote, Manchin once told Harry Reid, then the majority leader, "Harry, on my best day I can't sell this shit in West Virginia." His deal with Reid: "Harry, I think it's best if I just tell you how I'm going to vote so there's no surprises, so you always know where I'm at."

Biden and Manchin sat down in the Oval Office, alone late on February 1. Joe to Joe.

Joe, Biden said, I've lived through these situations and I'm trying to work through this. I prefer the bipartisan path, but that takes time. Unfortunately, we don't have time here because of the pandemic and the economy. There was a deadline ahead, March 14, when supplemental unemployment benefits would begin to lapse.

"This is so important," Biden said. He recalled working the Affordable Care Act for Obama in 2009. "I worked across the aisle, you know that."

"I know you do, Mr. President," Manchin said. "I know what's in your heart."

"I understand where you are," Biden continued. "But I want to explain to you. I had worked with them for seven or eight months trying to get a compromise on the Affordable Care Act, and at the end of the day I didn't get any Republicans. Now we have a Covid pandemic and it's time sensitive. I can't negotiate for six or eight months."

Manchin said he wanted President Biden, like all presidents, to succeed and would not let him fail.

It was not a negotiation. Few details were discussed. Manchin said he would want some changes, but he would help get something done.

Later that evening, Biden and Klain reflected on the separate sessions with the Republican senators and with Senator Manchin.

"I thought it went well," Biden said of the GOP meeting. "We're obviously very far apart."

"They never once in those two hours, never, came off their 618 billion dollars!" Klain said angrily. "They never once said, well, maybe we will go farther, or maybe we'll give you more money for that, or maybe we'll meet you halfway on schools."

The president was seeking $170 billion for school reopenings, the Republican offer was $20 billion. "Yes, it had been an amiable meeting," Biden said. But zero movement.

Klain did report that Portman said there would be a counteroffer.

"Well," Biden said, "that sounds good." Biden said he thought there was a 20 to 25 percent chance that something could be done with the Republicans. Low chance, but still possible.

One thing was certain. They did not want to get "Charlie Browned." They had seen this play before with the football snatched away at the last minute by the Senate Republicans. They could not wait indefinitely. Even if eight of the Republicans at the meeting voted with Biden, 58 total votes would not be enough—two short of the 60 needed to defeat a filibuster.

Both agreed the Democrats-only reconciliation path was maybe inevitable. The 10 Republicans were too far below Biden's number. What Biden had needed from them was a vivid overture, a sign of compromise—a recognition of his political capital and Democratic power in this new Washington. That could have maybe caused a spark. But there was none.

Even when Biden had brought up the Georgia win and his

promise on the checks, it was as if the Republicans did not want to acknowledge it.

Klain soon communicated privately to congressional leaders. They would keep the door open for Republicans to come back and work with them on aspects of the $1.9 trillion proposal, but Biden was determined to keep moving forward. No pause.

Speaker Pelosi was on board, telling her allies in the White House and at the Capitol she thought it was fine the Republicans had paid Biden a visit. But $618 billion? "They're not serious," she said.

"They don't understand what the president was saying," Pelosi said. She could not sell a modest deal to her members. "Who are you cutting out? Are you going to cut out the food for the children? The housing for their families? The direct payments? The unemployment insurance? You're going to cut out the vaccines?"

Pelosi had already expressed her feelings to Biden, one Sunday before the inauguration. They had been through decades of ups and downs in Washington. She had urged him to go big and fast, for the country and for Democrats, rather than waiting around for Republicans.

"Of all the times you have run for president, this is your time," Pelosi said. "We have always said of us, 'the times have found us.' The times have found you."

FIFTY-EIGHT

Senator Collins was in her office the next day, Monday morning, when one of her staffers came in and reported Leader Schumer had announced on the Senate floor that he would file to use the reconciliation process. It was a procedural move but signaled Democrats' intentions.

"I can't believe it," Collins said. It was less than 24 hours after the White House meeting with Biden that she had practically gushed over. In her view, she was expecting the White House to come back with a new number. "That means they're not going to do a counteroffer and we expected a counteroffer."

For Collins, this proved that Biden had moved firmly to the left. She liked to think she was down the middle, almost a perfect centrist. "I think I'm center-center," she told others. She was the only Republican senator who won in a state that Biden had carried.

Collins was sure Schumer's move on reconciliation had Biden's blessing. She believed that Biden's staff, especially Klain, and Schumer had pushed the president.

She also thought Schumer could be trying to solidify his liberal credentials because he faced a possible primary threat in his 2024 Senate race from a progressive star, Congresswoman Alexandria Ocasio-Cortez, who had become so famous she was now referred to as AOC, a leading member of the so-called "Squad" inside the House.

Progressives had been pressing Schumer for days. Senator Elizabeth Warren approached him after hearing of the Republican number of just $618 billion. "Don't take it," she urged.

Speaking on the floor on February 2, Schumer declared Senate Democrats ready to work with Senate Republicans but also said they were quite willing to go on without them, should they stall Biden's plan.

"We want this entire effort to be bipartisan. We do," Schumer said. "But helping the American people with the big, bold relief they need, that is job number one. That is job number one. So again: We're not going to dilute, dither, or delay."

The White House sent documents and papers to Collins attempting to justify some of their numbers. As best she could tell, one document had been prepared by the American Federation of Teachers, the teacher's union, to justify Biden's school aid number of $170 billion.

Schumer later that day confirmed Collins's suspicions, saying to reporters, "Joe Biden is totally on board with using reconciliation," he said. "I've been talking to him every day. Our staffs have been talking multiple times a day."

Collins and Schumer were not on speaking terms. She had absolutely loathed the way Senate Democrats targeted her during her 2020 reelection race. Democrats poured $180 million into the campaign, which she ultimately won by nine points. She thought the Democrats' ads were unnecessarily personal, dirty, calling her a fraud controlled by Trump and McConnell.

Collins, a Catholic, later quipped to friends, "For Lent, I gave up my anger at Chuck Schumer. It was either that or wine and I decided I'd rather have my glass of wine at night."

She approached McConnell at the Senate GOP's lunch later that day. The lunches were typically closed sessions where one senator picked the cuisine each week, usually something from their home state. Whenever southern senators catered the lunch, visitors to the Capitol and reporters in the halls could smell the hot brisket and corn bread.

Collins told McConnell the previous day's meeting with Biden seemed to have gone well, but she was completely caught off guard by Schumer's reconciliation announcement. It had blindsided her. It was such bad faith, Collins said. Getting 10 Republicans to agree on $618 billion and publicly stand by that kind of spending increase wasn't easy, she said. Didn't the White House get that?

McConnell was not surprised. He did not expect Biden and Schumer to move so quickly, to put their reconciliation card down that fast. But he expected they eventually would.

"Joe Biden has an A+ personality," McConnell said a few minutes later to the large group of Republicans at the lunch, "but you shouldn't assume he's a centrist."

So that became the Republican line. Biden was a nice fellow, a friend to many, but no moderate—and his staff was steering him further left.

As reconciliation picked up momentum, McConnell told senators and his aides he believed Biden was not going to coast. He was playing for history.

"He has a vision of what he wants America to look like and I do, too," McConnell said. "And it's different. And the reason we haven't been having any conversations this year is he's doing what every Democratic president wants to do, which is to push the country as far left as possible, as rapidly as possible.

"They all want to be the next FDR," McConnell said, referring to a long line of Democratic presidents. "They know they can't have three terms, but they're hoping there will be a monument."

"Look," McConnell told others, "if you've made it that far in politics, your second thought, after you say, 'My God, I can't believe it, I got to be president of the United States,' is, 'I'd like to be a great president of the United States.' "

As the lunch wrapped up on February 2, Collins went around the room and gave Republicans her personal pool report: their old friend seemed sympathetic to negotiating but the people around him did not.

Collins recounted Klain's head shakes, shaking her own head

about the chief of staff. She thought it was inappropriate for a chief of staff to provide a visible and negative head-shaking commentary during the president's meetings with the political opposition. And she was deeply offended for the Republicans and Biden himself. It was heavy-handed and rude.

As Biden pushed ahead, he called McConnell, ostensibly about Myanmar. The Senate Republican leader had long supported pro-democracy efforts in the country formerly known as Burma. It was one of the rare policy areas where they had real agreement.

Biden asked McConnell for policy recommendations and advice, then briefly switched to his $1.9 trillion rescue plan. What do you think?

McConnell said it was unlikely the president would see any Senate Republican support for another spending package as big as Biden had outlined. There was no way they could support something of that scope.

For McConnell, it was a statement of the obvious. He was not impolite. Just a summary judgment. A repeat of his public statements.

McConnell's influential and plugged-in chief of staff, Sharon Soderstrom, made similar points to senior Biden aides in private discussions in early February. She never gave them an exact vote count, but she told them Senate Republicans remained wary of more unemployment insurance because it hurt businesses that were trying to reopen. Too many people were making more money by not working and staying home.

Klain saw Biden did not have some special way of persuading McConnell, no magic power as the "McConnell whisperer," as some called Biden during the Obama years. But he did know how to negotiate with McConnell.

"For example," Klain once said, "you're not going to persuade

Mitch McConnell that he's wrong about the estate tax. That he didn't have the right class at the Kennedy School to explain to him the regressive nature. That's not what Joe Biden tries to do. He's like, 'Okay, you tell me what you need to get this done. I'll tell you what I need.' "

Inside the White House, there was a growing belief McConnell and Senate Republicans were stalling and holding to their position for a reason: They were not sure Biden could get the whole thing passed, hold all 50 Democrats.

Let him try, they seemed to be saying with their actions, and let us see if he can really keep Manchin and the progressives, with such different ideologies, together for a final vote. And if Biden can't do that, he might have to come groveling back to us to cut a smaller deal and save his first 100 days.

"His troops are lined up against it," Klain said within the White House. "Maybe we'll get a Republican vote, maybe we won't. I don't know. But the fundamental problem Republicans have in fighting it is it's popular" with the public, including with Republican voters.

In the West Wing, Klain talked up what he called his "little red hen theory" of Biden's rescue plan—and for the 2022 elections. He was taking names.

"If we pass this thing, we beat Covid, and get the economy moving, the people who helped pick the wheat and make the bread will share in the credit," Klain said. "The people who did not, will not."

McConnell told his staff, "When we will engage is when that fails." Maybe Biden would get this rescue bill through but there would come a point, now or later, where he would need the Republicans at the table. That was the leverage point.

"That's when we start dealing with each other," McConnell said about his strategy. "I don't blame him for not dealing with me now because I don't like anything he's doing."

McConnell believed the economy was picking up, the vaccine was going out. Senate Republicans could sit tight and not look like misers to the voters they wanted to win in 2022. This was not like March 2020, the beginning of the pandemic, or like the frightening lurch into the financial crisis in late 2008.

FIFTY-NINE

Senator Sanders, primary foe turned key supporter, and other Senate Democrats, such as Debbie Stabenow of Michigan, Jon Tester of Montana, and Brian Schatz of Hawaii, mingled outside the Oval Office on February 3. They looked around and laughed. Trump was gone.

"I would just have panic attacks sometimes walking out," Stabenow told them, recounting her past visits to see Trump. "No one was ever in a good mood either going in or coming out, and usually horrified when he came out. It was like, 'Oh my God, I can't believe this.' "

When Stabenow walked into the Oval, she told Biden, "You can't see my smile beaming under this mask, but I can assure you I'm beaming here."

Biden and his senior White House advisers had quickly turned their attention away from Collins, Portman and the other Republicans to Pelosi and Schumer, and to congressional Democrats. They were determined to keep this plan moving, to show movement on their side.

Schumer's reconciliation push for the rescue plan had the Senate Democrats in high spirits—a sign they mattered and would not be bit players this time. They were tired of watching Senate moderates and the busy "gangs" of centrists dominate the deals and headlines.

Biden got right to it. The United States was in the middle of a historic crisis, he told them. He pulled out his card with the number of vaccinations from the previous day—over 1.5 million people.

We are going to be able to do much better than we originally thought for the first 100 days, Biden said. But that is not all. We have this rescue plan, and we can't do it without you. All of us, as Democrats, need to be a cohesive team, he said.

Biden then went around the room, asking for input not only on the policy but on how to sell it to the country. This is an incredible moment for the nation and for us, he said.

It was part of Biden's style. Biden wanted details. Some saw Biden as a wonk. Others saw a president possibly worried about being caught unprepared or confused, as he had been a few times during the campaign. Trump had repeatedly challenged Biden to take a cognitive test and raised questions about his mental sharpness. "Something's going on," Trump told his aides.

Biden detested Trump's taunts and as president made sure to stay alert to reporters.

"What are they going to yell at me?" Biden would often ask his advisers before welcoming a press contingent into the Oval Office for a photo opportunity. "What are they going to ask?"

On February 3, Biden turned to the room of senators and nodded up at the portrait of FDR. Terrible times make great presidents, he said.

"I would have been much happier to be a good president, but here we are."

He brought up the February 1 meeting with Senate Republicans. If we can get the Republicans to join us, that'd be great, he said. But I just met with them and I don't get any sense that there is really a seriousness there. But we will try. In the end, it's going to be up to us to get this done.

I know some of you are talking to the moderate Republicans and that's great, he added. If you can get more support, we need it. You know me, I'd much rather do that. But the important thing is we get things done for people.

Stabenow said bipartisanship was now being redefined in the Biden era, away from deal cutting with Republican lawmakers to crafting policy that had appeal to both Democrats and Republican voters. Democrats should focus on those voters rather than the GOP's splintered, unsteady leaders in Congress. Biden agreed. Go right to the voters.

Senator Jon Tester of Montana, 64 years old, a gentle giant with a crew cut, told Biden this was his first time ever in the Oval Office. His voice was thick with emotion. He had been in the Senate since 2007. Fourteen years, through Obama and Trump, and this was his first time there.

"Pretty amazing room, it was pretty cool," Tester told a local news station later. He grinned. "It truly is an oval office. The doors are even oval."

Sanders, now the chairman of the Senate Budget Committee, spoke up. Stick with going big, he implored Biden. He argued it was not just about passing a huge rescue bill but about securing the working-class vote for a generation. It was about proving to them the federal government worked. Trump had stolen them away with his trade war and tariffs against China. To get them back, you had to convince them the Democrats were on their side, looking out for the working class.

The future of American democracy depends on which party is the party of the working class, Sanders, 79, added in his raspy, Brooklyn accent. Democrats must have deep appeal to people on the margins, the strugglers. He believed the Democratic Party was increasingly too cozy with the elites, the educated class with power and connections.

He was looking for that Scranton vein, not the Ivy League through line in Biden's inner circle.

"If we cannot deliver, authoritarianism may be on the march," Sanders said.

Sanders had grown up in Flatbush, Brooklyn, the son of a Polish immigrant paint salesman who never made enough money to fulfill his wife's dreams of not living in a rent-controlled apartment. Much of his family was wiped out in Poland during the Holocaust.

He told Biden and his colleagues they could not take anything for granted after January 6. Who says more horror could not happen here?

"As a kid, I read a lot about the Holocaust and Germany in the 1930s," Sanders later told others. "Germany was one of the most cultured countries in Europe. One of the most advanced countries. So how could a country of Beethoven, of so many great poets and writers, and Einstein, progress to barbarianism?

"How does that happen? We have to tackle that question. And it's not easy."

Biden called Collins on Super Bowl Sunday, February 7.

"It's a really bad move, Mr. President," Collins said, "that Chuck has gone to reconciliation." It was a lost opportunity. "Our offer was very sincere—and it wasn't the final offer."

She saw this was an unexpected chance to have a Susan to Joe, Joe to Susan talk. She and the group of nine other Republicans had increased their proposal by $32 billion, going from $618 billion to $650 billion. The new money would be used to increase the total amount going toward stimulus checks, with a targeted group of Americans now getting $1,400 checks. She and other Republicans believed that was a significant jump. That used to be real money.

Biden expressed interest in continuing to work with her and the other Republicans, but he made no firm commitments. It was only a 5 percent increase. They were more than miles apart.

Collins told him it was not an accident she had 10 Republicans in her group. Ten of them plus 50 Democrats equaled 60 votes, enough to stop a filibuster. The magic 60, she said.

"Mr. President, I just want you to be aware that I'm on the

call!" said a male voice breaking directly into the phone call. It was Brian Deese, Biden's director of the National Economic Council.

Biden seemed surprised. Collins was appalled. What was going on? How could this happen? She thought it was a private White House call. Did staff monitor, listen in or join all of Biden's phone calls?

Suddenly more chimes rang.

Bing! Bing! Bing! Bing!

Clearly others were joining.

Who? What? How?

Both Biden and Collins immediately became more cautious in their remarks to each other because of the intrusion. It was no longer Joe to Susan, Susan to Joe. Collins had no idea who else was listening. She, however, never asked or found out what was going on.

It sure was a conversation stopper. A snapshot of politics and their lives in 2021. Technology taking over, everyone on the line, running all their lives. Deese's interjection unnerved her—it was another staffer monitoring, another incident in the realm of Klain's head shakes. Another shadow over the shoulder of Joe.

To Biden and Klain, Collins was polite and gracious, but she never offered anything they could take seriously. Collins was always explaining why Biden was wrong, in a nice way. They gave her credit for her consistency. But they saw her latest floated offer, moving up a bit to $650 billion, as a very slow walk.

Biden and the White House staff were simultaneously working hard on Senator Murkowski to get her vote for the rescue bill. She was the last hope for a Republican vote, but they finally gave up on her.

"Listen," Biden said, "she's probably not going to be with us. But I like her, and I want to help her. She's not going to be with us on this vote. But it may very well be that somewhere down the road she will be with us. So, whether or not she's going to be with us on this package, I want to make sure we take care of her."

Alaska's share from the rescue bill was eventually increased from $800 million to $1.25 billion.

SIXTY

On Wednesday, February 3, Biden called together his national security team to begin a comprehensive review of the 20-year war in Afghanistan.

Biden wanted to make a big move: terminate the endless war. It would put his stamp on American foreign policy. He had strongly opposed large numbers of U.S. troops in Afghanistan since he was Obama's vice president. But he had not been the decision maker then. Now he was.

He knew the men and women of his foreign policy team sitting before him, most very well. Many were veterans of the Obama administration. As a group, they largely disdained Trump's foreign policy process, dismissing it as incoherent, amateurish and unnecessarily isolationist. Drawing on their muscle memory, they were determined to revive and restore the traditional foreign policy procedures and systems of the Obama years.

"Look," Biden told them, "I'm going to give it to you straight, where I'm at." He reminded them he had been a longtime skeptic, even a cynic, about staying in the war, which began after the September 11, 2001, terrorist attacks in the U.S.

But he promised, "I'm here to listen." He said he had asked Jake Sullivan, the national security adviser, to run a full review and to be the honest broker, leaving no stone unturned, and making sure everyone and every argument was heard. A full and fair debate might help prevent leaks during the process because each person could make their case to Biden and not feel the urge to go public to be heard.

Biden added, "I absolutely want to hear arguments to the contrary and I'm going to keep an open mind about this because if there is a compelling reason to stay, I will certainly consider it and listen to it."

Trump had announced a May 1, 2021, withdrawal of all U.S. troops, but Biden wanted to make his own decision on his own timetable.

Longtime Biden aides like Secretary of State Blinken and chief of staff Klain knew Biden was determined to bring all the troops home. He had wanted out, ever since 2009 when he believed the military and then Secretary of State Hillary Clinton had boxed in and overwhelmed President Obama in his first year. They insisted that Obama add tens of thousands of U.S. troops to the Afghanistan mission. Their resistance to any other option was so great, and often public, that Obama, who had little foreign policy or military experience, almost had no other choice.

Robert Gates, President George W. Bush's defense secretary whom Obama unexpectedly had asked to stay on, had hinted he might resign if Obama failed to approve more troops. Obama believed he could not afford to lose such an established national security figure.

Blinken even had heard Biden privately say in 2009 that the United States had to accept a brutal civil war if U.S. troops withdrew. "How bad can that be?" Biden had asked. Pressed on whether a civil war would break out among the ethnic Pashtuns, who make up nearly half the Afghanistan population, Biden had almost jumped in his chair.

"Bingo. Bingo, bingo, bingo!" he said confidently, grimly repeating one of his favorite expressions.

Biden had made his opposition known at the time to Obama,

as well as his disenchantment with how he believed the military had manipulated the president. Biden told others privately in 2009, "The military doesn't fuck around with me," more than implying they had with Obama.

Now in the 2021 review, Secretary of Defense Lloyd Austin, who knew Biden from the Obama years, told his staff that given Biden's strong feeling, American participation in the war would almost certainly be ending. But he believed there were strong military, intelligence and strategic arguments for keeping a small U.S. force there.

The first Black defense secretary, Austin was a 1975 West Point graduate from Georgia who had served in the Army for four decades. In 2009, he had been director of the Joint Staff, a key senior three-star post, during Obama's initial Afghanistan review when he became familiar with Biden's attitudes. The following year, the two men became even more entwined. Austin had been sent to Iraq as the commanding general of U.S. forces of Iraq in 2010 when Obama had asked Biden to oversee the withdrawal of most U.S. troops. Major Beau Biden was a lawyer on Austin's staff, and the major and the general got to know each other.

Biden and Austin were as steeped in the Afghanistan War history as anyone.

Thus began, over the next two months, an extraordinary series of 25 NSC meetings, large group and small group, one-on-one meetings with Biden, and meetings with his top advisers and cabinet members. Separate meetings of the NSC deputies and principals also were held without Biden. It was one of the most wide-ranging policy reviews ever held.

Emotional and contentious at times, the president seemed to want more certainty and clearer solutions than could be offered. Biden could be prickly and impatient. One top adviser found him almost impossible to work with, as Biden pressed for more detail and intelligence estimates.

Others thought the review was a textbook example of how foreign policy decisions should be made.

Biden's primary argument, the one that undergirded the debate, was that the mission had shifted from its original intent.

The war had been launched by President George W. Bush in October 2001 to root out the Al Qaeda terrorist organization responsible for the 9/11 attacks on the Twin Towers at the World Trade Center in New York City and the Pentagon.

The mission was to stop further attacks. But the war had expanded to a nation-building enterprise to defeat the religiously extreme Taliban, which had given Al Qaeda a safe haven to plot and stage attacks. The Taliban had ruthlessly ruled Afghanistan for five years before September 11, 2001. The hardline regime imposed Islamic law, oppressed women, and destroyed cultural sites, including sixth-century Buddhas which they regarded as forbidden religious idols.

A counterinsurgency effort called COIN grew to include not just defeating the Taliban but protecting the Afghan population and government. At one point, some U.S. military leaders hoped to have a platoon on every street corner in the capital of Kabul. At the height of the war a decade ago, the U.S. had 98,000 troops in Afghanistan. That number had dwindled in 2021 to 3,500, including regular and Special Operations forces.

Lingering over the whole Biden review was the basic question: What is the mission?

Biden had a particular disdain for counterinsurgency, viewing it as a classic example of mission creep.

"Our mission is to stop Afghanistan from being a base for attacking the homeland and U.S. allies by Al Qaeda or other terrorist groups, not to deliver a death blow to the Taliban," Biden said, reminding everyone of the war's original intent.

Simply put, for him the war had become a battle between the Afghan government and the Taliban. The U.S. military should have no part in a civil war in another country and needed to bring U.S. troops home, Biden told advisers.

As a preliminary step in the Sullivan-run policy review, Biden wanted answers to a few questions that deeply reflected his predisposition. As a practical matter, if at least one of them could not be answered positively, they had to face the reality that the U.S. troops had no attainable mission.

"One, do we believe that our presence in Afghanistan is fundamentally contributing to a significantly higher likelihood of a durable, negotiated political settlement between the Afghan government and the Taliban?

"Two, do we believe that the nature of the Al Qaeda and ISIS threat from Afghanistan is such that we have to keep thousands of troops on the ground there indefinitely?

"Three, if we go beyond the May 1 deadline and say we're just staying on an open-ended basis, what is the risk to the force and risk to the mission? And will I have to flow more forces back into Afghanistan?"

As part of the negotiated May 1 deadline with the Trump administration, the Taliban had agreed not to attack U.S. troops. There had been no attacks for one year. But, intelligence showed, they surely would resume if Biden decided to keep U.S. troops indefinitely.

He also said he wanted them to examine, in depth, the humanitarian consequences for the civilian population of Afghanistan if U.S. troops were withdrawn.

Sullivan privately said, "Being the president of the United States and making a decision like this you have to stare in the face the human and potential human costs of your decision."

In his 2020 memoir, *A Promised Land*, Obama recounted Biden's advice during the Afghanistan policy review the first year of Obama's presidency: "Listen to me, boss. Maybe I've been around this town for too long, but one thing I know is when these generals are trying to box in a new president." Biden brought his face a few inches from Obama's and stage-whispered, "Don't let them jam you."

Biden was now determined not to be jammed.

Over the course of the two months of meetings and private discussions in the Sullivan review, the Pentagon eventually laid out two main options. Secretary Austin said Biden could either execute an orderly withdrawal of all troops as quickly and safely as possible or he could approve an indefinite U.S. troop presence in Afghanistan.

U.S. troops were providing important coordination of surveillance and intelligence that helped stabilize the Afghan government of Ashraf Ghani, an academic who had been president of Afghanistan for six years. Austin said the U.S. presence also provided a situational awareness they could not get without being there. Being on the scene, on the ground, could make all the difference in early detection of a problem.

During the Sullivan process, Biden remarked, "If the mission is to preserve the Ghani government, I would not send my own son."

It was a sensitive issue. The president made several other references to his late son, Beau, as a benchmark for determining whether the mission was worthwhile and necessary.

Biden was the first U.S. president in decades to have had a child serve in a war zone, and Beau's experience seemed to heighten Joe Biden's sense of sacrifice and risk.

If the U.S. stayed, the intelligence forecast was that the Taliban would resume their attacks. Should that happen, Biden said he probably would be asked to send still more troops. "If we have 3,000 troops there and they're attacked, you guys"—he pointed to Austin and Milley—"will come in and say okay, we need 5,000 more."

That was the cycle he wanted to avoid. A troop presence became a magnet for more troops because the military leaders naturally would want to protect their own force. And the answer, not surprisingly, was always more troops.

Sullivan concluded that meant the question was not whether to stay or leave, but whether to add more troops or leave.

That gave powerful argument to getting out because it was crystal clear that Biden was not going to add more troops. That was not even an option.

SIXTY-ONE

Trump's Senate impeachment trial in February was showy and emotional. Footage of the Capitol riot presented by the Democrats jarred senators on both sides as they watched grainy clips of Pence and his family rushing down back steps, and Romney shuffling through hallways, both just steps away from rioters.

"You can hear the mob calling for the death of the vice president of the United States," said House impeachment manager Stacey Plaskett, a Democrat from the Virgin Islands.

Trump, who had been banned from Twitter and Facebook following the riot, watched the proceedings from his home in Florida. He hated it, and complained to aides about his defense lawyer, Bruce Castor of Pennsylvania, for wearing an oversized suit and for giving a long-winded and rambling opening statement that confused even Trump's supporters, some of whom wondered if he was improvising.

McConnell told his Republican senators it would be a vote of conscience for each of them. He did not reveal in advance how he was going to vote.

Trump was acquitted by a 57 to 43 vote, falling 10 votes short of the 67 votes needed to convict him. Seven Republicans, including Romney and Collins, voted to convict Trump.

After the vote, McConnell took the floor. He had been one of the 43 votes to acquit the former president. He had polished his speech to make sure what he was about to say was exactly what he wanted to say.

"January 6th was a disgrace," and an act of "terrorism," he said, fueled by people "fed wild falsehoods by the most powerful man on earth because he was angry he'd lost an election."

McConnell sounded exasperated but contained. He turned again and again to his colleagues, thrusting his hands toward them with emphasis. When he described the evidence of election fraud being offered by Trump's allies, he narrowed his fingers together until they were nearly touching, calling their claims extraordinarily thin.

"There is no question that President Trump is practically and morally responsible," McConnell said. "It was also the entire manufactured atmosphere of looming catastrophe, the increasingly wild myths about a reverse landslide election that was being stolen in some secret coup by our now president."

Still, he said, "by the strict criminal standard, the president's speech probably was not incitement."

Lindsey Graham told McConnell that he was surprised to see such emotion. "I didn't know you could get mad," Graham said.

McConnell, usually the Republican realist and cold-blooded operator, had been pushed into a zone where the party's raw wounds might not heal.

"Hatred of Trump knows no boundaries," Graham once said. "It makes people do things not in their self-interest. Like Mitch. I've never seen a person who could affect others as much as Donald Trump.

"I've seen it over and over. It's just the most amazing thing in politics. Smart, rational people break when it comes to Trump," he said. "He's not trying to get them to break. There is no magic. He's just being him. And he wears you down. He'll get you to do things that are not good for you because you don't like him."

Trump spoke with Graham the next day, Valentine's Day. He was the self-appointed middleman between Senate Republicans and a raging former president.

Graham's relationship with Trump had grown doubly complex after the January 6 insurrection. They shared a genuine friendship, fused by political talk and golf. They could have serious conversations. No other president had brought Graham inside like Trump. And the relationship also gave him increased visibility in the news and inside the GOP. He was a fixture on television, especially Fox.

But Graham also saw his engagement with Trump as a political necessity for the Republican Party. "I don't see how we come back without him," he said, "and I don't see how we get there without him changing."

On February 14, Trump was in a dark, sour mood about McConnell's floor speech. "I can't believe he would say those things given all we've done together," Trump vented to Graham. He went on and on. Tax cuts. Judges and the Supreme Court. Deregulation.

Graham said McConnell was still furious. He believes you cost the Republicans and him the Senate majority with the loss of the two Georgia seats.

Trump tore into McConnell again.

Graham worried if McConnell and Trump did not mend fences soon, it could cost Republicans a golden opportunity to win back power in 2022. Democrats would take the crack-up and use it to divide the party.

"They're going to take part of Mitch's speech and turn it into advertising in 2022 in Arizona, New Hampshire, Georgia and other contested areas," Graham predicted, "and say, 'Here is what Mitch McConnell says about Trump. What do you think?' "

Appearing on Fox News that night, Graham said if you think Trump is going away, or you think you can drive him out of the party, you are wrong. "He's ready to move on and rebuild the Republican Party," Graham said.

Days later, McConnell backed off, at least publicly, on Fox. He said he would "absolutely" support Trump if the former president won the Republican nomination in 2024.

Graham saw the remark as McConnell's way of keeping the peace. But he knew nothing had really changed. When McConnell's office put out a press release about his appearance on Fox News, it stressed his criticism of Biden. It did not even mention his promise to back a possible third Trump nomination.

Graham kept working Trump, trying to keep him engaged with Republicans.

"Mr. President, for us to be successful in 2022, we've got to put our best team in the field," Graham told Trump in another call, running through a list of Republican senators like John Boozman of Arkansas, John Hoeven of North Dakota and Roy Blunt of Missouri. All were low-key lawmakers up for reelection. They could use a Trump bump, he said. "The sooner that you can come out and support them, the better."

Trump said he would be happy to help them out. He seemed ready to be back in the fight. But he was far more interested in exacting revenge against House Republicans like Congresswoman Liz Cheney of Wyoming and others who had voted to impeach him. They were disloyal, irredeemable, traitors.

"The main thing you've got to do is repair the damage with Mike Pence," Graham told him. "I think there's universal belief that Mike Pence was incredibly loyal to you and you treated him poorly."

No way, Trump said.

"You got caught up in losing the election you thought you won," Graham said. "I get that. But you asked more of Mike Pence than he could deliver, and you said things about him that were unfair.

"And I think the best thing for you, Mr. President, is to fix that if you can."

Trump was silent.

That same weekend, Trump had dinner with friends at Mar-a-Lago, including Corey Lewandowski, Trump's brusque former campaign manager from 2016 who remained close to him, and former Florida attorney general Pam Bondi, one of Trump's defense lawyers in his first impeachment trial.

Members and guests approached Trump constantly, obsequious and enthralled. "You're the greatest president of my lifetime!" they fawned. "The best!"

Trump asked them about McConnell. Trump said he was still unhappy he had endorsed McConnell's 2020 reelection bid. "I know McConnell hates me. But what was I supposed to do? Endorse somebody else?"

He was angry with Kevin McCarthy, the minority leader, for talking him down about election fraud. "This guy called me every single day, pretended to be my best friend, and then, he fucked me. He's not a good guy."

Lewandowski later said privately he was surprised that Trump, of all people, did not seem to get that Republican leaders were self-interested.

"Kevin came down to kiss my ass and wants my help to win the House back," Trump said.

Trump looked around at his estate, packed with admirers and Palm Beach denizens. "Twitter took me down," he said. "It's been so relaxing without it. You know how many people I would have to go after if I still had it?"

Pence rented a home in Northern Virginia with an office in Crystal City, adjacent to Ronald Reagan Washington National Airport. It was a quieter life. The vice presidential motorcade was gone. Just a few Secret Service agents were assigned to him. A book and speeches were in the works. His real project was political visibility and rehabilitation. Trying to be in the game for 2024.

On February 23, Pence welcomed members of the Republican

Study Committee, a conservative faction in the House he once chaired, to his new office. It was an opportunity to play elder statesman.

No one brought up Trump, so Pence did. He assured them that he and the president had some good phone calls. Nobody asked for more details. It was like listening to a friend talk about a divorce when you hoped to find grounds to like both parties.

Pence grew nostalgic as he recalled his House days a decade earlier. He told them that when he was in the House in 2009, not one Republican voted for President Obama's stimulus package—and he said conservatives should try to oppose Biden's rescue plan in the same way this time around. Not one vote. It was an opportunity to unite the party on something.

"This is a defining moment for us, for Republicans," Pence said. "Obama left us out of the negotiations and if they didn't have us at the table, we said we're not going to be part of the bill.

"The party needs to reclaim our mantle on spending," Pence told them.

There were "complications" to this message, Pence added. But he did not explicitly acknowledge the hypocrisy. Republicans under Trump had spent trillions and all but abandoned fiscal conservatism. U.S. debt had surged. But returning to finger-wagging of years past was an easy play.

The conservative House members sitting around Pence nodded, from the group's chairman, Jim Banks of Indiana, to Lauren Boebert, a young, firebrand freshman from Colorado. They knew about the complications, too, but right now it was all about the fight.

SIXTY-TWO

On February 27, the House passed Biden's $1.9 trillion rescue bill, including the provision that raised the minimum wage to $15 an hour by 2025. The vote was narrow, 219 to 212, without one Republican yes.

Speaker Pelosi told others she saw what Democrats were doing in biblical terms.

"I see this as the gospel of Matthew. When I was hungry, you fed me," she said. "When I was homeless, you gave me shelter."

The Senate parliamentarian, Elizabeth MacDonough, had ruled days earlier that legislation raising the minimum wage to $15 an hour violated the rules for reconciliation and could not be included in the rescue bill.

While Biden had supported a $15 an hour minimum wage during the 2020 campaign, he and his top aides were not eager to go to war against the parliamentarian. But Pelosi knew that her members wanted it, so she kept it in. Senate Democrats would have to strip it out.

Keeping it in was also a blunt reminder to Senate Democrats: The House Democratic conference is more liberal than you. Don't forget it. Anything you do to water down this legislation could threaten its fate once it comes back for a final vote in the House.

Ron Klain kept small notecards in his jacket pocket. They had everything on them, in small print. The president's schedule, to-do lists, agenda for the White House staff, phone calls to be made.

In late February, one item at the top was winning over moderate Senate Democrats on Biden's rescue plan.

Klain had lots of meetings and talks with those lawmakers. He was astonished to find what he called a "complete inversion in American politics." Bernie Sanders and progressive allies wanted to make sure the stimulus checks went to people making six figures—$100,000—or more. Moderates, in contrast, were saying no, no, no, the money should be directed more to poor people.

They finally reached a compromise. Couples making $150,000 could get the full check, but a partial check would go to those making up to $200,000 with a sharper phasing out.

Manchin and about seven other Democrats had voiced some disagreement with aspects of the rescue plan. Klain and the White House staff were tracking the objections closely, from major concerns to small gripes. In a 50-50 Senate, each Democrat was a tall pole in the tent. Everyone was needed.

Klain recalled that they all thought that life in the Obama White House had been hard with 58 Democratic senators. He fantasized that if Biden had 58 Democrats, as chief of staff Klain would only have to work three days a week.

As Senate Democrats negotiated their version of Biden's plan, Senator Mark Warner, Democrat of Virginia, and others pushed for more money to expand broadband programs in rural areas where coverage was scarce. More than $3 billion had already been allocated in December's spending bill for broadband programs to expand Internet service, a sum considered huge.

But Warner and the others were pushing for more, citing how the pandemic had changed Americans' lives and made high-speed Internet access essential for health care, distance learning, and working from home.

The Biden White House agreed to increase the total amount of broadband spending for fiscal year 2021 to $20 billion.

At first, Warner and others thought that meant the White House would add $20 billion on top of the $3 billion enacted late last year for $23 billion total.

"You people are a little short," Warner said in a Zoom call soon after. "You said you would add $20 billion." It was evident that the rescue bill was becoming a goodie package for Democrats.

Steve Ricchetti and Warner had a little blow-out over this, and Ricchetti stuck to the $20 billion total for 2021. Warner and his allies ultimately agreed and secured an additional $17 billion in broadband spending.

It was a major commitment, the largest federal broadband investment ever.

The private spat among Democrats illustrated the large amounts of money at stake and how everyone wanted the most for their pet programs. The feeding frenzy was real.

While on the sidelines of the rescue plan, McConnell and Graham met regularly. The main topic continued to be Trump and what role the former president should play in positioning the party to win in 2022.

Graham said Trump was still the dominant force in the party. His 74 million votes still resonated, and his following was loyal and strong.

McConnell considered Graham the "Trump whisperer." He was fine with Graham playing the role. But he did not buy into Graham's strategy. McConnell said he saw Trump as a fading brand. Retired. "OTTB" as they say in Kentucky—"off-the-track Thoroughbred."

"There is a clear trend moving," McConnell said, toward a

place where the Republican Party is not dominated by Trump. "Sucking up to Donald Trump is not a strategy that works."

McConnell reminded Graham he had seen this dynamic play out before in 2014. That year, establishment Republicans beat back wild Tea Party challengers like Christine O'Donnell in Delaware. Many Republicans had warned him then the Tea Party was going to swallow the GOP whole, win every race.

Instead, Republicans maintained control of the House, gaining 13 seats, giving them the largest majority since 1929. In the Senate they won back control and gained nine seats, the biggest gain since Reagan's year of 1980.

And 2022 could end up being a lot like 2014, McConnell said. Republicans could hold firm and support normal, not crazy. Focus on electability, intervene in primaries when needed.

McConnell was confident his preferred candidates could eventually outpace any ragtag network that Trump might try to assemble. McConnell and his crew would out-organize them, outfundraise them, and avoid theatrical clashes.

"The only place I can see Trump and me actually at loggerheads would be if he gets behind some clown who clearly can't win," McConnell said sharply. "To have a chance of getting the Senate back, you have to have the most electable candidates possible."

It had to be about winning. If Trump was useful, great. If he were not useful, they would oppose his picks. Strictly business, McConnell said.

If Democrats tried to use McConnell as a cudgel against Republicans, he was confident it would fail as a tactic, even if they played his condemnation on February 13, when he said Trump was morally responsible.

"I'm not enough of a villain," he said, at least in the GOP, "to make that work."

Trump was going to try anyway.

SIXTY-THREE

For Biden, the tallest pole remained Joe Manchin. Biden knew it, Klain knew it, and Manchin knew it.

The night of Tuesday, March 2, Klain stopped by Manchin's 40-foot boat, *Almost Heaven*. Just the two of them for dinner. It was a nice but not super-fancy boat.

"Almost Heaven, West Virginia" is the first line of "Take Me Home, Country Roads" by John Denver, one of the state's anthems. The boat was the senator's floating citadel. "I can untie the ropes and away I go" home, he once told a reporter for *GQ* magazine.

I can't go home and explain to West Virginians, Manchin said, that if you stay unemployed one week longer, you'll get another $400, in addition to the $1,400 checks we're going to send their way.

The unemployment benefit was too much and for too long, Manchin argued. The $400 supplement had to be cut to $300 and the period shortened. That was his bottom line.

Klain knew that Manchin had promised President Biden that he would not let the bill fail, but Manchin was a genuine maverick who would not succumb to pressure. Klain left *Almost Heaven* that night after dinner believing that Manchin would somehow have to be accommodated.

Klain was not Manchin's only suitor. Senator Portman, with encouragement from McConnell, had been talking to Manchin since early February, after it became clear that the Group of 10 Republicans was being left behind.

Manchin was still in play. Portman had an amendment to the rescue bill to reduce the supplemental $400 weekly benefit to $300 for a shorter period of time.

Manchin liked it. The $300 figure was as much a psychological, symbolic stand as it was a policy position. He had spoken with more centrist Democratic economists in recent weeks, such as former treasury secretary Larry Summers, who had written an op-ed in *The Washington Post* warning of inflation that could be triggered by too much government spending. He had also spoken with former Obama economist Jason Furman.

Those conversations highlighted for Manchin his gut instinct that the labor force had to be willing to go back sooner rather than later. The economy was going to improve, and extended unemployment benefits were too much of an incentive for people to stay home.

Manchin gave Portman his word he would support the $300 amendment.

Jeff Zients, Biden's Covid coordinator, was giving the president daily reports. The Pentagon approved a request from FEMA for military assistance and would deploy more than 1,000 National Guard to help at vaccination sites. Community vaccination centers across the country were being set up. Biden had pledged to support 100 in his first month in office. They were at 441.

A pilot pharmacy program was being phased in to get retail pharmacies administering the vaccine. By using the Public Readiness and Emergency Preparedness Act, retired nurses and doctors and other health care workers could now give vaccinations.

But there was still not nearly enough testing, particularly on asymptomatic people. The United States was 32nd in the world on genomic sequencing, the testing method used to detect new variants. Spotting new mutations was key to slowing the spread of the virus because often the new mutations were more contagious. And the most important time to test was early, when the presence of variants was still minimal. Zients found this lag absurd, and he asked Biden for more money to eliminate the handicap.

Biden approved it but continued to push him hard. "Can you do it?" he asked Zients, sounding a little skeptical.

Zients said they would have hundreds of community health centers operating across the country by late March, using a hub-and-spoke model to make sure there was fair and equitable distribution of the vaccines into vulnerable communities.

"Are we really going to be able to have thousands of these? How many people are we reaching?" Biden asked. "Where are they coming from?" He even asked, "What do they look like?"

"Where are we on mobile units?" Biden asked at four meetings, one of about 40 Biden had on the virus early on. Zients followed up with four memos updating the president on the progress made, with 950 of the 1,385 community health centers set to administer vaccines by the end of March, many using mobile vans and pop-up sites.

Zients reported that $4 billion of FEMA assistance had been given to the states.

Sonya Bernstein, meanwhile, was still operating out of her basement apartment.

"Every time I would walk up the two steps as I left my front door, it was almost hard to look at the light," she joked with others. This was isolation. This was the operational end of the virus campaign, placing orders and giving directions across the federal government. Total mobilization.

SIXTY-FOUR

Leader Schumer called Speaker Pelosi as the rescue plan stalled in the Senate. No glee. Just business. It was time to finalize the legislation.

We are disappointed we can't get the minimum wage in there. It meant so much, Schumer told her. But this is the reality. Pelosi agreed. It was a disappointment, but they could not let it blow up Biden's bill.

"We will live to pass it again," Pelosi said of the minimum wage hike. "We will, and by the time we pass it, it's going to have to be more than $15 an hour."

Beyond taking out the wage hike, Schumer said, we're taking billions out of state and local aid and moving it into rural internet broadband.

And third, the weekly unemployment benefit is to be reduced from $400 to $300.

My liberals won't like that change, Pelosi said.

She knew her members. She kept close tabs on the House Progressive Caucus. They loved a big fight, especially with her, especially "the Squad" of younger female progressives such as Representative Ocasio-Cortez, who had broken ranks with Pelosi on an immigration bill she had backed. If told to take a $300 benefit, down from $400 and without any new incentives, she knew they could rebel.

Every change is a cut against the majority of my caucus, she said. If you want them to swallow this bill, you have to give us something.

Schumer came up with a change—a tax credit of $10,200, so people's unemployment insurance would not be taxable.

This made sense to Klain, who was involved in all the negotiations and monitored them closely. Without the tax credit, many unemployed people were going to get big tax bills on Tax Day. It would be a nightmare and there would be what he called "one of these stupid-Congress-should-do-something moments."

Schumer worked with Senator Tom Carper, Democrat of Delaware, to cobble together a new amendment: keep the benefit at $300 and extend it through October, along with the tax write-off up to $10,200.

Pelosi told Schumer and the White House that she could get it done, but things had to hold. No more tweaks. "Let's just end it," she said. "Let's just get it." Klain and others did not argue with her.

Schumer's whip team was muted and guarded about what would happen on Friday when all this was coming to a vote.

"As a whip, you don't assume anything until the roll call is made," Senator Dick Durbin of Illinois told CNN. "Whether or not we can hold it with 50 Democratic members staying loyal to the very end, and the vice president coming in to break the tie, that still remains to be seen."

When Manchin found out about the new amendment of $300 through October 4 with the tax credit of $10,200 that had been added to appease the House liberals, he blew up. "That wasn't our deal." Yes, he had promised Biden that he would not let the rescue plan fail. But he had never agreed to this lengthened unemployment timeline.

"Well," Manchin told his aides, as if he were speaking to Klain or Biden, "you're saying I'm not sticking to my deal, but you're not sticking to your deal." He stormed out of the office.

Klain arrived at the White House early on Friday, March 5, and saw that everyone was unhappy.

On the Senate floor, votes on Bernie Sanders's amendment to add in the minimum wage hike to $15 were taking place. It was likely to be a long vote. But Sanders wasn't threatening to vote against the rescue bill if it failed. A minimum wage hike only got 42 votes.

"If Bernie Sanders had said, 'You know, I'm dying on this hill,' that would have been the breaking point," Senator Richard Blumenthal of Connecticut told others. The rescue plan would have been killed. But Sanders was still sticking with the bill and standing with Biden.

Klain had engaged consistently with Sanders since the primaries. During the transition, Klain and Sanders had considered bringing Sanders into the cabinet as secretary of labor. Sanders privately told Klain he loved the idea. He could kick a little ass and show up at union rallies and outside Amazon facilities. But when the Democrats won the majority, both Klain and Sanders decided to shelve the idea. Sanders would instead be a committee chairman.

When Klain's ally, liberal think tank leader Neera Tanden, was facing sharp criticism for her aggressive anti-Sanders tweets in the wake of Biden nominating her to be director of the Office of Management and Budget, Republicans tried to bait Sanders to lash out at her.

"You called Sanders everything but an ignorant slut," alluding to the famous *Saturday Night Live* skit, Senator John Kennedy of Louisiana declared during her confirmation hearing.

In a gesture of goodwill toward the Biden White House, Sanders handled it quietly. He had Tanden over to his Senate office.

He printed out her tweets to go over with her. He wanted her to make sure she knew he was unhappy with them. But he did not want a public brawl.

"I'd like everyone to leave," Sanders said to his staff. "Just me in here."

Tanden ultimately withdrew.

Schumer had only been majority leader a short time, but Manchin had carefully laid out the terms of engagement and explained how he would operate as part of the majority.

Manchin repeated the approach he had used with Harry Reid: "If I can go home and explain it, I'll vote for it. If I can't explain it, I can't vote for it." He had always given Reid a heads-up on his voting decision to avoid surprises. Since West Virginia was the reddest state, he said, he would always be the most independent and the one who defected the most from party-line votes.

That morning, Manchin went to Schumer's leadership office in the Capitol.

"Hey, Chuck," Manchin said, "I just want you to know I'm not going to vote for this amendment you have on unemployment." He was referring to the Carper amendment which expanded the $300 supplemental through October 4, plus the $10,200 tax credit to satisfy the House. "This isn't the deal we agreed to." He instead would vote for Portman's amendment. "Let me tell you something. We just disagree. Do you understand that? We disagree."

Manchin strolled down to the floor. Word had gotten out. Senator Angus King of Maine, an independent who caucused with the Democrats, went up to him. "Joe, let's just take this deal. It's going to be fine."

No, no, Manchin said. It's not.

Manchin's chief of staff, Lance West, suggested to Manchin he work from his hideaway office in the basement of the Capitol.

It was near a small cafeteria where he could get food and avoid other senators.

Senator Amy Klobuchar, Democrat of Minnesota, was making her own soundings in the Senate and called Steve Ricchetti at the White House. Manchin was not playing around, she warned. The rescue plan could go down. Tonight. Biden's first 100 days, scarred by an intra-party showdown.

The call was a trigger.

Klain and others approached Biden. Maybe it was time for him to call Manchin, who had promised him he would not let the rescue bill fail.

Biden hesitated. He had been through hundreds of legislative fights. The presidential call had a special weight. It was the final twist of the arm.

"I can only make this call once," he said. "We've got to decide if this is the moment to do it. Is this right?"

Everyone seemed to think it was.

"I can only do this once," Biden repeated.

Biden called Joe Manchin around 1 p.m. Manchin was in his hideaway with his chief of staff Lance West.

"Joe," Biden said, "you wanted the unemployment smaller. We did that. You wanted certain dates" for the supplemental unemployment benefit. "We addressed that. You wanted checks targeted. We did that. You know, this is basically it. You need to come along."

Manchin corrected Biden. He said additional unemployment checks, though smaller, went for a longer time into the fall. People would be paid for not working for an extended period.

And then he voiced frustration about this new $10,200 tax credit, which he had just learned about. Someone who was not working was going to get an additional tax break, while someone who worked would not get it.

"Joe," Biden said, "if you don't come along, you're really fucking me. I need you on this. Find your way to yes on this."

"I don't know, I promised Rob Portman," Manchin said. He said he was talking to economists. They were telling him the economy would take off like a rocket. Mr. President, we need people ready to go back to work no later than July. Mr. President, you have said that we will have vaccines available to all citizens in our country who want it by May.

I can't lose this bill, Biden said. His voice was insistent, flecked with irritation. You're going to make me lose my bill, Biden said.

"You have to trust me," Manchin said. "You will not." He said his intention was not to kill the bill, only to get some parts removed. He was with Biden, but he wanted the White House to work with him.

"Joe, damn it," Biden said impatiently. "I just can't lose this bill."

"Mr. President," Manchin said, "in all due respect, you couldn't lose this bill with a keg of dynamite. A whole lot of nitroglycerin wouldn't blow it up. It's got so much good in it."

He added, "Every little municipality is going to get money. They are, for the first time, taking control of their destiny. They can fix their water lines, sewer lines, internet service. We've got a lot of good here, Mr. President."

"Joe," Biden said, "don't kill my bill." It was a personal request.

"Your bill is not going to be killed, Mr. President. I'm assuring you that." Then the Manchin stubbornness that the White House feared surfaced. "I'm not going to cave on this. I need something here. You know, we have to reach a deal. But don't worry, Mr. President. We'll get this done."

The call ended. Biden told his aides to make sure this thing got done. Klain said he was sure Manchin's refusal was about Portman.

In the hideaway, Manchin looked at chief of staff Lance West.

"They know where I've been, don't they?" Manchin asked. "They know I've been at $300. This isn't new for them."

"Of course, you've been saying that a long time," West said.

"Get to work, get it fixed," Manchin said. "Tell me who to call. I'll start calling. People will get this fixed."

Schumer realized it was time to maneuver. He proposed they sequence the amendments. Let Manchin vote for the Portman amendment first, keep his promise. Then they could put the Carper amendment on the floor. It would be drafted to supersede the Portman amendment and Manchin could vote for it. The bill would then have 50 votes and the tie broken by Vice President Harris.

Pelosi told Schumer he had to keep their deal in place. If Portman's amendment passed and was left as is, and the benefit went down to $300 and only through July, she could not guarantee passage in the House.

SIXTY-FIVE

Around 3 p.m. on March 5, Senator Debbie Stabenow of Michigan spotted Manchin heading quickly to his own hideaway office.

She knocked on his door. Manchin welcomed her to come inside and invited her to sit with him on the couch.

He started into his concerns about the bill—unemployment insurance too long in duration, a $10,200 tax credit.

Stabenow thought Manchin's complaints seemed minor—little issues, not big problems. Somebody had to speak some truth. Be blunt. She had been in elected office since Jimmy Carter was president. You can't let one person derail something that has already been decided, when the consensus is 99 percent there.

"You know what, Joe?" Stabenow asked. "Any one of us could do this. We have 50 people here. And do you think everything in this bill is perfect for me?"

Manchin was listening.

"The reality is, you've got a whole bunch of colleagues right down the hall who are pretty upset with you," she said. "Do you realize that?"

"I know, I know, I know, Deb," Manchin said. "But you don't understand. I represent West Virginia."

"Well, I represent Michigan. We've got a whole lot of people that kind of feel like, you know what? We're not a caucus of one. We're a caucus of 50. And we have to find a way to come together here, even if something is not perfect for our own state. Because you know what? This isn't a bill just for West Virginia. This is not a bill for Michigan."

Manchin started to talk about unemployment. With vaccines being rapidly distributed, he said he wanted to see people go back to work rather than choose to take their unemployment benefits and stay home. He was worried about businesses that could not find people to work.

"You know," she said, "you've been governor. Nothing's perfect. You try to get it to be good.

"You're being selfish."

Stabenow knew she had been forceful, maybe even a little much. But she felt it was appropriate. Everyone in the Senate Democratic Caucus was tiptoeing around Joe. Somebody needed to tell him how everybody else felt. The anger about the holdup was real. She also knew—everybody knew—that Manchin liked to be liked. He had people over to his boat. He was not the kind of senator who relished becoming a villain.

Stabenow next went to Virginia senator Tim Kaine's hideaway. Senator Kyrsten Sinema of Arizona, a moderate Democrat, was also there and looked up.

"Well?" Sinema asked.

"I don't know," Stabenow told her. "I don't know. I told him the truth. I told him what I thought he needed to hear. I don't know."

Lance West and Schumer's chief of staff began an informal shuttle diplomacy. West would walk from the hideaway to Schumer's office. Then back. Most reporters did not recognize him, so he could make the trip without fanfare, unlike Schumer's longtime chief of staff, Mike Lynch.

"Oh, shit, you're going to blow up the bill," Lynch, known for his calm demeanor, told West early in the day.

"How is that even possible?" West asked.

Lynch sketched out what Pelosi had said to Schumer. If this bill gets watered down any more, the House Progressive Caucus will take off.

"They'll send it back," Lynch said, "if it's not $400 through the end of September."

Really? West was skeptical. Did the Progressive Caucus have that much power?

"I don't want to find out," Lynch said.

West thought that was the best line of the afternoon. He reported back to Manchin, who did not buy it. They'd kill Biden's bill to spite him? Give me a break. Pelosi was being tough, as always. Democrats wanted to pass the bill ASAP. Unemployment benefits would expire in about a week on March 14. Manchin told him to go back. Find a deal. Keep the $300 but be flexible.

West and Lynch then talked about a $300 deal through early September, keeping the tax credit component with a cap on higher incomes. This kind of change would have a real effect for those who were struggling. Some 18 million Americans relied on the enhanced unemployment insurance.

Lynch perked up. Carper's original text had the benefit last through October 4, 2021. Manchin was now offering to support it if it went through September 6 instead. That was doable. And adding an income cap to who would be exempt from taxation? Fine.

Schumer was pleased at the development. Manchin seemed to be coming back.

West updated Louisa Terrell, Biden's legislative director. "Louisa, we have a deal I've presented to Mike," West said. "I just wanted you to know it as well because I think it's a good offer and I think it's something we can live with."

Terrell said she'd get back to him.

Biden had told everybody he only could make one call. That's what presidents did. One call to lean on a senator. You don't overdo it.

We need you to make another call, Biden's aides told him late Friday afternoon. Schumer had Carper's amendment ready to go, to come right after a vote on Portman's amendment. But Manchin had not yet formally signed onto Schumer's arrangement.

It was time to close, they said.

Biden sighed. All right.

He called Manchin, who was outside his hideaway when the phone rang. He slipped inside.

Biden was terse. This had gone on too long. And Manchin was still a wild card, regardless of what Schumer's and Manchin's aides were cooking up.

"What the fuck are you doing, Joe?" Biden asked him. "Come on, man.

"Look," Biden said. "We've worked it out so you can vote with Portman. It's time for this to be over. You've won, Joe. You're going to come out of this looking like you're the most powerful senator. You're going to come out of this looking like you're the dealmaker.

"Take yes for an answer," Biden said. "You get your vote with Portman. We modify the unemployment to fit what you wanted. But you have to let Carper go second. You have to support Carper. We have to have final say on this."

Manchin did not quite say yes.

"They act like they're going to shove it down my throat," Manchin said. "They can kiss my ass."

"Joe," Biden said, "I would never ask you to vote against your convictions."

Manchin thought that meant a lot coming from a former senator. There was too much pressure based on taking one for the party or the team. He said, "My team is West Virginia's team. Nobody hired me up here. Nobody can fire me up here. Only my team in West Virginia and I've got to answer to them."

Biden left the call feeling Manchin would get there. So did Klain and others.

Mike Lynch and Lance West spoke by phone. "Is there still a deal?" Lynch asked.

"Yes," West said. There was a deal.

Schumer called the White House. It was done.

Manchin and West left the hideaway to go see Schumer at his office. Manchin promised he would support the Portman amendment, then support Carper's. He would keep his word to his Republican friend but he would not sink Biden. They sat down to go over it one last time.

- Extend the existing $300 weekly jobless benefit to September 6.
- Provide a $10,200 tax credit for those with jobless benefits, but only if they are in a household making less than $150,000 a year.

"I still love you, buddy," Manchin told Schumer, after venting about the talks. He gave Schumer a hug.

When speaking to others later about his meeting with Schumer, Manchin said, "Chuck and I have great shouting matches. You got an Italian and a Jew in a room. New York and West Virginia." Enough said.

But the vote was still hours away, Schumer told the White House. They would need the evening and early morning hours to write and score the changes with the Congressional Budget Office. Calculations of the costs were required. Since there was no final bill, it was not possible to make those calculations. There were other amendments to vote on, part of what was being called a "vote-a-rama."

Manchin and Portman met up. "I got them from $400 to $300,

which is what you wanted," he told Portman. "The key thing was not to get $400."

Portman asked him to stick with his amendment: extend the $300 benefit through mid-July.

"I can't," Manchin said. "I'm the one who got these changes and can't go back on them."

Lynch held a conference call with Democratic chiefs of staff around 7:45 p.m. He thanked everybody for their patience.

Schumer's public announcement of the agreement, around 8 p.m. Friday, ended what had become a nine-hour standoff. By the time votes ended that evening, the Senate had broken its record for longest roll-call vote ever—nearly 12 hours. Almost two hours more than the previous record.

Democrats were exhausted and relieved.

Senator Blumenthal noticed Schumer's approach with Manchin. Yell, but keep him close, on the team. He and others wondered if Harry Reid, in the same position, would have been as patient. Manchin's chairmanship of the Senate Energy and Natural Resources Committee had never been threatened. Biden might have cursed—and the number of "fucks" Biden uttered seemed to multiply as the story went from senator to senator. But Biden or Schumer had never really threatened anything.

Portman was frustrated as he tangled that evening in a floor debate with Senate Finance Committee chairman Ron Wyden of Oregon. He felt like it was the longest eight hours of his life because he had to be on the floor in case his amendment was called up.

"Suddenly, if you're on unemployment insurance you don't have to pay taxes, but if you're working, you do have to pay taxes. How does that work?" Portman asked, speaking on the Senate floor.

Wyden dismissed Portman's criticism.

"The party that claims to want to help workers on their taxes won't lift a finger."

That night, Portman's amendment passed. Then Carper's did, too, superseding Portman's amendment, just as Schumer had orchestrated.

On Saturday, March 6, once it was all pulled together, the full rescue plan passed. 50 to 49. Senator Dan Sullivan of Alaska, a Republican, missed the vote due to a family funeral.

SIXTY-SIX

Biden watched the Senate vote on March 6 from the Treaty Room in the residence. He was working on a statement with Anita Dunn. Other aides made jokes that what was going down was a "big effing deal," a nod to his famous comment when Obamacare was passed.

Biden was ecstatic. He called up the Senate cloakroom and asked the attendant to put on any Democrat who was around. Bring them to the phone.

He called Schumer. "Took a genius to say wait until Friday to land the plane," Biden said. "Not forcing a final outcome, letting it play out." No rush. Sequencing the amendments with Portman and Carper. That solved the mess.

"Look, Chuck," he said. "I've seen a lot of this in my day. I've been around a long time. But what you've done here is about as masterful as anything I've ever seen."

He called Bernie Sanders.

"We need to take the time to sell this, do a tour around the country," Sanders said. Once rivals, now fellow salesmen. "Do some events, drive home what we have accomplished here."

Biden thanked Sanders for the advice and for sticking with him. Sanders's imprimatur had been critical in keeping progressives from fleeing.

The rest of the Senate Democratic Caucus was invited to join Biden on a Zoom call. Biden's camera was not working. Audio only. Schumer's video was on. He was emotional. He said he was proud they stuck together, called it one of the most historic bills they've ever passed.

"You should be very proud," he said.

The final vote was scheduled for the following week. The revised Senate version passed the House on March 10—220 to 211. Biden and Harris, and a small group of aides, watched that vote in the Roosevelt Room.

"Under ordinary circumstances, we'd have the entire staff watch this together like we did with the Affordable Care Act," Biden told them.

The next day, Biden delivered a nationally televised speech on the anniversary of the Covid-19 shutdown. "A year ago, we were hit with a virus that was met with silence and spread unchecked," he said. "Now because of all the work we've done, we'll have enough vaccine supply for all adults in America by the end of May. That's months ahead of schedule."

Biden did not give Trump even passing credit for the vaccines, a slight that seemed ungracious and unlike him. Zients felt that the credit belonged to the doctors and scientists who developed the vaccines, not Trump.

"It's truly a national effort, just like we saw during World War II," Biden said from the East Room. "Because even if we devote every resource we have, beating this virus and getting back to normal depends on national unity."

Biden's mood lifted after he signed the rescue bill. His presidency was off to a strong start. He was now 1–0 on big-ticket legislation.

He seemed pleased, but did not view the legislation as a personal accomplishment as he might have when he was a younger politician. He was 78 years old and his perspective had shifted.

I'm just doing what's right, he told aides. "It took me a long time to get here. I'm here to do this job." He said he was at ease with the rough and tumble of politics, but he did not have the same obsession he had in, say, 1987. He had watched too many other presidents zoom up and down. He was going to keep that sense of fate, take it all as it comes, day by day.

Mike Donilon remained close to Biden but stayed out of the news. When he went to a busy coffee shop in Alexandria one weekend to meet an old friend, no one noticed him. While Klain had a significant Twitter following, most Biden staffers were not becoming celebrities. In terms of intrigue, it was the opposite of Trump's first year.

Many of the Biden staffers on the press and policy sides were younger, and Pete Buttigieg, now in the cabinet as secretary of transportation, was just 39. Biden loved to be seen as a promoter of the next generation. But Donilon, Dunn, Ricchetti, Klain, along with Jill Biden, they reflected Biden's seasoned sensibility and politics.

On March 12, Biden held a celebration event in the Rose Garden. "It changes the paradigm," Biden said, standing with Vice President Harris.

"You got to tell people in plain, simple, straightforward language what it is you're doing to help," he said. "You have to be able to tell a story, tell the story of what you're about to do and why it matters because it's going to make a difference in the lives of millions of people and in very concrete, specific ways."

Leader McConnell was blasé about Manchin's "yes" vote on the rescue plan. He told associates that Manchin, as well as Senator Sinema, knew "it was not smart for them to get off the reservation" on Biden's first major initiative. Biden was too new, too popular.

McConnell wondered if Democrats' pressure on Manchin had soured Manchin on doing much more for Biden in 2021. Maybe he felt a little burned. Progressives assailed him daily, frustrated with his red-state politics.

"Mad as hell," McConnell told others about Manchin's mood on March 5, although some Republicans and Democrats thought it was wishful thinking.

Schumer made Manchin and his side look like fools, McConnell said, with the back-and-forth on the Carper and Portman amendments. He could see the campaign ads already. He said it would be remembered like when the 2004 Democratic presidential nominee, then Senator John Kerry, had voted for intervention in Iraq then voted against it.

SIXTY-SEVEN

On April 21, around 4 p.m. in the afternoon, Clyburn invited Manchin to meet in his Capitol office. It would be a serious, working meeting. Both men would have their chiefs of staff present and their chief counsels. Six people in the room, three facing three, sitting on dark cherry-colored leather couches and chairs.

Unlike the Capitol rioters, who seemed to easily find his office, Manchin needed directions.

Speaker Pelosi's "For the People Act," called H.R. 1, was idling in the Senate after being passed by the House in March. It called for early voting to last at least for two weeks, and for states to do more to register voters.

As they settled into the couches, Clyburn was blunt. Manchin could keep his position, broadly speaking, on preserving the filibuster. But it was intolerable for him to hold to that hard line on voting rights. Manchin had to give on voting rights, a clear constitutional and moral issue.

"I have never asked that you change your mind about the filibuster," Clyburn said. "But I would love to see the filibuster applied to constitutional rights in the same way we apply them to budgeting," with the reconciliation, majority-vote process. "We have the carve-out.

"Reconciliation. That's a word that applies more neatly to constitutional issues than it does to budgeting."

Manchin listened but did not make any promises. He was pleasant. We'll take a look.

"Look," Clyburn told him, "you don't have to be a racist country to tolerate racism. And that's what we're doing." He said the GOP voting proposals in the states were undoubtedly racist.

Clyburn said he knew Strom Thurmond, the late segregationist senator from his home state of South Carolina. He said even he and Thurmond were able to reconcile their differences. "Strom and I did get along very, very well."

Manchin said he was not aware of the pair's past work together.

"We worked together to do things that needed to be done in South Carolina," Clyburn said. "We still do with his children and his widow. I still work with his family. In fact, Strom had a sister named Gertrude," whom Clyburn had known from their work in state government decades ago.

"Gertrude and I worked together in the same office. Our desks were just about four or five steps apart. And he said to me, all the time, 'My sister, Gertrude, really loves you.' And I said, 'Well, show your love for your sister and let's do this together.' And we did a lot of things together," working on securing funds for their state.

Clyburn brought up his mentor, Judge Richard Fields. He was still alive. One hundred years old. He had gone to a historically Black college in West Virginia.

"Bluefield State," Manchin said.

"I remember when West Virginia State was 100 percent Black," Clyburn said. "These schools are now 80, 85 percent white."

Manchin said he wanted to be helpful. "I'm all for doing what is necessary to preserve and protect voting rights." He said the sweeping law passed in Georgia in March, signed by Republican governor Brian Kemp, disappointed him. That law restricted mail-in voting and beefed up voter identification requirements, although Republicans argued it expanded access by increasing early, in-person voting by one day.

What goes around, comes around, Manchin said. If we change

the rules, we do something, then the Republicans are in charge and they come back and do the same thing. I have a hard time believing we couldn't find Republicans on the other side of the aisle who agree we need to have fair, accessible and secure elections.

Well, Clyburn said, I'm just making this suggestion. Find a way to get it done.

The meeting lasted an hour. Manchin was friendly as he left, ever the amiable former quarterback. But he again made no commitments.

Clyburn told his aides he would keep at it.

Clyburn was increasingly disappointed and outraged. This was the biggest step backward in decades.

In all, nearly 400 bills to restrict voting had been introduced nationwide since the election. Since January, nearly 20 new laws had been enacted and dozens more had passed or were pending in state legislative chambers.

A GOP-pushed audit of the vote in Arizona's Maricopa County was also becoming a focal point for Trump and his allies, with Giuliani engaging state legislators and officials. In Georgia, Republicans were clamoring for more audits of hundreds of thousands of votes in the Atlanta area.

"We're going to make it a felony for you to give somebody a bottle of water if they stand in a line for eight hours to vote? What the hell is that? Come on," Clyburn vented.

By June, Manchin had not moved on the filibuster. He had issued a three-page memo as a foundation for more negotiations on a bipartisan voting bill. Stacey Abrams, the Georgia Democrat, said Manchin's memo was a "first and important step" to finding a compromise.

On June 22, Democrats failed to secure the necessary 60 votes to pass the House's voting rights legislation.

A silver lining, some Democrats said, the issue was now front and center. It could be a keystone for Biden and the party in the 2022 campaign.

Clyburn wanted more.

"Democracy is on fire and the Senate is fiddling!" he said to his aides as the Democrats struggled. "The head of the orchestra is a man named McConnell."

SIXTY-EIGHT

Biden dispatched his top foreign and defense policy cabinet officers, Blinken and Austin, to the NATO foreign ministers meeting in Brussels on March 23 and 24. The 36 NATO allies had nearly 10,000 troops left in Afghanistan. The U.S. contingent was the largest, at 3,500 troops. The allies had all shown firm commitment to the Afghanistan War over the last 20 years.

Genuinely listen and consult, Biden said. Robust working alliances were a tenet of Biden's worldview.

For Biden, one of Trump's worst mistakes was disparaging the NATO alliance and making it too much about nations' financial contributions for defense.

At a closed door meeting, Blinken took notes for three hours.

"Here's what I'm hearing, Mr. President," he told Biden in a secure call that night from Brussels. It was not totally a surprise, but it was a jolt. He said he heard a blast "in quadraphonic sound," which is surround sound. In other words, overwhelming. Blinken, a musician, had his own band, Coalition of the Willing, and played rock guitar.

The ministers' preference, he told the president, is that the U.S. leverage the departure of its troops to gain concrete moves by the Taliban toward a political settlement. Ideally, negotiate the basic contours of a future Afghan state, a constitution, and reform. The ministers had wildly ambitious hopes and talked about elections, human rights, and the rights of women and girls.

Biden and Blinken were in a serious pinch.

Back in Washington, Blinken consulted with his staff and State Department experts. He then changed his recommendation. Previously, he had been foursquare with Biden for a full withdrawal. His new recommendation was to extend the mission with U.S. troops for a while to see if it could yield a political settlement. Buy time for negotiations.

Defense Secretary Austin also came up with a new proposal, a variation on the same theme. He proposed a middle ground. Instead of all or nothing, why not have a slow, "gated" withdrawal in three or four stages to provide leverage for diplomatic negotiations. The "gated" withdrawals also would offer time and space for the political process and a hedge if the diplomatic talks fell apart.

As the internal debate on what to do with the Afghanistan War continued, Biden and Jake Sullivan asked everyone to answer another basic question: What would be the best-case scenario if U.S. forces left?

Intelligence officials inside the CIA and military described a possible negotiated settlement between the Afghan government and the Taliban without large-scale, sustained fighting. Population centers, Kabul and Herat, would have relative peace and enjoy the stability gains made over the course of the past 20 years. The central government would have much less, if any, control elsewhere in the country. That was the best case, but no one suggested it was the most likely.

Biden and Sullivan also asked, what do you think Russia and China would do if the U.S. left?

Those powers would generally prefer the U.S. to stay, U.S. intelligence agencies reported. China and Russia reaped the benefit of comparative regional stability without the work or cost.

Then there were the worst-case scenarios. Austin, Milley and the intelligence officials presented a long list of downsides of withdrawal. Their forecast was bleak:

- The civil war between the Afghan government and the Taliban extends and expands dramatically.
- The capital, Kabul, and other cities ultimately fall and the Taliban take over, amounting to a collapse of the Afghan state in months to years.
- A massive refugee exodus of at least 500,000 Afghans flee the country. Some thought it would be twice that at one million.
- Al Qaeda, now weakened, would reconstitute and reach full plotting capability to attack the United States or U.S. allies.

Biden asked, how much warning would we get of such terrorist capability? We should have six months warning, the intelligence officials said.

"We obviously can't trust that we'll have a full six months," Biden said. "I want you to build an over-the-horizon capability," referring to monitoring and attack capabilities from neighboring countries, "that allows us to suppress this and disrupt any reconstitution of Al Qaeda or other external plotting."

Austin reminded everyone that being "over-the-horizon" still denied the military and the intelligence services the critical situational awareness on the ground that has been so central to U.S. capability.

The presentation on the worst case continued:

- Afghans would lose their civil rights.
- The entire region would be destabilized.

What about Pakistan? Biden asked. He considered Pakistan the most dangerous state in the region because of their nuclear weapons stockpile.

A Taliban takeover of Afghanistan could put wind in the sails of Tehrik-i-Taliban or TTP, the Pakistani Taliban. The TTP was an active, armed resistance to the Pakistani government and was blamed for the 2007 assassination of former prime minister Benazir Bhutto.

The military leaders' and intelligence officials' warnings grew darker. They had spent decades tracking and studying the Taliban. They knew well what it would mean for the Afghan people, particularly women.

- Women's rights would be shredded, and Afghan women would be flogged in public and on their knees in the notorious Kabul soccer stadium, shot with bullets to their heads before shouting crowds, which happened during Taliban rule. Severed arms and legs of thieves would be on display for all to see.

- Some 16,000 schools opened in the last 20 years would be closed or destroyed.

It was a stunning list of possible human disaster and political consequences.

Okay, Biden said, let's talk through what tools we have available to us to reduce those possible consequences and risks.

If U.S. troops left, he said his goal, within six months, was to have sufficient capability in the Gulf region to respond to new problems without having U.S. forces based on the ground in Afghanistan. Then, the U.S. could continue to monitor terrorist targets in Afghanistan and have an accessible launching pad for U.S. military action to destroy them if necessary.

Sullivan and the NSC staff ultimately presented Biden with two memos: The strongest case for staying and the strongest case for leaving. The memos were based on the extensive interagency discussions. Equally important, if not more so, though, was Biden's own history with Afghanistan.

In a 2015 interview, Russian president Vladimir Putin was asked if his 16 years in the KGB influenced him. Putin's memorable answer: "Not a single stage of our life passes without a trace."

The same could be said of Biden's 20 years dealing with the Afghanistan War as chairman of the Senate Foreign Relations Committee, eight years as vice president, and his many trips to the country.

It was much more than a stage of Biden's life. Of particular significance was the three-month Afghanistan strategy review, which President Obama led in the first year of his presidency. As vice president, Biden participated in all the meetings, read the intelligence reports, and had a rare level of engagement in the policy review. Subtly and unsubtly, Biden let it be known that he thought few, if any, troops should be added.

The following year, 2010, Biden privately reviewed Obama's eventual decision to add 30,000 U.S. troops. He characterized it as a tragic power play executed by national security leaders at the expense of a young president. Obama, Biden said, had been rolled by the military and the "five blocks of granite," five key players at the time. The five were Secretary of State Hillary Clinton, Secretary of Defense Robert Gates, Chairman of the Joint Chiefs Michael Mullen, General David Petraeus, who was the Central Commander, and General Stanley McChrystal, the commander in Afghanistan.

McChrystal had written a classified assessment of the war saying there would be "mission failure" if he did not get tens of thousands more troops. He wanted 40,000 more. The four other blocks of granite—Clinton, Gates, Mullen and Petraeus—backed McChrystal.

Biden privately said if he were writing his memoirs, he would "accurately and concisely" state the problem he saw with the five's position.

"I was making the case over and over and over and over again that the Taliban was not Al Qaeda," Biden said. The insurgency was part of an internal civil war and not the terrorist group threatening the United States.

Biden recalled visiting Afghanistan while he was vice president-elect. He met with then–U.S. commander David McKiernan, who said they had not seen Al Qaeda in 18 months.

Biden said he then asked Secretary of Defense Gates, "Let me ask you a simple question. If there were no Al Qaeda, would we be spending 100 plus billion dollars sending tens of thousands of men and women to Afghanistan? The response was 'yes.' That was a crystallizing moment."

Gates argued the large U.S. troop presence contributed to the strategic stability on the subcontinent.

Biden had said, "Those blocks of granite had as one of the basic premises upon which they were building their argument that in order to stabilize Pakistan, we had to demonstrate we were prepared to defeat the Taliban. It's completely fucking illogical. They, the Pakistanis, created the goddamn Taliban. How are we solidifying Pakistan if we defeat the very people they created and continue to support?"

To back up the request of additional troops, the military had conducted a classified war game, "Poignant Vision," that showed sending anything less than 40,000 more troops would be a disaster in the region.

Biden told Obama that the military was selling him "bullshit" on the war. Biden knew from his years in the Senate the military was burying Obama in jargon.

"It's like the Catholic school kid. They teach you about confession and the priest. In third grade, when you're learning to go to do penance. Now you can't go in there and say I stole the gold chain and fail to tell the priest there was a gold watch at the end of the chain."

That's what the military leaders were doing, Biden said. "That's how these guys are. You've got to find out if they've got a goddamn gold watch at the end of the chain." He added, "A lot of this is new to the president," who had been elected to the Senate in 2004 and served there for just four years before winning the White House.

"There were four or five of their principles that I thought were just absolutely built on sand," Biden said.

One was to continue training the 400,000 Afghan security forces and police. But that would not guarantee an end to the counterinsurgency because the capacity of the U.S. troops was so much greater than that of the Afghan forces.

And if Afghan forces could never take control, the U.S. would be there forever. "The misrepresentation by omission constantly occurred," Biden said.

Biden spent hours and hours sitting alone with Obama, often during their regular weekly lunch.

"They thought they were outsmarting everybody. They're all over there having war games, but I was having lunch games."

Biden was not alone in his view. When military leaders argued they also needed the platforms in Afghanistan for Predator drones, the remote piloted and armed aircraft, CIA director Leon Panetta said the drones could be run from other countries.

"Thank God for old Leon," Biden said. "Leon basically speaks up and says, that's not the way I see it."

As the 2021 review was grinding on, Biden essentially agreed with Blinken that they had to make sure they had not unilaterally foreclosed a political settlement.

But a sense of dread was now pervading the review. The two sides of Biden were in conflict—get out or give negotiation every last opportunity.

As the military liked to say, "Every option is suboptimal." Now Biden had to chose the least suboptimal.

"Don't compare me to the Almighty," Biden told Blinken, "compare me to the alternative."

SIXTY-NINE

Blinken went back to the Taliban through intermediaries in Doha, Qatar, with the proposal of delaying the U.S. withdrawal.

The Taliban rejected it, saying that if the U.S. sought to delay when May 1 rolled around, if not sooner, the Taliban would start attacking U.S. forces and provincial capitals.

That was the last thing Biden wanted. New U.S. casualties after a one-year hiatus under Trump could be a political disaster.

Blinken shifted again, concluding that the 3,500 U.S. troops were a bare minimum and not sufficient leverage with the Taliban. While 10,000 U.S. troops might have provided that leverage, Blinken couldn't prove it.

Biden reminded Blinken that six years ago, in 2015, when Biden was vice president, they were in the Situation Room debating whether to extend the U.S. troop commitment.

Military leaders had made the case they needed to extend for another year. They said the last remaining piece to make the Afghanistan military self-sufficient and stand on its own feet was putting in place their ability to build supply lines and conduct aircraft maintenance. And that was supposed to take one year more.

"That was six years ago," Biden reminded Blinken and it still had not happened. "Six years ago!"

There was no better example of the military hiding the gold watch. Blinken consulted with some of the former secretaries of state. It's a very informal club. One asked, "Do people remember who was running Afghanistan on September 10, 2001, the day before the terrorist attacks? It was the Taliban. They'd been in charge for five years. Was the United States about to go to war to take down the Taliban because we didn't like what they were doing? No. Why now?"

"We didn't go to Afghanistan to make it a Jeffersonian democracy," Blinken finally concluded.

Austin also agreed the 3,500 U.S. troops was not sufficient leverage. By early April 2021, with Blinken and Austin back supporting the full withdrawal, Biden told his advisers he had decided to do just that. U.S. ground forces would leave by at least September 11, 2021, the 20th anniversary of the terrorist attacks.

He said no one had really told him the situation would be different in a year or two or three years. He said he saw a higher risk in staying than leaving. It came down to, if not now, when? There were too many maybes. Maybe it will get better. Maybe we could turn the corner. Maybe this, maybe that. The Al Qaeda threat had been significantly degraded, if not eliminated in Afghanistan, but the terrorism threat had shifted to other regions of the Middle East. The clear danger zones were in Somalia and in Iran.

Biden noted that his predecessors had wanted out. Obama had wanted out, Biden said, and Trump had wanted out and the easy decision was to keep some troops there.

"There's an easy way here and there's a reason we still have troops in Afghanistan. The easier call is just to punt," he said. "I didn't become president to do the easy thing."

But Biden said he did not know what would come next. The outcome was unclear, he acknowledged.

His decision and orders were not reduced to a single document, a traditional NSM, or National Security Memorandum. Secretary Austin transmitted military draw-down requirements to the commanders. Instead, a series of memos called SOCs, Summaries of Conclusions, summarized the meetings and specified the requirements for building over-the-horizon capability and also continuing the U.S. embassy presence in Kabul.

Biden told his advisers the decision was hard. But Sullivan did not think Biden anguished over it. Biden seemed at peace with his choice.

"What we can do is put ourselves in the best position to deal with the terrorist threat," Biden said, "and through our support, put the Afghan national defense and security force and the Afghan government in the best position to meet the threat from within Afghanistan."

Chairman Milley thought the review had been fair and open. "U.S. participation on the ground in this war in Afghanistan is ending," Milley said to his senior staff. "The question: Is this war over for America?" Milley's answer was similar to Biden's. It is too early to tell, and it was difficult to forecast the outcome.

Though he could see potentially gruesome and destabilizing outcomes, he felt comfortable that his advice was not taken. "Just because the general recommends it, doesn't make it right. The president has a much wider-angle view."

Milley spoke to the Joint Chiefs in the Tank about the issue of the president's authority to make the final national security decisions.

"Here's some thoughts for us to think about as the senior leaders of the military," Milley said. "You're dealing with a president who was the vice president under Obama and the guys like Blinken and Sullivan and all these other guys. These guys were all in the second and third tier positions in the Obama administration. And all of them have a searing memory of the first year of Obama." That was when the military and Secretary of State Hillary Clinton strong-armed Obama to send 30,000 more U.S. troops to the Afghanistan War.

"I was a colonel at the time and Mullen was the chairman and I was in the basement. I was a witness to some of this. Admiral Mullen, McChrystal and Petraeus, the uniform guys, had tried to box in a president, a new, young president from Chicago that maybe, I can't read minds, they thought they could take advantage of and box him in on a surge in Afghanistan.

"Here's what I take from that as Colonel Milley. Here's a couple of rules of the road here that we're going to follow. One is you never, ever ever box in a president of the United States. You always give him decision space. Number two, you don't play cute and you don't give your advice on the front page of *The Washington Post*. And you don't, you damn sure don't give it in speeches. You just don't do that. You give candid, honest advice. You give it in private and you give it to the president, you know, face-to-face or through professional documents. We don't play games. That's not what we do as a military. We don't undermine the president. We don't box a president in. That's the rules that we play by. It's that simple. And if someone can't abide by those, they're going to be gone."

On Biden, Milley said, "You're dealing with a seasoned politician here who has been in Washington, D.C., 50 years, whatever it is. The reason that a lot of the tight decision making took place in the Obama administration and it shifted to the White House is because of that negative first year and there was a breach of trust. And that's why you get, you know, the complaints from the generals during the Obama administration about micromanagement."

Austin and Milley decided to expedite the withdrawal because it would be safer for the U.S troops. They hoped all troops would come home by mid-July. A visitor to Austin's office said he found the new secretary "scared to death" that a terrorist strike might originate from Afghanistan someday.

"When someone writes a book about this war," Ron Klain said to others, "it's going to begin on September 11, 2001, and it's going to end on the day Joe Biden said, 'We're coming home.' "

As a practical matter, Biden was abandoning Afghanistan to civil war and potential collapse, but Klain, at one of the final meetings, said it was essential that the American families who sacrificed in the war, especially those who lost loved ones, not feel that Biden was turning his back on them. After making a public announcement of the withdrawal decision, Biden should personally visit Section 60 of Arlington National Cemetery and pay his respects to those who had given their lives to the mission, Klain recommended. And make sure the families saw him.

Biden gave a 16-minute address to the nation on April 14. Instead of the high drama of an evening Oval Office address, he spoke from the Treaty Room in the afternoon.

"I'm now the fourth United States president to preside over American troop presence in Afghanistan: two Republicans, two Democrats," he said. "I will not pass this responsibility on to a fifth.

"For the past 12 years, ever since I became vice president, I've carried with me a card that reminds me of the exact number of American troops killed in Iraq and Afghanistan. That exact number, not an approximation or rounded-off number, because every one of those dead are sacred human beings who left behind entire families. An exact accounting of every single solitary one needs to be had.

"As of this day, 2,448 U.S. troops and personnel have died in our Afghanistan conflicts, 20,722 have been wounded.

"It's time to end the forever war," he said.

Biden then visited Arlington National Cemetery and, wearing his mask, walked alone through Section 60 where the dead from Afghanistan and Iraq are buried.

"I have trouble these days even showing up at a cemetery and not thinking of my son Beau," Biden said. He turned to the hundreds of white tombstones, extended his arms, and said, "Look at them all."

Lindsey Graham was furious with both Biden and Trump, given the final decision to withdraw all U.S. forces from Afghanistan. He believed both did not recognize the full consequences.

"I hate Joe Biden for this," Graham said. "I hate Trump. I've lost all respect for Biden. I've lost a lot of respect for Trump," who tried to get all the U.S. troops out but faced massive resistance from his military leadership.

Graham, who had made more than two dozen trips to Afghanistan in the last 20 years, believed he knew more about the conflict than anyone in Congress, and more than most in the military.

The problem, Graham said, was, "Radical Islam cannot be accommodated. It cannot be appeased. The Taliban is a radical Islamic movement, inconsistent with any of the values that we hold near and dear. That is oppressive to women, completely intolerant of religious diversity, and would take Afghanistan back to the 11th century if they could. All I can say is that a movement like this eventually will come back to haunt us.

"We thought that the Taliban were just a bunch of nut jobs. But the Taliban is a regional, radical Islamic movement that doesn't have extraterritorial designs, but that creates a permissive environment for international terrorism. They will create instability so Al Qaeda can come back.

"I think the Taliban is going to give safe haven to people that will come after us.

"We gave up the best listening post you could ever have regarding international terrorism," he said, "which are the CIA bases along the Afghan–Pakistan border."

But he said he understood. "The American people want us to come home. People are tired.

"I fear for Pakistan's stability because of Afghanistan going south. But there will be a civil war. Women in certain parts of the country will fall into very dangerous hands and the entire shit show will play out on American television. Biden and Trump will be seen as having given life to the movement that created 9/11."

Graham said he had a more fundamental objective. "My job is to maintain what's left of the John McCain wing of the Republican Party, the Ronald Reagan wing of the Republican Party that believes that America is an indispensable leader. That we will sacrifice whatever it takes to maintain our security and values throughout the world. That this idea that you can withdraw from over there and be safe over here is folly. That if you don't understand the best way to protect America is to be involved in the enemy's backyard in partnership with people who reject radical Islam, you're an idiot."

If there is no Afghanistan rescue effort, Graham said, "The translators and all the people who came to our aid to fight for their country are going to be slaughtered. It's going to be a stain on our honor. That's what I believe."

Retired General David Petraeus, who had commanded U.S. forces in Afghanistan and been the modern architect of the counterinsurgency strategy Biden loathed, immediately blasted the decision.

"Are we really going to allow major cities to fall to the Taliban?

"I do expect a civil war that will be brutal, bloody and have all the terrible manifestations of uncivil war.

"We have an administration that talks about bringing back support for democracy and human rights. Well, so much for that. Here's a place where we actually can be defending it and where the alternative is pretty bleak. And we're not willing to maintain 3,500 troops? It shows that the support for democracy, human rights, women's rights is hollow."

The over-the-horizon surveillance and attack capability was a fiction. "Drone flights would be six to eight hours and drones aren't refuelable in the air. This is dire stuff. And it's not worth 3,500 troops?

"A major, tragic mistake," he said, "reflecting ignorance of the importance of U.S. forces on the ground and surveillance from fixed wing aircraft, close air support, and other intelligence platforms. It will be like Saigon 1975 when helicopters evacuated the last Americans from Vietnam. Only this time it will be helicopters rescuing Americans from the roof of the American embassy in Kabul just before the fall 2022 House and Senate elections."

Former President George W. Bush said publically Biden's decision was a mistake. "I'm afraid Afghan women and girls are going to suffer unspeakable harm."

Biden did not expect to see on television and in the newspapers so much critical commentary. People who had been clamoring to end the longest war were now fixated on the future of various groups in Afghanistan, including women and girls.

To him, they seemed to have pivoted from "we've got to end this war" to "what are we going to do about these people?" There was a lot of piling on. Several days after the announcement, Blinken and Sullivan were with the president in the Oval Office.

Though the decision was made, Blinken could see that Biden was still struggling with the damned-if-you-do, damned-if-you-don't nature of the decision.

"Mr. President," Blinken said, trying to provide some comfort, "this was an incredibly hard decision." It was done in the presidential style. "I admire the fact that you made it." As they had discussed, he could have ducked it as his predecessors had. But it had been made eyes wide open.

Biden was standing by the Resolute Desk. Blinken could see the president was still carrying the burden of the decision. Presidents lived in the world of the suboptimal.

Standing there alone, the president lightly tapped the desk.

"Yeah," Biden said, "the buck really does stop here."

SEVENTY

Trump, Lindsey Graham and Gary Player, the 85-year-old South African golfing great and winner of nine major tournaments, stood on the fairway of the 10th hole of Trump International in West Palm Beach, Florida, on Saturday, May 8.

Trump had left the White House 108 days earlier and was living in his Florida enclave, surrounded by standing ovations from patrons and guests at Mar-a-Lago and his golf club. As he sat eating his well-done steak or hamburger, people would approach and flash him a thumbs-up and call him the rightfully elected president. They passed him printouts of articles alleging election fraud.

Player, 5-foot-6, was a legendary fitness fanatic. He could still leg press 350 pounds and joked, "Sir, lose a couple of pounds," when Trump awarded him the Presidential Medal of Freedom the day after the Capitol insurrection.

A Trump friend and supporter, Player selected a rescue club from his bag, a club meant to get a golfer out of trouble.

"This is how to hit 150 yards," Player said, instead of the usual 250 yards. "Weaken your grip. Open the clubface and take a smaller swing. That gets the ball up and it's better than hitting your nine iron."

Player, nicknamed the Black Knight for his all-black clothing, lined up and took a compact, controlled swing. The ball arced up perfectly, hit the green, took one bounce and rolled into the cup.

Whoa! Whoa! Trump and Graham whooped. They laughed hard.

Player's approach—backing off, toning it down, swinging less extravagantly with a smaller club, asserting more control—was almost a perfect metaphor for what Graham had been preaching to Trump since the election.

"Mr. President," Graham had said earlier that morning, "there's just no way this party can grow without you. You are the leader of the Republicans. But we've got some damage to repair here."

Grievance and hate, an unending barrage, had, in Graham's view, derailed Trump. Graham often wondered whether Trump realized the damage. Was he capable of repairing it?

Trump brushed off talk of the upcoming 2022 midterm elections. The 2020 election was still on his mind. He had been cheated, he repeated. The election was stolen. Republicans had not sufficiently supported him.

He again angrily denounced Mitch McConnell and Congresswoman Liz Cheney. Trump would never forgive McConnell for saying his actions in the lead-up to January 6 were a "disgraceful dereliction of duty." It was a stab in the back.

Pence could have saved him by kicking the election to the House, Trump added.

"No," Graham said. "Mike Pence did his job."

Trump ignored him.

Graham had become used to the routine. Trump would say rigged, cheated and stolen.

"You lost a close election," Graham said for what seemed like the 100th time. Trump ignored that remark, too.

Graham thought that Trump just might never acknowledge he had lost and was convinced he could be of more help to Trump and the Republican Party by staying part of Trump's orbit, tempering his worst impulses. The Republicans needed Trump's help in 2022 to regain the House and Senate.

He could be a go-between for those who couldn't stand to be

in the same room as Trump, but had the same goal—winning. Plus, Trump was fun. His enemies just did not see the charm.

Between shots, Player told Trump and Graham about a new golf course he was thinking of building in the wilds of South Africa. It was a beautiful place where golfers could spot all kinds of animals—buffalo, lions, zebras, elephants—roaming the grasslands.

"What happens, Gary, when two lions look out and say, 'You know, that's a pretty thick guy. I'd like to eat him. Let's go eat him,'" Trump joked.

"Well, they've got fences and stuff," Player said.

"You mean they can't climb over a fence?" Trump asked skeptically.

"If you get in a Jeep, they won't come into the Jeep," Player assured him. "But if you get out of the Jeep, they'll eat you."

"How do you know they won't come into the Jeep?" Trump asked.

"I'm not betting my life on it," Graham said.

Trump persisted.

"Do you carry a gun?"

"No," Player said.

"Well, I'm carrying a gun," Trump said.

Graham had not heard Trump laugh and enjoy himself so much in a long time. He was in a good mood, chipper. No presidency. No flurry of tweets. His Twitter and Facebook ban was surprisingly liberating, he claimed.

"I've found I've got hours a day just to do other things," Trump had said.

Golf was the ultimate recreation, and that day Trump also had brought along a donor and a caddy. Player brought his grandson. Six men, their golf carts crisscrossing the course for hours with golf balls flying everywhere, like an airport with so much overhead traffic.

Player shot 68, four under par. Trump maybe six over. Graham had six good holes, six bad holes, and six in the middle. Standard, no real score, he said. Trump had criticized Graham's swing. "You're lunging at the ball."

After the golf, Graham kept up his drumbeat. "You're strongest when you're talking about your policies," he said. He had a list: "Securing the border versus chaos on the border, tax reform, smaller government, staring down the Iranians, standing up to China."

The Democrats and Biden were overreaching, too radical, Graham said. "The Democrats are doing their part to put us back in the game." Graham even went further, "If the election were held next Tuesday, we'd win the House. We're going to have a decent chance of coming back and picking up a seat in the Senate.

"We can't do it without you, Mr. President. You have to help us. But you're going to have to focus on the future, not the past to maximize our chance at success."

Graham was like an addiction counselor, struggling to keep his patient from taking one more drink. Trump wanted to sip the past.

"You've got to figure out who to endorse and who not to endorse," Graham said. "You want your best team on the field. It's in your interest for us to win the House and Senate. That means January 6 is not your obituary if the party can come back."

And here was the key: "The best way to do that is to pick people who can win in their states, in their districts. And maybe not the person you like best, but the person who can win." Trump was going to have to endorse some people who were not always-Trumpers or even Trump allies.

"You need to endorse most of my colleagues," Graham said. In all, 15 Republican senators were up for reelection at that point, including Lisa Murkowski, who had voted to convict Trump in February.

No, Trump said emphatically on Murkowski, absolutely not. She had been very disloyal and unappreciative of all he had done for Alaska, such as opening oil and gas exploration.

In Georgia, Graham told Trump he was working to recruit Trump favorite Herschel Walker. A three-time All American and 1982 Heisman Trophy winner, Walker was considered one of the greatest football players of all time. He was also a longtime friend to Trump.

A Walker candidacy would present a test case for Republicans. He was famous and conservative and a Black American. But in Washington, many veteran consultants were worried about Walker's past and mental health. He once told ABC he liked to play "Russian Roulette" with a loaded gun pressed to his temple when he had houseguests. He had cheered Trump's claims of election fraud and his fight to "Stop the Steal." The Georgia race in 2022 would likely demand discipline.

Graham also told Trump he should draft an America First policy agenda modeled on Newt Gingrich's 1994 "Contract with America," the important conservative plan that laid out specific legislation Republicans would enact if they won back the House. Six weeks after being unveiled, Republicans trounced Democrats in the midterm elections, gaining 54 seats in the House and control of both chambers.

After an hour and a half Graham's post-golf seminar ended. He had made his points.

"I can throw a punch," Graham said after Trump left, "and I stand up for him. But I'm always the guy pushing him to take the less confrontational approach.

"For 2024, if he wants to run, then he's going to have to deal with his personality problems. The problems created with Trump's personality are easier to fix than if the party blew completely up and we had a civil war. A third-party movement would start if you tried to kick Trump out of the Republican Party.

"We are in a pretty good spot on policy. But we've got a very damaged team captain."

Trump saw himself as anything but.

"Are my numbers really that good?" Trump asked one of his longtime pollsters, John McLaughlin, on June 16 during a political briefing at his Bedminster, New Jersey, golf club.

"Yes," McLaughlin said, nodding and pointing to his printout of his firm's May 21 poll of Republican primary voters that said 73 percent wanted him to run again in 2024. And 82 percent said they would support him in the primary campaign if he jumped in.

McLaughlin turned to the next page. The question posed to GOP voters: "Thinking ahead to the 2024 Republican primary election for President, if that election were held today among the following candidates, for whom would you vote?"

The result showed Trump dominating the field of potential contenders, with 57 percent choosing him from more than a dozen others. Mike Pence came in second place with just 10 percent. Florida governor Ron DeSantis, a rising star, came in third place with 8 percent.

"Have you ever seen any numbers like this?" Trump asked.

"No," McLaughlin said. "These numbers, your numbers, are better than what Reagan had."

"In many ways, you were a more conservative president than Reagan," he said. "Tougher on immigration and trade, more pro-life, in many ways. You've really transformed the Republican Party into the party of the working men and women of America, whereas Reagan was always working to get Reagan Democrats and attract working-class voters."

This was not a one-off session. Trump was keeping his political operation fully active, even if its size had significantly shrunk since he left the presidency.

Other public polls showed Trump had deep Republican support, but also significant liabilities. An NBC News/*Wall Street Journal* poll in April, among registered voters nationwide, showed Trump with 32 percent positive ratings and 55 percent negative ratings, compared to 50 percent positive and 36 percent negative for Biden.

"The more you get attacked, the more your base gets solidified," McLaughlin told Trump. "More intensified. Your support is not going anywhere."

McLaughlin had been arguing to Trump for weeks that Biden's support could eventually crater like Jimmy Carter's ahead of the 1980 election, when the Iran hostage crisis overwhelmed his presidency and Ronald Reagan won.

"The pendulum is going to swing back, Mr. President," he said. "Just be patient. Hang back and wait and see what happens, and there will be buyer's remorse about Biden.

"These are *your* vaccines. *You're* the one who left the country in a position for a rebound on the economy. Biden is not going to be able to take credit for that."

Kellyanne Conway was still in Trump's inner circle. "My Kellyanne, my Kellyanne," he would begin, calling her up after a summer round of golf.

Since she left the White House the previous year and did not formally join the 2020 campaign, she had some distance from his defeat, now five years after serving as his campaign manager in 2016.

"It's fine for you to say my Kellyanne," she said. "But I need you to see me as somebody else." She was not on the payroll and she was suspicious of the advisers who counted on Trump's behemoth fundraising apparatus for their post-campaign livelihood. "I am a person, if not the person, close to you who did not take a dime, not a penny from your $1.4 billion reelection campaign."

Okay, Trump said, understood.

"There are eight or 10 things you need to know. Got to get back to basics. How did you win in the first place in 2016? You won because you have this connective tissue with people. The people are forgotten. You've elevated them. They actually benefited financially, culturally, emotionally. They had upward economic and social mobility while you were president. And they are the most hurt by your loss.

"They're the most hurt because they're the coal miners and the steelworkers and the energy workers. They're the middle-wage people. They're the ones who have not one kid, but three and four who now are going backward in their economic mobility."

Stop with the grievances. No more obsession with the election. Speak to real anxieties. Win back the support of suburban women who backed you in 2016. Get back to talking angrily about China instead of Georgia.

Trump said he appreciated the advice and felt nostalgic about his 2016 campaign. At the end, it was just a handful of aides flying around on his private plane, going from rally to rally. He wanted that back, be the outsider. His campaign in 2020 had a corporate feel.

"That's why you're going to be in charge of everything, honey, the next time," Trump said.

Conway laughed and made no promises.

"Listen, you were the underdog both times even though you were the president of the United States the second time. But what you didn't have this time was the hunger and the swagger. And you weren't under-resourced and understaffed. If anything, Arlington," where the Trump campaign had its headquarters, "became Brooklyn," where Hillary Clinton housed her 2016 campaign.

"What do you mean?" Trump asked.

"Trump 2020 resembled Hillary 2016. You had too much money, too much time, too much ego."

Later, again on the golf course with friends and donors, Trump told his golfing group he was thinking about using his private Boeing 757 airplane as a way of taunting Biden. A shadow Air Force One, flying around the country ahead of the 2022 midterm elections.

"The American people love that plane," he said. "I am thinking of getting it repainted in red, white, and blue. Like Air Force One, the way I believe Air Force One should look.

"That's my brand. I don't do the corporate jet thing. I'm not going to show up in a little Gulfstream like a fucking CEO."

SEVENTY-ONE

"I'm upset you called me a killer," Russian president Vladimir Putin told President Biden in an April 13 phone call. Biden had been asked in an ABC News interview if he thought Putin was a "killer" and said, "I do."

"I was asked a question," Biden told Putin. "I gave an answer. It was an interview on a totally different topic. And it was not something premeditated," as if that ameliorated the meaning. The Kremlin had called the insult unprecedented and summoned its ambassador in the United States back to Moscow for further discussions.

Putin also punched back publicly, saying, "It takes one to know one," and rattled off the U.S. government's treatment of Native Americans and its decision to drop atomic bombs on Japan during World War II.

The call was part of Biden's effort to put Putin on notice to expect a chillier relationship than the one Putin had had with Trump.

Earlier on, before the call, Biden had told Jake Sullivan that he wanted a new strategy for dealing with Russia. What are we trying to accomplish?

"Let's take a step back," Biden said. "I'm not looking for a reset," a reference to Obama's approach to Russia. "I'm not looking for some kind of good relationship, but I want to find a stable and predictable way forward with Putin and Russia."

As a first step, Biden asked the U.S. intelligence agencies to assess the quality of information about some alleged recent Russian actions.

The intelligence agencies reported they had determined with high confidence that Russia was behind three major acts of aggression: the poisoning of opposition leader Alexey Navalny, the massive cyberattacks that allowed Russia to spy on or disrupt some 16,000 computer systems worldwide, and the interference in the 2020 U.S. presidential election to help Trump.

During his call with Putin in April, Biden laid out the accusations.

"You're wrong about everything," Putin said. "You have no evidence. We didn't interfere in your election. We didn't do any of these things."

Biden dismissed the denials. "I'm warning you we are coming at you with these responses," Biden said. He described a series of aggressive sanctions. "They will happen this week and I want you to hear it from me directly. And it's because of the specific things you've done. I've said I would respond and I'm responding."

He also warned Putin not to start a new military incursion into Ukraine.

Putin continued his categorical denials and said he was upset about the killer accusation.

"Let's meet," Biden said, proposing a summit between the two of them. "Let's you and I sit down. You bring your concerns, and I will bring mine." On any and all topics. "And we'll sit face to face, and we'll talk about all of it."

"Let me get this straight," Putin said. "You want to meet and talk about all the issues in our relationship? All of them?"

Sullivan, who was listening on the call, thought Putin, always suspicious, wanted to make sure it was not some kind of trap.

Biden assured Putin it would be an open dialogue. He knew Putin realized a meeting would show he is respected by the American president. They had met a decade earlier, in 2011, when

Biden was vice president and Putin was temporarily serving as prime minister.

Biden later told *The New Yorker* that during that meeting, he said, "Mr. Prime Minister, I'm looking into your eyes and I don't think you have a soul."

Putin smiled and told Biden, through an interpreter, "We understand one another."

For Biden, it was standard for American presidents to meet with the Russian leader. Though a declining economic power with less than 10 percent of the U.S. GDP, Russia still had more than 2,000 strategic nuclear weapons and thousands of smaller tactical nuclear weapons. Russia also had significant conventional and nonconventional military units deployed around the world.

"Okay," Putin finally said to Biden, "I would like to have the summit also. Let's have our teams work on it."

Biden frequently cited former House Speaker Tip O'Neill's adage that all politics is local. "You know," Biden said, "all diplomacy is personal. At the end of the day, you've got to develop these personal relationships."

On April 15, the White House and Treasury Department announced sanctions on the Russian Central Bank, its Finance Ministry, wealth fund, six technology companies, 32 entities and individuals for attempts to influence the 2020 presidential election, and eight individuals and groups involved in Russia's occupation and repression in Crimea.

Biden and Putin later announced they would meet June 16 in Geneva, Switzerland.

"I know there were a lot of hype around this meeting, but it's pretty straightforward to me—the meeting," Biden told reporters on June 16 on the Swiss lakeside after the meeting ended. "One, there is no substitute, as those of you who have covered me for a while know, for a face-to-face dialogue between leaders. None. And President Putin and I had a, share a unique responsibility to manage the relationship between two powerful and proud countries, a relationship that has to be stable and predictable."

"Why are you so confident he'll change his behavior, Mr. President?" CNN's chief White House correspondent, Kaitlan Collins, then asked.

Biden, who had started to walk away, turned back with irritation.

"I'm not confident he'll change his behavior," he said, glowering at Collins and wagging his finger. "Where the hell—what do you do all the time? When did I say I was confident? I said—"

"You said in the next six months you'll be able to determine—" Collins said.

"I said, what I said was, let's get this straight. I said: What will change their behavior is if the rest of the world reacts to them and it diminishes their standing in the world. I'm not confident of anything; I'm just stating a fact."

"But," Collins pressed, "given his past behavior has not changed and, in that press conference, after sitting down with you for several hours, he denied any involvement in cyberattacks; he downplayed human rights abuses; he even refused to say Aleksey Navalny's name. So how does that account to a constructive meeting, as President—President Putin framed it?"

Biden snapped at the 29-year-old reporter, "If you don't understand that, you're in the wrong business."

Clips of the back-and-forth went viral on Twitter. Standing outside Air Force One later that day, Biden said, "I owe my last questioner an apology. I shouldn't have, I shouldn't have been such a wise guy with the last answer I gave." Collins said an apology was unnecessary.

The episode was a snapshot throwback to Biden's history of self-inflicted gaffes, which had mostly been dormant as he stuck to scripted events during his presidency.

That side of Biden—his tendency to at times be testy or mangle statements—was still him and now part of his presidency. Several Biden aides privately said Klain and Dunn worked to address this issue by keeping him away from unscripted events or long interviews. They called the effect "the wall," a cocooning of the president.

But the unscripted Biden occasionally appeared.

"The progressives don't like me because I'm not prepared to take on what I would say and they would say is a socialist agenda," he told *New York Times* columnist David Brooks in May. His comments upset many progressives for linking the word "socialist" to them.

In late June, Biden announced he had struck a major bipartisan deal on infrastructure with Republican senators, but shortly after seemed to upend the agreement by saying the deal was contingent upon a more liberal spending package that would be passed through reconciliation.

"Both need to get done," he said, "and I'm going to work closely with Speaker Pelosi and Leader Schumer to make sure that both move through the legislative process promptly and in tandem. Let me emphasize that: and in tandem."

His remarks surprised some Democrats, who always saw a two-track strategy. And they annoyed Republicans, who were unhappy he added a caveat after making a splash about striking a big, bipartisan deal.

Steve Ricchetti worked the phones for days, repairing the White House's relationships on both sides of the aisle and keeping talks alive. Biden ultimately issued a 628-word statement to clarify his position.

McConnell pounced on the runaround. "It almost makes your head spin," he said.

Biden carried on. Infrastructure was central, a must-pass part of his agenda. You make a mistake, you move on.

"Get up!"

And sometimes, you even had to deal with a literal stumble.

Biden fell to his knees on March 19 as he climbed the steps of Air Force One, boarding a flight to Atlanta. He got up, climbed a few more steps, then fell again.

Republicans ridiculed Biden and savored the video footage, particularly since Biden's campaign had mocked Trump's at times halting gait during the 2020 race.

The White House assured reporters Biden was "100 percent fine."

Biden, however, was frustrated. He later told others that once he got up the steps and ducked inside the cabin, he muttered to himself.

"Fuck," Biden whispered. "Fuck!" He was loud enough for others to hear him.

Russia lingered. U.S. intelligence traced a massive number of ransomware attacks to Russian criminals. Electronically blocking access to computers until money, often millions of dollars, was paid was a huge problem. The attacks were not only cyber war but economic war. There was not yet evidence tying Russian intelligence and Putin directly, but like everything in Russia, Putin had iron grip control.

President Biden and Putin spoke by secure phone on July 9. Biden demanded that Putin crack down on the Russian-based criminals involved in the corrupt and malicious attacks.

"If you can't or won't, I will," Biden said. "I just want to be clear about that so there's no ambiguity."

At the end of the conversation, Biden added, "You know, Mr. President, great countries have great responsibilities. They also have great vulnerabilities."

U.S. offensive cyber capability was formidable, as Putin knew. Biden left it at that. It was as close as Biden came to delivering a direct threat to the Russian president.

Biden had spent his life angling for the presidency. But once he arrived at 1600 Pennsylvania Avenue, his top aides could see he was uncomfortable. He missed Delaware. His own house.

Biden privately started calling the White House "the tomb." It was lonely. Cold. The virus made social events impossible, at least at the start, when it was just him and Jill, and their two German shepherds. Family members made sure to visit, but relaxing with the grandkids back in Delaware, where he liked to eat chocolate ice cream out of the freezer at night, seemed appealing in comparison.

Biden made sure to tell aides and friends that the staff at the White House was great. Everybody was kind. They were always asking him what he wanted, or if they could get him a snack. It was like a fancy hotel. Even the residence, which he never visited during his eight years as vice president, was laid out that way. The beautiful carpets. The paintings on the wall. The ornate chandeliers. It reminded him of the Waldorf Astoria.

"I'm just not used to taking off my coat and someone grabbing it and hanging it up," Biden said. "But they're very nice people." The vice presidential mansion, tucked away by trees and up on 13 acres, two and a half miles from the White House, suited his casual tastes.

Weekends in Wilmington quickly became the norm. Get on Marine One, head over to Andrews, and get back home. He could wander around and make those long, winding phone calls to old Senate pals and people in Delaware who still called him Joe.

"He is not comfortable living in the White House," Ron Klain told others. The valets and staff at 1600 Pennsylvania, "that's just not who he is. He likes to go live in a house.

"Joe Biden has always been, I'm either at work or I'm at home. And being upstairs at the White House feels like you're staying at someone else's house."

With his closest advisers, who had worked with him for decades, Biden retained a tight-knit sense of trust. They knew each other. They knew him. No bad day, or disaster, could really rattle that, or him.

There was hope. When they launched on Inauguration Day, January 20, the United States had 191,458 new Covid-19 cases and 3,992 new deaths. By late June, the daily coronavirus death total in the U.S. had dropped under 300, a dramatic reduction of more than 90 percent. This was largely due to the successful vaccine program.

The Centers for Disease Control announced that fully vaccinated people could gather and go about their activities without a mask. Businesses reopened and cafés and restaurants welcomed people inside. A hustle and bustle began to return to the streets.

Yet the future trajectory of the pandemic remained uncertain. The aggressive and highly contagious Delta variant threatened the world. Vaccine hesitancy and opposition still might prevent the U.S. from reaching herd immunity. The long-term effectiveness of the vaccines against a mutating coronavirus remained unknown.

"Now he comes into the office every day kind of in a midrange emotional space," Klain once said privately.

It was as much hope as reality. As president, Biden remains an emotional man, expressing himself openly on everything. "Midrange emotional space" was not natural.

"There is no news I can walk in and give him in the morning," Klain said, "that is worse than the news he's been given many other times of his life." The death of his first wife and young daughter in 1972, the death of Beau in 2015.

"Conversely, there's no news I can walk in and give him in the morning that's better than the news he's gotten at some other time in his life."

After finishing fifth in the New Hampshire primary, for example, Biden was elected president of the United States nine months later.

SEVENTY-TWO

"Your problem is too much drama," Lindsey Graham told Trump in another one of their endless and now routine phone calls later in the summer. "Too much volatility. You could, if you choose to, fix your problem easier than Biden.

"You keep saying the election was rigged and you were cheated. You lost a close election.

"You fucked your presidency up."

Trump abruptly hung up the phone.

About a day later, he called Graham back.

"Listen, I don't blame you," Graham said. "I would have hung up, too!"

It was tough medicine, but Graham reminded Trump he was on his side, his friend forever. He was trying to rehabilitate him. But if Trump came back with a recalibrated pitch and approach, who knew what could happen?

Trump responded by saying his supporters loved his personality. "I'll lose my base," if I change. They expect me to fight, to be disruptive. It was built in. This was not a fuck up. The election was stolen.

The night of Tuesday, June 22, Trump and Graham had another long phone conversation.

Graham wanted to shift Trump's focus to Biden. He said Biden's policies were disastrous and provided an opening for Republicans.

But Trump had failed to define Biden in the presidential campaign and had let Biden define himself. Now Biden was defining himself again.

"You can prosecute the case against Biden better than anybody," Graham said. "But you can't do that and complain about losing at the same time. The media is not your friend. They're going to take the throwaway line you give in a speech about 2020, and that just wipes out all the other things you say about how Biden is driving the country in the wrong direction.

"If we come back in 2022 and recapture the House and take back the Senate, you'll get your fair share of credit. If we fail to take back the House and the Senate in 2022, Trumpism, I think, will die. January 6 will be your obituary.

"If we don't win in 2022, we're screwed."

In the House, the Republicans were only down five seats. But House Minority Leader Kevin McCarthy had a job managing the unmanageable. So many factions. Graham had been in the House for eight years before moving to the Senate in 2003 and knew them well. "You've got the Republican Study Groups. You've got the moderates. The House is just a constant shit show."

Graham believed Trump would not have won the 2016 Republican presidential nomination without his hardline stance on immigration. Americans wanted more control of their borders. Trump understood that. He had made the issue work for the GOP and win over those voters who did not identify with the Paul Ryan or Mitch McConnell school of Republican politics. Biden, who wants to expand and simplify the legal immigration process, was already facing GOP salvos for the latest surge of migration from Central America.

On economics and government spending, Graham believed people instinctively understand that everything can't be free all the time. People were being incentivized not to work. Inflation is the enemy of the middle class.

"An out-of-control border," Graham said, summarizing his position. "A crime wave and increased prices of gas and food could lead to a Republican blowout in 2022."

"Do you think it could be that big?" Trump asked.

"Yes," Graham said.

But Trump then said again that he got cheated in the election. "You know, I won Georgia," he said.

"No," Graham said, "I missed that one. I missed that story."

"They purged 100,000 people from the rolls," Trump said.

"Mr. President," Graham said, "with all due respect, that doesn't mean you won Georgia." Some 67,000 Georgia residents had been dropped from the voting rolls because they had filled out change-of-address forms, and 34,000 had been eliminated because election mail sent to their homes had been returned. "There's nothing that's going to happen that will give you Georgia or Arizona. Period." Nothing that will give you any other state.

"The allegations you're making about the election don't hold water," Graham said. A few minor ballot problems, that was it, not anywhere close to something that could change the outcome in any state. He reminded Trump that he and his staff had checked. "There weren't 60,000 people in Georgia that voted under 18 or 8,000 felons that voted in Arizona from prison. That's not true."

Trump persisted. He was cheated.

"You agree with me that you've got a chance to come back," Graham said, again shifting his approach.

"Yes."

"Let's focus on that. Mr. President, the greatest comeback in American history is possible. You've been written off as dead because of January the 6th. The conventional wisdom is that the Republican Party, under your leadership, has collapsed. If you, as the party leader, could lead us to a 2022 victory and you came back to take the White House, it would be the biggest comeback in American history.

"I don't pretend to know the mood of the country," Graham said, "but I do know the mood of the Republican primary voter in South Carolina. Rock solid Trump." But it would not last forever.

"Mr. President, there's a growing group of people who wonder if you've been too damaged to win again. And these are pretty much Trump people. You've got to prove to them that you can change."

Trump was entertaining a parade of authors of Trump books at Mar-a-Lago for interviews, even multiple interviews.

"They're going to write a shitty book about me," Trump said.

"Yeah, you're probably right," Graham agreed.

"But I thought there will maybe be one line in the book that'd make it less shitty."

"I'm with you," Graham said. "Why not?"

"I'm talking to everybody."

It seemed to Graham that Trump had opened the door to everyone but the Uber driver.

"At least I get to tell my side of the story," Trump said. He appeared to love the interviews.

"If you don't think you did a good job, why should anybody else think you did a good job?" Graham asked.

"I think I did a good job."

"Go tell people why. Go defend your presidency. Do you think your presidency's worth protecting?"

"Yeah."

"Well, go defend it.

"I enjoyed your presidency. It wore me out. I turned gray during the last three years."

Trump played the media successfully about half the time and the other half, "he's just his own worst enemy," Graham concluded.

Dealing with Trump was like being near the sun. You could really get burned. For Republicans like himself, the question was: "How close do you want to get to the sun without melting?"

"I think he's redeemable. I think he's got magic and I think he's got darkness. I've said that a thousand times.

"His desire to be successful and to be seen as being successful is my best hope. He wants to be remembered as a good president."

When Trump would say he thought he was a good president, Graham once said, "You're right, you were. But you lost."

"I got cheated."

But before any comeback was possible, it was essential for Trump to purge himself of January 6, Graham believed.

"January 6th was a horrible day in American history. It was 1968 all over again. Every day you woke up, you thought, what could happen? What's going to happen next? You had Bobby Kennedy killed. You had Dr. King killed. You had riots in the streets. You had a Democratic convention that was in complete chaos. We made it then. We'll make it now."

Graham told Trump to please stop excusing the behavior of the Capitol rioters.

But Trump would not stop.

"They were peaceful people. These were great people," he said in a July 11 interview with Fox News. "The love, the love in the air, I have never seen anything like it.

"You have people with no guns that walked down. And frankly, the doors were open and the police, in many cases, you know, they have—they have hundreds of hours of tape. They ought to release the tape to see what really happened." Yet more than 100 police officers had been injured during the riot.

Graham did not want to hear this. By the summer, federal prosecutors had charged more than 500 people in the riot.

"How you doing, boss?" Brad Parscale said to Trump in a phone call in early July.

Though Parscale, Trump's former campaign manager, had been all but banished from his circle a year earlier after the Tulsa rally debacle, he was now back in. Trump often went from hot to cold to hot with advisers.

"Sir, are you going to run?"

"I'm thinking about it," Trump said. He sounded restless. Impatient. He leaned into the idea. "I'm really strongly thinking about running."

"Well, that's all I need to hear," Parscale said.

"We've got to keep doing this, Brad." He wondered aloud if Biden was suffering from dementia.

"Decrepit," Trump spat, speaking of Biden.

"He had an army. An army for Trump. He wants that back," Parscale later told others. "He feels a little pressure of not being in the fight like he was and he's wrapping his head around how to get back there.

"I don't think he sees it as a comeback. He sees it as vengeance."

EPILOGUE

Across the Potomac River at Quarters 6, inside his second-floor, top secret Sensitive Compartmented Information facility, surrounded by multiple secure video screens connected to the White House and the world, Chairman Milley was still trying to sort out the meaning of the January 6 riot.

"The 6th of January was one of the days of high risk," Milley told senior staff. "Neither I, nor anyone that I know of, to include the FBI or anybody else, envisioned the thousands of people who assaulted the Capitol.

"To basically encircle the Capitol and assault it from multiple directions simultaneously, and to do what they did, that was something else.

"The 6th was pretty dramatic. That's about as dramatic as you're going to see it, short of a civil war."

The conventional wisdom, which had settled into Washington, was that there had been warnings. But Milley knew the internet chatter had lacked coherence and did not provide the specific, credible intelligence that could avert a catastrophe.

It had been a grave U.S. intelligence failure, comparable to the missed warnings prior to the September 11, 2001, terrorist attacks and to Pearl Harbor, and exposed glaring gaps and weaknesses in the American system.

What did Milley and others miss? What did they not understand?

Milley, ever the historian, thought of the little remembered 1905 revolution in Russia. The uprising had failed, but it had set the stage for the successful 1917 revolution that led to the creation of the Soviet Union. Vladimir Lenin, the leader of the 1917 revolution, had later called the 1905 revolution "The Great Dress Rehearsal."

Had January 6 been a dress rehearsal?

Milley told senior staff, "What you might have seen was a precursor to something far worse down the road."

Milley knew that history moves slowly but then often without warning lurches suddenly forward so it seemed impossible to stop. Whether the country was witnessing the end of Trump or the beginning of the next phase of Trump would only be known in retrospect.

Trump was not dormant. He was out holding campaign-style rallies across the country in the summer of 2021. More than 10,000 people in Trump hats and waving signs that read "Save America!" attended his June 26 rally in Wellington, Ohio.

"We didn't lose. We didn't lose. We didn't lose," Trump told the crowd.

"Four more years! Four more years! Four more years!" they roared.

"We won the election twice!" Trump said. This was the latest way to claim he had beaten Biden. The crowd erupted. "And it's possible we'll have to win it a third time."

About 90 minutes into the rally, Trump whipped them up again. This was not a farewell.

"We will not bend," Trump said, adopting a Churchillian cadence. It was a war speech. "We will not break. We will not yield. We will never give in. We will never give up. We will never back down. We will never, ever surrender. My fellow Americans, our movement is far from over. In fact, our fight has only just begun."

Milley wondered, was this just Trump's desire to project strength? Or a desire for absolute power?

Presidents live in the unfinished business of their predecessors. No one could be more aware of that than Joseph R. Biden Jr.

Biden and his advisers hated to utter Trump's name. Aides frequently warned each other to please avoid the "T" word.

But Trump's existence permeated the White House, even the residence. One night, Biden wandered into a room where a huge video screen covered the wall. To relax, Trump used to upload programs to virtually play the world's most famous golf courses. "What a fucking asshole," Biden once said as he surveyed the former president's golf toys.

A prior president burdened by the heavy shadow of his predecessor was Gerald Ford in 1974. Ford called Watergate the "national nightmare." Watergate disappeared but Nixon did not. In his first 30 days as president, Ford was increasingly beleaguered as Nixon dominated the news.

"I needed my own presidency," Ford later said.

His remedy was a full pardon of Nixon. Ford believed it was in the national interest and the only way to shed the Nixon past. The decision was greeted with almost universal outrage, and Ford lost the presidency two years later, largely due to suspicions that he worked to save his political mentor and predecessor from prison.

Biden has said he would never pardon Trump. But he faced Ford's dilemma: How do you get the country to move on? How do you have your own presidency?

Biden kept watch on Trump, though he held his observations close. His aides noticed he could be prickly and tough at times and would walk into the Oval Office unhappy some mornings about another round of Trump talk on MSNBC's pundit roundtable, *Morning Joe.*

Five years ago, on March 31, 2016, when Trump was on the verge of winning the Republican presidential nomination, we worked together for the first time and interviewed Trump at his then unfinished Trump International Hotel on Pennsylvania Avenue in Washington.

That day, we recognized he was an extraordinary political force, in many ways right out of the American playbook. An outsider. Anti-establishment. A businessman. A builder. Bombastic. Confident. A fast-talking scrapper.

But we also saw darkness. He could be petty. Cruel. Bored by American history and dismissive of governing traditions that had long guided elected leaders. Tantalized by the prospect of power. Eager to use fear to get his way.

"Real power is—I don't even want to use the word—fear," Trump told us.

"I bring rage out. I do bring rage out. I always have. I don't know if that's an asset or a liability, but whatever it is, I do."

Could Trump work his will again? Were there any limits to what he and his supporters might do to put him back in power?

Peril remains.

Note to Readers

All interviews for this book were conducted under the journalist ground rule of "deep background." This means that all the information could be used but we would not say who provided it.

The book is drawn from hundreds of hours of interviews with more than 200 firsthand participants and witnesses to these events. Nearly all allowed us to tape-record our interviews. When we have attributed exact quotations, thoughts or conclusions to the participants, that information comes from the person, a colleague with direct knowledge, or from government or personal documents, calendars, diaries, emails, meeting notes, transcripts, and other records.

President Trump and President Biden declined to be interviewed for this book.

Acknowledgments

We have profound gratitude for Jonathan Karp, the CEO of Simon & Schuster. He oversees an enterprise that publishes thousands of titles a year, but he was also our hands-on editor. He engaged with us at every step—conception, drafting, and even the photo captions and book-jacket copy. He pushed us and himself, always asking the important questions: Do we have this right? Do we understand this? Who else might speak to us?

Jon is an editor of conscience and compassion, a seeker of truth and clarity. He loves books, authors, and readers, and sees publishing as both civic duty and moral responsibility.

Special thanks to Kimberly Goldstein, who oversaw the organizational and technical efforts of getting this book published. She is a master. And thanks to other executives and leaders at Simon & Schuster who were unflagging in their support: Dana Canedy, Julia Prosser, Lisa Healy, Lisa Erwin, Paul Dippolito, Irene Kheradi, Stephen Bedford, Kate Mertes, Richard Shrout, W. Anne Jones, Jackie Seow, Rafael Taveras, Mikaela Bielawski, and Elisa Rivlin.

Copy editor Fred Chase came to Washington from his home in Texas and gave the manuscript multiple reads with his keen eye and sense of language. Mary E. Taylor spent hours skillfully and professionally assisting us in this project. We will forever be thankful to her.

Robert B. Barnett, lawyer and counselor, has earned the title Senior Publishing Guru of Washington. He guided us through this project at every turn, always wise, always devoted, and always available.

Woodward has 50 years with *The Washington Post*. Costa eight years. The *Post* is one of the great, ever-growing institutions in the United States—demanding, traditional yet also experimental. Jeff Bezos, the *Post*'s owner, has brought dynamism and much needed stability to the *Post*. Publisher Fred Ryan has supported both of us and has been an unflinching defender of press freedom.

In the newsroom, we appreciate former executive editor Marty Baron and managing editors Cameron Barr and Tracy Grant for encouraging this collaboration, and are excited to support Marty's successor, Sally Buzbee, as she leads and bolsters the *Post* in the coming years. National editor Steven Ginsberg is valued by both of us, as is the whole National team.

Thanks to the *Post*'s director of photography, MaryAnne Golon, and photo editor, Thomas Simonetti, who expertly assisted us with the photos included in this book.

We cherish the relationships we have with hundreds of other *Post* colleagues, from the copy aides to the reporters who have worked closely with us to the veteran editors who make it all happen every day. There are far too many names to list here. But we hope they know how much they mean to us. We are honored to be part of the *Post* family.

Writing a book on the White House and campaigns necessitates constant study. We learned much from the reporting published by *The Post, The New York Times, The Wall Street Journal*, CNN, NBC News and MSNBC, ABC, CBS News, the Associated Press, Reuters, Axios, *The Atlantic*, and Politico, among many others.

We were also reporting on the final months of the Trump presidency at the same time as other authors. Naturally, our reporting paths sometimes took us down similar roads, and we respect the work they have done in their books on this period, particularly *I*

Alone Can Fix It by Carol Leonnig and Philip Rucker, *Landslide* by Michael Wolff, and *"Frankly, We Did Win This Election"* by Michael C. Bender.

Woodward

Many thanks to former colleagues and continuing friends: Carl Bernstein (for nearly 50 years of counsel and friendship), Don Graham, Sally Quinn, David and Linda Maraniss, Rick Atkinson, Christian Williams, Paul Richard, Patrick Tyler, Tom Wilkinson, Steve Luxenberg, Scott Armstrong, Al Kamen, Ben Weiser, Martha Sherrill, Bill Powers, John Feinstein, Michael Newman, Richard Snyder, Jamie Gangel, Danny Silva, Andy Lack, Betsy Lack, Rita Braver, Carl Feldbaum, Anne Swallow, Seymour Hersh, Richard Cohen, Steve Brill, Tom Boswell, Wendy Boswell, Judy Kovler, Peter Kovler, Ted Olson, Lady Olson, Karen Alexander, Brendan Sullivan, Bill Nelson, Jim Hoagland, Jane Hitchcock, Robert Redford, David Remnick, David Martin, Gerald Rafshoon, Cheryl Haywood, George Haywood, Jim Wooten, Patience O'Connor, Christine Kuehbeck, Wendy Woodward, Sue Whall, Catherine Joyce, Jon Sowanick, Bill Slater, Cary Greenauer, Don Gold, Kyle Pruett, Marsha Pruett, Veronica Walsh, Mickey Cafiero, Grail Walsh, Redmond Walsh, Diana Walsh, Kent Walker, Daria Walsh, Bruce McNamara, Josh Horwitz, Ericka Markman, Barbara Guss, Bob Tyrer, Sian Spurney, Michael Phillips, Neil Starr, Shelly Hall, Evelyn Duffy, Dr. William Hamilton, Joan Felt, Ken Adelman, Carol Adelman, Tony D'Amelio, Joanna D'Amelio, Matt Anderson, Brady Dennis, Jeff Glasser, Bill Murphy, Josh Boak, Rob Garver, Stephen Enniss, Steve Milke, Pat Stevens, Bassam Freiha, Jackie Crowe, Brian Foley, Cyrille Fontaine, Dan Foley, Betty Govatos, and Barbara Woodward.

Rosa Criollo's generous spirit throughout this project was appreciated.

Robert Costa, 35, is half my age, 78. But he exceeds my

understanding of politics, Washington, and journalism. He is a marvel. He taught me so much, always driving us to ask penetrating, honest questions and then examine the answers. I would feel good doing one or two interviews a day. Many days, he would do seven. No one has more energy or curiosity. He found a structure to this story, immediately seeing the relationship between Biden and Trump, and the connective politics of the Republican and Democratic parties, the White House, and Congress.

My family is in my thoughts daily: daughter Diana, daughter Tali and her husband Gabe, and my grandchildren, Zadie and Theo.

Elsa Walsh, my wife, devoted many days and weeks to this book. Formal and informal talk, and more talk. But most important, she is a brilliant, informed and very intense editor. Costa and I were treated to regular and compelling rewrite suggestions. He learned, as have I over the years, that it is possible to have more suggestions and edits on a page than the original typed words.

There is still a degree of mystery to Elsa's genius. In doing more than 200 interviews, nearly all of them recorded, Costa and I have 6,200 pages of transcripts. That could be about 20 long, serious books—a virtual library of the Trump and Biden presidencies. At times, we lost track of what might be important and what might not be important. Not Elsa. She zeroed in on who had critical information and who was providing it. One evening, she took a stack of transcripts and retired with her green pen. She soon started peppering us with questions. Why is this not in the latest draft? Don't you see how this connects with what another person said? Each day, she forwarded choice clips from our own paper, or the *New York Times*, or the *Wall Street Journal* or special political and military publications, and she even had assignment lists and reading lists for us.

Everything is related, she said in dozens of ways. I suggest you contact this person or go back to that person, she said. Does this section go far enough? Her work enlarged every scene and the whole book.

As I always remind myself, Elsa is a disciple of Henry James and his assertion on the importance of kindness. She is always kind. There is no sufficient way to thank her for all she contributes to our lives together and my writing, and the 17 books I have written since we have been together.

When we were married in 1989, a Wallace Stevens poem was read:

> *So great a unity, that it is bliss*
> *Ties us to those we love*
> *Be near me, come closer, touch my hand*
> *Phrases compounded of dear relation, spoken twice,*
> *Once by the lips, once by the services.*

Costa

My siblings James Costa, Ellen Duncan, and Tim Costa are the pillars in my life, along with my parents, Tom and Dillon Costa. My siblings' spouses, Meghan Daly Costa and Paul Duncan, and my nieces, Dillon and Sloane Duncan, add joy to our lives.

Special thanks to the extended Dalton and Costa families. My wonderful aunts and uncles and cousins are too many to list here. You know how much you all mean to me.

I am grateful for my longtime family friends in Bucks County and across the country, and for my friends in the Washington area.

I've been blessed to have bright and caring colleagues in my print and television work. Since 2014, I've been lucky to call the *Post* my professional home. Many thanks to the reporters and editors who have become partners as we have covered the big stories, and to Tammy Haddad and the Post Live team.

At PBS and WETA, Sharon Rockefeller opened the door and gave me the privilege of moderating *Washington Week.* Many thanks to the program's excellent team, PBS executives, and the board at the Corporation for Public Broadcasting.

Being part of MSNBC and NBC News as a political analyst for five years was terrific. Many thanks to Rashida Jones, Elena Nachmanoff, Andy Lack, and the anchors, reporters, and tireless producers who have become close friends.

Rev. John Jenkins, C.S.C., president of the University of Notre Dame, encouraged me to be a reporter at a critical time in my career. He has remained a mentor for over a decade. My journalism professor Robert Schmuhl continues to be a wise and guiding presence in my work.

The author Michael Bamberger taught me so much about writing and listening and finding the emotional truth in the smallest of moments.

Special thanks to three of my teachers at Pennsbury High School: Al Wilson, Steve Medoff, and Frank Sciolla. Due to their vision and commitment, I was introduced to journalism.

It's hard to put into words how much I've enjoyed getting to know Bob, Elsa, and Diana Woodward. My gratitude is lifelong. And Bob, you've truly given me a master class on reporting and leadership. Every day was a gift.

Source Notes

The information in this book comes primarily from deep background interviews conducted by the authors with firsthand participants and witnesses, or from contemporaneous notes and documents. Additional and supplemental source notes follow.

PROLOGUE

xiv *The scenes of a screaming:* Full Metal Jacket, Stanley Kubrick, June 17, 1987, Warner Bros.

xv *The Chinese were investing:* See "Military and Security Developments Involving the People's Republic Of China," Office of the Secretary of Defense Annual Report to Congress, 2020.

xv *military parade in Tiananmen Square:* Helen Regan and James Griffiths, "No Force Can Stop China's Progress, says Xi in National Day Speech," CNN, October 1, 2019.

xv *latest "game changing" weapon:* Tetsuro Kosaka, "China Unveils ICBM Capable of Reaching U.S. With 10 Warheads," *Nikkei Asia,* October 2, 2019; Rajeswari Pillai Rajagopalan, "Hypersonic Missiles: A New Arms Race," *The Diplomat*, June 25, 2021.

xvi *sending military planes daily:* Steven Lee Myers, "China Sends Warning to Taiwan and U.S. With Big Show of Air Power," *The New York Times,* September 18, 2020; Yimou Lee, David Lague and Ben Blanchard, "China Launches 'Gray-Zone' Warfare to Subdue Taiwan," Reuters, December 10, 2020.

xvi *resolutely smash:* Yew lun tian, "Attack on Taiwan and Option to Stop Independence, Top China General Says," Reuters, May 28, 2020.

xvi *In the South China Sea:* "China's Military Aggression in the Indo-Pacific Region," U.S. Department of State, 2017-2021, State.gov.

xvii *ABLE ARCHER:* See Ben Macintyre, *The Spy and The Traitor* (New York: Broadway Books, 2018), pp.178–182.

xvii *later the CIA director:* Ibid, p.182.

xix *"Reichstag moment":* Jeffrey Herf, "Emergency Powers Helped Hitler's Rise.

Germany Has Avoided Them Ever Since," The Washington Post, February 19, 2019.

xxiii *but I'm going to say that I asked you:* Letter from Speaker Nancy Pelosi to Democrat Colleagues, "Dear Colleague on Events of the Past Week," January 8, 2021, speaker.gov.

xxv *had been saying for years:* See William J. Perry and Tom Z. Collina, *The Button* (Texas: BenBella, 2020).

xxvi *In an article published:* William J. Perry and Tom Z. Collina, "Trump Still Has His Finger on the Nuclear Button. This Must Change," *Politico*, January 8, 2021.

xxvi *Two weeks after:* Bernard Gwertzman, "Pentagon Kept Tight Rein in Last Days of Nixon Rule," *The New York Times,* August 25, 1974.

xxvi *Nixon had grown increasingly irrational:* Bob Woodward and Carl Bernstein, The Final Days (New York: Simon & Schuster, 1976).

xxviii *Suddenly, about:* Video: Manu Raju, CNN Breaking News, 12:03 p.m., January 8, 2021.

CHAPTER ONE

1 *Speaking before four American flags:* "Trump Condemns Hatred 'On Many Sides' in Charlottesville White Nationalist Protest," CBS News, August 12, 2017.

1 *look and manner of a neighborhood priest:* Annie Karni, "In Biden White House, the Celebrity Staff Is a Thing of the Past," *The New York Times,* May 18, 2021.

1 *His mother was a local union organizer:* Scott MacKay, "Commentary: From South Providence to the Biden Campaign, Meet Mike Donilon," Rhode Island Public Radio, October 12, 2020.

2 *Heather Heyer, a 32-year-old:* Harmeet Kaur and Hollie Silverman, "Charlottesville Police to Remove Same Version of Car That Killed Heather Heyer from Its Fleet," CNN, December 13, 2019.

3 *Biden issued a tweet:* @JoeBiden, "There is only one side. #charlottesville," 6:18 p.m., August 12, 2017, Twitter.com.

3 *Trump would not let go:* "President Trump News Conference," C-SPAN, August 15, 2017.

3 *"big fucking deal":* "Remarks by Vice President Biden at Health Care Bill Signing Ceremony at the White House," C-SPAN, March 23, 2010.

4 *Within two weeks:* Joe Biden, "We Are Living Through a Battle for the Soul of This Nation," *The Atlantic*, August 27, 2017.

CHAPTER TWO

5 *Ryan publicly said he was "sickened":* David A. Fahrenthold, "Trump Recorded Having Extremely Lewd Conversation About Women in 2005," *The Washington Post,* October 8, 2016.

5 *Ryan liked to call himself a "policy guy":* Julie Hirschfeld Davis, "Bidding Congress Farewell, Paul Ryan Laments Nation's 'Broken' Politics," *The New York Times,* December 19, 2018.

6 *The memo:* The reference material was obtained by the authors.

6 *Ryan tested out his research:* "Paul Ryan at Trump Tower." Remarks to reporters available at C-SPAN.org. Posted on December 9, 2016.

7 *Ryan got word that Trump was ready:* Damian Paletta and Todd C. Frankel, "Trump Says No Plan to Pull Out of NAFTA 'At This Time,'" *The Washington Post,* April 27, 2017.

7 *Ryan began to dictate:* Austin Wright, "Ryan, House and Senate GOP Outraged by Trump News Conference," *Politico,* August 15, 2017.

8 *On March 21, 2018:* Mike DeBonis and Erica Werner, "Congressional Negotiators Reach Deal on $1.3 Trillion Spending Bill Ahead of Friday Government Shutdown Deadline," *The Washington Post,* March 21, 2018.

9 *On Fox News that morning:* Video: "Pete Hegseth: This Is a Swamp Budget," Fox News, March 23, 2018, foxnews.com.

9 *Trump tweeted:* @realDonaldTrump, "I am considering a VETO of the Omnibus Spending Bill . . . and the BORDER WALL, which is desperately needed for our National Defense, is not fully funded," March 23, 2018, Twitter.com.

10 *Growing up, his dad had died when he was a teenager:* Robert Costa, "My Brother, Paul Ryan," *National Review,* August 20, 2012.

10 *On April 11, 2018:* Paul Kane, John Wagner, and Mike DeBonis, "Speaker Ryan Will Not Seek Reelection, Further Complicating GOP House Prospects," *The Washington Post,* April 11, 2018.

CHAPTER THREE

11 *plagued by plagiarism charges:* Neena Satija, "Echoes of Biden's 1987 Plagiarism Scandal Continue to Reverberate," *The Washington Post,* June 5, 2019.

11 *his 365-page campaign autobiography:* Joe Biden, *Promises to Keep: On Life and Politics* (New York: Random House, 2007).

11 "Get up!": Ibid., pp. ii–iii.

12 *He gave Biden important roles:* See Bob Woodward, *The Price of Politics* (New York: Simon & Schuster, 2013).

12 *President Obama was hinting strongly:* Peter Baker, "Biden and Obama's 'Odd Couple' Relationship Aged into Family Ties," *The New York Times,* April 28, 2019.

12 *a brief October 2014 story:* Luis Martinez and Arlette Saenz, "Joe Biden's Son Hunter Biden Discharged from Navy After Positive Cocaine Test," ABC News, October 16, 2014.

13 *In his 2021 memoir:* Hunter Biden, *Beautiful Things* (New York: Gallery Books, 2021), pp. 215–17.

13 *A few months later:* Michael D. Shear, "Beau Biden, Vice President Joe Biden's Son, Dies at 46," *The New York Times*, May 30, 2015.

13 *a life that included:* Steve Holland, "Standing Among U.S. Graves, Biden Explains Afghanistan Decision in Personal Terms," Reuters, April 14, 2021.

14 *The following day:* "Full text: Biden's Announcement That He Won't Run for President," *The Washington Post,* October 21, 2014.

CHAPTER FOUR

15 *Jill and Joe Biden:* Jill Biden, *Where the Light Enters* (New York: Flatiron Books, 2019).

16 *As the evening wore on:* Lauren Easton, "Calling the Presidential Race State by State," Associated Press, November 9, 2020.

16 *"You didn't hear":* Video: "Conversation with President Amy Gutmann & The Honorable Joseph R. Biden, Jr.," Irvine Auditorium, University of Pennsylvania, March 30, 2017, president.upenn.edu/bidenevent-3-30-17.

16 *Biden stopped through:* "Donald Trump Inauguration Speech Transcript," *Politico*, January 20, 2017; Joe Biden, *Promise Me, Dad* (New York: Flatiron Books, 2017).

16 *On March 1, the* New York Post*:* Emily Smith, "Beau Biden's Widow Having Affair with His Married Brother," *New York Post,* March 1, 2017.

17 *"Worse yet, I started backsliding" into drugs:* Hunter Biden, *Beautiful Things* (New York: Gallery Books, 2021), p. 183.

17 *Richmond was a rising star:* Bryn Stole, "As Congressional Black Caucus Chair, Cedric Richmond Steps Forward to Cut a National Figure," *The Advocate,* August 10, 2018.

18 *a center fielder and pitcher:* Ben Terris and National Journal, "The Fiercest Battle in D.C. Is on the Baseball Diamond," *The Atlantic,* June 11, 2013.

18 *bestseller list for one week:* "Hardcover Nonfiction," *The New York Times,* December 3, 2017.

19 *the Black architect:* Roy S. Johnson, "Overlooked No More: Joseph Bartholomew, Golf Course Architect," *The New York Times,* February 5, 2020.

CHAPTER FIVE

20 *Don McGahn, who worked closely:* Robert Costa, "McGahn's Last Stand," *The Washington Post,* October 4, 2018.

20 *She accused Kavanaugh:* Emma Brown, "California Professor, Writer of Confidential Brett Kavanaugh Letter, Speaks Out About Her Allegation of Sexual Assault," *The Washington Post,* September 16, 2018.

21 *November 6 brought blue gains:* Jane C. Timm, "Democrats Gain 40 House Seats, as NBC Projects TJ Cox Wins California's 21st District," NBC News, December 6, 2018; Harry Enten, "Latest House Results Confirm 2018 Wasn't a Blue Wave. It Was a Blue Tsunami," CNN, December 6, 2018.

23 *a detailed 11-page memo:* This Biden political memo was obtained by the authors.

23 *A mammoth beast:* Annie Karni, "A Peek Inside Hillary Clinton's Brooklyn HQ," *Politico,* July 16, 2015.

CHAPTER SIX

24 *President Trump appointed:* Shannon Van Sant, "Trump Appoints Gen. Mark Milley Chairman of the Joint Chiefs of Staff," NPR, December 8, 2018.

24 *Trump made it clear:* David Brown, Daniel Lippman, and Wesley Morgan, "Trump's Newest 'Central Casting' General," *Politico,* July 10, 2021.

24 *a West Point graduate and lobbyist:* Kenneth P. Vogel, Michael LaForgia, and Hailey Fuchs, "Trump Vowed to 'Drain the Swamp,' but Lobbyists Are Helping Run His Campaign," *The New York Times,* July 6, 2020.

24 *During Milley's confirmation:* "Hearing to Consider the Nomination of General Mark A. Milley, for Reappointment to the Grade of General and to Be Chairman of the Joint Chiefs of Staff," Committee on Armed Services, United States Senate, July 11, 2019, armed-services.senate.gov.

25 *Mattis once called:* See Bob Woodward, *Rage* (New York: Simon & Schuster, 2020), p. 136.

26 *served as general counsel:* Michael Kranish and Hamza Shaban, "In Corporate Role, William P. Barr Clashed with Justice Department That He Now Seeks to Lead," *The Washington Post,* December 8, 2018.

26 *he had publicly criticized:* Andrew Prokop, "Trump's Attorney General Nominee Wrote a Memo Expressing Deep Suspicion of the Mueller Probe," *Vox*, December 20, 2018.

27 *"Under the regulations":* U.S. Government Publishing Office, "Confirmation Hearing on the Nomination of Hon. William Pelham Barr to Be Attorney General of the United States," Senate Hearing 116-65, January 15 and 16, 2019, Congress.gov.

28 *Mueller finally finished his report:* Robert S. Mueller, "Report on the Investigation into Russian Interference in the 2016 Presidential Election," United States Department of Justice, March 2019.

29 *Mueller wrote one of the most convoluted lines:* Ibid., p. 2.

29 *Barr released a letter:* "Read Attorney General William Barr's Summary of the Mueller Report," *The New York Times*, March 24, 2019.

29 *"It was a complete and total exoneration":* President Trump, C-SPAN, March 24, 2019.

29 *Mueller himself complained:* Devlin Barrett and Matt Zapotosky, "Mueller Complained That Barr's Letter Did Not Capture 'Context' of Trump Probe," *The Washington Post,* April 30, 2019

29 *700 former federal prosecutors:* Dartunorro Clark, "Hundreds of Former Prosecutors Say Trump Would Have Been Indicted if He Were Not President," NBC News, May 6, 2019.

29 *In a Freedom:* Aaron Blake, "A GOP-Appointed Judge's Scathing Review of William Barr's 'Candor' and 'Credibility,' Annotated," *The Washington Post*, March 5, 2020.

30 *"It ended in dust":* Bob Woodward interview with President Donald J. Trump, December 20, 2019, in *Rage* (New York, Simon & Schuster, 2020), p. 164.

CHAPTER SEVEN

31 *a veteran of the Obama White House:* Jordan Fabian, "Biden Hires Former Obama Official Anita Dunn as Senior Adviser," Bloomberg News, January 15, 2021.

31 *estate he rented:* Kristen Schott, "See the NoVA Home Where the Bidens Used to Reside," *Northern Virginia* magazine, January 8, 2021

31 *she was not in lockstep:* Ryan Lizza, "Why Biden's Retro Inner Circle Is Succeeding So Far," *Politico,* December 19, 2019.

32 *Pay attention to Biden-type Democrats:* Nate Cohn, "Moderate Democrats Fared Best in 2018," *The New York Times,* September 10, 2019.
33 *Klain had backed:* Alex Thompson and Theodoric Meyer, "Ron Klain's Possible Resurrection," *Politico: West Wing Playbook,* November 11, 2020.
33 *The email was part of a trove:* Ibid.
34 *Kathleen, had accused him of squandering:* Margie Fishman, "Divorce Filing Details Split of Kathleen, Hunter Biden," *The News Journal,* March 2, 2017.
35 *whose progressive credentials made her a force:* Gabriel Debenedetti, "Rising Stars Collide in Shadow 2020 Primary," *Politico,* January 29, 2018.
35 *was drawing rave reviews:* Eric Bradner, "Pete Buttigieg Makes Star Turn in Town Hall Spotlight," CNN, March 11, 2019.

CHAPTER EIGHT

36 *"What do you think?":* Jill Biden, *CBS This Morning,* May 7, 2019.
36 *We understand, Pop:* Naomi Lim, "'Pop, you Got to Run,'" *Washington Examiner,* September 26, 2019.
36 *Corners of the right wing online:* Samantha Putterman, "Fact-checking the Pedophilia Attacks Against Joe Biden," *PolitiFact,* August 12, 2020.
36 *"We do everything by family meetings":* "Biden School Celebration: Conversation with Joe Biden and Presidential Historian Jon Meacham," University of Delaware, February 26, 2019.
37 *What Biden did not disclose:* Hunter Biden, *Beautiful Things* (New York: Gallery Books, 2021), pp. 204–17.
37 *"One day, out of the blue":* Ibid., p. 215.
38 *"ran and ran and ran":* Ibid., p. 217.

CHAPTER NINE

39 *as an idea with a bestselling following:* Jon Meacham, *The Soul of America: The Battle for Our Better Angels* (New York: Random House, 2018).
39 *Meacham told him:* Video: "Biden School Celebration: Conversation with Joe Biden and Presidential Historian Jon Meacham," University of Delaware, February 26, 2019.
40 *the informal Arthur M. Schlesinger Jr.:* Annie Karni and John Koblin, "Helping to Shape the Words of the President-Elect: A Presidential Historian," *The New York Times,* November 9, 2020.
40 *Blunt Rochester was the first woman:* Christina Jedra and Xerxes Wilson, "Lisa Blunt Rochester Wins Second Term in Congress," *The News Journal,* November 6, 2018.
43 *His penchant for hugging:* Natasha Korecki, Marc Caputo, and Alex Thompson, "'Friendly Grandpa' or Creepy Uncle? Generations Split over Biden Behavior," *Politico,* April 1, 2019.
43 *as the Me Too movement:* Hailey Fuchs, "Me Too Is Still a Movement," *The Washington Post,* August 11, 2019.
43 *"An Awkward Kiss Changed How I Saw Joe Biden":* Lucy Flores, *New York* magazine, March 29, 2019.
43 *Then, in a speech:* Lisa Lerer, "Joe Biden Jokes About Hugging in a Speech, Then Offers a Mixed Apology," *The New York Times,* April 5, 2019.

43 *In her book:* Jill Biden, *Where the Light Enters* (New York: Flatiron Books, 2019), p. 53.

43 *"He needs to give people their space":* Jill Biden, *CBS This Morning*, May 7, 2019.

CHAPTER TEN

44 *the largest field in decades:* Matthew Yglesias, "The Comically Large 2020 Democratic Field, Explained," *Vox*, December 17, 2018.

44 *In a suit jacket and open-collared shirt:* @JoeBiden, "The core values of this nation . . . our standing in the world . . . our very democracy . . . everything that has made America—America—is at stake. That's why today I'm announcing my candidacy for President of the United States. #Joe2020," 6:00 a.m., April 25, 2019, Twitter.com.

44 *Progressives outwardly detested him:* Elana Schor, "Joe Biden Faces a Challenge Winning Over Progressives," Associated Press, March 22, 2019.

45 *Biden jumped on the Amtrak:* Michael Scherer and John Wagner, "Former Vice President Joe Biden Jumps into White House Race," *The Washington Post*, April 25, 2019.

45 *Biden then headed:* Michelle Ye Hee Lee, "Joe Biden Campaign Reports Raising $6.3 Million in 24 Hours," *The Washington Post*, April 26, 2019.

46 *Trump's margin of victory:* Tim Meko, Denise Lu, and Lazaro Gamio, "How Trump Won the Presidency with Razor-Thin Margins in Swing States," *The Washington Post*, November 11, 2016.

46 *"Welcome to the race Sleepy Joe":* @realDonaldTrump, April 25, 2020, Twitter.com.

46 *"I just feel like a young man":* Video: @thehill, President Trump: "I just feel like a young man. I'm so young. I can't believe it. I'm the youngest person—I am a young, vibrant man. I look at Joe—I don't know about him," 12:37 p.m., April 26, 2019, Twitter.com.

47 *When Biden, appearing:* Video: "Joe Biden on Why He's Running for President," *The View*, ABC News, April 26, 2019.

47 *"I am a union man":* "Joe Biden Campaign Rally in Pittsburgh," C-SPAN, April 29, 2019.

47 *Anzalone came back with poll results:* Campaign polling documents obtained by the authors.

CHAPTER ELEVEN

48 *his days as a public school teacher:* Gillian Brockell, "A Civil Rights Love Story," *The Washington Post*, January 10, 2020.

48 *eating fried whiting filets:* Jonathan Martin, "Hoping to Woo Black Voters, Democratic Candidates Gather at James Clyburn's Fish Fry," *The New York Times*, June 21, 2019.

48 *Biden had said there was "some civility":* Isaac Stanley-Becker, "'We Got Things Done': Biden Recalls 'Civility' with Segregationist Senators," *The Washington Post*, June 19, 2019.

48 *"I was in a caucus with James O. Eastland":* Ibid.

49 *When later pressed:* Justin Wise, "Biden Defends Remarks About Segregationist Senators: 'Apologize for What?,'" *The Hill,* June 19, 2019.
49 *Clyburn made sure to defend:* Emma Dumain, "Biden Said He Found Common Ground with Segregationists," McClatchy, June 19, 2019.
49 *Emily, a librarian:* Emma Dumain, "Emily Clyburn—Librarian, Activist, Wife of SC Congressman Jim Clyburn—Dies at 80," *The State,* September 19, 2019.
50 *"So on the issue of race":* "Transcript: Night 2 of the First Democratic Debate," *The Washington Post*, January 28, 2019.
50 *By the next week:* "Harris Gets Big Debate Bounce While Biden Sinks Quinnipiac University National Poll Finds," *Quinnipiac University Poll*, July 2, 2019, poll.qu.edu.

CHAPTER TWELVE

51 *Senator Harris's bump to the top tier did not last:* Astead W. Herndon, Shane Goldmacher, and Jonathan Martin, "Kamala Harris Says She's Still 'In This Fight,' but out of the 2020 Race," *The New York Times,* December 3, 2019.
51 *the two leading lights*: Jonathan Martin, "Elizabeth Warren and Bernie Sanders Have a Problem: Each Other," *The New York Times,* December 16, 2019.
51 *His October 1 heart attack:* Sean Sullivan and Amy Gardner, "Sanders's Heart Attack Raises Questions About His Age, Potential Damage to Campaign," *The Washington Post,* October 5, 2019.
51 *and concentrated on Biden:* Robert Costa, "Ascendant Bernie Sanders Turns His Focus to Joe Biden as Iowa Nears," *The Washington Post,* January 2, 2020.
51 *out-of-nowhere victory:* April McCullum, "As Mayor, Bernie Sanders Had to Wait for a Revolution," *Burlington Free Press,* February 27, 2016.
53 *was sinking millions of dollars:* Asma Khalid, "In a Month, Michael Bloomberg Has Spent More than $100 Million on Campaign Ads," NPR, December 27, 2019.
53 *During a December 5, 2019, Oval Office interview:* Bob Woodward interview with President Donald J. Trump, December 5, 2019, in *Rage* (New York: Simon & Schuster, 2020), p. 189.

CHAPTER THIRTEEN

55 *Blinken had served as No. 2:* Graeme Wood, "Biden's Sleepily Reassuring Appointments," *The Atlantic,* November 23, 2020.
55 *played in a dad-rock band:* Claire Shaffer, "Yes, Biden's Secretary of State Hopeful Antony Blinken Has a Band," *Rolling Stone,* November 23, 2020.
55 *That January, news:* See Bob Woodward, *Rage* (New York: Simon & Schuster, 2020), pp. xiii–xv.
55 *Klain had led efforts:* Juliet Eilperin and Lena H. Sun, "Ebola Czar Ron Klain to Leave Feb. 15 After Leading U.S. Response to Outbreak," *The Washington Post,* January 29, 2015.
56 *Biden and his team drafted an op-ed:* Joe Biden, "Trump Is Worst Possible Leader to Deal with Coronavirus Outbreak," *USA Today*, January 27, 2021.

56 *"This will be the biggest national security threat":* Woodward, *Rage*, p. xiii.

56 *Trump's angst about Biden:* Natasha Korecki, "How Trump's Biden Mania Led Him to the Brink of Impeachment," *Politico,* September 27, 2019.

57 *In the call, a transcript:* "Telephone Conversation with President Zelensky of Ukraine," July 25, 2019, transcript, declassified September 24, 2019, White House.gov.

57 *Trump was acquitted:* Seung Min Kim, "In Historic Vote, Trump Acquitted of Impeachment Charges," *The Washington Post,* February 5, 2020.

58 *Greg Schultz was under mounting pressure:* Alexander Burns, Jonathan Martin, and Katie Glueck, "How Joe Biden Won the Presidency," *The New York Times,* November 7, 2020.

58 *The Iowa caucuses on February 3 were a drubbing:* Nathan Robinson, "Joe Biden Flopped in Iowa," *The Guardian,* February 4, 2020.

58 *Buttigieg, surging in the polls:* Chris Sikich, "Pete Buttigieg Surges in New Hampshire After Seizing Iowa Narrative with Claim of Victory," *Indianapolis Star*, February 7, 2020.

58 *"Pete's Record":* Adam Shaw, "Brutal Biden Campaign Ad Mocks Buttigieg's Experience as South Bend Mayor," Fox News, February 8, 2020.

CHAPTER FOURTEEN

60 *the Congressional Black Caucus had a gathering:* Matt Viser and Cleve R. Wootson Jr., "Eighteen Days That Resuscitated Joe Biden's Nearly Five-Decade Career," *The Washington Post,* February 29, 2020.

60 *"My second point is about 10-20-30":* Tracy Jan, "Reparations, Rebranded," *The Washington Post,* February 24, 2020.

61 *a Sanders nomination:* Jonathan Martin and Alexander Burns, "Bernie Sanders Wins Nevada Caucuses, Strengthening His Primary Lead," *The New York Times,* February 22, 2020.

62 *"Everyone should be represented":* "Read the Full Transcript of the South Carolina Democratic Debate," CBS News, February 25, 2020.

62 *Clyburn spoke in North Charleston:* "Representative Jim Clyburn Endorses Joe Biden Ahead of South Carolina Primary," C-SPAN, February 26, 2020.

62 *For months, there were constant complaints:* Jeff Zeleny and Arlette Saenz, "Joe Biden Grapples with Attacks from Trump and the Rising Warren Threat," CNN, October 7, 2019.

63 *During an interview:* Transcript, "Clyburn on Biden Endorsement," CNN, February 28, 2020.

64 *Biden was moved:* "'He Reminds Me of My Son Beau,'" CNN, March 2, 2020.

CHAPTER FIFTEEN

66 *Super Tuesday:* "Live Results: Super Tuesday 2020," *The Washington Post,* washingtonpost.com/elections.

66 *warred with Clinton's campaign:* Alex Seitz-Wald, "How Sanders Delegates Organized a Walkout Under Everyone's Nose," NBC News, July 26, 2016.

67 *Biden suspended in-person campaigning:* Sydney Ember, Annie Karni, and Maggie Haberman, "Sanders and Biden Cancel Events as Coronavirus Fears Upend Primary," *The New York Times,* March 10, 2020.

67 *The shift was strange:* Matt Viser and Annie Linskey, "Live from His Basement, Joe Biden Pushes for Visibility as Democrats Worry," *The Washington Post,* March 25, 2020.

67 *Trump made fun of Biden:* Aaron Sharockman, "Biden Isn't in the Basement, but the Trump Campaign Keeps Saying So," *PolitiFact*, October 4, 2020.

67 *Warren's older brother:* Jess Bidgood, "Elizabeth Warren's Oldest Brother Dies of Coronavirus in Oklahoma," *The Boston Globe,* April 23, 2020.

68 *an unvarnished and pointed three-page memo:* Campaign memo obtained by the authors.

69 *the rumor that Democrats would replace Biden:* Douglas MacKinnon, "Bye Bye Biden? Democrats Could Replace Joe Biden with John Kerry as Presidential Candidate," *The Sun*, July 31, 2020.

70 *Parscale was close to Trump's son-in-law:* Ashley Parker and Josh Dawsey, "Adviser, Son-in-Law and Hidden Campaign Hand," *The Washington Post,* July 26, 2019.

CHAPTER SIXTEEN

71 *close friends with Robert Mueller's wife:* Dareh Gregorian, "Who Is Attorney General William Barr?," NBC News, April 18, 2019.

71 *Barr had gone to see Bush:* "William P. Barr Oral History," Miller Center, University of Virginia, April 5, 2001.

CHAPTER SEVENTEEN

76 *Trump convened a meeting:* Kaitlan Collins, Joan Biskupic, Evan Perez, and Tami Luhby, "Barr Urges Trump Administration to Back Off Call to Fully Strike Down Obamacare," CNN, May 5, 2020.

77 *Other Republicans also shook their heads:* Jessie Hellmann, "GOP Senator: DOJ's Obamacare Argument 'as Far-fetched as Any I've Ever Heard,'" *The Hill,* June 12, 2018.

78 *Groundhog Day:* Harold Ramis, *Groundhog Day*, Columbia Pictures, 1993.

79 *On the morning of May 14, Trump told:* Donald J. Trump interview with Maria Bartiromo of Fox News, May 14, 2020.

80 *Durham, who was probing:* Michael Balsamo and Eric Tucker, "Barr Appoints Special Counsel in Russia Probe Investigation," Associated Press, December 1, 2020.

80 *Barr prepared a little speech:* Matt Zapotosky, "Barr Says He Does Not Expect Obama or Biden Will Be Investigated by Prosecutor Reviewing 2016 Russia Probe," May 18, 2020.

CHAPTER EIGHTEEN

81 *"Deep in the heart of Delaware":* Marc Caputo and Christopher Cadelago, "Dems Warm to Biden's Bunker Strategy," *Politico,* June 24, 2021.

81 *"Punxsutawney Joe":* Ibid.

81 *Biden's lead widened:* Justin Wise, "Poll: Biden Widens Lead over Trump to 10 points," *The Hill,* May 31, 2020.

81 *Trump mused about injecting:* Allyson Chiu, Katie Shepherd, Brittany

Shammas, and Colby Itkowitz, "Trump Claims Controversial Comment About Injecting Disinfectants Was 'Sarcastic,'" *The Washington Post,* April 24, 2020.

82 *"I wanted to always play it down":* Bob Woodward interview with President Donald J. Trump, March 19, 2020 in *Rage* (New York: Simon & Schuster, 2020), p. xviii.

82 *Trump had tweeted earlier:* @realDonaldTrump, 2:47 p.m., March 9, 2020, Twitter.com.

82 *"Our country wasn't built to be shut down":* "President Trump with Coronavirus Task Force Briefing," C-SPAN, March 23, 2020.

83 *cell-surface receptors called ACE2:* Kate Sheridan, "The Coronavirus Sneaks into Cells Through a Key Receptor," STAT News, April 10, 2010; Krishna Sriram, Paul Insel, and Rohit Loomba, "What Is the ACE2 receptor," *The Conversation,* May 14, 2020.

83 *During an interview with Trump:* Bob Woodward interview with President Donald J. Trump, March 19, 2020, in *Rage*, pp. 287–88.

84 *He would write a book:* Dr. Vivek Murthy, *Together: The Healing Power of Human Connection in a Sometimes Lonely World* (New York: HarperCollins, 2020).

CHAPTER NINETEEN

86 *in more than 140 cities:* Derrick Bryson Taylor, "George Floyd Protests: A Timeline," *The New York Times,* March 28, 2021.

86 *seven minutes and 46 seconds:* Paul Walsh, "7 Minutes, 46 Seconds: Error in George Floyd Killing Timeline Won't Affect Charges, County Says," Minneapolis *Star Tribune,* June 18, 2020.

86 *Trump told Woodward, "These are arsonists":* Bob Woodward interview with President Donald J. Trump, June 3, 2020, in *Rage* (New York: Simon & Schuster, 2020), p. 343.

86 *one of Trump's most conservative senior advisers:* Nick Miroff and Josh Dawsey, "The Adviser Who Scripts Trump's Immigration Policy," *The Washington Post,* August 17, 2019.

88 *as the 1968 riots in Washington, D.C.:* Denise Kersten Wills, "'People Were Out of Control': Remembering the 1968 Riots," *Washingtonian* magazine, April 1, 2008.

88 *the 1993 FBI siege:* Tara Isabella Burton, "The Waco Tragedy, Explained," *Vox*, April 19, 2018.

88 *President Lyndon B. Johnson had deployed:* Lauren Pearlman, "A President Deploying Troops at Home Subverts Local Control and Accountability," *The Washington Post,* June 5, 2020.

89 *Trump to the underground bunker:* Jonathan Lemire and Zeke Miller, "Trump Took Shelter in White House Bunker as Protests Raged," Associated Press, May 31, 2020.

91 *he told the governors:* Robert Costa, Seung Min Kim, and Josh Dawsey, "Trump Calls Governors 'Weak,' Urges Them to Use Force Against Unruly Protests," *The Washington Post,* June 1, 2020.

92 *"You have to dominate":* "President Trump's Call with US Governors over Protests," CNN, June 1, 2020.

CHAPTER TWENTY

93 *Joe Lengyel, who was the chief:* "Guard Chief Stresses Strategic Use of Force, Parity with Active Force," Defense.gov, March 4, 2020.

93 *Around 6:30 p.m.:* U.S. Government Publishing Office, "Oversight Hearing Before the Committee on Natural Resources, U.S. House of Representatives, June 28–29, 2020.

94 *"Pepper balls":* Ibid.

94 *Trump spoke for seven minutes:* Transcript of "President Trump's Rose Garden Speech on Protests," CNN, June 1, 2020.

97 *Dozens of National Guard troops:* Phillip Kennicott, "The Dystopian Lincoln Memorial Photo Raises a Grim Question: Will They Protect Us, or Will They Shoot Us?," *The Washington Post,* June 3, 2020.

CHAPTER TWENTY-ONE

99 *"We must be vigilant about the violence":* "Joe Biden's Remarks on Civil Unrest and Nationwide Protests," CNN, June 2, 2020.

100 *"I've always believed":* Matthew Impelli, "U.S. Secretary of Defense Breaks with Trump, Says He Doesn't Support Invoking Insurrection Act," *Newsweek,* June 3, 2020.

CHAPTER TWENTY-TWO

106 *Milley decided to apologize publicly:* Transcript: "General Mark Milley's Message to the National Defense University Class of 2020," *Joint Staff Public Affairs,* June 11, 2020.

107 *like the Victrola Dog:* Michael P. Farrell, "A Visual History of Albany's Top Dog: Nipper Through the Years," Albany *Times Union*, January 25, 2021.

107 *the issue of Confederate flags:* Dan Lamothe and Josh Dawsey, "U.S. Military Faces a Reckoning on How to Handle Its Confederate Symbols Without Provoking Trump," *The Washington Post,* June 12, 2020.

109 Wag the Dog*:* Barry Levinson, United States: New Line Cinema, 1997.

CHAPTER TWENTY-THREE

111 *City health officials:* Nicole Sganga, Musadiq Bidar, and Eleanor Watson, "Oklahoma Officials Worry About Trump's Rally as Tulsa County COVID Infections Rise to Record Levels," CBSNews.com, June 18, 2020.

111 *A day before, Trump told Woodward:* See Bob Woodward, *Rage* (New York: Simon & Schuster, 2020), p. 357.

111 *a sea of empty blue seats:* Philip Rucker and Robert Costa, "Trump Rallies in Red-State America—and Faces a Sea of Empty Blue Seats," *The Washington Post,* June 20, 2020.

113 *The pandemic "is disappearing," he insisted:* Annie Karni and Maggie Haberman, "Away from Gridlock in Washington, Trump Puts on a Show for His Club," *The New York Times,* August 7, 2020.

113 *"The deep state":* @realDonaldTrump, August 22, 2020, 7:49 a.m., Twitter.com.

113 *He also was a regular donor*: Sarah Karlin-Smith, "Trump to Pick Texas Cancer Doctor to Head FDA," *Politico*, November 1, 2019.

CHAPTER TWENTY-FOUR

116 *Biden had publicly pledged:* Brian Schwartz, "Joe Biden Pledges to Pick a Woman to Be His Running Mate," CNBC, March 15, 2020.

116 *And she was a member:* Stephanie Saul, "Kamala Harris's Secret Weapon: The Sisterhood of Alpha Kappa Alpha," *The New York Times*, July 1, 2019.

117 *the pair collaborated:* Edward-Isaac Dovere, "The Battle That Changed Kamala Harris," *The Atlantic*, August 19, 2020.

118 *"We had each other's backs":* Kamala Harris, *The Truths We Hold: An American Journey* (New York: Penguin, 2019).

118 *She posted a picture on Instagram:* @kamalaharris, "Over the weekend, I attended the memorial service for my dear friend Beau Biden. It was a moving tribute to Beau, who cared so deeply for his family, the people of Delaware, and our country. I feel fortunate to have known Beau as a friend as to have had the opportunity to work closely with him as Attorneys General. My heart and prayers go out to his family, which he loved so passionately," June 8, 2015, Instagram.com.

118 *"Beau always supported her":* Scott Bixby, "Kamala Harris Was in Biden Circle of Trust. Then Came Debate Night," *The Daily Beast*, July 13, 2020.

118 *Harris was the daughter:* Ellen Barry, "How Kamala Harris's Immigrant Parents Found a Home, and Each Other, in a Black Study Group," *The New York Times*, September 13, 2020.

118 *voting record was unabashedly liberal:* David Lightman, "How Liberal Is She? Watchdog Groups Rate the Senate Record of Kamala Harris," *The Sacramento Bee*, August 12, 2020.

119 *Biden's note card was photographed:* Colby Itkowitz, "Joe Biden's Personal Notes on Kamala Harris: No Grudges," *The Washington Post*, July 28, 2020.

119 *Even Harris's rivals:* Julie Pace, David Eggert, and Kathleen Ronayne, "How Biden Decided: Whitmer Pulled Back, Pushing Pick to Harris," Associated Press, August 12, 2020.

119 *On August 11, Biden sat in front:* Philip Elliott, "How Joe Biden's Enduring Grief for His Son Helped Lead Him to Kamala Harris, *Time*, August 12, 2020.

119 *On his desk rested:* Michel Martin, "Joe Biden Remembers His Son in His New Memoir," NPR, November 8, 2017.

120 *There were about 10 million more women than men registered to vote:* "Elections: Data and Analysis for Current and Past Races with Women Candidates, by Election Year," Rutgers: Center for American Women and Politics, cawp.rutgers.edu; Ruth Igielnik, "Men and Women in the U.S. Continue to Differ in Voter Turnout Rate, Party Identification," Pew Research Center, August 18, 2020.

120 *The campaign raised $48 million in the 48 hours:* James Oliphant and Kanishka Singh, "Biden Campaign Raises $48 Million in 48 Hours After Naming Kamala Harris as VP Choice," Reuters, August 13, 2020.

120 *On August 12:* "Joe Biden Introduction of Senator Kamala Harris as Running Mate," C-SPAN, August 12, 2020.

CHAPTER TWENTY-FIVE

121 *A Secret Service agent interrupted:* Clarence Williams, Anne Gearan, Carol D. Leonnig, and Martin Weil, "Secret Service Shoots Man Near the White House," *The Washington Post,* August 10, 2020.

121 *Trump tweeted*: @realDonaldTrump, 7:33 a.m., August 12, 2020, Twitter .com.

121 *The Trump campaign followed up with a video:* Donald J. Trump for President, August 11, 2020, youtube.com.

122 *Bill Stepien after Brad Parscale was demoted:* Andrew Restuccia and Rebecca Ballhaus, "Trump Replaces Campaign Manager," *The Wall Street Journal,* July 15, 2020.

122 *In late September, the FDA submitted:* Noah Weiland and Sharon LaFraniere, "F.D.A. to Release Stricter Guidelines for Emergency Vaccine Authorization," *The New York Times,* September 22, 2020.

123 *Seven former FDA commissioners published:* Robert Califf, Scott Gottlieb, Margaret Hamburg, Jane Henney, David Kessler, Mark Mclellan, and Andy von Eschenbach, "7 former FDA commissioners: The Trump Administration Is Undermining the Credibility of the FDA," *The Washington Post*, September 29, 2020.

123 *Later that same evening:* Transcript of Presidential Debate, The Commission on Presidential Debates, September 29, 2020, debates.org.

123 *Bourla joined the chorus:* "Moving at the Speed of Science: An open letter from Pfizer Chairman and CEO Albert Bourla to U.S. colleagues," October 1, 2020, Pfizer.com.

124 *"Will you shut up, man?":* Vice President Joe Biden, Transcript of Presidential Debate, The Commission on Presidential Debates, September 29, 2020, debates.org.

124 *Trump had resisted going:* Noah Weiland, Maggie Haberman, Mark Mazzetti, and Annie Karni, "Trump Was Sicker than Acknowledged with Covid-19," *The New York Times,* February 11, 2021.

125 *"antibody cocktail":* Katie Thomas and Gina Kolata, "President Trump Received Experimental Antibody Treatment," *The New York Times,* October 2, 2020.

125 *U.S. health officials went into a frenzy:* Yasmeen Abutaleb and Damian Paletta, *Nightmare Scenario: Inside the Trump Administration's Response to the Pandemic That Changed History* (New York: HarperCollins, 2021).

125 *The White House remained a hot zone:* Josh Margolin and Lucien Bruggeman, "34 People Connected to White House, More Than Previously Known, Infected by Coronavirus: Internal FEMA Memo," ABCNews.com, October 7, 2020.

127 *In 2017, the State Department had strongly denied:* Meghan Keneally, "State Department Denies Tillerson called Trump a 'Moron,'" Associated Press, October 4, 2017.

CHAPTER TWENTY-SIX

128 *In 1987, Admiral William J. Crowe:* See Bob Woodward, *The Commanders* (New York: Simon & Schuster, 1991), p. 40.

129 *"I beat this crazy, horrible China virus":* Donald J. Trump in an interview with Maria Bartiromo, Fox News, October 11, 2020.

130 *"We need you to join ARMY FOR TRUMP's election security operation":* Team Trump, September 21, 2020, Facebook.com.

CHAPTER TWENTY-SEVEN

131 *like other Trump parties:* Annika Merrilees, "President Donald Trump Once Again Serves Fast Food to College Athletes at White House Celebration," ABCNews.com, March 4, 2019.

131 *On June 22, he had tweeted:* @realDonaldTrump, 5:16 a.m., June 22, 2020, Twitter.com.

131 *In his own Republican National Convention speech:* "Full Transcript: President Trump's Republican National Convention Speech," *The New York Times,* August 28, 2020.

131 *19 minutes after midnight:* Patrick Maks, "Calling the 2020 Presidential Race State by State," Associated Press, November 8, 2020.

132 *Fox News's decision desk called Arizona for Biden:* Elahe Izadi, "Who Won Arizona? Why the Call Still Differs by Media Organization," *The Washington Post,* November 5, 2020; David Bauder, "Two Fox News Political Executives Out After Arizona Call," Associated Press, January 19, 2021.

132 *He predicted victory:* Grace Segers, "Joe Biden Expresses Confidence in Election Night Speech: 'We Feel Good About Where We Are,'" CBS News, 1:15 a.m. November 4, 2020.

133 *"This is a fraud":* Transcript of President Trump's U.S. 2020 Election Night Speech, November 4, 2020.

133 *a switch of 44,000 votes:* Benjamin Swasey and Connie Hanzhang Jin, "Narrow Wins in These Key States Powered Biden to the Presidency," NPR, December 2, 2020.

133 *A* Washington Post *analysis noted:* David Brady and Brett Parker, "This Is How Biden Eked Out His 2020 Victory," *The Washington Post,* February 12, 2021.

134 *House Republicans had won a net of 10 seats:* Nick Vlahos, "After Close Shave, Cheri Bustos Furious About Polling That Missed GOP Gains in House," *The Journal Star,* November 6, 2020.

CHAPTER TWENTY-EIGHT

137 *On Saturday, November 7:* Brian Slodysko, "Explaining Race Cals: How AP Called the Race for Biden," Associated Press, November 7, 2020.

137 *"Joe Biden Is Elected the 46th President of the United States":* Katie Glueck, *The New York Times,* November 7, 2020.

138 *Biden said, smiling in a dark suit:* Amber Phillips, "Joe Biden's Victory Speech, Annotated," *The Washington Post,* November 7, 2020.

138 *Adopting a theme:* See, for example, "A Time to Heal: Gerald Ford's America," C-SPAN, January 31, 2010.

139 *the classic Jackie Wilson R&B song:* "(Your Love Keeps Lifting Me) Higher and Higher," Columbia Studios, 1967.

139 *Biden's Senate press secretary for 10 years:* Margaret Aitken Interview with Jim Gilmore, *Frontline,* July 21, 2020.

141 *he wanted to recite:* Seamus Heaney, "The Cure at Troy: A Version of Sophocles' Philoctetes" (New York: Noonday Press, 1991).

141 *Matt thought it had been an amazing call:* Biden also sent a personal letter, which was provided to the authors:

Joseph R. Biden
November 9, 2020

The Manlove Family,

On behalf of the entire Biden family, I extend my deepest condolences to you on the sudden passing of your beloved Elaine and Wayne. Their loss leaves us heartbroken, as it does for so many people throughout Delaware.

A loving wife, mother, grandmother, friend and public servant, Elaine's legacy as Delaware's elections commissioner is embodied in the very democracy she gave her life to making better, more inclusive and more equal. Whether as a voter or a candidate, I knew, and my vote knew that their most fundamental right to vote would be protected under her watchful eye and deep love of country.

Appointed and beloved leaders of all political stripes, Elaine embraced our state's unofficial creed that all politics is personal no matter how difficult the task. Her joy was infectious enough to bring people together, to strengthen our bonds as fellow Americans. And we just saw in the most recent historic election that more Delawareans vote than ever before. But we all know that the only bond deeper was her bond with her Wayne. A good, decent, honorable man.

Matthew, Joe, Michael, we share unfortunate bonds of losing loved ones suddenly and far too soon. I know that there are no words that can ease the pain you are feeling, but I want you to know that one day the memories of your parents will bring a smile to your lips before a tear to your eye. It will take time, but I promise you that that day will come. And on this day and for the difficult days ahead, I hope you find solace in a hymn that has sustained our family and which I believe sustains our state and country.

"And he will raise you up on eagle's wings, bear you on the breath of dawn, make you shine like the sun and hold you in the palm of his hand."

May the spirit of your dear parents be raised on eagle's wings, shine like the sun and be held in the palm of God's hand.

With love and sympathy,
Joe Biden

CHAPTER TWENTY-NINE

142 *Biden, while vice president, had told President Obama:* Bob Woodward, *Obama's Wars* (New York: Simon & Schuster, 2010), p. 62.

142 *For Biden, anything relating to family:* "Senator Graham Speaks to Reporters" Calling for a Special Counsel to Investigate Hunter Biden, C-SPAN, December 16, 2020.

144 *Photographs of Giuliani and serious-looking:* Katelyn Burns, "The Trump

Legal Team's Failed Four Seasons Press Conference, Explained," *Vox*, November 8, 2020.

144 *Giuliani rambled at length:* Video: "Four Seasons Total Landscaping Press Conference," AP Archive, November 17, 2020.

145 *When a reporter told Giuliani:* Ibid.

147 *Powell asserted:* "Election Drama Unfolds as Counting Continues," Sidney Powell on *Lou Dobbs Tonight,* Fox Business, November 6, 2020.

CHAPTER THIRTY

148 *About eight seconds later:* @realDonaldTrump, "I am pleased to announce that Christopher C. Miller, the highly respected Director of the National Counterterrorism Center (unanimously confirmed by the Senate), will be Acting Secretary of Defense, effective immediately. . . . Chris will do a GREAT job! Mark Esper has been terminated. I would like to thank him for his service," 12:54 p.m., November 9, 2020, Twitter.com.

148 *In anticipation of being fired:* Meghann Myers, "Exclusive: Esper, on His Way Out, Says He Was No Yes Man," *Military Times,* November 9, 2020.

149 *Kathrin Jansen:* Katie Thomas, David Gelles and Carl Zimmer, "Pfizer's Early Data Shows Vaccine Is More Than 90% Effective," *The New York Times*, November 9, 2020.

149 *But Trump refused to believe it:* @realDonaldTrump, November 10, 2020, Twitter.com.

150 *"It ain't over til it's over":* @Mike_Pence, Told @VP Team Today, "it ain't over til it's over..and this AIN'T over! President @realDonaldTrump has never stopped fighting for us and we're gonna Keep Fighting until every LEGAL vote is counted!," 1:41 p.m., November 9, 2020, Twitter.com.

151 *Trump had made to* Breitbart News*:* "Exclusive—President Donald Trump: Paul Ryan Blocked Subpoenas of Democrats," *Breitbart*, March 13, 2019.

152 *at a public State Department session with reporters:* Video: Secretary of State Mike Pompeo, "'There Will Be a Smooth Transition to a Second Trump Administration,'" *The Washington Post,* November 10, 2020.

CHAPTER THIRTY-ONE

154 *Milley arranged to speak:* "Remarks by General Mark A. Milley at the Opening Ceremony for the National Museum of the United States Army," *Joint Staff Public Affairs*, November 11, 2020.

155 *Hollyanne, Milley's wife:* Courtney Kube, "Gen. Milley's Wife Saved Vet Who Collapsed at Veterans Day Ceremony in Arlington," NBC News, November 13, 2020.

155 *"almost a 'Zelig' figure":* David Ignatius, "How Kash Patel Rose from Obscure Hill Staffer to Key Operative in Trump's Battle with the Intelligence Community," *The Washington Post*, April 16, 2021.

158 *Jonathan Swan and Zachary Basu:* "Episode 9: Trump's War with His Generals," Axios, May 16, 2021.

159 *The next day, Thursday:* "Joint Statement from Elections Infrastructure Government Coordinating Council & The Elections Infrastructure Sector Coordinating Executive Committees," November 12, 2020, cisa.gov.

159 *Trump soon fired:* @realDonaldTrump, "The recent statement by Chris Krebs on the security of the 2020 Election was highly inaccurate . . . Therefore, effective immediately, Chris Krebs has been terminated as Director of the Cybersecurity and Infrastructure Security Agency," 7:07 p.m. November 17, 2020, Twitter.com.

159 *The International Atomic Energy Agency had just reported:* "UN Agency: Iran Uranium Stockpile Still Violates Atomic Deal," Associated Press, November 11, 2020.

CHAPTER THIRTY-TWO

162 *In a letter:* The authors obtained a copy of the Giuliani team's letter to the Trump campaign.

163 *The next day, November 19:* "Trump Campaign News Conference on Legal Challenges," C-SPAN, November 19, 2020.

163 *The headline:* Bess Levin, "Rudy Giuliani's Hair Dye Melting Off His Face Was the Least Crazy Part of His Batshit-Crazy Press Conference," *Vanity Fair,* November 19, 2020.

163 *"When we kept pressing":* Tucker Carlson, "Time for Sidney Powell to Show Us Her Evidence," Fox News, November 19, 2020.

164 *Abrams:* David Marchese, "Why Stacey Abrams Is Still Saying She Won," *New York* magazine, April 28, 2019.

164 *He had lost his White House job in 2018:* Carol D. Leonnig and Josh Dawsey, "Trump's Personal Aide Apparently Lost White House Position over Gambling Habit," *The Washington Post,* March 15, 2018.

168 *"So far, it's not good":* Mike Lillis, "Clyburn: Biden Falling Short on Naming Black Figures to Top Posts," *The Hill,* November 25, 2020.

CHAPTER THIRTY-THREE

169 *Balsamo filed the story:* Michael Balsamo, "Disputing Trump, Barr Says No Widespread Election Fraud," Associated Press, December 1, 2020.

172 *Comey giving two memos:* Zachary Cohen, "The Tweet That Got James Comey to Go to the Press," CNN.com, June 8, 2017.

175 *"Amazing time":* @Donald Trump Junior, December 8, 2020, Instagram.com.

175 *Cortes's Twitter profile:* @CortesSteve, Twitter profile as at July 7, 2021, Twitter.com.

175 *The "deplorables":* Hillary Clinton in a speech to journalists at a New York fundraiser, September 9, 2020; Katie Reilly, "Read Hillary Clinton's 'Basket of Deplorables' Remarks About Donald Trump Supporters," *Time*, September 10, 2016.

CHAPTER THIRTY-FOUR

177 *Rove was also publicly dismissive:* Karl Rove, "This Election Result Won't Be Overturned," *The Wall Street Journal*, November 11, 2020.

177 *"They have not earned your vote":* Joey Garrison, "'They Have Not Earned Your Vote': Trump Allies Urge Georgia Republicans to Sit Out Senate Runoffs," *USA Today, December 3, 2020.*

178 *Trump was losing:* Alison Durkee, "Trump and the GOP Have Now Lost More than 50 Post-Election Lawsuits," *Forbes*, December 8, 2020.

178 *The high court's rejection:* Justice Samuel Alito order in *Mike Kelly, United States Congressman, et al., Applicants et al. v. Pennsylvania, et al.*, delivered December 8, 2020.

179 *"A picture is worth a thousand words":* @realDonaldTrump, 8.55 p.m., March 23, 2016, Twitter.com.

179 *Trump later told* New York Times *columnist:* Maureen Dowd, "Trump Does It His Way," *The New York Times,* April 2, 2016.

180 *Barr wrote a resignation letter:* "Read William Barr's Resignation Letter to President Trump," *The Washington Post,* December 14, 2020.

181 *Trump accepted the resignation and tweeted:* @realDonaldTrump, "Just had a very nice meeting with Attorney General Bill Barr at the White House. Our relationship has been a very good one, he has done an outstanding job! As per letter, Bill will be leaving just before Christmas to spend the holidays with his family . . ." 5:39 p.m., December 14, 2020, Twitter.com.

181 *But due to Trump's various legal and legislative challenges:* See, for example, Ann Gerhart, "Election Results Under Attack: Here Are the facts," updated March 11, 2021, washingtonpost.com.

181 *nearly two-thirds of the House GOP:* Sarah Binder, "Why So Many House Republicans Co-Signed Texas's Lawsuit to Overturn the Election," *The Washington Post,* December 15, 2020.

182 *"Many millions of us":* "McConnell Applauds President Trump & Congratulates President-Elect Biden," December 15, 2020, mcconnell.senate.gov.

183 *Biden said the crowd:* Video: "Vice President Joe Biden Visits McConnell Center," University of Louisville, February 11, 2011.

CHAPTER THIRTY-FIVE

184 *But Trump soon sent off a tweet:* @realDonaldTrump, 7:11 a.m., December 11, 2020, Twitter.com.

185 *Pfizer-BioNTech was authorized:* "Pfizer and BioNTech Celebrate Historic First Authorization in the U.S. of Vaccine to Prevent Covid-19," Pfizer, December 11, 2020.

185 *One week later:* "FDA Takes Additional Action in Fight Against COVID-19 by Issuing Emergency Use Authorization for Second Covid-19 Vaccine," U.S. Food and Drug Administration, December 18, 2020.

185 *But distribution lagged:* "Trends in Number of Covid-19 Vaccinations in the U.S.," Centers for Disease Control and Prevention, covid.cdc.gov/covid-data-tracker/#vaccination-trends.

185 *Coronavirus infections and deaths:* See Centers for Disease Control and Prevention Data Tracker, covid.cdc.gov.

185 *Klain watched:* Ibid.

185 *More than 140,000 Americans:* "The Employment Situation: December 2020," U.S. Bureau of Labor Statistics, January 8, 2021.

186 *17 Ebola treatment units:* "Fact Sheet: The U.S. Response to the Ebola Epidemic in West Africa," October 6, 2014, Obamawhitehouse.archives.gov.

187 *As a businessman, Zients's philosophy:* Chad Day, Luis Melgar, and John McCormick, "Biden's Wealthiest Cabinet Officials: Zients, Lander, Rice Top the List," *The Wall Street Journal,* March 23, 2021.

189 *These are state and locally run organizations:* "Fact Sheet: President Biden Announces Community Health Centers Vaccination Program to Launch Next Week and Another Increase in States, Tribes, & Territories' Vaccine Supply," Briefing Room, February 9, 2021, WhiteHouse.gov.

189 *More than 91 percent:* U.S. Department of Health and Human Services, "Ensuring Equity in COVID-19 Vaccine Distribution: Engaging Federally Qualified Health Centers," Hrsa.gov.

190 *He said checks should be:* Rachel Siegel, Josh Dawsey, and Mike Debonis, "Trump Calls on Congress to Approve $2,000 Stimulus Checks, Hinting He Might Not Sign Relief Bill Without Changes," *The Washington Post*, December 22, 2020.

CHAPTER THIRTY-SIX

191 *A historic number of Republican women:* "Results: Women Candidates in the 2020 Elections," Rutgers University: Center for American Women and Politics, November 4, 2020.

191 The New York Times *later called it a "stinging setback":* Adam Nagourney, "A Stinging Setback in California Is a Warning for Democrats in 2022," *The New York Times,* December 26, 2020.

CHAPTER THIRTY-SEVEN

193 *Byrne, a business gadfly:* Cade Metz and Julie Creswell, "Patrick Byrne, Overstock CEO Resigns After Disclosing Romance with Russian Agent," *The New York Times*, August 22, 2019.

193 *He also claimed:* Sheelah Kolhatkar, "A Tycoon's Deep-State Conspiracy Dive," *The New Yorker,* December 7, 2020.

195 *Truman had tried to use it: Youngstown Sheet & Tube Co. v. Sawyer,* 343 US 579 (1952).

196 *That Monday, December 21:* Reuters video: "'No Plan to Do So,' Barr Says of Appointing Special Counsels," *The New York Times,* December 21, 2020.

CHAPTER THIRTY-EIGHT

198 *Instead, the amendment:* U.S. Constitution, Amendment XII.

199 *Republicans now controlled more delegations in the House:* Kyle Kondik, "Republican Edge in Electoral College Tie Endures," University of Virginia, Center for Politics, January 9, 2020.

200 *Pence told Quayle that he had studied the video:* "Electoral Ballot Count," C-SPAN, January 6, 1993.

200 *There was a lawsuit in federal court:* Jacques Billeaud, "US Supreme Court Asked to Decertify Biden's Win in Arizona," Associated Press, December 13, 2020.

CHAPTER THIRTY-NINE

206 *becoming the first senator to do so:* "Sen. Hawley Will Object During Electoral College Certification Process," December 30, 2020, Hawley.senate.gov.

206 *"JANUARY SIXTH, SEE YOU IN DC!":* @realDonaldTrump, 2:06 p.m., December 30, 2020, Twitter.com.
206 *His allies:* Brian Schwartz, "Pro-Trump Dark Money Groups Organized the Rally That Led to Deadly Capitol Hill Riot," CNBC, January 9, 2021.
207 *In August, Bannon had been charged:* Matt Zapotosky, Josh Dawsey, Rosalind S. Helderman, and Shayna Jacobs, "Steve Bannon Charged with Defrauding Donors in Private Effort to Raise Money for Trump's Border Wall," *The Washington Post,* August 20, 2020.

CHAPTER FORTY

209 *Lee received a two-page memo:* Memorandum by John Eastman, "Privileged and Confidential: January 6 scenario," sent to Mike Lee on January 2, 2020, obtained by the authors.
210 *"faithless" electors:* Robert Barnes, "Supreme Court Considers 'Faithless' Presidential Electors and Finds More Questions than Answers," *The Washington Post,* May 13, 2020.
210 *Trump adviser Stephen Miller:* Mark Joyella, "On Fox News, Stephen Miller Says 'An Alternate Set of Electors' Will Certify Trump as Winner," *Forbes,* December 14, 2020.
212 *Mark Meadows grew up as a self-described "fat nerd":* Gabriella Muñoz, "Mark Meadows' Journey from 'Fat Nerd' to Trump Chief of Staff," *The Washington Times,* March 12, 2020.
212 *He openly cried:* Maggie Haberman, "For Mark Meadows, Transition from Trump Confidant to Chief of Staff Is a Hard One," *The New York Times,* April 16, 2020.
213 *Several states had recorded:* Reuters staff, "Fact check: Clarifying the Comparison Between Popular Vote and Counties Won in the 2020 Election," Reuters, December 29, 2020.
214 *Trump's lawyers had now lost:* Zoe Tillman, "Trump and His Allies Have Lost Nearly 60 Election Fights in Court (And Counting)," BuzzFeed News, December 14, 2020.

CHAPTER FORTY-ONE

216 *The first memo*: Memorandum sent to Lindsey Graham from Mayor Rudy Giuliani, Trump Legal Defense Team, "Deceased People Who Voted in the 2021 Election in GA," January 4, 2021, obtained by the authors.
217 *A second:* "Voting Irregularities, Impossibilities, and Illegalities in the 2020 General Election," January 4, 2021, obtained by the authors.
218 *Turning to a PowerPoint printout:* "Analysis of Vote Irregularities in Georgia's 2020 General Election," January 2021, obtained by the authors.
219 *another "confidential" memo:* "Confidential Memo on Voting Irregularities in Georgia," January 3, 2021, obtained by the authors.
219 *Holmes received an email:* Email to Lindsey Graham from Rudolph Giuliani, "Voting Irregularities, Impossibilities, and Illegalities in the 2020 General Election," January 4, 2021.
219 *that touted conspiracies:* Rachel Abrams, "One America News Network Stays True to Trump," *The New York Times,* April 18, 2021.

220 *He found a 2013 Supreme Court case: Arizona v. Inter Tribal Council of Ariz., Inc.,* 570 U.S. 1 (2013).

CHAPTER FORTY-TWO

224 *"I know we all":* "Vice President Pence Remarks at Georgia Senate Campaign Event," C-SPAN, January 4, 2021.

226 *That night in Georgia, Trump tore:* "President Trump Remarks at Georgia U.S. Senate Campaign Event," C-SPAN, January 4, 2021.

CHAPTER FORTY-THREE

233 *Metropolitan Police arrested five people:* Marissa J. Lang, Emily Davies, Peter Hermann, Jessica Contrera, and Clarence Williams, "Trump Supporters Pour Into Washington to Begin Demonstrating Against Election," *The Washington Post,* January 5, 2021.

233 *Trump directed his campaign:* Maggie Haberman and Annie Karni, "Pence Said to Have Told Trump He Lacks Power to Change Election Result," *The New York Times,* January 5, 2020.

234 *"If Vice President @Mike_Pence":* @realDonaldTrump, 1:00 a.m., January 6, 2021, Twitter.com.

234 *Trump had promised a "wild" protest:* @realDonaldTrump, "Peter Navarro releases 36-page report alleging election fraud 'more than sufficient' to swing victory to Trump. A great report by Peter. Statistically impossible to have lost the 2020 Election. Big protest in D.C. on January 6th. Be there, will be wild!" December 19, 2020, Twitter.com.

235 *"To be clear":* Letter from D.C. Mayor Muriel Bowser to Acting Attorney General Rosen, Secretary McCarthy, and Acting Secretary Miller, January 5, 2021. See @MayorBowser, 1:53 p.m., January 5, 2021, Twitter.com.

CHAPTER FORTY-FOUR

237 *"All Mike Pence has to do":* @realDonaldTrump, 8:17 a.m., January 6, 2021, Twitter.com.

239 *Before Trump took the stage:* Video of Rudolph Giuliani's Remarks: "'Let's Have Trial by Combat' over Election," Reuters, January 6, 2021.

240 *Pence released his two-page letter:* @Mike_Pence, 1:02 p.m., January 6, 2021, Twitter.com.

240 *Following Trump's hour-long speech:* "Former President Donald Trump's January 6 Speech," CNN Transcript, February 8, 2021.

241 *"No, I want to be here":* Lesley Stahl, "Nancy Pelosi on the Riot at the Capitol, Congress' Mandate Under Joe Biden and the Youth in the Democratic Party," CBS News transcript, from CBS's *60 Minutes,* January 11, 2021.

CHAPTER FORTY-FIVE

244 *removed from the Senate floor at 2:13 p.m.:* Elyse Samuels, Joyce Sohyun Lee, Sarah Cahlan, and Meg Kelly, "Previously Unpublished Video Shows Pence, Romney, Schumer and Others Rushing to Evacuate the Capitol," *The Washington Post,* February 10, 2021.

245 *Trump tweeted:* @realDonaldTrump, "Mike Pence didn't have the courage to do what should have been done to protect our Country and our Constitution, giving States a chance to certify a corrected set of facts, not the fraudulent or inaccurate ones which they were asked to previously certify. USA demands the truth!" 2:24 p.m., January 6, 2021, Twitter.com.

248 *Ashli Babbitt was shot and killed:* Dalton Bennett, Emma Brown, Atthar Mirza, Sarah Cahlan, Joyce Sohyun Lee, Meg Kelly, Elyse Samuels, Jon Swaine, "41 Minutes of Fear: A Video Timeline from Inside the Capitol Siege," *The Washington Post,* January 16, 2021.

248 *And one remark stood out:* Aaron Blake, "9 Witnesses Who Could Have Offered Vital Testimony at Trump's Impeachment Trial," *The Washington Post,* February 13, 2021.

249 *At 3:13 p.m., Trump sent out a tweet:* @realDonaldTrump, 3:13 p.m., January 6, 2020, Twitter.com.

251 *Biden shelved plans:* "President-elect Biden Remarks on U.S. Capitol Protesters," C-SPAN, January 6, 2021.

CHAPTER FORTY-SIX

253 *Pence called Christopher Miller:* Lisa Mascaro, Ben Fox, and Lolita C. Baldor, " 'Clear the Capitol,' Pence Pleaded, Timeline of Riot Shows," Associated Press, April 10, 2021.

254 *They decided on a video:* "President Trump Video Statement on Capitol Protesters," C-SPAN, January 6, 2021.

254 *Seven minutes later*: @USMarshalsHQ, 4:24 p.m., January 6, 2021, Twitter .com.

255 *A photo of Hawley, his fist raised:* Katie Bernard, "A Photographer and a Fist Pump. The Story Behind the Image That Will Haunt Josh Hawley," *The Kansas City Star,* January 7, 2021.

255 *ready to just end the drama:* Matthew Choi, "Loeffler Reverses on Challenging Biden's Win After Riot at Capitol," *Politico,* January 6, 2021.

256 *"These are the things":* @realDonaldTrump, "These are the things and events that happen when a sacred landslide election victory is so unceremoniously & viciously stripped away from great patriots who have been badly & unfairly treated for so long. Go home with love & in peace. Remember this day forever!," 6.01 p.m., January 6, 2021, Twitter.com.

256 *"When I arrived in Washington this morning":* Senator Kelly Loeffler floor statement, "I Cannot Now in Good Conscience Object," C-SPAN, January 6, 2021.

257 *Senator Mike Lee was solemn:* "Sen. Lee Speaks on Counting Electoral Votes," January 6, 2021, lee.senate.gov.

257 *"Trump and I, we've had a hell of a journey":* "Graham Addresses Electoral Results on Senate Floor," January 6, 2021, lgraham.senate.gov.

258 *Shortly after 3:40 a.m.:* CBS News staff, "Pence Announces Biden's Victory After Congress Completes Electoral Count," CBS News, January 7, 2021.

258 *Pence headed out to his motorcade:* Josh Dawsey and Ashley Parker, "Inside the Remarkable Rift Between Donald Trump and Mike Pence," *The Washington Post,* January 11, 2021.

CHAPTER FORTY-SEVEN

259 *Pelosi and Schumer:* "Joint Statement on Call to Vice President Pence on Invoking 25th Amendment," January 7, 2021, speaker.gov/newsroom.

260 *Pence worked:* The Editorial Board, "Donald Trump's Final Days: The Best Outcome Would Be for Him to Resign to Spare the U.S. Another Impeachment Fight," *The Wall Street Journal*, January 7, 2021.

260 *Trump's secretary of transportation:* @SecElaineChao, "It has been the honor of a lifetime to serve the U.S. department of Transportation," Resignation letter, 1:36 p.m., January 7, 2021, Twitter.com.

260 *Later, at the airport:* Paul P. Murphy, Gregory Wallace, Ali Zaslav, and Clare Foran, "Trump Supporters Confront and Scream at Sen. Lindsey Graham," CNN, January 10, 2021.

262 *In actuality, South Korea is 29 percent Christian:* Phillip Connor, "6 Facts About South Korea's Growing Christian Population," Pew Research Center, August 12, 2014.

CHAPTER FORTY-EIGHT

The information in this chapter comes from deep background interviews.

CHAPTER FORTY-NINE

270 *Some 4,000 people:* "Trends in Number of COVID-19 Cases and Deaths in the US Reported to CDC, by State/Territory," CDC Data Tracker, covid.cdc .gov.

270 *losing 140,000 jobs in December:* "U.S. Current Employment Statistics Highlights: December 2020," U.S. Bureau of Labor Statistics, January 8, 2021, bls.gov.

270 *earning Trump the distinction:* Glen Kessler, "Biden's Claim that Trump Will Be the First President with a Negative Jobs Record," *The Washington Post*, October 2, 2020.

271 *An expansion of the child tax credit:* "DeLauro, DelBene, Torres Introduce Legislation to Expand the Child Tax Credit to Permanently Give Families Monthly Payments and Cut Child Poverty Nearly in Half," February 8, 2021, delauro.house.gov.

272 *and long an outspoken advocate for children:* Congresswoman Rosa L. DeLauro, *The Least Among Us: Waging the Battle for the Vulnerable* (New York: The New Press, 2017).

CHAPTER FIFTY

274 *They all read it:* Unclassified "Memorandum for the Joint Force," The Joint Chiefs of Staff, January 12, 2021.

274 *Media coverage of Milley's letter:* Alex Ward, "US Military Chiefs Warn Troops Against 'Sedition and Insurrection' Before Biden Inauguration," *Vox*, January 12, 2021.

275 *with a 144-foot by 14-foot screen:* "Historic Conmy Hall Transformed with Christie LED Wall," Christie Digital Systems, September 24, 2020, christiedigital.com.

277 *the Boogaloo Boys:* Craig Timberg, Elizabeth Dwoskin, and Souad

Mekhennet, "Men Wearing Hawaiian Shirts and Carrying Guns Add a Volatile New Element to Protests," *The Washington Post,* June 4, 2020.

CHAPTER FIFTY-ONE

279 *canceling its plans to hold a future major:* Doug Ferguson, "PGA Championship Leaving Trump National in '22 Tournament," Associated Press, January 11, 2021.

279 *Another blow came:* Steve Gardner, "Patriots' Bill Belichick Declines Medal of Freedom from Donald Trump, Says He Has 'Great Reverence' for Democracy," *USA Today,* January 11, 2001.

280 *Pence, in an unusually emotional letter:* Transcript, "Read Pence's Full Letter Saying He Can't Claim 'Unilateral Authority' to Reject Electoral Votes," PBS, January 6, 2021.

280 *The second move:* "H.Res.24—Impeaching Donald John Trump, President of the United States, For High Crimes and Misdemeanors," *Congressional Record*, January 11, 2021, Congress.gov.

280 *"He must go":* "The Latest: Pelosi Wants Fines for Bypassing House Security," Associated Press, January 13, 2021.

281 *McConnell would not say:* Nick Niedzwiadek, "McConnell Says He Hasn't Ruled Out Convicting Trump in Senate Trial," *Politico,* January 13, 2021.

282 *"My fellow Americans":* "A Message from President Donald Trump," Trump White House Archives, January 13, 2021.

CHAPTER FIFTY-TWO

284 *He couched it as an emergency response:* Video: "Biden Unveils $1.9 Trillion COVID Relief Bill," CBS News, January 15, 2021.

284 *The plan's core components:* "President Biden Announces American Rescue Plan," Briefing Room, January 20, 2021, WhiteHouse.gov.

285 *Some House members criticized:* Letter to President Biden and Vice President Harris, January 28, 2021, signed by Representative Ilhan Omar and more than 50 Other House Democrats, omar.house.gov.

285 *But despite understanding:* Mitch McConnell, *The Long Game: A Memoir* (New York: Sentinel, 2016).

286 *Near the end of the call:* Audio of the conference call was obtained by the authors.

287 *On January 15:* "A Pillow Salesman Apparently Has Some Ideas About Declaring Martial Law," *The Washington Post*, January 15, 2021.

289 *Over 140 people were granted clemency:* Rosalind S. Helderman, Josh Dawsey, and Beth Reinhard, "Trump Grants Clemency to 143 People in Late-Night Pardon Blast," *The Washington Post,* January 20, 2021.

289 *For a split second, Biden's voice cracked:* "President-elect Biden Departure from Delaware," C-SPAN, January 19, 2021.

CHAPTER FIFTY-THREE

292 *Trump had unexpectedly signed a final pardon:* Alayna Treene, "Trump's Final Act as President: Pardoning Jeanine Pirro's Ex-Husband," Axios, January 20, 2021.

292 *a crew was setting up Biden's office:* Annie Linskey, "A Look Inside Biden's Oval Office," *The Washington Post,* January 21, 2021.

294 *Harris had two Bibles:* Chelsea Jane and Cleve Wootston Jr., "Kamala Harris Sworn into History with Vice-Presidential Oath," *The Washington Post,* January 20, 2021.

295 *as Amanda Gorman, a young Black woman:* Amanda Gorman, *The Hill We Climb: An Inaugural Poem for the Country* (New York: Penguin Young Readers Group, 2021).

296 *a family Bible with Celtic cross:* Shane O'Brien, "Celtic Cross Featured on Joe Biden's Irish Ancestors' Bible Used in Inauguration," January 21, 2021.

296 *Biden's 2,552-word speech:* "Inaugural Address by President Joseph R. Biden, Jr.," January 20, 2021, WhiteHouse.gov.

297 *191,500 of them:* Jason Samenow, "Inaugural 'Field of Flags' on the Mall Seen from Space," *The Washington Post,* January 20, 2021.

297 *Breakfast of southern-style steak:* Menu obtained by the authors.

298 *"You know, we have a tradition on Air Force Two":* "Former VP Mike Pence and Former Second Lady Karen Pence Return Home to Indiana," WLKY News Louisville, January 20, 2021.

CHAPTER FIFTY-FOUR

299 *Jen Psaki later noted:* Seung Min Kim, "On His First Day, Biden Signs Executive Orders to Reverse Trump's Policies," *The Washington Post,* January 20, 2021.

301 *Biden decided to announce:* "Remarks by President Biden on the Fight to Contain the COVID-19 Pandemic," Briefing Room, January 26, 2021, WhiteHouse.gov.

302 *Biden had announced:* "Biden Says He Will Ask Americans to Wear Masks for the First 100 Days He's in Office," CNN, December 3, 2021.

CHAPTER FIFTY-FIVE

305 *Greene had also promoted:* Camila Domonoske, "QAnon Supporter Who Made Bigoted Videos Wins Ga. Primary, Likely Heading to Congress," NPR, August 12, 2020.

CHAPTER FIFTY-SIX

306 *Senator Susan Collins:* Statement: "Group of 10 Republican Senators Outline Covid-19 Relief Compromise, Request Meeting with President Biden," January 31, 2021.

309 *One light touch:* Ashley Parker, Matt Viser, and Seung Min Kim, "'An Easy Choice,'" *The Washington Post,* February 7, 2021.

312 *Bill Clinton's rebuke, in 1992:* Thomas B. Edsall, "Clinton Stuns Rainbow Coalition," *The Washington Post,* June 14, 1992.

314 *Biden's plan called for:* "President Biden Announces American Rescue Plan," Briefing Room, January 20, 2021, WhiteHouse.gov.

CHAPTER FIFTY-SEVEN

317 *Collins was delighted:* "Senate Republicans on Covid-19 Relief Talks with President Biden," C-SPAN, February 1, 2021.

317 *Later,* The Washington Post*:* Ashley Parker, Matt Viser, and Seung Min Kim, "Inside Biden's Decision to Go It Alone with Democrats on Coronavirus Relief," *The Washington Post,* February 7, 2021.

CHAPTER FIFTY-EIGHT

323 *Speaking on the floor:* "Majority Leader Schumer Remarks on the Urgent Need to Begin the Process of Passing COVID Relief Legislation by Advancing the Budget Resolution Today," February 2, 2021, democrats.senate.gov.

323 *Democrats poured $180 million into the campaign:* Ellen Barry, "The Democrats Went All Out Against Susan Collins. Rural Maine Grimaced," *The New York Times,* November 17, 2020.

CHAPTER FIFTY-NINE

330 *"Pretty amazing room":* Maritsa Georgiou, "Tester Discusses Stimulus Proposal Talks, First Visit to Oval Office," NBC Montana, February 3, 2021.

330 *Sanders had grown up:* Bernie Sanders, "As a Child, Rent Control Kept a Roof over My Head," CNN, July 30, 2019.

331 *Republicans had increased their proposal:* "Group of 11 Republican Senators Push for Targeted $650 Billion COVID-19 Relief Plan," March 5, 2021, collins.senate.gov.

CHAPTER SIXTY

335 *Trump had announced:* "Agreement for Bringing Peace to Afghanistan Between the Islamic Emirate of Afghanistan Which Is Not Recognized by the United States as a State and Is Known as the Taliban and the United States of America," February 29, 2020.

338 *In his 2020 memoir:* Barak Obama, *A Promised Land* (New York: Crown, 2020), pp. 318–19.

339 *Biden was the first U.S. president:* "Remarks by President Biden on the Way Forward in Afghanistan," Treaty Room, April 14, 2021, WhiteHouse.gov.

339 *the Taliban would resume their attacks:* Jacob Knutson, "Taliban Threatens to Attack U.S. Troops as Trump Withdrawal Date Passes," Axios, May 1, 2021.

CHAPTER SIXTY-ONE

341 *"You can hear the mob calling":* "Trump Impeachment Trial Day Two," transcript, CNN, February 10, 2021.

342 *"January 6th was a disgrace":* "McConnell on Impeachment: 'Disgraceful Dereliction' Cannot Lead Senate to 'Defy Our Own Constitutional Guardrails,'" February 13, 2021, mcconnell.senate.gov.

343 *Appearing on Fox News:* "Trump Is Ready to 'Move on and Rebuild the Republican Party,' Sen. Graham," *Fox News Sunday*, February 14, 2021.

344 *he would "absolutely" support:* Axios staff, "McConnell Says He'll 'Absolutely' Support Trump if He's 2024 GOP Presidential Nominee," Axios, February 26, 2021.

CHAPTER SIXTY-TWO

347 *The Senate parliamentarian:* Emily Cochrane, "Top Senate Official Disqualifies Minimum Wage from Stimulus Plan," *The New York Times*, February 27, 2021.

348 *Couples making $150,000:* "Fact Sheet: The American Rescue Plan Will Deliver Immediate Economic Relief to Families," U.S. Department of Treasury, March 18, 2021, treasury.gov.

348 *Warner and the others:* "Federal Reserve Chair to Sen. Warner, Broadband Is an Economic Necessity," February 23, 2021, warner.senate.gov.

349 *$20 billion:* "Three programs—the Emergency Broadband Benefit, the ARP Emergency Connectivity Fund, and the ARP Capital Projects Fund—exclusively set aside funding for digital equity policies. These three programs together total $20.371 billion," Adie Tomer and Caroline George, "The American Rescue Plan Is the Broadband Down Payment the Country Needs," Brookings, June 1, 2021, brookings.edu.

349 *It was a major commitment:* "Statement of Sen. Warner on Senate Passage of the American Rescue Plan," March 6, 2021, warner.se.

350 *Instead, Republicans maintained control:* "House Election Results 2014," *The New York Times,* December 17, 2014.

350 *largest majority:* Phillip Bump, "It's All but Official: This Will Be the Most Dominant Republican Congress Since 1929," *The Washington Post,* November 5, 2014.

CHAPTER SIXTY-THREE

352 *Manchin liked it:* Larry Summers, "The Biden Stimulus Is Admirably Ambitious. But It Brings Some Big Risks, Too," *The Washington Post*, February 4, 2021.

352 *Biden had pledged:* "Fact Sheet: 441 Federally-Supported Community Vaccination Centers in First Month of Biden-Harris Administration," Briefing Room, February 26, 2021.

CHAPTER SIXTY-FOUR

354 *who had broken ranks with Pelosi:* Susan Page, "Inside Nancy Pelosi's War with AOC and the Squad," *Politico,* April 15, 2021.

355 *Schumer worked with Senator Tom Carper:* Kristina Peterson, Andrew Duehren, and Richard Rubin, "Senate Democrats Overcome Impasse, Reach Agreement to Advance Covid Relief Bill," *The Wall Street Journal,* March 5, 2021.

355 *"As a whip":* Transcript of *The Situation Room*, CNN, March 4, 2021.

356 *On the Senate floor:* U.S. Government Publishing Office, Legislative Session, *Congressional Record*, Vol. 167, No. 42, United States Senate, March 5, 2021, "Amendment No. 972," S1219.

356 *"You called Sanders":* "Office of Management and Budget Director Confirmation Hearing," C-SPAN, February 10, 2021.

357 *Tanden ultimately withdrew:* Seung Min Kim and Tyler Pager, "Tanden Withdraws as Budget Nominee in Biden's First Cabinet Defeat," *The Washington Post*, March 2, 2021.

CHAPTER SIXTY-FIVE

363 *Manchin seemed to be coming back:* Emily Chochrane, "Senate Is on Track for Stimulus Vote After Democrats Agree to Trim Jobless Aid," *The New York Times*, March 5, 2021.

366 *Schumer's public announcement:* U.S. Government Publishing Office, Legislative Session, *Congressional Record*, Vol. 167, No. 42, United States Senate, March 5, 2021, S1230; Erica Werner, Jeff Stein, and Tony Romm, "Senate Democrats Announce Deal on Unemployment Insurance, Allowing Biden Bill to Move Forward," *The Washington Post*, March 5, 2021.

366 *Portman was frustrated:* "Senators Wyden and Portman on Extending Unemployment Benefits to September," C-SPAN, March 5, 2021.

367 *On Saturday, March 6:* H.R.1319—American Rescue Plan Act, as amended, passed in the Senate by Yea-Nay Vote 50–49, March 6, 2021, 12:12 p.m.

CHAPTER SIXTY-SIX

369 *The next day:* "Remarks by President Biden on the Anniversary of the COVID-19 Shutdown," East Room, White House, March 11, 2021, White House.gov.

370 *On March 12:* "Remarks by President Biden on the American Rescue Plan," Rose Garden, White House, March 12, 2021, WhiteHouse.gov.

CHAPTER SIXTY-SEVEN

372 *Speaker Pelosi's: For the People Act of 2021,* H.R.1, 117th Congress (2021–2022).

374 *In all, nearly 400 bills:* "Voting Laws Roundup: May 2021," Brennan Center for Justice, May 28, 2021, brennancenter.org.

374 *Since January, nearly 20 new laws:* Ibid.

374 *A GOP-pushed audit:* "Arizona Election Audit Enters New Phase as Ballot Count Ends," Associated Press, June 25, 2021.

374 *In Georgia:* Mark Niesse, "More Ballot Reviews Pending in Georgia, Sowing Doubts in Elections," *The Atlanta Journal-Constitution,* June 10, 2021.

374 *On June 22, Democrats failed:* Dave Morgan, "Democrats Hope a Voting Rights Failure Sparks Change on Senate Filibuster," Reuters, June 22, 2021.

CHAPTER SIXTY-EIGHT

380 *In a 2015 interview:* "President Vladimir Putin Part 1," interview with Charlie Rose, September 28, 2015, charlierose.com. The Kremlin reported the quote somewhat differently: "You know every stage of your life has an impact on you. Whatever we do, all the knowledge, the experience, they stay with us, we carry them on, use them in one way or another. In this sense, yes, you are right." See "Interview to American TV channel CBS and PBS," September 29, 2015, en.kremlin.ru.

380 *McChrystal had written:* Bob Woodward, *Obama's Wars* (New York: Simon & Schuster, 2010), p. 161; Bob Woodward, "McChrystal: More Forces or 'Mission Failure,'" *The Washington Post*, September 21, 2009, p. A1.

381 *To back up the request . . . "Poignant Vision":* Woodward, *Obama's Wars*, pp. 244–45.

CHAPTER SIXTY-NINE

387 *They hoped all troops . . . home by mid-July:* Thomas Gibbons-Neff, Eric Schmitt, and Helene Cooper, "Pentagon Accelerates Withdrawal from Afghanistan," *The New York Times*, May 25, 2021.

388 *Biden gave a 16-minute address:* "Remarks by President Biden on the Way Forward in Afghanistan," Treaty Room, April 14, 2021, WhiteHouse.gov.

388 *Biden then visited:* Anna Gearan, Karen DeYoung, and Tyler Page, "Biden Tells Americans 'We Cannot Continue the Cycle' in Afghanistan as He Announces Troop Withdrawal," *The Washington Post,* April 14, 2021.

391 *Biden's decision was a mistake:* Kate Martyr, "George W. Bush: Afghanistan Troop Withdrawal 'A Mistake,'" DW, July 14, 2021.

CHAPTER SEVENTY

392 *Player, 5-foot-6:* "Donald Trump Cracked Fat Joke with Golf Legends at Private Ceremony Day After Insurrection," *TMZ Sports*, February 25, 2021.

395 *In all, 15:* "Senators up for Re-Election in 2020," U.S. Senate Press Gallery, July 9, 2021, dailypress.senate.

396 *he liked to play "Russian Roulette":* Bob Woodruff, Jamie Hennessey, and James Hill, "Herschel Walker: 'Tell the World My Truth,'" ABC News, April 15, 2008.

396 *He had cheered Trump's:* Bill Barrow, "In Georgia, Herschel Walker Puts GOP in a Holding Pattern," Associated Press, June 26, 2021.

396 *gaining 54 seats:* Martine Powers and Reuben Fischer-Baum, "How to Flip the House," *The Washington Post,* June 26, 2018.

397 *his firm's May 21 poll:* "National Survey Results General Election Likely Voters Political Environment, Trends & Analysis," McLaughlin & Associates, May 2021, mclaughlinonline.com.

CHAPTER SEVENTY-ONE

401 *Biden had been asked:* "Transcript: ABC News' George Stephanopoulos Interviews President Joe Biden," ABC News, March 16, 2021.

401 *The Kremlin had called:* Sarah Rainsford, "Putin on Biden: Russian President Reacts to US Leader's Criticism," BBC News, March 18, 2021.

401 *"It takes one to know one":* Video: "Putin on Biden Killer Remark," Reuters, March 18, 2021, youtube.com.

403 *Biden later told:* Evan Osnos, "The Biden Agenda," *The New Yorker,* July 20, 2014.

403 *Biden frequently cited:* Former House Speaker Tip O'Neill, *All Politics Is Local* (New York: Random House, 1995).

403 *On April 15:* "Fact Sheet: Imposing Costs for Harmful Foreign Activities by the Russian Government," Briefing Room, April 15, 2021, WhiteHouse.gov.

403 *Biden and Putin later announced:* "Statement by White House Press Secretary Jen Psaki on the Meeting Between President Joe Biden and President Vladimir Putin of Russia," Briefing Room, May 25, 2021, WhiteHouse.gov.

403 *"I know there were a lot of hype":* "Remarks by President Biden in Press Conference," Hôtel du Parc des Eaux-Vives Geneva, Switzerland, June 16, 2021, WhiteHouse.gov.

404 *"Why are you so confident":* Ibid.

404 *"But," Collins pressed:* Ibid.

405 *"The progressives don't like me":* David Brooks, "Has Biden Changed? He Tells Us," *The New York Times,* May 20, 2021.

405 *In late June, Biden announced:* "Remarks by President Biden on the Bipartisan Infrastructure Deal," East Room, June 24, 2021, WhiteHouse.gov.

405 *Biden ultimately issued a 628-word:* Seung Min Kim and Sean Sullivan, "Biden Tries to Move Beyond Flubbed Rollout of Infrastructure Deal," *The Washington Post,* June 29, 2021.

405 *McConnell pounced:* "Democrats Pull the Rug out from Under Bipartisan Infrastructure Negotiators with 'Unserious Demands,'" June 24, 2021, republicanleader.senate.gov.

406 *Biden fell to his knees:* "President Biden Departure from Joint Base Andrews," C-SPAN, March 19, 2021.

406 *The White House assured:* Katie Rogers, "Biden Is 'Doing 100 Percent Fine' After Tripping While Boarding Air Force One," *The New York Times,* March 19, 2021.

408 *There was hope:* CDC Data Tracker, "Trends in Number of COVID-19 Cases and Deaths in the US Reported to CDC, by State/Territory," covid.CDC.gov.

408 *The Centers for Disease Control announced:* "Remarks by President Biden on the COVID-19 Response and the Vaccination Program," Rose Garden, White House, May 13, 2021, 3:58 p.m., WhiteHouse.gov.

CHAPTER SEVENTY-TWO

410 *Republicans were only down five seats:* Nathan L. Gonzales, "These 4 States Could Decide Control of Congress in 2022," *Roll Call,* June 16, 2021.

413 *"They were peaceful people":* Transcript of Donald J. Trump interview with Maria Bartiromo, *Sunday Morning Futures,* Fox News, July 11, 2021.

413 *had charged more than 500 people:* "Six Months Since the January 6th Attack on the Capitol," United States Attorney's Office, District of Columbia, justice.gov.

EPILOGUE

416 *"We didn't lose":* "Former President Trump Holds Rally in Ohio," C-SPAN, June 26, 2021.

416 *About 90 minutes into the rally:* Ibid.

417 *burdened by the heavy shadow:* See Bob Woodward, *Shadow* (New York: Simon & Schuster, 1999), p. 13.

417 *Five years ago:* Bob Woodward and Robert Costa on-the-record interview with Donald J. Trump, March 31, 2016.

Photo Credits

Jabin Botsford (*The Washington Post*): 3, 4, 5, 8, 9, 10, 12, 13, 15
Jahi Chikwendiu (*The Washington Post*): 2
Al Drago (for *The Washington Post*): 7
Demetrius Freeman (*The Washington Post*): 5, 10
Salwan Georges (*The Washington Post*): 9, 14
Andrew Harnik (AP Photo): 11
Evelyn Hockstein (for *The Washington Post*): 1
Calla Kessler (*The Washington Post*): 14
Melina Mara (*The Washington Post*): 13
Khalid Mohammed-Pool (Getty Images): 11
Bill O'Leary (*The Washington Post*): 2
Astrid Riecken (for *The Washington Post*): 6
Michael Robinson Chávez (*The Washington Post*): 6
Toni L. Sandys (*The Washington Post*): 8
Patrick Semansky (AP Photo): 4
Brendan Smialowski (AFP): 16
Alex Wong (Getty Images): 1, 12

Index

Page numbers in *italics* indicate illustrations and document reproductions.

About the Authors

Bob Woodward is an associate editor at *The Washington Post*, where he has worked for 50 years. He has shared in two Pulitzer Prizes, one for his Watergate coverage and the other for coverage of the 9/11 terrorist attacks. He has authored 21 national bestselling books, 15 of which have been #1 *New York Times* bestsellers.

Robert Costa is the Chief Election & Campaign Correspondent for CBS News, where he has worked since 2022. He previously served as a national political reporter at *The Washington Post* and as moderator and managing editor of *Washington Week* on PBS. He holds a bachelor's degree from the University of Notre Dame and a master's degree from the University of Cambridge. He is from Bucks County, Pennsylvania.